PC DISASTERS, MISHAPS, ANd BLUNdERS

Horror Stories

To help you prevent disasters, mishaps, and blunders from occurring (and to help you when they do occur), we've compiled a few of our eye-opening horror stories for you to read here. As you read through the book, you'll encounter many more of these stories as you learn how to protect yourself.

Horror Story: Having your PC stolen under any circumstance can be devastating, especially if you don't have your critical data backed up. But losing your PC can also turn into a disaster of epic proportions if your life depends on what you had stored on your PC. Consider the situation that happened to actor Robert Blake, who has been on trial for murder. During his trial, Blake's lawyer had his computer stolen which contained "the heart and soul of the defense case." The moral here is that if you hire an attorney to defend you, make sure your attorney has a good backup system and knows how to use it.

Horror Story: Laptops are the greatest invention since the discovery of electricity. We take them everywhere and we use them as much as we can. There's nothing better than sitting on the coach with your laptop on your lap, checking email while you are watching your favorite TV show, and having a few bites of your favorite snack. Unfortunately, some medical researchers have recently determined that laptops can threaten male fertility. Laptop computers pose a long-term threat to the fertility of young men who use them because they can reduce sperm formation by raising temperatures in the genital area.

Horror Story: Professional identity thieves do exist, and they can be very successful until they are caught. In 2001, Abraham Abdallah was sent to prison for committing a string of serious thefts he pulled while stealing the identities of some very high-profile people. While he was working as a busboy in a Brooklyn restaurant, he took on the identities of some of the richest people in the U.S. His target was the *Forbes* 400 list. Before he was caught, Abdallah was on a mission to steal $1 billion in assets. You might not be on the *Forbes* 400 list, but there are plenty more Abdallahs out there who are very skillful at cracking the security of major financial institutions to steal your identity.

Horror Story: We heard a story on NPR recently that will make anyone who travels with their laptop worry more than they should. A frequent business traveler was rushing off to the airport to catch his plane. When the taxi arrived at his house, he rushed out and put his bags in the trunk. He unfortunately forgot to put his laptop in the trunk; he left it on the ground, behind the taxi. When the taxi driver had to back up out of the driveway, he heard a terrible crunch and he knew instantly that his trip was ruined.

Horror Story: On the local news recently, we heard a story that will likely send chills down your spine if you are an avid eBay shopper. A family just moved across the country to Arizona. As they were moving into their new house over a two-day period, some thieves broke into their garage and stole a number of cartons containing their belongings. The family likely thought their stuff was safe because no one would steal basic items such as dishes, bath towels, books, clothes, and other items. A few days later, one of the family members was scanning auctions on eBay and came across many of the items that were stolen from their garage. How stupid is that? The moral of the story is: Online services such as eBay have opened up many new channels for fencing goods. Watch your stuff closely. Internet fraud is not limited to thieves who operate only online.

Horror Story: We work with someone who spent over $2,000 on a powerful computer system so that they could be really productive with their work. Then they got cheap and decided to buy a very inexpensive wireless network card. (This would be like buying the top-of-the-line Mercedes and then putting cheap gas in it!) Soon they discovered that the cheap card shorted out the motherboard, rendering the computer useless. The moral of this story: It's okay to look for a good deal but do your homework and don't buy junk.

SURVIVING

PC DISASTERS,
MISHAPS, ANd
BLUNdERS

Jesse M. Torres

Peter Sideris

PARAGLYPH™
PRESS

President
Keith Weiskamp

Editor-at-Large
Jeff Duntemann

Vice President, Sales, Marketing, and Distribution
Steve Sayre

Vice President, International Sales and Marketing
Cynthia Caldwell

Production Manager
Kim Eoff

Cover Designers
Kris Sotelo

SURVIVING PC DISASTERS, MISHAPS, AND BLUNDERS

Limits of Liability and Disclaimer of Warranty

The author and publisher of this book have used their best efforts in preparing the book and the programs contained in it. These efforts include the development, research, and testing of the theories and programs to determine their effectiveness. The author and publisher make no warranty of any kind, expressed or implied, with regard to these programs or the documentation contained in this book.

The author and publisher shall not be liable in the event of incidental or consequential damages in connection with, or arising out of, the furnishing, performance, or use of the programs, associated instructions, and/or claims of productivity gains.

Trademarks

Trademarked names appear throughout this book. Rather than list the names and entities that own the trademarks or insert a trademark symbol with each mention of the trademarked name, the publisher states that it is using the names for editorial purposes only and to the benefit of the trademark owner, with no intention of infringing upon that trademark.

Paraglyph Press, Inc.
4015 N. 78th Street, #115
Scottsdale, Arizona 85251
Phone: 602-749-8787
www.paraglyphpress.com

Paraglyph Press ISBN: 1-932111-98-0

Printed in the United States of America
10 9 8 7 6 5 4 3 2 1

PARAGLYPH
P R E S S

The Paraglyph Mission

This book you've purchased is a collaborative creation involving the work of many hands, from authors to editors to designers and to technical reviewers. At Paraglyph Press, we like to think that everything we create, develop, and publish is the result of one form creating another. And as this cycle continues on, we believe that your suggestions, ideas, feedback, and comments on how you've used our books is an important part of the process for us and our authors.

We've created Paraglyph Press with the sole mission of producing and publishing books that make a difference. The last thing we all need is yet another tech book on the same tired, old topic. So we ask our authors and all of the many creative hands who touch our publications to do a little extra, dig a little deeper, think a little harder, and create a better book. The founders of Paraglyph are dedicated to finding the best authors, developing the best books, and helping you find the solutions you need.

As you use this book, please take a moment to drop us a line at **feedback@paraglyphpress.com** and let us know how we are doing— and how we can keep producing and publishing the kinds of books that you can't live without.

Sincerely,

Keith Weiskamp & Jeff Duntemann
Paraglyph Press Founders
4015 N. 78th Street, #115
Scottsdale, Arizona 85251
email: **feedback@paraglyphpress.com**
Web: **www.paraglyphpress.com**

Recently Published by Paraglyph Press:

Degunking eBay
By Greg Holden

Small Websites, Great Results
By Doug Addison

A Theory of Fun
For Game Design
By Raph Koster

Degunking Your Email, Spam, and Viruses
By Jeff Duntemann

Perl Core Language Little Black Book
By Steven Holzner

Degunking Windows
By Joli Ballew
and Jeff Duntemann

Degunking Your Mac
By Joli Ballew

3D Game-Based Filmmaking: The Art of Machinima
By Paul Marino

Windows XP Professional: The Ultimate User's Guide,
Second Edition
By Joli Ballew

Jeff Duntemann's Wi-Fi Guide
By Jeff Duntemann

Visual Basic .NET Core Language Little Black Book
By Steven Holzner

The SQL Server 2000 Book
By Anthony Sequeira
And Brian Alderman

To my family, I love you all.
—Jesse M. Torres

ે

To Billie Jean, Big Al, and Nathan. You are my motivation, inspiration, and support system. And to my Uncle Constantine, many thanks for planting the "Tech Bug" in me at an early age.
—Peter Sideris

ે

About the Authors

Jesse M. Torres' experience in the computer industry includes the private, corporate, and government sectors. He served six years in the Air National Guard working in computer maintenance and has since worked for large corporations such as PricewaterhouseCoopers and United Technologies. His education includes a specialist's certification in electronic switching systems from the U.S. Air Force, a B.A. in Versatile Technology from the University of Connecticut, a specialist's certification in Lotus application development, and an MCSE and MCAD certification from Microsoft. He has also written the books *Windows Admin Scripting* and *Windows Admin Scripting 2nd Ed* (both available from Paraglyph Press). Currently, Jesse is working for Bridgewater Associates, a global investment manager located in Westport, CT.

Peter Sideris has earned numerous certifications including A+, MCSE, MCDBA, and MCAD. He started his career as a field technician and quickly became an IT department Assistant manager with Prudential CT Realty managing the helpdesk, creating network documentation, providing technology needs assessment, and troubleshooting. Peter is currently working as a Systems Engineer for General Technology Group, Inc. in Meriden Connecticut specializing in security, disaster recovery and planning and client needs assessment.

Contents at a Glance

Contents

Chapter 3
Software Disasters and Mishaps 57

Chapter 5
Wireless Networking 113

Chapter 11
Travel Mishaps and Disasters 267

Chapter 14
Digital Lifestyle Hazards 345

Chapter 15
Piracy 373

Introduction

Most people assume that those of us who work in the technology industry never have problems with their PCs and other tech gadgets. They probably think that our homes are filled with the quiet humming sound of working technology—PCs that never crash, printers that never have problems, fast and reliable Internet connections, tangle-free wires, and PCs free of junk, viruses, and spam. Things couldn't be further from the truth. In fact, it's safe to say that we suffer from PC disasters and mishaps just as much as anyone else. And because we have to solve our own problems, as well as all the other problems we confront at work and the ones that our friends and neighbors bring us, we know first hand how painful a disaster or mishap can be. We also know how embarrassing it is to have to deal with a blunder such as spilling a can of soda on a PC or dropping a laptop. We feel your pain, and then some!

We wrote this book to help you expertly deal with any PC-related disaster, mishap, or blunder that might come your way. A disaster is something really bad that can happen such as your PC getting stolen or your hard drive crashing. A mishap is a problem that isn't as serious as a disaster, such as your printer giving you fits because the ink cartridge has gone bad (and yes there is something you can do about this!). A mishap is something you might do that is really stupid and you wouldn't want to even tell your best friends about it. And if you are not really careful, your blunders can turn into real disasters and cost you a lot of time and money.

Other books have been written on PC disaster and recovery topics but they typically focus on the obvious topics—backing up data, operating system crashes, and so on. They cover technology as if it is used in a vacuum. Our approach is very different. We focus more on the activities that you might do with your PC and the digital lifestyle that you likely have. Let's face it; our PCs impact every part of our lifestyle and because we are so dependant on them, a disaster or a mishap that we are not prepared for can have a significant impact on us. You'll also find that this book is jam-packed with numerous practical tips to help you with the different ways that you use your PC, such as how you travel with your technology, how you use email, how you share files with your friends, how you install and configure software, how you use devices like PDAs and digital cameras with your PC, how you access the Internet, and much more.

If It Ain't Broke Yet, It Might Be Soon!

All PCs and tech devices certainly have their share of problems, even the most expensive, jaw-dropping, cutting-edge pieces of technology. If your PC is crashing, slowing down, or simply not turning on, then it's likely that your spouse or best friend has dropped it, your kids have damaged something by sticking crayons inside it, or you've been victimized by a hacker or some other thief. To make matters worse, it seems like technology always fails just when you need it the most, such as when your laptop battery dies as you are flying home and trying to finish up an important report or when your printer refuses to print just before that big meeting. Technology is great when it works but when it doesn't, you might feel like tossing your PC, printer, PDA, and other devices out the window. Hold that thought for a few minutes because we think we can help.

We Can Help You Fix It!

When tech problems first occur, most people either try to cry, scream, or curse their way out of it (we admit it, we also try these options). After this fails, there are usually three different paths you can take:

1. *Ignore it.* Most people choose this path first. They figure the problem isn't a big deal, the problem is too complicated, or the problem simply isn't worth spending money on to fix it. Unfortunately, no matter how small the problem, it won't likely go away on its own. This is especially true for problems like spam, viruses, and junkware.

2. *Find someone to fix it.* This is usually the second stop. Typically, people get help from a family member, a coworker, or even pay a tech support person to solve the problem. While this may work initially, most people can't keep paying for or soliciting help from others.

3. *Fix it yourself.* This is usually the last resort and is typically done by the very brave or technically efficient. Hopefully, you can build a track record of being able to fix more things than you break.

We're here to tell you to stop your cursing and start your fixing. With a little help along the way, you can solve most of your disasters and mishaps and gain the knowledge you need to keep from making blunders.

So What's the Real Problem?

To be honest, most tech problems are quickly and easily fixed (but you'll never hear that from the repair technician who charges $50 per hour). So why don't more people fix their own PC problems? Besides fear of the unknown, we think the answer is very simple—most people are afraid to read the manual and they are afraid to do something they haven't tried before. These manuals are really boring and complicated. The same goes for computer books. Most of them are written in some strange technobabble, as if they were written for rocket scientists. That's where this book takes a different approach.

Our goal is to provide you with an interesting, easy to read guide for preventing and surviving today's top PC problems. We wanted to create a fun book that our family and friends could read and enjoy, as well as being helpful and informative. We also worked hard to remove the "fear factor" of fixing your own tech problems by providing easy to follow solutions. Just like taking medicine when you're sick, this book shows you how to recognize the symptoms and apply the right fix.

How to Use This Book

This book covers the types of problems all PC users will face sooner or later, from the embarrassing to the truly stupid accidents and mistakes. For something that is smashed, hacked, in flames, virus-laden, or just plain slow and unreliable, this book covers it all with helpful tips to prevent problems from occurring, as well as lifesaving advice for rescuing a burning device. While this book is primarily focused on the PC and related devices (printers, monitors, keyboards, and so on), it also helps you solve and avoid problems with today's more popular tech devices (cell phones, PDAs, MP3 players, digital cameras, and wired/wireless networking devices).

In each chapter, we'll show you how to deal with the disasters, mishaps, and blunders that can occur for a particular topic area such as hardware, software, viruses, and travel. In each chapter, you'll find a set of scenarios with practical, hands-on solutions that are designed to help you solve your problems quickly. We've also included in each chapter a number of real-world "Horror Stories" to help you get a good perspective on what can go wrong if you are not prepared to deal with disasters and mishaps.

You'll want to keep this book in a safe place and use it if a problem occurs. But better yet, use it to help you put good preventative measures in place so that you can keep disasters from occurring in the first place. For example, if you learn how to protect your PC from being stolen, you likely won't ever have to follow up on the solutions that we present in the book.

Theft and Loss

Disasters to avoid:

- Having your PC hacked into and losing sensitive data that could cost you a lot of headaches.
- Getting your identity stolen by criminals who run up large bills on your credit cards and steal from your bank account.
- Having your PC, laptop, PDA, or cell phone stolen.

Mishaps and blunders to run from:

- Losing sensitive data about credit card and other financial accounts because this information was left in your wallet.
- Getting devastated because your PC was stolen and you failed to back up all of your important data.
- Losing important data because you let someone that you couldn't trust use your PC.

Some of the most painful disasters and mishaps that can occur are related to theft and loss. This is something we fear as computer users. Think about it: What would happen if someone broke into your house and stole your PC? Would you have all of your data backed up and copies of your major software programs stored in a safe place? Or would you lose everything, including all of your valuable work, and have to start over? And what about your sensitive, personal data? Do you really have a way to protect the information that is stored on your computer, such as your bank accounts, credit card information, social security number, and so on, if an enterprising thief got his hands on it?

Physical theft is something that most of us are familiar with, but other kinds of theft, such as data theft and identity theft, which are just as devastating, can occur. With data theft, for example, hackers and other criminals can break into your computer and steal your valuable data without you ever realizing it. In some ways this is the worst kind of theft because you won't know a crime is even taking place until it is too late, and thus you won't know how to protect yourself. In recent years, a new form of data theft has emerged due to the widespread use of the Internet and this has led to wide-scale identity theft. Criminals can sneak onto your computer, access your valuable data (such as one of your credit card numbers and your social security number), and then they can go out into the world and take on your identity. If you think this is just a scenario for a Hollywood movie (remember *The Net* with Sandra Bullock?), think again. Identity theft has rapidly become one of the largest types of crimes around the world.

In this chapter, we'll show you how to really protect yourself from data, identity, and hardware theft. You'll learn about the types of disasters and mishaps that can occur because of theft and you'll learn how to protect yourself to keep your data and hardware as safe as possible. And just in case you do get ripped off at some point, we'll show you what you can do. Prevention is always the best measure, but bad things do happen from time to time, and we want to make sure that you can recover from anything that might come your way.

Data Theft

- Learn how data theft occurs.
- Learn how to prevent and detect data theft.
- Learn how to deal with data theft if it occurs.

In the world we live in today, data is much more valuable than money. Most of us don't carry around lots of cash anymore. If our wallets or purses were stolen, we wouldn't lose too much. But the data we carry around or store on our computers, personal digital assistants (PDAs), cell phones, and other devices, such as credit card numbers, bank account numbers, social security numbers, and so on, can really open up doors for thieves. We need to change our thinking a little and learn how to really protect this data because it is the new currency.

Data theft involves having your personal or work files read or taken by others without your knowledge. The type of data that can be stolen includes bank account numbers, social security numbers, usernames and passwords, and company secrets. Unlike hardware theft, where your device is physically missing, data theft is nearly an "invisible" crime. Unless you are standing over the shoulder of the person doing the stealing, you likely won't realize it has happened. Further compounding this problem, most of us think our data is safe because data theft could never happen to us. Statistics prove that this thinking is dead wrong.

HORROR STORY! A friend was just about to leave on a month-long vacation to Australia. The night before he was about to hop on a plane, he got a call from his credit card company. Some thief had acquired his main credit card number over the Internet during the day and had gone on a wonderful shopping spree on the Internet. Fortunately, the credit card company caught the thief in the act, but the company decided to cancel the credit card right before our friend was leaving on his trip. Imagine having to deal with something like this just as you are about to walk out the door, knowing that you'll be traveling without a credit card. This is one reason why it is never a bad idea to have a backup credit card account.

How Does Data Theft Occur?

When you normally think of data theft, you probably just think of a physical loss such as a missing CD, a stolen laptop, and so on. The fact is that data theft can occur in a number of ways:

- *Reading:* If you have sensitive data that should be viewed only by a select few, then it is data theft if an unauthorized individual merely reads it. Whether this person looks over your shoulder, uses your computer when you go to get coffee, or hacks into your computer, just viewing your files can cause you or your company embarrassment. In an extreme case, it could cause you or your company to fall into financial ruin.

- *Copying:* Copying a file, CD/DVD, or memory stick and even making a photocopy of a piece of paper are ways others can steal your data without you even knowing it.

- *Intercepting:* While the physical location and logical location of your data should be secured, you also need to pay attention when sensitive data is transmitted. Email, faxes, instant messages, and even print jobs are not inherently secure. If you are sending sensitive data, try to always send it yourself. Don't hand a fax with highly sensitive data to a friend at work or a clerk at a copy or mail shop. This is just asking for trouble. If it is that important, that paper should never leave your sight.

- *Stealing trash:* Digging through the trash is something we all joke about, but it is one of the major successful strategies (known as "dumpster diving") that thieves use for data and identity theft. If you write down computer passwords, access codes, your email address, or other critical data on a sheet of paper and then later throw it away, your data could be at great risk. This is the type of blunder you want to make sure you avoid, so invest in a shredder and use it. Don't think that you are safe just because you work in a big office. The garbage cans still get emptied and thieves are really good at finding the stuff they are not supposed to see. You should also securely dispose of old computers, cell phone, CD/DVDs, or anything else that may contain sensitive data.

- *Stealing a device:* Why go through the trouble of hacking into a computer when you can just steal the whole thing? Having an entire device stolen is one way to lose a lot of valuable data all at once. See the section on hardware theft later in this chapter for more information.

HORROR STORY! Recently a medical company in Arizona that went out of business made headline news for making a ridiculous blunder that helped a set of criminals steal a lot of data and go on an identity theft shopping spree. After closing down, the company placed all of its confidential personal files in a dumpster behind its vacated building—right next to a strip mall. Imagine how pleased the thieves were to come across this wonderful data—social security numbers, birth dates, even credit card accounts that were still open. The thieves sold all of the data to a noted hacker ring and weeks later the police discovered that over $500,000 of goods were purchased on the Internet with the stolen data.

What Are Common Data Theft Targets?

We could easily tell you to just secure anything that contains sensitive data, but this strategy isn't always the most practical. The problem is that we live in an age of information overload and information is everywhere. It's difficult to keep track of it. This is especially true for the average person who doesn't realize how prevalent data theft is and how vulnerable they are. Consider the following list of common data theft targets:

- *Removable storage:* CDs, DVDs, floppy disks (who still uses them?), hard drives, memory sticks, backup tapes
- *Portable devices:* Cell phones, digital cameras, PDAs, and laptops
- *Unsecured transmissions:* Faxes, emails, instant messages, printing, cell phone text messaging
- *Paper:* Legal documents, manuals, theses, birth certificates
- *Personal items:* Wallets, purses, credit cards, bank cards, checkbooks, social security cards

---

TIP: When doing business with a company, be sure that the company verifies that your account number does not contain any part of your social security number.

You should make sure you have a strategy for keeping any of these targets in a safe place far away from untrusting eyes. Don't just leave valuable data in a desk drawer. If you work with a lot of sensitive data, you should consider investing in a safe and keeping your most sensitive data locked up.

WARNING! While small safes may keep your data safe from the casual thief, any good thief will just take the entire safe home and use a drill and crowbar to get at your data.

You should also be very careful about putting sensitive electronic data (email accounts, passwords, and so on) in your wallet or purse. If a thief steals your wallet or purse, you might not only lose your credit cards, but you could be handing over the keys to your electronic kingdom in the process.

HORROR STORY! A friend was vacationing in the Caribbean. While snorkeling on a secluded cove, she left her wallet hidden with her possessions on the beach. A thief came by and stole her wallet, walking away with a pile of cash and a credit card. She quickly called the credit card company and figured everything was taken care of. When she got home a week later, she discovered that her troubles were far from over. It turns out she had her email accounts, passwords, and bank account in her wallet. The thieves had a field day cleaning out her bank account and her $2,000 vacation quickly became a $20,000 affair that she is still paying for. In our book, this is what we call a real blunder!

TIP: You can use a program like eWallet to secure your passwords, personal identification numbers (PINs), credit card numbers, and so on. Not only does it protect this information even when stolen, it also provides a central place to store the numerous passwords, URLs, and so on that we use daily. The program is available for Windows, the Pocket PC, the Palm, and even a Smartphone cell phone. You can find more information at **www.iliumsoft.com/site/ew/ ewallet.htm.**

How Can I Detect Data Theft?

As we stated earlier, data theft is a silent crime and difficult to detect, but there are some tell-tale signs that you should watch for by using the following methods:

- *Keeping a close eye on your electronic accounts:* Many banks, credit card companies, and investment companies now send out their statements electronically. In fact, some of these statements are not even issued in print form anymore. You should set up a system to regularly review these accounts and look for any suspicious activity.

- *File auditing:* You can enable file audit of your files using Windows and NTFS combined. This will tell you which users are touching your files (and from where) in addition to what they are doing and when they are doing it. If you are on a business network, talk to your local tech support staff to enable file auditing.

- *Logon auditing:* Logon auditing can record who is accessing your computer, from where, and when. If you are on a business network, talk to your local tech support staff to enable logon auditing.

- *Antivirus software:* Use antivirus software to detect, remove, and prevent viruses and Trojans attempting to access your data. See Chapter 8 for more information about protecting yourself against viruses.

- *Anti-junkware:* Use anti-junkware software to detect, remove, and prevent spyware and malware attempting to access your data. See Chapter 9 for more information about how to deal with junkware.

- *Cameras:* While auditing and antivirus detect data file theft, cameras will detect physical data theft. The use of cameras is commonly found in the office environment, but sites like X10.com make it easy and affordable to add home security cameras. You can even use an existing webcam and possibly your camcorder to catch thieves in the act.

How Do I Know If My Keystrokes Are Being Logged?

One way that thieves can get access to your sensitive data is to monitor your keystrokes. This might sound creepy, but it happens more than you might think. Thieves use a technology called *keylogger*, which is essentially a program or hardware device that silently records every keystroke you make. While some employers may use these as a security measure, hackers use them in hopes of stealing confidential information and company secrets, passwords, account numbers, and anything else they may find useful. Here are some situations you should be on the lookout for to help you determine if a keylogger is in place:

- *Is your keyboard plugged directly into your PC?* Some hardware keyloggers plug directly into your computer's keyboard input and then your keyboard plugs into it.

- *Is your keyboard a standard keyboard?* Some hardware keyloggers look like regular keyboards. If your keyboard has been replaced or is suspect, replace it.

- *Are there strange files continually increasing in size?* Some keyloggers store data to text files that increase in size as you type. You can use the advanced file search features in Windows to track these files down.

- *Look for recently modified files.* Some advanced keyloggers may have a set file size in which they can store data, preventing you from seeing it grow in size. Again, the Windows advanced file search tool can you help find these.

- *Disable your network connection.* Some keyloggers instantly transmit keystrokes on the fly to a server located on the Internet. If your computer is not connected to the Internet, the link will be broken. This will give you the time you need to figure out what is going on.

- *When in doubt, rebuild your system.* Some keyloggers use tactics that are difficult to detect (storing data on remote network locations, running as drivers, encryption, and so on). Your best bet is to erase your system and start from scratch.

Do I Need to Be Concerned about Spyware?

Spyware is software that can be downloaded from the Internet to your computer without you even knowing it. It runs in the background and collects data and in turn transmits the data back through the Internet. We'll be looking at spyware and harmful software techniques in Chapter 9.

When Should I Clear My Personal Information from a Device?

Sensitive data can be stolen not only from your computer, but it can also be stolen from any device that you use. A PDA is one such device, as are many of the newer cell phones, which allow you to store all kinds of data. You should therefore be careful about where you put your data. Devices such as PDAs and cell phones are easy to lose or misplace.

When electronic devices break, are upgraded, or have reached the end of their useful life, most people just get rid of them. Years ago you could throw away your calculators and typewriters without the slightest amount of concern about where they ended up (unless you went to the extreme by burning your typewriter ribbons). In today's high-tech world, the junk heap is a dangerous place. Companies now spend a large amount of money conditioning their old equipment for retirement. You should also use these practices when disposing of your unwanted equipment. You never know whose hands your device could end up in and what data they are going to extract. Here are some situations in which you should be careful to remove sensitive data from a device:

- *Getting your device repaired:* Most manufacturers send you a refurbished device as a permanent replacement while they fix your device and then send it to the next customer. Not only is your personal information available to the repair technicians, it may even be available to the customer who gets your repaired device. Also, remember to remove any auxiliary storage cards you may have installed on the device. These can include secure digital cards, compact flash cards, and other types of removable storage.

- *Selling, donating, or disposing of your device:* Your device should be thoroughly wiped of any and all data in these cases. You never know whose hands they will end up in. Some thieves go to extremes to get their hands on people's discarded tech gadgets just for the personal information.

- *Loaning your device to others:* This is just plain common sense. Do not give your device to someone that you cannot trust. They may steal data themselves or may lose it.

HORROR STORY! I (Jesse) typed this book on a refurbished laptop that I purchased from a major manufacturer. To my surprise, the laptop came complete with the previous owner's information (full name, email address, and even financial information). The previous owner was extremely lucky because any data thief could use the information to financially and even socially ruin them. While the manufacturer should have erased this information and given me a clean computer (not only for the previous owner's protection, but for mine as well—viruses, and so on), the previous owner should have taken the extra effort to wipe the system of their personal information. See the next section for information on how to clear personal information from your computer.

How Can I Clear Personal Information from My Computer?

Effectively removing data from your computer is a tricky proposition. There are many factors to consider. Is there any valuable data on the drive that you want to protect? Your answer to this question may increase or decrease the need to remove the data. Naturally, if you have no important information, then the need to clear the drive is diminished. However, if you have been emailing, shopping online, or doing your finances on your computer, the need to clear it should be paramount. After you have made the decision to remove the data, you can choose from among several options:

- *Physical destruction*: This is self-explanatory. Remove your hard drive and damage it beyond repair. There are many ways to accomplish this. One of our favorites involves a hammer and some good old elbow grease. Go ahead and smash the life out of it! Do it after you have a bad day at the office; just be careful of flying shrapnel. Remember, the bigger the hammer, the better the smashing. Other suggestions include drilling through it with an electric drill, using it for target practice, and melting it down. Just remember to remove the drive from the computer first.

WARNING! Be sure to wear eye protection when using the hammer method. It won't do you any good to go blind while trying to secure your data.

- *Reformat*: Reformatting is another way to get rid of your old data, provided the formatting is done thoroughly. You can just do a plain old format, but that will not completely remove the sensitive information. Someone with enough experience and resources will still be able to extract data. One way to do this is to format your hard drive in a Windows machine and then install it in a MAC or Linux machine and format it again. This duel formatting using two different file systems will do the trick. You can also use software like Active@ KillDisk (**www.killdisk.com**) to securely format your drives.

- *Use Eraser*: When you delete data, the data is marked deleted but is not removed from the media. When you place new data on the media, your old deleted files may eventually be overwritten. While formatting and FDISKing are better, ultimately you need a method to ensure your deleted, confidential data is overwritten. Eraser is a free Windows utility you can use to overwrite your deleted files several times. It can be downloaded from **www.heidi.ie/eraser/**.

Myth Buster:

- Can I clear my hard drive by using a magnet? The answer is yes and no. Magnetism can be used as a method to wipe information from the surface of a hard drive. The only problem is that you would need an extremely powerful conventional magnet or an electromagnet.

How Can I Clear Personal Information from My PDA?

Clearing information from your PDA is not as difficult as removing it from your PC. The information is stored in RAM that can be wiped with the press of a few buttons. Most PDAs have a "hard reset" mechanism. A hard reset clears all personal information and programs and leaves a fresh operating system install (just as when you bought it). To perform a hard reset, you may have to press and hold the reset button (tiny hole accessible with a paper clip) while also holding other buttons. This method varies by device and manufacturer, so consult your owner's manual for more information.

WARNING! Although a "hard reset" will clear the information from your PDA, it will not clear the information from any memory cards (SD, compact flash, memory stick, and so on) in the PDA.

How Can I Effectively Protect My Personal Information?

The following list outlines the key to keeping your sensitive data from prying eyes:

- *Know what's sensitive and where it is.* Don't let yourself get lazy about where you store your sensitive data.
- *Watch your device.* Do not leave your device anywhere or allow others to use it unsupervised.
- *Protect your device.* Use the password/lock features of your PC, PDA, and cell phone. Lock your device when it's not in use. Consult your owner's manual for more information.
- *Protect your account.* Password-protect your account and change your password frequently.
- *Protect your files.* Use NTFS permissions and encryption to secure your files.

- *Use the password protection features included in your installed software.* This will provide you with an extra level of protection, especially if you let others use your PC.

- *Use IRM.* Information rights management (IRM) is a feature of Office 2003 that helps prevent sensitive documents and emails from being copied, edited, or forwarded.

- *Use a firewall.* Firewalls are software or hardware devices that sit between you and the Internet and prevent unauthorized Internet users from accessing your PC. See Chapter 4 for more information.

- *Keep your device and software up-to-date with the latest fixes.* You can use **www.windowsupdate.com** to apply fixes to Microsoft Windows computers. See Chapter 3 in this book for more information.

- *Secure your transmissions.* Do not fax or email secure information. Email may be used for confidential information transmission if properly encrypted.

Identity Theft

Identity theft can potentially make your life a living hell. It is a crime that occurs when a thief obtains your personal information and uses it to their advantage. Once the thief has enough information, they may apply for credit cards, a driver's license, car loans, and even mortgages in your name. Unfortunately, most victims do not realize their identities have been stolen until after months or sometimes even years of abuse. The results can be devastating and lead to financial ruin. The following sections will help you understand, recognize, and help prevent identity theft.

DID YOU KNOW 27.3 million Americans were victims of identity theft during the period from 1998 through 2003? For more information, visit **www.ftc.gov/opa/2003/09/idtheft.htm**.

What Kind of Information Does an Identity Thief Look For?

The practice of identity theft might seem a little nebulous or like something out of a scary movie, but there are special techniques that thieves employ. They basically gather up information about an individual so that they can create a profile of the person and then use that profile. They typically look for information such as the following:

- Social security number

- Birth certificate
- Date of birth
- Current and previous addresses
- Mother's maiden name
- Bank and credit card account numbers
- Phone number

In many cases, all of this information is needed to be able to build up a profile on a person. Therefore, you should never include all of this information in a single place (such as your wallet) that could end up in the wrong hands. If this kind of information is stored on your computer or some other electronic device, you should make sure that it is stored in a file that can be encrypted and password-protected. If the information is easily accessible on your computer and your computer is stolen, you could be at great risk.

HORROR STORY! Professional identity thieves do exist, and they can be very successful until they are caught. In 2001, Abraham Abdallah was sent to prison for committing a string of serious thefts he pulled while stealing the identities of some very high-profile people. While he was working as a busboy in a Brooklyn restaurant, he took on the identities of some of the richest people in the U.S. His target was the *Forbes* 400 list. Before he was caught, Abdallah was on a mission to steal $1 billion in assets. You might not be on the *Forbes* 400 list, but there are plenty more Abdallahs out there who are very skillful at cracking the security of major financial institutions to steal your identity.

How Does an Identity Thief Obtain My Personal Information?

Identity thieves make it their job to know you. The more they know, the more they can pretend to be you. Here are some of the methods identity thieves use to obtain information about you:

- *Stealing personnel records from your place of employment.* This can include phone calls to your employer under the guise of a financial institution or credit agency.
- *Contacting you by telephone.* These callers often pose as a representative of a government agency or some other legitimate business (retail store, bank, credit card company, utility company, and so on). This is known as "social engineering" or "pretext calling."
- *Searching for your personal information on the Internet.*
- *Finding personal info in your home or automobile.*

- *Posing as a retailer to obtain your credit report.*
- *Searching your garbage.* This can occur at home or at work, and thieves look for information (old bills and receipts, pre-approved credit cards and applications, personal letters, and so on).
- *Submitting a change of address form to have your mail sent to another location.*
- *Stealing your property (wallet, purse, computer, cell phone).* These items can be a true treasure-trove of personal information.

DID YOU KNOW up to 70 percent of identity theft cases occur from personal data taken from the workplace? For more information, visit **http:// msnbc.msn.com/id/5015565/.**

What Are Some of the Signs of Identity Theft?

Often there are no warning signs to indicate that a person's identity is being stolen until it is too late. But, there are clues you can be on the lookout for, and the sooner you recognize the signs, the sooner you can report and stop a thief. Be aware of the warning signs:

- Some or all of your mail might be missing.
- You receive a letter or phone call discussing accounts you did not open.
- Your accounts have unexpected charges.
- You apply for credit and are denied due to overwhelming debt.

How Can I Help Prevent Against Identity Theft?

Unfortunately, no one can completely prevent identity theft. Until we are solely identified by our fingerprint, retinal (eye) pattern, or heat signature, identity theft will continue to be a problem. Taking a proactive approach against identity theft is the best way to prevent it. The following list describes a few ways to help prevent identity theft:

- *Check your credit report.* This should be done regularly. You could invest $4 to $10 per month with one of the three larger credit-monitoring companies (Equifax, Experian, or TransUnion) and they will monitor your credit information and let you know if activity is occurring (such as someone trying to open an account in your name).

WARNING! Do not go overboard on checking your credit report. Excessive checks can harm your credit rating.

- *Sign your important cards.* Sign your credit, debit, and ATM cards. Check them often to make sure your signature did not rub off. This would allow a thief to just sign your name in their handwriting.

- *Shred it.* Buy a shredder and shred any documents you plan to dispose of that contain your personal information, such as bills, receipts, statements, and address books.

- *Cut it.* Cut up pre-approved credit cards sent to you in the mail.

- *Memorize it.* Memorize your PIN. Never write it down, even if you plan to store it in a "safe place" (your wallet, purse, or safe).

- *Keep it.* Never give your password out, even if the request comes from the company you use the password for.

- *Change it.* Change your PIN frequently.

- *Mix it.* Use different passwords for each site/service.

- *Remove it.* When traveling, remove your hard drive and memory media from your laptops and PDAs and carry them on you.

- *Complicate it.* Do not use PINs or passwords that reflect birth dates, children's ages, names of pets, and so on. These are the first items a hacker or identity theft will try when attempting to break into your accounts. Choose a more complicated PIN or password. Consider using upper- and lowercase letters in a password because combining the two provides you with an extra layer of security. You should also consider using different passwords for different accounts. If you use one master password for all of your accounts and the password is stolen, you'll really feel stupid.

- *Google it.* Search the Internet for your name, phone number, and other personal information and see what shows up. Do this periodically. See the next section for details.

How Can I Tell If My Personal Information Is Posted on the Internet?

Your personal information may end up on the Internet at one point or another. You could have posted a message in a newsgroup, responded to a message on a message board, wrote a product review on Amazon, sold something on eBay, or even just signed up for something and didn't realize your information would be posted on the Internet. The following list will help you determine if and where your personal information is posted on the Internet:

1. Go to **www.google.com.**
2. Enter the information you are searching for in the text box and click the Google Search button.
3. If your information is listed on any Internet web page, it should be displayed to you now.

If you find your information listed on a web page, you should contact the webmaster of the website and demand that they remove it immediately.

You can also search the newsgroups to see if your information is posted there:

1. Go to **www.google.com** and click the Groups link on the top of the page.
2. Enter the information you are searching for in the textbox and click the Google Search button.
3. If your information is listed in any newsgroup posting, it should be displayed to you now.

Unfortunately, you cannot have your information removed from a newsgroup posting. These postings do not reside on one server; they are replicated to every news server the moment they are posted. Once the message has been posted, the server does not allow updates to the posting.

What Should I Do If I Am a Victim of Identity Theft?

Since there is no time to waste, let's get right to it:

- *Contact one of the three major credit bureaus and report the theft (that company's representatives will notify the other two to you).* The company should have a hotline dedicated for fraud notification.

  - Ask that your file be marked with a "fraud alert" and that the default time period (90 to 180 days) be extended to the maximum of seven years. You can always call back and cancel the fraud alert at any time.

  - Ask them to mail you a copy of your credit report (which is free to anyone whose file is marked with a "fraud alert").

- *Contact your creditors and report the theft.* This includes but is not limited to banks, credit card companies, mortgage holders, and retail stores. Inform them of the theft and work with them to have accounts canceled and billing statements mailed to you. The identity thief may have contacted these companies and changed your contact information, so make sure these companies have your correct contact information, including your mailing address. If the information is incorrect, record the incorrect information, save it for your records, and give to the police when filing your police report.

- *Go to the post office.* See if the identity thief has been rerouting your mail to their address. Obtain the address where your mail is being delivered, save it for your records, and give it to the police when filing your police report. Have the post office send your mail to the correct address if it is being fraudulently delivered to another address.

- *Go to the police:*

    - Give them any information and evidence you have (always give them a copy when possible and keep a copy for yourself).

    - File a police report and obtain a copy. Some police departments may choose not to (or not know how to) file a police report for identity theft. This report is extremely important because it may be required to prevent having to pay for false charges. So be persistent, follow up, and go over some heads if you have to. Make sure the police report contains a list of all accounts that were affected.

- *Contact a lawyer.* You may need one to fight creditors who insist that you pay for fraudulent charges.

- *For more information, visit* ***www.idtheftcenter.org***.

What Should I Do If My PIN/Password Is Stolen or Compromised?

Whether you use an ATM card or online website, you simply cannot escape the good old ID and PIN/password combination. Using this combination is the most common method to secure an electronic account. Your ID (account number, username, real name) is generic, easy to obtain (old bill, memorizing the account number, easy guess, and so on), is not usually changed, and is for the most part common knowledge. Your password, on the other hand, is the one thing that really secures your account. If you think your PIN/password has been stolen or compromised, you should do the following:

- Immediately inform your provider.

- When contacting your provider, take note of the day, time, and names of the people you talk to. Save all emails. You may need to be armed with this information if you find yourself later fighting with your provider against charges you did not make.

- Change your PIN/password.

What Should I Do when Someone Asks Me for My PIN/Password or Personal Information?

A common fraud tactic is to send someone an email stating that their account is about to close or their account is missing information and you must contact them immediately with your PIN, password, or personal information. (We'll be covering this in more detail in Chapter 6 when we present phishing and other types of Internet fraud.) No matter how official the email, website, or letter looks or how legitimate the person over the phone sounds, a legitimate business will never contact you asking you for your PIN/password. If contacted, here are the different approaches you should take:

- If contacted by phone, hang up. If you have caller ID, record the phone number.

- If contacted by email, do not delete it. Your provider may request it.

- If contacted via mail, do not throw the letter or the envelope away. Your provider may request it.

- Contact your provider. Provide them with the phone number, email, letter, and envelope.

- Contact the police if necessary.

Hardware Theft

Having your personal property get lost or stolen is a very distressing event. It can cause anger, anxiety, confusion and fear, and it almost always seems to happen at the worst time. If you've ever had something stolen, you know you're more emotional than rational. Every second counts to get your device back, catch the thief, and prevent charges in your name from occurring. This section will present steps that you can follow if your PC or other device is stolen or lost. We'll also show you how to prevent your device from being stolen in the first place.

How Can I Help Prevent My PC or Other Device from Being Stolen?

When something of yours gets stolen, it's not your fault. Even if you forgot your PDA in the public restroom and came back five minutes later to discover it missing, it's still not your fault. The fault lies in the person who took something that did not belong to them. Because it's not your fault, you don't want to waste precious time beating yourself up with guilt. The important thing to do is take action, and we'll show you what to do later in this chapter. Fortunately, there are things you can do to prevent the theft from occurring in the first place (such as not leaving your belongings unattended in a public restroom). The following list outlines a few steps you should take to prevent your device from being stolen:

- *Transport your device in a discrete bag.* Using traditional laptop and camera carry cases is the same as spray painting "Valuable tech device here, come get it!" right on the side of your bag.

- *Never leave your device in plain sight when stored in your car or hotel room.* Secure it in the trunk or hotel safe.

- *Never leave your device unattended (even if the bathroom attendant looks trustworthy).*

Most items get stolen when you are not looking.

- *Lock it down.* Use a cable lock to secure your laptop. Make sure you lock your laptop in a way that it cannot be easily removed.

- *Do not store sensitive data on a portable device.* If you must, store it on removable storage (i.e., removable hard drive, memory stick) and keep it separated from your device when not in use.

- *Encrypt your sensitive data.* While this won't prevent the device from getting stolen, it will prevent others from viewing your personal data.

- *Mark your territory.* Engrave or etch your equipment. This will make it easier for the police to identify and more difficult for a thief to pawn/sell.

TIP: For more information, see Chapter 11 to learn about travel disasters and mishaps.

What Should I Do If My PC or Other Device Is Stolen or Lost?

Losing your laptop, computer, or PDA can actually be worse than having your wallet/purse stolen. Your wallet/purse may have a couple of bucks, some phone numbers, and a few credit cards in it, but your device probably costs more than the money in your wallet/purse, plus it contains tons of personal data (credit card numbers, financial data, address books, and so on). If your device is stolen or lost, you should follow the important steps here as quickly as possible:

- *Quickly assess your loss.* Did you have sensitive data stored on the stolen device (passwords, financial data, bank accounts)? Take steps to secure these items. You may need to notify your credit card companies and banks as quickly as possible.

- *Inform the local security force in your immediate area (mall security, airport security, store security, hotel security).* They may be quick enough to act and recover your device.

- *Contact and file a police report.* Also contact the device manufacturer. They may keep a database of stolen serial numbers it can reference if the thief calls in to get it serviced.

What Should I Do If My Cell Phone Is Stolen/Lost?

Every minute that goes by after your cell phone is lost or stolen is a minute of long distance charges you will be responsible for. The moment you think your cell phone has been lost or stolen, you should take these steps:

- *Verify that the phone is lost or stolen before reporting it.* Try calling your cell phone from another phone and listen for the ring or vibration.

- *Inform the local security force in your immediate area (mall security, airport security, store security, hotel security).* They may be quick enough to act and recover your device.

- *Immediately contact your service provider and have your phone disconnected.*

- *When contacting your service provider, take note of the day, time, and names of the people you talk to.* Save all emails. You may need to be armed with this information if you find yourself later fighting with your service provider against costly phone calls you did not make.

- *File a police report and obtain a copy.* This report may be required to prevent having to pay for false charges.

What Preventative Measures Can I Take to Reduce My Loss in Case of a Stolen/Lost Cell Phone?

Besides the cost of replacing your phone (which by itself can be quite expensive), a stolen/lost cell phone can end up costing you big time. The person who stole or found your phone can rack up tons of 1-900, roaming, long distance, email, text/picture messaging, and minute charges. With today's modern cell phones, the person can also purchase ring tones, games, and even retail items, ultimately costing you a small fortune. The following information will help minimize your loss in case your cell phone is stolen or lost:

- *Insure your phone.* Make sure the policy covers both loss and theft and that you are aware of the deductible costs.

- *Know your contract.* To avoid being liable for calls and purchases you did not make, you may need to take specific steps required by your service provider when your phone is stolen/lost.

- *Password/PIN-protect your cell phone.* Most cell phones can be locked, preventing someone from using it without first entering the correct password/PIN. Consult your owner's manual for more information.

- *Contact your service provider and disable features that you do not need.* This includes international, 1–900 calling, text/picture messaging, and so on.

In addition to taking these steps, follow the instructions in the preceding section.

HORROR STORY! My (Jesse's) mother-in-law purchased a new cell phone and decided to protect it with a PIN (sounds reasonable). Unfortunately, she forgot her PIN, entered it incorrectly three times, and caused her phone to completely stop working. How did this happen? Newer cell phones have subscriber identity module (SIM) cards that hold your personal information. If you enter the wrong PIN a few times, the SIM card sets itself into block mode and you must go to your cell phone provider to have it reset. This little incident cost her $25 but taught her a valuable lesson: read the manual.

What Preventative Measures Can I Take to Reduce My Loss in Case of a Stolen/Lost Computer/PDA?

We already discussed the preventative measures that you can take to help keep your PC or other devices from being stolen. Unfortunately, no matter how careful you are, bad things can still happen. You can't always control when something will happen, but you can take steps to reduce your loss:

- *Keep your personal data secure. Any personal data that you store on your PC or a device such as a PDA should be stored in secure files.* If you use programs like Quicken to process your financial data, make sure that you pass-word-protect your files. If your computer gets lost or stolen, at least your most precious data will be safe.

- *Back up, back up, back up.* Keep reminding yourself that all of your impor-tant work data and software programs need to be backed up and stored in a manner that ensures easy access. When you lose a computer (and once you get over the shock), you'll need to get a new computer and get it set up quickly.

- *Record your device serial numbers.* Keep a copy in your wallet/purse. You may need this information to file a police report.

Summary

People used to keep receipts, phone numbers, and credit cards in their wallets, which were ready to burst at any second. But because wallets held every piece of personal information, folks usually knew where they were at all times, and they were fairly easy to protect. Nowadays, our personal information is everywhere. It's in our wallets and purses and on our computers, laptops, PDAs, and cell phones. The list is almost endless, which makes it very difficult to protect.

In this chapter, we reviewed where folks usually keep personal information and how to protect those locations. We showed you where thieves may strike (even going through your garbage) and how to stay one step ahead of them. You learned how to prevent accidentally handing over your personal property and information to thieves (why make their work easy for them?). While you can't prevent every possible theft, you can minimize and recover your losses in case a theft actually occurs.

2

Hardware Disasters and Mishaps

Disasters to avoid:

- Having your hard drive fail, especially if your important data isn't fully backed up.
- Having your PC catch on fire.
- Having your PC fail to start up.

Mishaps and blunders to run from:

- Spilling water on your device.
- Dropping your laptop or other device.
- Getting a DVD stuck in a DVD drive.

The hardware we'll be covering in this chapter consists of PCs and the other physical devices we have grown to love and hate. That's right; we love them when they work (hopefully most of the time) and hate them when a big disaster occurs, such as dropping your laptop at the airport. We'll be looking closely at the physical devices that connect to the outside of your desktop PC, laptop, and PDA. We will also examine the components inside of them (video cards, network cards, memory). To help you deal with problems most effectively, we've arranged this chapter into general hardware failure issues (hard drives, monitors, and so on), desktop PC issues, and laptop issues.

In the dawn of the PC age (experts place this around 1981), computers seemed to be as fast and powerful as we would ever need them to be. They were also extremely expensive. One of our first computers was a hand-me-down IBM PC Junior. This computer had no hard drive, no modem, and very limited capabilities by today's standards. Yet it retailed for well over a thousand dollars when released. By today's standards, these first PCs were toys. In fact, Bill Gates once said that 640K of memory should be plenty. Now you can't even fire up a cell phone with that amount of memory.

Improvements in materials and manufacturing methods have allowed great advances in the area of computer hardware. For you, that means huge performance gains and much lower prices. A system that cost $3,000 a few years ago can now be replaced by one twice as powerful, for under $1,000.

With all of this progress, you would think that your hardware would always work correctly. Think again! Disasters and mishaps still occur with hardware, and occasionally you get caught committing a blunder such as spilling a soda on your keyboard.

Using Windows Help and Support Center

Before we dive in and look at the various hardware problems you might encounter, let's discuss a few of the resources that are available to help you with disasters and mishaps related to PC hardware.

Debuted in Windows ME and continued in Windows XP and 2003, the Help and Support Center (HSC) is the centralized help system for various computer issues, hardware and software. This help system is far more advanced than those in the previous versions of Windows. In addition to the typical search and index features, it includes wizards, troubleshooters, walk-throughs, updated content via an Internet connection, and a user-friendly interface. Depending on your computer manufacturer, the interface may vary slightly because manufacturers are allowed to customize it. Figure 2.1 shows the Windows Help and Support Center home page customized by Hewlett Packard (HP).

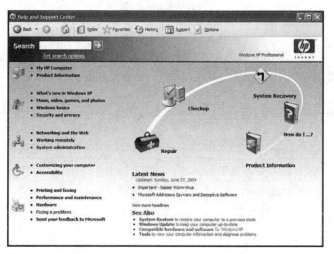

Figure 2.1
Windows Help and Support Center home page.

You are probably now scratching your head in amazement that you never knew about this helpful feature before. Don't feel bad; you are not alone. Microsoft is very good at hiding the best features and utilities from the average user. To access this useful Windows feature, do the following:

1. Click Start.
2. Click Help and Support.

Believe it or not, this feature has been available in every version of Windows that we can remember.

Windows Device Manager

The Windows Device Manager (see Figure 2.2) made its debut in Windows 95, took a brief leave of absence in Windows NT 4.0, and has been in every subsequent release of Windows since then. It can be accessed by following these simple steps:

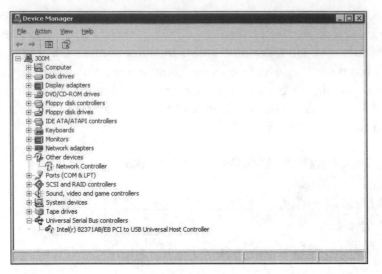

Figure 2.2
Windows Device Manager.

1. Right-click My Computer.

2. Select Properties.

3. Click the General tab.

4. Click the Device Manager button.

Here are some of the tasks you can perform using the Device Manager:

- Check the current status of hardware. Look for symbols next to a particular device to see if there are problems with it.
- Configure device properties and settings.
- Uninstall and reinstall hardware.
- Update, view, and roll back device drivers.

TIP: If you open the Device Manager and see the error shown in Figure 2.3, you will not be able to make any changes using this tool. You will only be able to view installed devices and their properties. Making changes in Device Manager requires you to have administrative privileges on your computer.

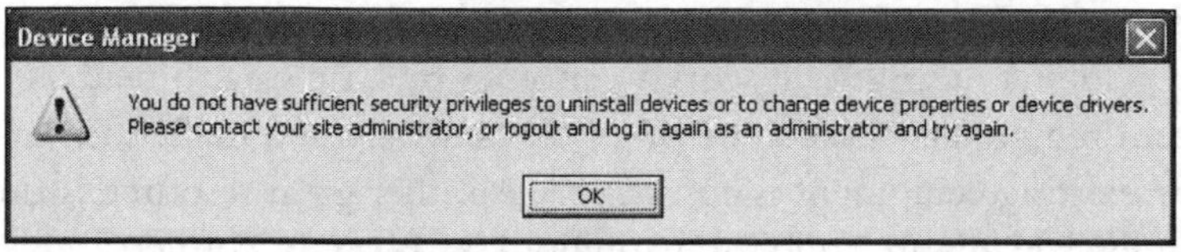

Figure 2.3
Device Manager Error Message.

Hardware Failure

- Learn about the causes of hardware failure.
- Learn what to do if your PC won't boot.
- Learn how to prevent hardware failures.

What Are the Common Causes of Hardware Failure?

Just when we have our PCs and other devices working exactly the way we want them to, *boom*—hardware failure occurs. Why? Why can't these products be built properly? Stronger? More reliable? For decades, no one has been able to create a piece of electrical hardware that won't break and will never become obsolete. The problem is that they can't see into the future to determine what technology will be hot in a few years or what manufacturing process will help them to make better, cheaper, faster, and more reliable computers and other devices. To start, let's review some of the common causes of hardware failure (you've probably experienced one or two of these already!):

- *Age:* Nothing lasts forever. This holds especially true for technology. Age has multiple effects on devices. Some break because they get old, others become obsolete. Most manufacturers establish a life expectancy for their devices—anywhere from one year to five years. These companies are smart and want their old devices to take early retirement so you have to buy new ones. Hardware also ages quickly because of cost factors. Manufacturers research what they expect the average consumer to pay for their products, and they design around that. In other words, they design for the moment and not for the future.

- *Faulty development:* Here problems range from out-of-box failures to poorly and cheaply designed, second-rate devices. Cheap, second-rate devices not only break easier than more reliable, common devices, but drivers and third-party support are more difficult to find.

- *Incompatible devices:* Just because a piece of hardware works in one computer doesn't mean it will work in another one. Be sure to read all system requirements when buying new hardware and make sure that your existing equipment is compatible. Another great resource is the Windows Hardware and Compatibility List. It can be found at **www.microsoft.com/whdc/hcl/default.mspx**.

- *Damage:* For some reason, most things on this planet don't like to be bumped, kicked, dropped, stomped, cut, and scratched. This is especially true for tech devices. Tech devices are extremely intricate, containing millions of microscopic transistors, tons of interconnected working parts, and complex power management features. The slightest upset makes the difference between the device you love and an overpriced paper weight. Treat your devices with care.

HORROR STORY! We work with someone who spent over $2,000 on a powerful computer system so that they could be really productive with their work. Then they got cheap and decided to buy a very inexpensive wireless network card. (This would be like buying the top-of-the-line Mercedes and then putting cheap gas in it!) Soon they discovered that the cheap card shorted out the motherboard, rendering the computer useless. The moral of this story: It's okay to look for a good deal but do your homework and don't buy junk.

What Should I Do If My Computer Won't Boot?

This is the nightmare scenario we all worry about from time to time. Unfortunately, the way disasters work, something like this typically happens when you need your computer the most, such as when you have to make an important presentation in front of 500 people. When your computer won't boot, the first thing you need to figure out is if you are having a hardware problem or a software problem. If your computer powers up and starts to boot the operating system (Windows), you likely have a software problem. We'll show you want you can do then in Chapter 3. If your computer won't power up, you likely have a problem related to electricity. See the sections "What Should I Do If My Desktop PC Won't Turn On?" and "What Should I Do If My Laptop Won't Turn On?" later in this chapter.

The final category of boot failures relates to the low-level systems (BIOS) and the hardware that work off them. Here's a course of action to follow if you are experiencing difficulties that fall into this category:

- *Make sure your power is working.* As silly as this might sound, don't forget to check that your power cord is plugged in properly. Check your wall socket and check the back of your PC. Inspect your power cord to make sure you don't have a defective cord. If your computer has a "power on" light, make sure that it is on.

- *Try turning the power switch on and off on your computer a few times.* This action just might do the trick.

- *Make sure your monitor is on.* Just because you see nothing on the screen doesn't mean that your computer is at fault. Check to make sure that your monitor is powered up and connected to your computer.

- *Make sure your computer runs the power-on self test (POST).* Look for any sort of output on your screen and a single beep. If you get the single beep, skip the next step. If not, then you may have some serious problems on your hands. Go to the next step.

- *Unplug everything that plugs into your computer on the outside with the exception of the power cord.* Try booting it up while listening for any beeps. If you hear a single beep, then something you unplugged must be causing a problem. If you hear no beep or hear multiple beeps, then the problem is inside the computer. If you feel comfortable doing this, remove your computer's side cover and remove the memory, processor, video card, all PCI cards, and drive cables. Now go ahead and plug everything back in and turn your computer back on. Did you get the single beep? If you did get the beep and your computer boots, you have fixed your problem. If not, you have a serious problem on your hands. Bring your computer to a qualified computer repair shop.

- *Make sure that your hard drive is working correctly.* A dead hard drive will certainly stop your computer in its tracks. Make sure that you follow the instructions presented later in this chapter for dealing with failed drives.

What Can I Do If I Forget My BIOS Password and I Can't Access It?

Some of us get nuts with setting passwords in as many places as possible. One of these obscure places is the computer's BIOS (which stands for basic input/output system). We can set a password on these to prevent others from making changes to our system. Unfortunately, this is one of those passwords that can easily be forgotten. It is not as if you type this password in every time you boot up the computer. Forgetting it usually is not a big deal, but in some cases it may be necessary to get into the BIOS. Here are some tips on how to get into the system BIOS if you have forgotten the password:

- *Use default passwords.* Most BIOS manufacturers have a back-door password that can be used to bypass the password you put in place. A quick search on the Web for "BIOS default passwords" will turn up hundreds. The tip at the end of this section shows you how to determine who made your system BIOS. Then, just look up your manufacturer's default passwords in these lists.

- *Use password cracking software.* Some clever people have written programs that allow you to crack the BIOS password. One of our favorites can be downloaded from **http://natan.zejn.si/rempass.html**.

- *Use the jumper.* Most motherboard manufacturers provide you with a jumper on the motherboard that can be used to reset the BIOS. Shorting out these pins will automatically reset your BIOS. Check your system manual for more information. You may also find this information on a label affixed to the inside of your system.

- *Remove the battery.* Somewhere on your computer's motherboard you will find a battery. It will look like a large watch battery. Removing it for about 10 minutes may do the trick and reset your BIOS.

- *Overload the keyboard buffer.* Some older systems can be reset by pressing the Esc key rapidly during boot or by unplugging both the keyboard and mouse before booting up.

- *Use a service.* As a last resort, you can use a professional service to crack the password.

TIP: You can determine the manufacturer of your system BIOS by paying close attention when you start your computer. Look at the first few lines of text that appear. Usually most BIOS manufacturers will put a blurb about themselves here.

How Can I Recognize If My Hard Drive Is Dying?

The scenarios presented in this section and the next two are perhaps the most important ones in this book, so read them carefully! Hard drives are being used on more and more devices these days, including laptops, desktops, MP3 players, DVRs (TiVo, Replay), Xbox, iPods, and even certain DVD recorders. Hard drives are sensitive devices, easily damaged by heat, dust, and shock. If your device is acting strangely, it may be because the hard drive is dying. Keep a close eye out for any of these symptoms, and if you detect any, follow the advice in the next section:

- Your hard drive is talking! If you hear your hard drive screaming, squealing, or clicking, chances are it is dead or well on its way. If you hear these sounds and your device will not boot, please proceed to the next section.

- It is taking longer than usual for your device to get up and running.

- The hard disk is silent for long periods after you try to open a file or folder.

- Error messages appear much more frequently, particularly when you perform tasks such as copying, pasting, and deleting files and folders.

- File and folder names are changing to weird names.

- Your files are missing or inaccessible.

- It is taking longer than usual to access your files.

- The contents of files are jumbled or you get irregular output when printing files.

- The video on your DVR skips or locks up.

- Devices that blue-screen (or green-screen if you own a TiVo) or even lock up frequently may be suffering from a bad hard drive. If you used Windows 95, 98, or ME you will be familiar with blue-screens. Usually they occur when you are working on a very important document and all of a sudden your screen turns blue and displays a cryptic error message. If we only had a nickel for every time this has happened.

What Should I Do If My Hard Drive Is Having Problems?

Basically, hard drives are compact, electromechanical storage devices comprising metal discs that store data. In the early days of personal computers, it didn't take much to damage them. Today, hard drives are much more reliable, but they do fail, and when they do, you might feel like you should break down in tears. Here are some things you can do if your drive is starting to act up:

- *Run a BIOS checking utility.* Most newer computers come with a utility in the BIOS that can scan for errors. The term for this is Self-Monitoring, Analysis and Reporting Technology (SMART). Most modern hard drives come standard with this technology. Here are instructions on how to use these types of utilities. Keep in mind that your system may be a little different, so always double-check your documentation.
    - Look for something that says "Press F10 for setup" or "Setup F2." The exact keystroke can vary from system to system.
    - Once you are in the system BIOS, you should see a section called "Utilities." Once again, this can vary greatly from system to system.
    - Run any tests that are offered for hard drives.

- The results of these tests will give you a good indication of whether your hard drive is any good.

- *Run the Checkdisk utility to scan and repair any errors.* You can run this from Windows, but we prefer to use it from the command prompt—you know, that black screen with the white letters that everyone is so fearful of. You can start the command prompt by clicking Start, clicking Run, typing in **CMD**, and pressing Enter. At the prompt type **CHKDSK *x*: / R**, where *x* is the drive letter you want to check, and press Enter. If you are prompted to reboot, go right ahead and do so. This is necessary because the utility needs full access to your drive. Things like Weather Bug, antivirus software, and other programs that load at startup can prevent it from finishing.

- *Use scanning software provided by your drive manufacturer.* Most companies provide software that you can use on your drive to check it. We highly recommend Western Digital's Data Lifeguard Diagnostics. The nice people at Western Digital have designed this utility to run on any hard drive regardless of the manufacturer. It is very easy to use and does error checking, surface scans, and SMART diagnostics. You can download this tool for free at **http://westerndigital.com**.

What Should I Do If My Hard Drive Has Completely Failed?

Welcome to the land of "last resort," or so it may seem. You may have been experiencing some failure symptoms that you've ignored or you may turn your device on only to discover that it won't start up. Here's what you need to do:

- *Use our "defibrillator" method.* This might seem drastic, but give it a try. First, unplug your computer. Then, remove your computer's cover, yell "CLEAR!" and give the face of your hard drive a light tap with a screwdriver or small hammer. Sometimes this will give you a few more minutes for you and your hard drive to be together.

- *Remove the hard drive and place it in your freezer.* Let it get nice and cold to the touch. Put it back into your machine. As crazy as this sounds, it may sometimes give you the precious time you need to extract your important data from the drive.

- *If none of the previous methods worked, chances are the drive is dead.* If you still absolutely have to get at the data on the drive, there are people that can help. There are companies that specialize in removing data from bad drives. It is not a cheap alternative, though. Expect to pay a premium.

How Can I Help Prevent Hard Drive Failure?

Hard drive failures usually render their associated devices useless, especially if it is the main drive. While certain failures cannot be prevented (death by age, manufacturer's defect, most other failures are all things that can easily be prevented. Here are a few ways you can help prevent hard drive failure:

- *Proper ventilation*: Keep your device's vents open and clear from debris. Properly cooling your device's internal components is paramount.

- *Physical impact*: Don't drop your device or subject it to severe shock. This can cause damage to the drive's platters and reading heads.

- *Voltage*: Use a surge protector or UPS. This will prevent any voltage spikes or drops from damaging your computer. A small increase or drop in system voltage can wreak havoc in electronics. This is especially true during the summer months when air conditioners are running. Also, try not to plug large appliances (air conditioners, refrigerators, and so on) into the same outlet your computer is plugged into.

- *RAID*: Purchase and install drive mirroring hardware. Basically, this is a card you install in your PC. You attach your current drive to this card and add another drive of equal or greater capacity. The card then creates a mirror image of the main drive on the fly. If your main drive dies, it switches over to the backup. This type of setup is highly recommended if the PC is being used for important tasks such as business uses.

TIP: Back up and restore your data on a frequent basis. There is no sense in doing backups if you are not sure that they are working. Windows comes with a free tool called Windows Backup that can back up your data to a tape drive or a file that can be stored on CD-ROM, DVD, Zip disks, or many other formats. To run, click Start | Run, type **NTBACKUP**, and click OK. Figure 2.4 shows the Windows Backup utility in action.

Why Won't My Monitor Turn On?

For the most part, the monitor is a reliable device. Other than advances in video types and resolutions, they have not changed much. This has allowed manufacturers to perfect how they are made and the quality of the components going into them. Every once in a blue moon you will run into one that does not work properly. The following suggestions should help you get out of a jam:

- *Make sure the monitor is actually turned on.* Is the power light on?

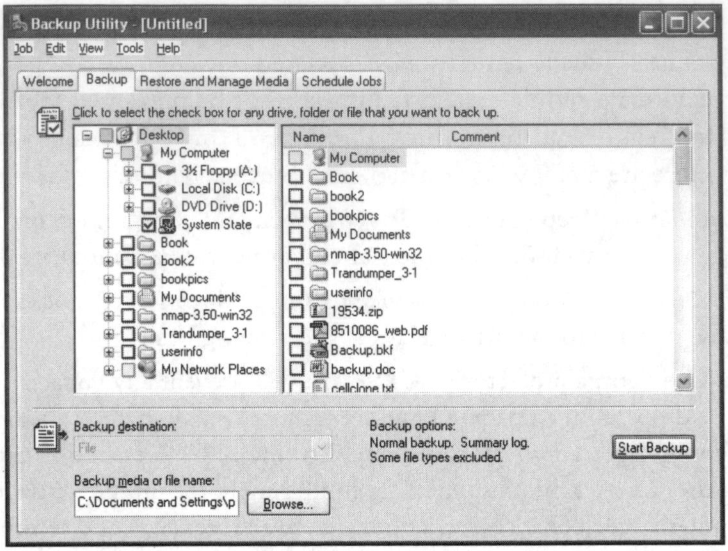

Figure 2.4
Windows Backup.

- *If the monitor is connected to a laptop, you may be having laptop display problems.* See the sections on laptops later in this chapter for more information.

- *Check to see that everything is connected properly.* Make sure the power cord is connected firmly to the monitor. Some computers have an on-board video card and a third-party video card. Make sure your monitor is connected to the right connector on the desktop or laptop.

- *Check to make sure that the connector pins aren't bent or broken.* Most monitor connectors have tiny pins that connect to your computer or laptop. These pins can be easily bent or broken if you're not careful. Examine the connector to see bent, broken, or missing pins. Video graphics array (VGA) monitors (traditional cathode-ray tube, or CRT, monitors) have 15 pins, while liquid crystal display (LCD) monitors (newer flatscreen) have 24 pins.

- *Make sure you have power.* Verify the monitor is plugged into a power source. If it is plugged into a power strip or uninterruptible power supply (UPS), make sure that the power strip or UPS is switched on. Try plugging the monitor directly into a wall outlet to be on the safe side. If all else fails, try plugging a known working device (for example, a lamp) into the outlet to verify that the outlet is working. If the known working device does not power on, you may have blown a fuse or have a bad outlet.

- *Make sure the monitor's power switch is on.* Some monitors have a separate power switch on the back. Make sure it is switched on.

- *Make sure the power button doesn't feel funny.* Power buttons are very prone to failures. They are one of the places some computer manufacturers look to cut corners. If you cannot press it in completely or it feels unusually springy, it may be broken.

- *Try replacing the power cord.*

- *Get help.* If none of these steps have helped, you should seek assistance from your local tech support or computer manufacturer. Under no circumstances should you try to open or attempt to repair a CRT monitor. There are several hazards in doing this. You can be electrocuted by large capacitors inside the case, and the picture tube itself can implode if improperly handled. Please leave these types of repairs to a professional. Don't try to be a hero.

Why Does My Monitor Have Spots or Discoloration?

If you have ever put a magnet near a television, you know exactly what we are talking about here. The screen image distorts and the colors change drastically, leaving you with an image that resembles a tie-dyed T shirt. Most of the time it looks like a color stain on your screen. Keep in mind this only happens to CRT monitors; LCD displays are exempt from this phenomenon. Here's how you can fix this problem:

- *Most modern monitors have built-in degaussing mechanisms.* It usually can be accessed by using the menu controls or by pressing the degauss button. Check your monitor's documentation for specific instructions.

- *If degaussing does not work immediately, try doing it for about a week every time you boot up.* It may take several degaussing sessions to clear some cases of this up.

- *In extreme cases, the built-in degaussing tool in monitors will not work.* These will require the use of a manual degaussing tool. Most TV repair shops (if you can find one still in business) can do this for you for a nominal fee.

How Can I Prevent Monitor Spots or Discoloration?

When a monitor is spotted or discolored, it is due to magnetism. This usually doesn't occur on its own but as a result of an outside force. Here's how you can prevent magnetism in your monitor:

- *Keep stereo speakers, telephones, and other magnets away from your monitor.*

- *Some computer speakers provide shielding to prevent this from happening.* Generally, the cheaper the speaker, the less shielding you get (if any at all). When in doubt, just move the speakers an adequate distance from the monitor.

- *Screens can also become magnetized as a result of physical shock to the monitor.*

- *An extreme change in the orientation of the monitor can cause this effect.* Try not to move it around too much.

- *Some types of very strong magnets can permanently damage a monitor.*

Why Does My Monitor Make Noise?

CRT monitors (monitors that look like traditional tube televisions with a glass screen) traditionally make noise when turned on or when the resolution/refresh rate is changed. This noise is usually a buzzing or clicking sound. The noise is caused by the voltage changes that occur. They are perfectly normal. If your monitor is making noise even when you do not change resolutions/refresh rates, this may indicate a hardware problem and you should have your monitor serviced.

What Should I Do If My Input Devices Stop Working?

This can be one of the most debilitating failures. Your $2,500 desktop or laptop has been rendered useless by a faulty mouse, keyboard, or touchpad. Here are some fixes to help you when your input devices stop working:

- *Make sure it is plugged in.* Most modern keyboards and mice use either a PS2 or Universal Serial Bus (USB) connection.

- *Check connections.* If your keyboard is not plugged in, you may have to reboot in order for the computer to recognize the keyboard.

- *Check for reversed connections.* Make sure your keyboard and mouse connections are not reversed. On most systems, keyboard connections are green while mice connections are purple.

- *Check your drivers.* For PDAs, make sure you download and install the latest drivers from the manufacturer's website.

- *Check for wireless.* For wireless keyboards and mice, ensure that the batteries are charged. Also ensure you are in range for the keyboard to work correctly.

- *Use the Windows Help and Support Center.* Click the Windows Start button and then Help and Support. When the help center appears, click Fixing a problem. In the left menu, click Hardware and system device problems. In the right pane under Pick a task, select Input Device Troubleshooter.

PREVENTATIVE MAINTENANCE: Cleaning is a simple thing that you can do to extend the life of any device. You can use compressed air, a computer-safe vacuum, or some cotton swabs with alcohol (isopropyl please) to clean most input devices. Make sure your computer is off and consult your owner's manual before cleaning.

What Should I Do If My Device Can't Read or Write to a CD/DVD?

Whether you are using your computer, DVD player, or CD player in your car, in your lap, or in your living room, CD and DVD players have become the top tech toys in the average home. They bring us music, movies, and data in a small, inexpensive package. The following solutions describe what to do if your device can't read or write to a CD or DVD:

* *CD players can only read CDs.* CD players use a specific type of laser to read the data from a disc. Placing a DVD in them will cause an error.

* *Certain types of drives can only read certain types of discs.* The standard formats are CD, CD-R, CD-RW, DVD-R, DVD+R, DVD-RW, DVD+RW. Just because your device is a CD or DVD burner doesn't mean it can read all these types. Check your owner's manual for more information.

* *Older CD and DVD players may not be able to read recordable media.* Even newer players may not be able to. Consult your owner's manual for more information.

* *Insert a disc into the drive and see if any LEDs light up on the drive.* In addition, check to see if the eject mechanism works properly. If no lights are visible on the front of the drive, check the power connection on the drive.

* *A dirty laser lens can cause the drive to have difficulty reading the disc.* See the preventative maintenance section for tips on how to clean these.

* *Is your computer mounted sideways?* Most drives have "catches" to allow sideways mounting, but they do not always work. This depends on your drive's speed and catch mechanism (center catch or rim). To see if this is the cause of the problem, turn your computer right side up and try again.

PREVENTATIVE MAINTENANCE: Drive lenses can be cleaned in a couple of ways. You can purchase cleaning discs. And if you are feeling adventurous, you can also disassemble the drive and clean the lens with isopropyl alcohol and a lint-free cloth.

What Can I Do If My CD/DVD/Hard Drive Doesn't Work After I Install It?

Installing new hardware can be tricky business. Here are a few things to check if a drive fails to work after it's installed:

- *Check the power.* Ensure that the power is connected properly.

- *Make sure the IDE cable is installed correctly.* The red stripe on the cable should line up with pin #50 of the drive's connector.

- *Make sure the drive's master/slave jumper is positioned correctly.* It can be set to master, slave, or cable select, depending on your particular setup. Check your computer's documentation for more info.

- *Try installing the drive on a different IDE channel.* This option is available only on desktop models. If it works on another channel, you more than likely have a bad IDE channel.

- *Check the status of the device in Device Manager.* If it is listed but has an exclamation point, question mark, or red *X* next to its name, the problem may be driver-related.

Why Won't My CD Drive Play Music?

Some computers live hidden lives as expensive CD players. This is most common in offices where Barry Manilow and Neil Diamond are played through the office Muzak system. A disgruntled employee will throw in a Led Zeppelin disc to drown out the other music. But what happens when this does not work? Does the person have to go nuts? Follow these instructions to find out:

- *Check the audio interface cable.* If you just replaced your CD drive and it suddenly will not play music or your PC was never able to play music, then this is the culprit. This cable runs between the CD drive and either the motherboard or sound card. Without it, you will have no audio running out of your CD drive.

- *Check the speakers.* Make sure your speakers are hooked up correctly and are powered on.

- *Make sure your computer has a sound card in it.* Without this crucial device, you will never be able to play music in your computer.

What Should I Do If My USB Ports or Connected Devices Don't Work?

Universal Serial Bus (USB) technology has been around since about 1995. It was originally touted as the successor to serial and parallel ports. It has lived up to its billing but still has its fair share of problems. These solutions show you what to do if you have trouble with USB ports or connected devices:

- *Using Windows NT or Windows 95?* Sorry, but Bill Gates says USB is not supported on these operating systems. Time to upgrade.

- *Try connecting fewer devices.* USB ports have a maximum bandwidth and voltage limitation. This is true even if you have a USB hub.

- *Try a different port.* The USB port you are currently plugged into may be broken. Try using a different one to determine if this is the problem.

- *If using a USB hub, try bypassing the hub.*

- *Check the length of your cable.* Your device manufacturer may have a maximum length of cable that can be used before errors and interoperability occur.

- *Check the status of the device in Device Manager.* If it is listed but has an exclamation point, question mark, or red *X* next to its name, the problem may be driver related.

PREVENTATIVE MEASURE: Be very careful when removing or inserting cables from the USB ports because the connectors are easily broken.

What Can I Do If My Floppy Drive Won't Work?

Although floppy drives are definitely on their way out, many of us still depend on them for sharing files with others and backing up important data. Only minor changes have been made to them over the years, mostly in the area of capacity. The hardware has remained pretty much the same. Here are some things to check if you are having problems with the floppy drive:

- *Your floppy drive LED should blink when you are booting your machine.* If it doesn't, you should check to make sure it is plugged into the power supply.

- *On the flip side, an LED that stays on solid more than likely indicates that the interface cable is not plugged in correctly.* Your floppy drive has a connector with 34 pins. This connector will probably have pin #1 clearly marked. Pin #1 should line up with the colored stripe on the interface cable.

- *Make sure the drive is being detected by the BIOS.*

- *Make sure a shield from a floppy disk has not been left in the drive.* We have personally seen this a number of times and it is very difficult to diagnose. If you do discover that this has happened, removing the shield may or may not be difficult. Try first opening the drive flap and fishing it out with an envelope opener or other thin, long object. Be careful not to bend any internal components of the drive. If this does not prove fruitful, then removing the drive should be next on your list. Once the drive is out, carefully pry off the upper cover and remove the shield. Also be on the lookout for the tiny spring that operates the shield. It may have dropped into the drive and should be removed. If it is left in the drive, it may cause damage to any floppy disks that are inserted. Other items to be on the lookout for include Post-it notes, address labels, and disk labels.

- *Clean the drive using a cleaning disk and some isopropyl alcohol.* In most cases, this will cure a floppy drive that will not read from a disk.

How Can I Prevent My Floppy Drive from Destroying My Floppies?

Floppies are so delicate and unpredictable that the slightest mistreatment can make then completely unusable. This is particularly important if you have been storing data on a floppy. The following tips will minimize the chances of this happening to you:

- *Make a sacrifice to appease the floppy gods.* If you haven't used your floppy drive in a while, chances are that a great deal of dust has accumulated inside of it. This dust can end up on a floppy disk and will contaminate the disk, resulting in data loss. You can minimize this damage by first inserting a blank or unimportant floppy to take the brunt of the dust attack.

- *Clean house.* Clean your drive with a vacuum cleaner. Then thoroughly blow it out with compressed air. This will dislodge any dust and particles that have made a home in your floppy drive.

- *Rotate your floppies.* Note the date that you started using the floppy disk. You can mark this on the label with a pen or marker. Only use the floppy for about six months. After this time, copy all files to another floppy.

Unfortunate Hardware Mishaps

- Learn what to do if your device catches fire.
- Learn what to do if you drop your device.

Why Did My Device Catch on Fire or Start Smoking?

As ridiculous as this might sound, it does happen. Plastic, metal, and flowing electricity can make for a very combustible combination under the right circumstances. When products are tested by the manufacturers, it is usually done in pristine laboratory conditions that are nothing like the conditions in your homes and offices. Here are some of the common causes of a smoky or fiery device so that you can avoid the embarrassment:

- *Old electrical wiring:* Older homes are notorious for having less than adequate electrical systems. Peter's home is a prime example. The home was built in 1920 and, for the most part, still has most of the original electrical system in place. This electrical system was designed for one light bulb and one clock per room. It simply cannot consistently provide enough electricity for today's power-hungry hardware.

- *Overloaded electric sockets:* Yes, we've all done this at one time or another— plug 14 items into an adapter connected to a 2-socket outlet. Christmas is a popular time of year for this phenomenon (see the movies *Christmas Story* and *Christmas Vacation* for re-enactments). Try to avoid doing this at all costs; it just isn't worth the risk. Power strips cost around $7 these days, are readily available at most stores, and may even protect your device from power surges. See Chapter 12 for more information about power surges.

- *Incorrect power supplies:* One of our father's was famous for this one: substituting a lost adapter with an adapter that looked similar or even modifying the connector to make it fit. Sometimes it would work, but most of the time he just ended up destroying the adapter and the device. The moral: Always use the proper power supply. When buying or using a replacement, make sure the replacement matches the voltage and amperage requirements and is Underwriters Laboratories listed.

- *Inadequate ventilation:* Remember that your machines need to breathe just as you do. Storing hot, running computers in a small space (such as a cabinet or a closet) may cause it to overheat and catch fire. In addition, humid conditions will cause the device to moisten, short out, and possibly catch fire. Your device needs to be in a location that is room temperature, but preferably a little cooler. Keep that in mind when choosing a location for your devices.

- *Blocked ventilation:* Laptops are crammed with all sorts of stuff and run very hot. They contain multiple fans needed to keep the machine at a reasonable temperature. Placing the laptop directly on your lap or atop a pillow or blanket may cause the fans on the bottom to be blocked, ultimately causing the device to overheat, catch fire, or worse, catch your pillow, blanket, and even clothes on fire.

- *Foreign objects in the case:* Kids, pets, and even gravity can cause nasty stuff like coins, paper clips, and other little goodies to find their way into the case. If you are lucky, they will just float harmlessly in there. But do you want to count on luck?

- *Overclocking:* This is the act of modifying a device's clock speed to have it run faster than the manufacturer originally intended. Gamers are notorious for this, forcing their CPU and video card to run at top speeds. While we all want our hardware to run at top speeds, the manufacturer has set its recommended speed to avoid errors, shortness of life, and overheating.

- *Liquids:* Water will cause serious damage to your device and may even cause fire. One of water's natural properties is its capability to conduct electricity. Unless your device is waterproof, keep it away from liquids. See the section called "What Should I Do If My Device Gets Wet?" later in this chapter for more information.

HORROR STORY! This is one of the most unusual mishaps described in this book, and each time we think about it we start to laugh. A newspaper in California ran a story with this headline: "Girl Burned when Cell Phone Catches Fire." According to the story, a 16-year-old girl suffered second-degree burns when her cell phone caught fire in her back pocket. Witnesses say they saw smoke, an explosion, and fire coming from her pants. I think we can safely assume that the fire was caused by the cell phone and not by her pants.

What Should I Do If My Device Catches Fire or Starts Smoking?

If your device catches on fire or starts smoking, first avoid the obvious responses (like screaming, crying, or running). Try to take a calm and systematic approach. In situations like these, your life or the life of others may depend on it. Here's exactly what to do:

- *Stop, drop, and roll.* If the device is in your pocket, you have no time to waste. If you have access to water, immediately jump in or soak up. If there is no water, take your shirt or pants off immediately and stomp out the fire. All portable devices are low voltage and are not an electrocution threat. Never try to take the device out of your pocket. You'll just increase your chance of getting burned and spreading the fire.

- *Disconnect power.* By disconnecting power, you may be able to limit the amount of damage. Be careful with the power cord; it may have built up a considerable amount of heat in a very short time. You may be tempted to unplug it, but we recommend leaving it. If the cord is hot enough, just touching it may cause the plastic shielding to separate and may lead to electrocution. To be safe, always disconnect power at the breaker box. You may also try disconnecting power by switching your UPS or power strip off, provided you can tell they are not affected by the fire.

- *Get the device outdoors.* If possible, place the device outdoors on concrete, asphalt, or some other nonflammable surface. Placing a fiery computer on your lawn is a bad idea. Besides, you don't want to upset the neighbors!

- *If the device if plugged in to an outlet, DO NOT USE WATER TO PUT OUT THE FIRE.* Water will only lead to electrocution and rusting of salvageable components. You should use a fire extinguisher that has been rated for all types of fires. See the next section for more info.

- *Call the fire department.* If you have any doubts about your ability to put the fire out immediately, call the fire department. They are trained in dealing with every type of emergency.

How Can I Prevent a Fire from Happening in the First Place?

If Smokey the Bear was employed by the electronics industry, here's the advice he would likely give:

- *Use only a UL approved, adequate power supply.* This is extremely important because the wrong power supply can quickly lead to disaster. An incorrect adapter can build up heat very quickly, melt through wiring, and start a fire.

- *Use a lap desk.* Use a lap desk to avoid burns and provide proper ventilation. Laptops get hot, and placing one directly on your lap or on a pillow or other flammable item may cause burns or a fire.

- *Buy yourself a fire extinguisher.* This is probably one of the most overlooked safety devices you should have in your house. Having a fire extinguisher handy during a fire can mean the difference between a little fire damage and your home burning to the ground. They can be purchased at local home improvement stores or shops that specialize in fire safety. Be sure to buy one that is rated for all types of fire. Using one rated for wood fires won't help you much with electrical fires.

WARNING! Fires spread very quickly when in the right environment. Besides the danger of the fire itself, burning plastic can quickly release deadly poisonous fumes. When in doubt, get out and call the fire department. Despite what your boss might say, no device is worth losing your life.

HORROR STORY! We recently came across a story of a fellow who had a small fire at his house. He calmly walked over to where he kept his trusty fire extinguisher, pulled it off the wall, pulled the pin, pressed the handle down, and...nothing happened. So what went wrong? He had neglected to have his fire extinguisher recharged every year. This is necessary to keep them in proper working order. Plan on doing this when you change the batteries in your smoke alarms.

What Should I Do If My Device Gets Wet?

Unless your device has gills, swims, is not electric, is made of stainless parts, and is basically a fish, getting it wet is not a good idea. So until someone decides to invent electronics that work underwater, we need to follow these guidelines:

- *Disconnect power.* By disconnecting power, you may be able to limit the amount of damage. If the device is plugged into a power source, *do not unplug or touch the device.* Water + Electricity = Electrocution. To be safe, always disconnect power at the breaker box. You may also try disconnecting power by switching your UPS or power strip off, provided you can tell that they are not wet.

- *Disconnect the battery.* If the device is powered by a low voltage battery (laptop, PDA), disconnect the battery. You can reduce the chances of the device being permanently destroyed by removing power as soon as possible.

- *Discharge the device.* Once it's disconnected from power and out of the' "wet zone," discharge the device. By pressing the power button a few times, you can discharge (drain the electricity from) the internal components. This will allow all of the electricity to dissipate from the internal circuitry of the device. Believe it or not, some components may stay charged for up to several weeks.

- *Dry it off.* Wipe off any water with a towel. Try to be as thorough as possible. Any water that you miss may end up finding its way back into the device.

- *Let it dry out.* Let the device dry out completely, not just the outside. It could take up to 24 hours for your device to dry out thoroughly. If you have water under a screen, do not press the screen to try to get the water out. Let the water evaporate on its own.

- *Do not shake it dry.* Do not vigorously shake your device to remove the water because you may spread the water damage and additionally damage other shock-sensitive components, such as hard drives and internal speakers.

- *Get help.* If none of these steps have helped, you should seek assistance from your local tech support or computer manufacturer.

HORROR STORY!

This is a story that was sent to us by Joli Ballew, the author of the bestselling book, *Degunking Windows*. Last January, I was in Seattle at a conference. No one was home. The next weekend, I stepped out to lunch with my parents. During the hour and a half we were gone, the hot water heater burst. Apparently, water just kept streaming out of it until the water got turned off at the street. It was disastrous, and when we got home, the water was all the way down in the hallway and only inches away from the computer—whose tower sits on the floor in the first bedroom. It was making its way back to the other rooms. We saved everything, but one week later and the whole house would have been a goner. We used a lot of towels. Can you believe we actually had a wet-dry shop vac in the garage we never even drug out?

What Preventive Measures Can I Take to Keep Water Away?

In addition to the obvious—don't get it wet in the first place—here's what you can do:

- *Don't drink and compute.* This is a common cause of wet devices.
- *Don't store your devices in or near areas where they can get wet.* This includes a pool, toilet, bathtub, fish tank, the outdoors, and so on.
- *Don't expose your device to extreme temperature changes.* Doing so will cause condensation (water) to form on the case and internals and eventually it will fail.

What Should I Do If I Drop My Device?

After dropping your device, you must first cleanse yourself of any violent thoughts directed at the device. After all, it was not the device's fault. It was your own clumsiness. Swear a little, compose yourself, and follow these steps:

- *Try powering it on.* You would be surprised at the resilience of technology (but make sure you cross your fingers first—this can really help!).
- *Check connections.* If it does not power up immediately, verify that a component has not become dislodged (battery, hard drive, and so on).
- *Shake and listen.* Shake it lightly and listen for loose pieces. If you hear any pieces rattling around inside your machine, chances are that you have broken it.

TIP: If you are prone to accidents, you should purchase an extended warranty or insurance for your device. Most manufacturers offer complete coverage for a price. You can also buy a protective case for your device.

HORROR STORY! Our publisher told us about this mishap he had with his laptop recently. He traveled from Arizona to Shanghai, China, for an important presentation that he was giving. The presentation was on his laptop, and he didn't have a backup. When he got to his hotel, he dropped his laptop and the laptop refused to boot. He started taking components out of the laptop and eventually he took out the internal accessory drive and the computer booted right up. It turned out that dropping the computer damaged a component in the accessory drive. Sometimes you get lucky!

What Should I Do If a CD/DVD Is Stuck in My Device?

This happens more often than you can possibly imagine. To make matters worse, it is usually your least favorite CD or DVD that gets stuck in the player—you know, that Hanson CD you picked up from the discount bin at Wal-Mart. So does this mean that you must spend the rest of your life listening to "MmmBop"? Before you take drastic measures to avoid this aural torture, try these solutions:

- *Is the power on?* Almost every CD/DVD drive requires power to eject the disc. Make sure you have power before trying to eject the disc. If you hear grinding noises, shut off power and skip to the last step.

- *Clippy to the rescue.* No, we're not referring to that annoying cartoon character Microsoft promised would be removed from Office but never was. We're talking about a paper clip. Most desktop and laptop CD/DVD drives have a manual eject hole, a tiny hole big enough to fit a paper clip. Stick a paper clip all the way in there and the CD will eject. You may have to remove the front bezel to get at it.

- *Use a slight pry.* If you have a player with a tray mechanism (a tray comes out and you place the disc on it), you can try to pry open the tray. With the power off, try to gently pry the tray open. Take care not to break the bezel or drive mechanism by prying too hard. If a gentle pry does not open the tray, do not apply more force. You can proceed to the next step and prevent yourself from breaking the drive.

- *Take it apart.* If you have some mechanical skill and a little guts, you can try to take the drive apart and remove the obstruction. For most CD/DVD players, you can remove the screws from the bottom or back, take off the cover, and then remove the obstruction (and of course put the thing back together). This may void your warranty, so do this as a last resort.

Why Do CDs/DVDs Get Stuck in My Device?

Here are a few reasons why a disc may get stuck in a drive:

- *Heat:* Excessive heat can damage and warp your discs, causing them to get stuck in the drive. Keep your disc out of the sun and away from heat to reduce warping.

- *Labels:* Custom labels pasted on a disc can come off (even partially) and cause your disc to get stuck in the drive. Whether the glue does not adhere properly (bubbles, humidity), cheap glue was used on the label or label kits, or the heat from the drive causes the label to lift, custom labels aren't worth the damage they can cause. Use a permanent marker instead.

- *Disc present:* Putting multiple discs into a single drive mechanism will cause a jam. Even if your player is a changer (able to read multiple discs), it can only read one at a time (since it truly has only one drive mechanism). Always ensure that there is no disc in the drive and that the drive is ready before inserting a new disc.

- *It's broken:* The mechanism to eject the disc or tray may be broken. This can include the motor, the gear, or the power supply line that feeds the motor.

Desktop PCs

- Learn about the common causes of desktop failure.
- Learn how to resolve desktop failure issues.

What Should I Do If My Desktop PC Won't Turn On?

Desktop computers are the easiest devices to troubleshoot when it comes to power. Unlike laptops or PDAs, desktops usually have all of their components firmly secured inside the case and aren't moved often. Here's a list of tasks you can perform if your desktop will not turn on:

- *Are you pressing the right button?* Most PCs have both a reset and a power button, usually on the front of the computer and usually right next to each other. These buttons can be confusing because most of the time they are not labeled and just have some hieroglyphic picture next to them. When in doubt, press one. If your PC still does not turn on, press the other one.

- *Do you hear that?* Do you hear or even see the fans inside the power supply turning? Can you feel the air coming out? The power supply is usually located at the back of the computer, right where the power cord connects to the computer. If you cannot hear, see, or feel the power supply fan and you follow all the following steps, you may need to replace your power supply.

- *What's that smell?* Does the power supply or the computer emit a burning smell? If so, chances are the power supply has burned out and needs to be replaced.

- *Is everything connected properly?* Make sure the power cord is connected firmly to the computer power supply and to the source of power.

- *Do you have power?* Verify that the computer is plugged in to a power source. If it is plugged in to a power strip or uninterruptible power supply (UPS), make sure that the power strip or UPS is switched on. Try plugging the computer directly into a wall outlet to be on the safe side. If all else fails, try plugging a known working device (a lamp, for example) into the outlet to verify that the outlet is working. If the known working device does not power on, you may have blown a fuse or have a bad outlet.

- *Is the computer's power switch on?* Some computers have a separate power switch on the back. Make sure it is switched on.

- *Does the power button feel funny?* If the power button feels funny or is permanently stuck in the on or off position, chances are that it is broken.

- *Try replacing the power cord.*

- *Get help.* If none of these steps have helped, you should seek assistance from your local tech support or computer manufacturer.

What Should I Do If My Computer Keeps Shutting Off?

A desktop computer that shuts off on its own can be very difficult to diagnose. The failure can be a result of hardware, software, or a combination of both. Here are some common things to look out for:

- *Make sure that you have a good constant flow of power to your PC.* If at all possible, use a line conditioning device or a UPS.

- *Make sure your power supply is providing enough current to feed the computer and all of its accessories.* If you have recently added new hardware, you may be pushing the envelope. Also, if you smell anything suspicious coming from the computer, suspect a failing power supply.

- *Check the connections going from the power supply to your computer's mainboard.* Make sure the connector is fully inserted and is making good contact.

- *Install all Windows critical updates.* There are some vulnerabilities in Windows that can cause this to happen under the right circumstances.

- *Reseat any connectors or components you can get your hands on.* This can include memory, video card, PCI cards, connectors, processors, and BIOS chips.

If you have tried all of these suggestions but continue to have problems, it may be time to get help.

HORROR STORY!

A client once called complaining that one of their computers was constantly shutting itself down. The computer would then mysteriously reboot itself after a little while. After arriving on the scene, we spent a good deal of time waiting for the computer to shut down. After about a two-hour wait it finally did it. The computer just died. After some careful diagnosis, we discovered that the outlet the computer was plugged into was controlled by a light switch. The catch was that the light switch was located in an adjacent office.

What Should I Do If My Desktop Computer Has No Sound?

Most desktop computers come with only an internal "speaker," which provides the lovely beeps that occur when your computer powers on. Computer speakers are usually external and can be as simple as a two-speaker setup or as complex as a five-speaker setup with a subwoofer (boy, could we use one of those). Here are the steps to take if you have no sound from your desktop:

1. *Make sure your speakers are on.* Verify that the speakers are connected to power and switched on. Most desktop speakers have a power light (usually green) that allows you to see if they have power.

2. *Pump up the volume.* Verify that the volume is turned up and not muted. You need to check in several places for this. First, make sure that the volume control on the speakers is turned up. Also, check to see whether the volume is turned down or muted in Windows. You can do this in Control Panel.

3. *Make sure the speakers are connected.* Make sure the speakers are connected to the proper output jack. The jack and connector are usually color-coded according to the following table:

Pink or red	Microphone input
Green	Line Output
Light Blue	Line Input
Orange	Digital Output
Black	Line Out 2, analog, for rear speakers

4. *Check for crackling.* If you hear crackling coming from the computer speakers, the cables and connectors are loose or need replacement. Blown speakers can also cause this. Try borrowing a set from a friend to see if the problem persists.

5. *Open up Device Manager and check the status of sound card.* It will be listed under "Sound, video and game controllers." Check the section at the beginning of this chapter to determine what the problem is. If the sound device does not show in Device Manager, try rescanning for hardware. If this does not work, you may have a faulty sound card.

6. *Use the Windows Help and Support Center.* Click the Windows Start button and then click Help and Support. When the help center appears, click "Fixing a problem." In the left menu, click "Games, sound, and video problems." In the right pane, select "Sound Troubleshooter."

Laptops

- Learn the common causes of laptop failure.
- Learn how to resolve laptop failure issues.

There is no tech device we treasure more than our laptop computers. Their portability, size, and weight make many people choose them over desktop computers. Yet, others still have a bias against laptops. When they first became popular, laptops had many issues. Poor display and battery life, heavy weight, and slower processors were just some of the problems that plagued the early laptops. With advances in micro circuitry, display technologies, and battery life, the laptop is an equal competitor to the desktop. This section will help you troubleshoot some common problems experienced with laptops.

What Should I Do If My Laptop Won't Turn On?

While laptops provide the functionality of a desktop, they provide so much more since they have to be small, portable, and versatile. This extra layer of functionality means more areas to check when something goes wrong. Here are the key steps you should take if your laptop will not turn on:

1. *Is the battery charged?* This is the most common cause of a laptop not turning on. Attach power to the laptop and try turning it on. If the battery is fully drained, you may have to leave the device charging for a few hours before you can turn it on (even if it's plugged in). Also keep in mind the fact that batteries may discharge even though the laptop is turned off.

2. *Are you pressing the right button?* Most laptops have multiple buttons and switches that control power. For example, a laptop may have a slider switch to provide power to the computer but a button to actually turn on the computer. When in doubt, consult your owner's manual.

3. *What's that smell?* Does the laptop emit a burning smell? If so, chances are something has burned out and needs to be replaced.

4. *Is everything connected properly?* Make sure the power cord and battery are connected firmly to the laptop and to the source of power. Some laptop power supplies even have a power cord that connects between the laptop and the transformer (black box), and then the transformer plugs into the wall. While the power cord may be connected to the laptop and the transformer plugged into the wall, you may have a disconnect between the laptop power cord and the transformer.

5. *Do you have power?* Verify that the laptop is plugged into a power source. If it is plugged into a power strip or UPS, make sure that the power strip or UPS is switched on. Try plugging the laptop directly into a wall outlet to be on the safe side. If all else fails, try plugging a known working device (such as a lamp) into the outlet to verify that the outlet is working. If the known working device does not power on, you may have blown a fuse or have a bad outlet.

6. *Does the power button feel funny?* If the power button feels funny or is permanently stuck in the on or off position, chances are that it is broken.

7. *Get help.* If none of these steps have helped, you should seek assistance from your local tech support or laptop manufacturer.

What Should I Do If My Laptop Display Won't Turn On?

Laptops have come a long way in terms of durability and longevity. However, laptop displays are still a weak link in the chain. The fact that they are constantly opening and closing puts a good deal of wear and tear on them. This constant use causes the connections that transfer power and other information to your monitor from the laptop to break. If yours will not turn on, follow these steps:

1. *Toggle display modes.* Most laptops have a three-state display mode that allows you to send video output to the laptop screen, external monitor, or both. Consult you owner's manual on how to toggle these modes.

2. *With the computer on, try slowly opening and closing the screen.* Did the display turn on or flicker? On laptops, ribbon cables are used to connect from the main motherboard (located under the keyboard) to the screen. Sometimes these cables get bent or torn around the hinge area just below the screen. If this is the case, contact the manufacturer for repair.

3. *My laptop is sleeping.* If your display will not turn on, it may be in power save mode. Depending on your laptop, you can pull your laptop out of power save mode by moving the mouse, pressing a key, pressing the power button, or pressing some key combination (for example, FN+F5).

4. *Power your computer off, disconnect the battery and power cord, and press the power button a few times.* This should discharge any electricity in the laptop. Reconnect the battery and power cord, and then try turning on the computer to see if the display is back.

5. *Make sure the display button is off.* Laptop displays have a tiny button that turns the display off when the top is closed. This is done to save power if the laptop is still on. Make sure that this button is not stuck in the down position. Look for this button near the point where the monitor hinges to the laptop.

What Should I Do If My Laptop Has No Sound?

With advances in audio systems, laptop owners now have some pretty decent sound systems installed in their machines. Although they probably do not provide the low-end grunt of some desktop systems, they do a good job of reproducing sound. If your laptop has no sound, try these options:

- *Some laptops have volume control wheels or buttons.* These are also usually hidden in some place where they can be difficult to find. They allow you to adjust or mute the volume completely. Consult your owner's manual on how to adjust the volume through these controls.

- *Some laptops require you to press the function key (FN) and another key simultaneously to raise and lower the volume.* You may also be able to mute the sound completely using a similar combination of keystrokes. Consult your owner's manual for details.

- *Connect a pair of headphones and see if there is volume.* Remember to plug the headphones into the correct jack. If your laptop has speakers, chances are it has a microphone and line out jack as well. Check your manual for details.

- *Open up Device Manager and check the status of the sound card.* It will be listed under "Sound, video and game controllers." Check the Device Manager section at the beginning of this chapter to determine what the problem is. If the sound device does not appear in Device Manager, try rescanning for hardware. If this does not work, you may have a faulty sound card.

- *Use the Windows Help and Support Center.* Click the Windows Start button and then Help and Support. When the help center appears, click "Fixing a problem." In the left menu, click "Games, sound, and video problems." In the right pane, select "Sound Troubleshooter."

Printers

- Learn the common causes of printer issues.
- Learn how to correct printer issues.

There is no other tech device we despise more often than the printer. It serves such a simple purpose and yet printer makers never seems to get it right. Smeared ink, messy toner, and paper jams are just a few of the things we hate about printers. We thought the "digital age" was going to get rid of the "paper age." Wrong. We are actually printing more now than we ever did. Looks like the printer is here to stay. The following sections will help you deal with various printer issues.

What Should I Do If My Printer Won't Turn On?

We wish we had the Fonzie touch—give it a little kick and voila, it's working. Unfortunately, printers don't like to be kicked. Here are some procedures you can try if your printer will not turn on:

- *Check the power cable.* Make sure it is firmly seated and plugged in.
- *If the cable is plugged into a surge protector, make sure the surge protector is on as well.* If you have any doubts, just plug the printer directly into a wall outlet.
- *Check to see if the display says "Online" or that the main status LED is green.*
- *Make sure you let the printer warm up properly.* You may have to wait a few minutes after turning your printer on before you can use it.
- *Use the Windows Help and Support Center.* Click the Windows Start button and then Help and Support. When the help center appears, click "Fixing a problem." In the left menu, click on "Printing problems." In the right pane, select "Printing Troubleshooter."

What Should I Do If My Printer Won't Print?

People usually do not print documents ahead of time; they usually print them right when they need them. Whether it's a presentation, movie show times, or driving directions, you need your printouts now, not later. Here are some tasks to perform if your printer refuses to print:

- *Turn the printer and the computer off and then on again and then try printing again.* This fixes most printing problems.
- *Makes sure the printer is on, has ink, and has paper.*

- *Check to see if the display says "Online" or that the main status LED is green.* If this is not the case, check the following:

  - Make sure all compartments are closed.

  - Make sure you have paper loaded in the paper tray.

  - Make sure you have ink cartridges or toner loaded.

  - Make sure there is nothing obstructing the path of any moving objects.

- *Check to see if the main display shows any error messages or if the main status LED is blinking.* If either of these occurs, check either your documentation or the manufacturer's website for additional info.

- *Check for a possible paper jam.*

- *Make sure you are printing to the correct printer.*

- *Check to see if the printer is physically connected to the computer.* Most modern printers use either a USB or parallel cable.

- *Try a different/spare cable if you have one handy.*

- *Try printing from DOS.* Printing from DOS will rule out the printer, cables, or computer hardware from being at fault:

  1. Click Start.

  2. Click Run.

  3. Type in the word Command and click OK.

  4. Type in **dir>lpt1** and press Enter.

  5. A page should print from your printer.

NOTE: *This will not work if your printer is connected to your computer with a USB cable.*

- *Open Notepad, type some text, and try printing.* If this works, the problem is with the file type/application you are trying to print from and has nothing to do with the setup in Windows.

- *Print a test page directly from the printer.* Your printer manual or the manufacturer's website can give you the details on doing this. If you are able to successfully print a test page from the printer, then your problem is computer-related.

- *Check the status of the device in Device Manager.* If it is not listed there, it is probably caused by one of the previous problems we listed. If it is there but there is an exclamation point, question mark, or red *X* next to it, the problem may be driver-related.

- *Use the Windows Help and Support Center.* Click the Windows Start button and then Help and Support. When the help center appears, click "Fixing a problem." In the left menu, click on "Printing problems." In the right pane, select "Printing Troubleshooter."

What Should I Do If My Printer Stops Picking Up Paper?

Older printers commonly have problems with the paper feeding mechanism. When it happens, your printer is rendered useless. Here are a few reasons a printer would stop picking up paper and how to resolve it:

- *Overfilled paper tray:* Overfilling your printer's paper tray may cause jams and possibly damage your printer's roller mechanism. Check your printer's documentation for the exact maximum-allowed paper count. If you need the added paper holding capacity, consider investing in an additional paper tray. Most higher-end printers support these.

- *Paper type:* Make sure the type of paper you are using is supported by your printer. Using a paper that is too heavy can lead to damaged rollers or other printer internals. Using an unsupported paper type may cause extreme permanent damage to your printer. For example, cheap slide-show transparencies can melt inside a laser jet printer.

- *Lift.* Some printers have a lift mechanism that raises the paper into the paper path. Make sure this lift mechanism is doing its job. If it is not, the rollers don't stand a chance of grabbing any paper.

- *Gravity:* If your printer is of the gravity-feed type (the paper sits in a slot on the top of a printer and drops into it), make sure nothing has fallen in and jammed the paper path.

- *Paper jam:* Make sure there is no paper stuck and causing a paper jam inside of the printer.

- *It's dirty:* A printer's transfer rollers carry the paper on its journey through the printer. You should be able to see these in most printers. They are usually a dark gray in color and are made of rubber or hard plastic. Periodically cleaning your printer rollers will extend their life and help avoid paper feed issues. This can be accomplished by using a clean, lint-free cloth and some isopropyl alcohol.

- *It's broken:* There are several interconnected pieces that your printer uses to pick up paper—rollers, gears, and paper lift to name a few. If you've tried all the fixes described here, you may have a broken component. Contact the manufacturer for more information.

WARNING! Laser printers work by burning (fusing) the ink onto the paper. They can also cause severe burns if you are not careful. Never work on your printer with the power connected or if it has been used recently.

Summary

If you have taken one thing away from this chapter, we hope it is that there are a number of things that you can do to avoid and protect yourself against hardware disasters and mishaps. Your PC and other devices will certainly not last forever but you can make them last longer by taking care of them. And if a disaster strikes when you least expect it, like having a hard drive crash, there are always steps you can take to minimize your losses and pain.

3

Software Disasters and Mishaps

Disasters to avoid:

- Having your PC refuse to start up because your operating system has failed.
- Having to reinstall Windows as a clean install and having all of your data wiped out.
- Having a software installation fail after you've spent hours working on it.

Mishaps and blunders to run from:

- Improper software installations.
- Losing your master installation CD for Windows.
- Not being able to use a program because it has expired.

Software. It's that magic thing that makes your computer work. Or it's that thing you curse under your breath, as in, "My darn software isn't working." But software isn't really magic, and it is usually more reliable than we give it credit for. Software consists of the games, programs, and even operating systems we use every day. Software tells our PCs how to do things. Here's an analogy: Think of a marriage where the wife (the software) tells the husband (the computer) what to do. The husband (if he is smart) follows his wife's instructions, thus making everything work. And we all know what happens when he chooses not to follow these instructions—the blue screen of death shows its ugly head.

Now that you have a good understanding of the kinds of hardware disasters and mishaps that can occur with PCs and other devices, it's time to peel away the onion a little more and discuss software disasters and mishaps. We'll first look at the basic issues surrounding software, and then we'll discuss problems that occur with installing software, updating software, and using new operating systems with older software.

Why Do I Need Software?

Most experts agree that the earliest use of software was by a Frenchmen named Jaquard. He developed a machine that could loom textiles by running a series of punched cards through a reading device. The punch card remained the dominant form of software for a very long time because the hardware evolved very slowly.

Sometime during the early 1980s (our favorite decade, by the way), software started creeping away from large corporations, the military, and educational institutions and made its way into your home. About 20 years have passed since that time and software has made a remarkable change in the way we live. One thing has stayed the same though: software is very prone to failure. That's why we're here!

Software has found its way into every nook and cranny of our lives. Whether you realize it or not, you probably could not make it through a day without interfacing with computer software on some level. There is software in your alarm clock, coffeemaker, and maybe even your electric toothbrush. You probably can't even make it past breakfast without using software. Here is a breakdown of some of the types of software you may encounter as you use computer-related electronic equipment:

- *Operating system:* This piece of software is responsible for controlling a PC and other devices. It manages memory, printing, networking, those silly smiley faces you send using AIM, disk drives, and a myriad of other things. You see the hardware through the operating system. (We sometimes think the operating system is at the other end laughing as we spill coffee on our keyboard or fall asleep playing video games.) Examples of operating systems include Windows, Mac OS, Unix, and DOS.

- *BIOS:* BIOS stands for basic input/output system. It's what a device uses until it loads the operating system. Most of you have seen the black and white screens that scroll past as you boot up your computer. That is the BIOS hard at work, waiting for the operating system to grab the baton.

- *Drivers:* Drivers are a type of software that allows the operating system to communicate with hardware. Every single piece of hardware inside of and connected to your PC needs a driver or it will not work.

- *Applications:* Applications are a type of software that is designed to perform a specific purpose. This is probably what comes to mind when you hear the word *software*. Applications have been written for word processing, databases, spreadsheets, gaming, email, and countless other purposes. The amount of software available these days is truly daunting. You could probably spend a lifetime trying to use every piece of software ever created.

Types of Software Installations

When software is installed, the installer may add, modify, or delete files, Registry entries, or even text within files. There are many different types of software installation packages:

- *Single executable installation:* This is probably what comes to mind when you think of software installations. It consists of a single, compressed file (usually an EXE, or executable, file) that includes all of the instructions that are needed to install the program.

- *Web-based installation:* This type of installation has become very popular in recent years, most likely because of the proliferation of broadband Internet access. We imagine at some point that all software installation will take place over the Web (and we will all have flying cars and work for Spacely Sprockets or Cogswell Cogs).

- *Media-based installation:* This type of installation places all of the necessary files on a span of discs. Also included is an executable file that knows where to copy the files and what changes to make to the system.

- *Windows installer:* Windows Installer was introduced with Windows 2000. It can install, repair, and remove software using instructions that are provided in MSI files.

Types of Operating Systems

An operating system of any kind is one of the biggest software applications around (some with over 45 million lines of code). The operating system is what people interact with and the environment on which other programs run. Operating systems all fall into one or more of the following categories:

- *GUI:* The graphical user interface operating system is what most of you will be familiar with. It consists of graphics and icons that are manipulated using a mouse or other input device.

- *Multiprocessing:* These operating systems are designed to use more than one processor. Once only a privilege of supercomputers, you can now find these powerful operating systems running servers in a doctor's office.

- *Multiuser:* The multiuser operating system allows many people to use it all at once or at different times.

- *Multitasking:* A multitasking operating system can run multiple programs at the same time.

- *Multithreading:* A multithreading operating system allows different parts of software to be run concurrently.

Major Software Failure

- Learn about the causes of software failure.
- Learn how to recognize software failure.
- Learn what to do when software failure occurs.

What Are the Common Causes of Software Failure?

The worst kind of software failure you can have is when your computer refuses to start up because your operating system (Windows) refuses to work. The other type of failure you might experience is that an application refuses to run. Both of these types of failures can really stop you in your tracks and ruin your day. When a failure occurs, it's important to diagnose your disaster carefully so you don't end up wasting a lot of time and money. Here are some of the common causes of software failure that you should put on the top of your troubleshooting list:

- *Registry problems:* The good news with Windows is that it has a built-in database and control system to keep track of all of the software and critical information that lives on your PC. This feature is called the Registry. You've probably heard it mentioned now and then by the tech geeks you know. Usually they make comments under their breath like "Oh, it's a Registry problem" or "Damn, the Registry is really screwed up again." The bad news is that the Registry is known to have problems from time to time, and when the Registry has a "bad hair day," your PC might not start up or an important program installed on your PC might not work. We'll show you some things that you can do if you suspect that you are having a Registry "bad hair day."

- *Improper installations:* Software can be really fussy. If it isn't installed just right, it might not ever run at all or it might run inconsistently. This is why we have devoted a lot of attention to showing you how to properly install your software and how to deal with software installation issues in this chapter. If you are having problems with software, you can usually fix them by simply reinstalling your software. This is something we often put off doing because it is a pain, but it does work better than anything else.

- *A change in the weather (a.k.a., a recent software installation):* It might seem that just out of the blue your operating system or an important application (like your word processor) starts acting up. The only thing you can attribute the problem to is that it is suddenly raining or the wind has picked up. The real truth is that computers aren't really that unpredictable. Usually, a problem like this occurs because you've recently done something such as install some new software, a new hardware device like a printer, or you've been attacked by a virus (as mentioned later in this list). When you install new software or hardware, internal changes are made to your operating system, and these changes can affect the balance of power on your computer. When we suspect problems like this, we like to make a list of all of the changes that we've made to our PCs over the past week or two. Then we see if we can work through the list to try to find what went wrong.

- *Expired software:* Software, like hardware, doesn't always last forever. Many programs that users install on their PCs are often downloaded from the Internet. Many are trial versions. Programs like this run fine and offer all of the features of the commercial version until one day when they simply stop running. Software that needs to be activated may be fully functional for a few days and then may completely cease to function until you activate it. Finally, subscription-based software (such as antivirus software) may continue to work after it expires (typically one year) but not fully (it's not updated).

- *Viruses and other gunk:* Viruses can create havoc on a PC (especially when you have an important deadline like getting a report done for the boss a few days before your big review). Because of the importance of viruses, we've devoted an entire chapter to them. Chapter 8 covers viruses in great detail.

- *Poorly written code:* Contrary to what software developers tell you, their products are flawed. The majority of software packages are released to the general public prematurely. As a result, they are riddled with code flaws, bugs, and security holes. Proof of this is the fact that they release so many hot fixes and patches. If they had it right the first time, there would be no need for these.

HORROR STORY! We were on an important deadline to get some critical work completed. We were using some trial software that we downloaded from the Internet. (We bet you know where this is going!) The night before the project was due, we were traveling without having any type of Internet connection and the expiration date for the trial software came due. Talk about the mother of all helpless feelings. You click on the software to start it up and all you see is a little alert window telling you to insert another quarter, so to speak. Why is it that software like this always seems to expire when (a) you need it the most and (b) you are stuck in a situation where you can't pay for an upgrade or download another trial version? What we learned is that if you are using trial software for a critical project, always be mindful of its expiration date. Better yet, don't be cheap. If you use the software for important projects, buy the full version!

What Should I Do If My Operating System Will Not Start?

A two-week vacation in Hawaii might be ready to move to the top of your priority list. But before you call your travel agent and pack up your swimsuit collection, you'll need to run some diagnostics. You might get lucky and be able to fix your problem so that you can get back to work (or perhaps we should say that getting back to work could be the unlucky outcome). An operating system that fails to start could be suffering from something as simple as a minor problem with Windows or as complex as a corrupted Registry. Here's what you need to do:

- *Make sure that you have investigated all of the hardware failure problems presented in Chapter 2.* You never know; you might just get lucky and discover the problem is due to a faulty power cord.

- *Try to return your system to an earlier state.* This solution will work only if your computer is still booting up and you are using Windows XP. Windows XP provides a special feature that allows you to return it to a state it was in prior to its current state. If you installed some new software or hardware drivers recently, for example, your computer might be acting up. You can then use the Windows System Restore feature to restore your computer without losing any of your personal data. System Restore is covered in detail in Chapter 13, "Backup and Recovery."

- *Use the Windows Setup CD that came with your PC.* This is another important solution that can be used if you are running Windows XP. Your Windows XP Setup CD provides a repair option that can fix startup problems, problems with system files, and more. To use this feature, you'll need to boot from the Setup CD. After the Setup software starts, you will be given an option to select the repair feature. It is important that you select the repair option and not the option to reinstall Windows. The repair software feature will check your computer and try to fix the problems that it finds so that your computer can then boot up on its own.

- *Try to fix a Registry boot problem.* Your computer may be suffering from having a corrupted Registry. This is a problem that can be fixed, so you won't have to fully reinstall Windows. See the section that follows for advice on how to do this.

- *Use the Windows Upgrade feature.* This is another nice trick you can try if you are running Windows XP. You'll need to locate your Windows Setup CD (you didn't lose it, right?), boot from it, and run the Install/Upgrade option. This option will install Windows XP, but it will treat the installation as an upgrade and therefore it will preserve your installed programs, data files, computer settings, and so on. Running this procedure is similar to using the repair option; it simply takes longer. It is a good fallback position if the repair procedure won't work for you.

- *Perform a clean install of Windows.* This is your last resort. If you've tried everything else and you still can't get your PC to boot, you'll need to use your Windows Setup CD and perform a clean install. The really bad news is that this procedure will reformat your hard drive and you'll lose all of your data and programs.

HORROR STORY! A friend of ours purchased a laptop recently. He got it all set up, installed all of his favorite programs, and put quite a bit of his work files and personal data on the computer. Of course, since the laptop was fairly new, he hadn't taken the time to back anything up. After investing hours of his time, the laptop refused to boot up. He figured he could easily use the Windows install CD that came with the laptop and run the diagnostics and fix his problem. Big surprise. The laptop, like many these days, didn't come with the full Windows installation CD because the operating system was preinstalled by the laptop manufacturer. The only CD that was provided was a "worst case" CD that is used to return the computer to the state it was in when it was sold, which means that everything gets wiped out. Our friend had to run out and purchase an actual installation version of the Windows operating system. The moral: When you buy a computer, read the fine print and make sure you understand exactly what software is provided. As our friend learned, the original equipment manufacturer (OEM) version of Windows is a really bad idea!

How Can I Tell If I Have a Registry Boot Problem?

The nice thing about Windows is that when it has Registry problems, it isn't shy. It will likely scream at you using its full set of lungs. As Windows tries to boot up, the error message that you'll receive will read something like this:

Windows XP could not start because the following file is missing or corrupt:

\WINDOWS\SYSTEM32\CONFIG\SYSTEM

What the operating system is telling you is that it can't start because something that is stored in the Registry has become corrupted or unreadable. Reasons for this include a dying hard drive, a virus, a software install gone bad, or just plain old bad luck.

Can I Fix a Corrupted Registry That Is Keeping My PC from Booting?

Yes, but we won't lie to you and tell you this is easy to do. In fact, most people shouldn't try to do this on their own. Usually the problem is caused by software that was previously installed and run on your computer and corrupted the Registry in some manner. Because the Registry is now corrupted, you can't fix the problem by simply removing the troublesome software. Besides, your computer won't start up in the first place, so you now have a bigger problem to solve!

The process required to repair the Registry involves restoring your Registry to the state it was in on an earlier date. This involves moving some low-level system files around. Our best advice in learning how to do this is to either call Microsoft tech support (if you have a registered copy of Windows, they will gladly help you) or visit the website that Microsoft provides for customer support. The Registry problem that we have been discussing here must happen to a number of people because Microsoft makes available a fairly detailed instruction guide on how to fix a Registry boot problem (**http:// search.support.microsoft.com/kb/c.asp?fr=0&SD=GN&LN=EN-US**).

What Can I Do If My Computer Boots Really Slowly

We have to think that the real reason Starbucks got its start was because of all of the PC users out there who were tired of waiting for their PCs to boot up and didn't have anything else to do. The more you use your PC, the more cluttered it can get with all of the software that you have installed, and this can really slow it down. In fact, this has become such a big issue that our publisher recently released a book titled *Degunking Windows* that has rapidly become one of the top-selling computer books. (Get a copy if you don't have one yet!)

If your computer is booting slowly or if the booting process occasionally stalls, it is likely that Windows is having difficulty loading one of its system-related files or you may have too many programs loading in the system tray at boot-up. Figure 3.1 shows an example of a normal system tray.

Figure 3.1
The Windows System Tray.

If your system tray has an exorbitant amount of items in it, chances are they are having an adverse effect on your computer. Here's what you can do to speed things up:

* *Remove some of the programs that get loaded when Windows starts*: Every item in the system tray can slow down the time it takes Windows to boot. You can keep them from loading when Windows starts by following these simple instructions:
  1. Click Start.
  2. Click Run.
  3. Type in msconfig and click OK.
  4. Click the Startup tab.

5. Everything on this list will start when Windows fires up. The majority of these programs are unnecessary and can really slow down your system. You can stop them from loading by unchecking the box next to each item. Although none of these items are critical to Windows, some of them perform important functions. For example, un-checking VPTray will disable Symantec Real-Time File Protection on your system. The bottom line is to be very careful when removing things from here.

6. Click OK and restart.

- *Clean the Registry using a commercial Registry cleaning utility.* The Registry can start looking like your garage if you're not careful. Cleaning the Registry on your own is a really bad idea, even if you think you know what you are doing. We suggest you invest in a good Registry cleaning tool such as Norton SystemWorks or Registry Clean Pro and use this software on a regular basis.

- *Check your antivirus software.* Sometimes those pesky antivirus programs will try to run a full system scan at startup. This is especially true if you have not started your computer for a few days.

What Should I Do If I Can't Run an Application?

Problems in this section deal with software you have just recently installed and software that has been installed and operating for quite some time but won't run now. Here's what you can do:

- *Application shortcut:* Make sure the shortcut is pointing to the correct executable file. You can do this by following these simple instructions:

1. Right-click the application's startup icon.

2. Select Properties.

3. Check the Target field and make sure it contains the name of the correct executable file. Figure 3.2 shows this information for Microsoft Word.

- *Software expiration:* The trend with software these days is that you pay money online and then download the software from the Internet. The software will typically run for a year or so and then expire. If you have a program that suddenly stops working, make sure you check to see that the software hasn't expired. If it has, you'll need to visit the company's website and renew your software.

- *Administrative privileges:* Some applications will not run unless you have administrative privileges on the computer you are running it on. This may not be apparent at first. You may be allowed to start the program and work with it a little and then all of a sudden it may stop while you are doing some tasks. It may be accompanied by an "access denied" error

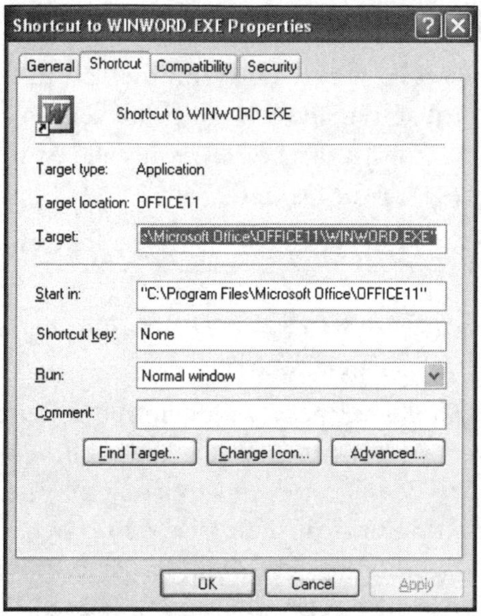

Figure 3.2

Application icon properties.

message. You must provide your account administrator rights or have your system administrator do it for you.

- *Repair:* Some programs allow you to repair an installation by running a special utility. They basically reinstall all of the critical files that are a part of your application.

- *DLL hell:* Dynamic Link Libraries (DLLs) are common files that applications share to provide familiar functionality. Things like the Save As, Print, and Open File dialog boxes are the work of DLL files. The problem with them is that they can be replaced with a different version by a recent file install. This can make programs that are dependant upon them not work properly. Contact your software's manufacturer if you suspect DLL problems.

- *Reinstall:* If everything we have suggested up to this point has failed, you will probably have to reinstall the software.

Installing, Uninstalling, and Repairing

- Learn the proper methods for installing software.
- Learn what to do if an install fails.
- Learn how to safely uninstall software.

What Should I Do Before Installing Software?

No one can accurately predict when or why a software installation fails. If we had a crystal ball, we could probably make a large profit lending ourselves out to software companies. Until that day comes, you will just have to follow these guidelines to improve your success rate:

- *Check compatibility.* Make sure your software can run on the PC you are installing it onto.

- *Reboot first.* This clears out any in-memory errors. Besides, it is the first thing any tech support person will suggest you try.

- *Clear the Temp folder.* This folder holds temporary files created and used by applications when they are opened or installed. When the application is closed, these files are supposed to be deleted. Unfortunately, this is not always the case. Some programs do not clear these files, or a program may have been closed abruptly, leaving files in this folder. All of this junk collecting in there spells trouble for any software install.

- *Close any applications running in the background.* Programs running in the background can wreak havoc with software installs. Antivirus, sound programs, and IntelliPoint (Microsoft mouse software) are at the top of this list.

- *Make sure you have administrative privileges on the computer.* Confirm this before attempting to install a program. You won't be able to install most programs if you don't have the proper security permissions.

- *Do not open any applications or files.* This will only slow down or possibly interrupt your install.

- *Turn off your screen saver.* Nothing is more annoying then being halfway through an install when the screen saver starts. Not only is it a nuisance, it may also cause you to cancel your install inadvertently.

- *Connect power.* If you're using a laptop, is the laptop plugged in? When on battery, your laptop may go into power save mode, operating your hardware at lower speeds to save power.

- *Keep your kids away from the keyboard.* They just seem to hit the right key every time. We think kids are born with a sixth sense of how to break things.

What Happens During a Software Installation?

The main purpose of an installation is to transfer all of the relevant files to your computer and configure the software to run on a particular operating system and use your installed hardware. A setup does all or some of the following:

- *Gathers system information.* It determines your current operating system version and a whole slew of other information. It uses this to configure itself and to determine if your computer meets its requirements.

- *Gathers user information.* The setup also asks for your input. It may ask you for product key information, installation path, advanced installation options, and a host of other variables. Sometimes it may feel like an interrogation, especially when its starts asking you for your age or gender.

- *Creates program shortcuts and folders.* Program shortcuts are the icons you double-click to launch a program. Folders are created to contain the program files.

- *Updates the Windows Registry.* This is where all of the specific details of the software are stored so that Windows can have easy access to them.

- *Shows installation progress.* This usually manifests itself as the blue status bar we have all grown accustomed to.

- *Completes the setup and restarts the computer.* Usually, it will ask your permission before it does this. However, some installs don't care if you have a very important spreadsheet open that has not been saved. So be very careful about what you have open when installing software.

HORROR STORY! One of the authors of this book (who shall remain unnamed) was installing Windows 2000 Service Pack 4 on a computer he was re-loading. To save time, he decided to also simultaneously install Microsoft Office 2000. Sounds like a good idea right? WRONG!!!!!!!!!!!!!!!!!!!! The Office install came to a grinding halt with an error message and promptly reversed itself. "Not a big deal," he thought," I will just install it after I reboot." After the reboot, he started to install Office and quickly found out that he could not. After two hours of fooling around with the Windows Installer Service, he finally got it right. The moral of this story is obvious, so we will not mention it here.

How Do I Start a Software Install?

Starting a software install is usually very simple or extremely difficult. We're not quite sure why this is the case. You would figure software companies would have made up their minds by now. Here are a few common methods:

- *Auto run:* This method involves putting a CD-ROM in your drive and closing it. Your drive will blink and make whirling noises signifying that it is reading data off of the disc. You should shortly see a splash screen for the program you are installing.

- *Executable file:* Executable files are another way to start an installation. They are typically named setup.exe, update.exe, or a host of other names. They can normally be found on the root of the disc. However, sometimes they may be hidden inside of a folder named Install.

- *Archive:* Some programs are archived inside of another file such as a ZIP file. In such a case, you should extract the contents of the archive to a normal folder and then run the install program. Many times this program will start automatically.

Why Is This Install Taking So Long?

A typical software install usually takes from 2 to 15 minutes. Some may take longer depending on the size of the program. If it seems to be taking an excessive amount of time, the install may have crashed. Here are some indications your install has failed:

- *The hard drive LED is not flashing at all.* In most cases your hard drive will be busy cranking away writing files. If there is no activity from it, chances are the install has failed.

- *The install program says, "Not responding."* This is another good indication that something is not right. It is usually accompanied by a lack of hard drive activity.

- *The progress bar is not moving.* Most installation programs have a status or progress bar to let you know how far along the installation is. If this has not moved in a while, the install may have failed.

- *The install is prompting you for information.* Some installation programs will prompt you for information at some point where you least expect it. It will not proceed until you have given it an answer. The problem here is that the box asking the question might be hidden behind the main install screen where you cannot see it. Simultaneously pressing the Tab and Alt keys will allow you to switch to this hidden screen.

Why Did My Install Fail?

Here are the reasons why your install may have failed:

- *Incompatibility.* Most modern software installs can automatically detect if the system and the software are fully compatible. Things like the operating system, memory, hard drive space, and service pack version can play a part in determining compatibility. Look on the side or rear of the box your software came in to locate the list of everything that is necessary to run the software.

- *Check the install log.* Don't you wish there was some magical install log that would tell you exactly why an install failed? Actually, there is a log on your computer for this very purpose, but the software manufacturer doesn't always put all of its information (or information that is understandable) there. The main application log is coincidentally called the application log, but you may also need to check the system log for errors. Before you look at the logs, be aware that there is a lot of information in there. Some errors and warnings are normal (if you can believe that). To view the logs, you need to start the Windows Event Viewer. Click Start, click Run, enter **EVENTVWR**, and then click OK. Click on any log and then on any event for more information.

- *You may have files or applications open that need to be closed.* Many installs require you to close any open programs. The open programs may be using shared files or consuming valuable system resources that are needed for the install process.

- *You may have started the install twice.* We've done this countless times. Look for multiple copies of the install program showing in your taskbar. Closing one of them should allow you to proceed.

- *Make sure your CD/DVD is free of dirt and scratches.* A CD/DVD drive will have trouble reading from a dirty or scratched CD/DVD-ROM. Unfortunately, it will not tell you this directly. It will just sit there trying to read from the disc while you are left in limbo. We almost wish drive manufacturers would add another LED to indicate a problem reading the media.

- *If you are installing software on a laptop, make sure the laptop is plugged in.* When it's running on battery power (not charging), your laptop may go into power save mode, operating your hardware at lower speeds to save power. This results in slower system performance and a slower install. For optimal speed and performance, run your laptop off of the charger when installing software.

- *Make sure you are using the correct install files.* Sometimes software companies will include several extra disks with the software they sell. These other disks may contain optional files, other products, or even advertisements. Make sure you are not using one of these.

HORROR STORY!

A friend of ours who works in the information technology industry was installing Microsoft Exchange server for a client. The install kept failing almost immediately. He tried several different things to move the install along but everything failed. Eventually, he was forced to call Microsoft. (This call cost him two hundred dollars, by the way.) After some investigative work, it turned out the disk he was using was actually a service pack of Microsoft Exchange server and not the install media. The moral here is to not assume you have the correct disk if your install bombs.

Why Is My System Slow After Something Was Installed?

You have just installed some software and rebooted your computer, and you have now found that your computer has become slow and unresponsive. Well, we have good news and bad news. The bad news is that the software you just installed may have caused this. The good news is that we may be able to help. Here are some possible causes:

- *You may have installed a virus or spyware.* This usually applies to software installed via the Internet. If you went to a website and were prompted to install software, you may have been tricked into installing a piece of software that can do great harm to your system. See Chapters 8 and 9 for more information.

- *You may have replaced a critical system file.* The software may have overwritten or deleted a critical system file. The System Restore utility should be able to help you out of this jam. See Chapter 13, "Backup and Recovery," for more information on this utility.

- *You may have replaced a driver.* The installation may have replaced a hardware driver. See the section "Software for Hardware" for more on device drivers.

What Should I Do If I Can't Find a Program After Installing It?

Most applications that you will install will place a shortcut on your desktop. Some even go so far as to install a shortcut in the Quick Launch menu and taskbar. However, some are adept at hiding themselves from all but the most well-informed computer users. Here are some places to check if your installed program is playing hide-and-seek with you:

- *Start menu:* This should be the first place you look. Just click Start in the lower left-hand corner. You may even be greeted by a tooltip stating "New programs installed" in the Programs or All Programs menu. This will depend on whether you have the classic or modern Start menu enabled. Look through this menu to find your software. It may be listed by the program name or software publisher.

- *Program Files folder:* Most Windows applications install themselves under this main folder. You can find the folder by double-clicking My Computer and then Local Disk (C:). You will see a folder named Program Files. Your program may be installed there. Once you locate the software's folder, look for an executable file (the name of the file will end with .exe). Some examples of this would be Winword.exe (Microsoft Word), Acrobat.exe (Adobe Acrobat), and Realplay.exe (Real Player).

- *Root of your hard drive:* Some software will create a folder on the root of your C: drive. This is normally the case with older DOS and Windows applications, although some newer programs may do this too. Open up My Computer and double-click the icon for your hard drive. Look for a folder name that resembles the program you installed or the company that made it.

- *On a different partition or hard drive:* If you have multiple partitions or multiple drives, the software may have been inadvertently installed there.

What Should I Do If I Delete a Program Shortcut?

Don't panic. Losing a shortcut won't hurt you—it is simply a pointer to something valuable. Deleting a shortcut does not delete the program installation, so you won't need to reinstall the program itself. Here are a few ways to recover or re-create the shortcut to your program:

- *Use the Recycle Bin.* If you didn't permanently delete the shortcut (hold the Shift key while pressing the Delete key), you should be able to recover it from the Recycle Bin. To do this, double-click the Recycle Bin, find and select the shortcut, right-click it, and choose Restore.

- *Follow the instructions in the previous section to locate the program.* If you find the program listed in your Start menu, you can copy the shortcut to the location of your choosing. Once you find the installed program, right-click its icon and choose Create Shortcut. You can then move the shortcut to a location of your choosing.

HORROR STORY! A workplace friend was cleaning her Windows desktop off one evening when she deleted a file named access.mdb. She thought it was for some program she did not use or need and emptied the Recycle Bin and shut down the computer. The next day her husband fired up the computer and was going to start work on the database project he was working on. Well, he was a little surprised to say the least. Luckily, he had a backup copy stored on a ZIP drive. The moral here is to not delete anything unless you are completely sure it is unnecessary.

Why Can't I Install/Uninstall Software?

If you are unable to start or complete an installation, you may be having a permissions issue. No, we're not talking about getting a note from your mother. We are referring to the built-in security accounts that Windows uses. At some point, someone at Microsoft said, "Wouldn't it be great if we could keep people from installing software?" Microsoft created different levels of permissions in order to accomplish this:

- *Are you an administrator?* To install software, you need to be a member of the Administrators or Power Users group. When you first set up the computer, you may have been prompted to create additional accounts. These accounts may have not been given administrative privileges and are just normal users.

- *Are you in Terminal Services?* Terminal Services is a technology that allows multiple people to log into a server and access a Windows desktop. It has many benefits, including allowing companies to keep older equipment longer, easier administration, and a slew of others. One of the security options built into it prevents users from installing software. Only administrators can install software in a terminal services environment. A quick way to determine if you are using terminal services is to click Start in the lower-left corner. It may say "Terminal Services" on the Start menu. Figure 3.3 shows an example of this. If it does, then forget about installing any software on your own. Chances are the system administrator has it locked down tight.

Figure 3.3
Finding Terminal Services.

- *Are you logged on as administrator?* Here is where it gets really confusing. Some programs require that you are actually logged on as the administrator account. Logging on with an account that is a member of the Administrators security group alone is not sufficient. When in doubt, just log on as administrator to avoid any potential trouble. You can log on as administrator by doing the following:

  1. Click Start.
  2. Click Log Off.
  3. Confirm that you wish to log off by clicking Log Off.

This is where it gets a little tricky. Depending on if you are using Windows 2000 or Windows XP the instructions vary. We have broken them down for you as follows:

- Windows 2000 or Windows XP Professional that are part of business network (Domain):

  1. Simultaneously press CTRL, ALT, and DEL.
  2. Type in Administrator in the username box.
  3. Type in the password for this account.
  4. Click OK.

- Windows XP Home Edition or Professional that are not part of a business network (Workgroup):

  1. Click the icon for the administrator account.
  2. If prompted, provide the password and click OK.

What Can I Do If My Software Install Fails?

A failed software install can lead to frustration and anger very quickly, especially if you have tried it a few times with no luck. Give the following list a shot:

- *Reboot and retry.* Rebooting a computer somehow seems to fix 95 percent of all Windows failures.

- *Check the event log.* The event log keeps a history of errors and warnings that are generated by the software and hardware installed on your computer. It can be found by using Control Panel and double-clicking Administrative Tools. In particular, the application log may have some information that pertains to the failed software install.

- *Check the install log.* During most software installs, a record is kept of all of actions and any error messages that were generated during the installation. It can usually be found on the root of your C: drive and is usually named Install.txt or Install.log.

- *Make sure your system is up-to-date.* Old hardware drivers or an out-of-date system BIOS may be causing the problem.

- *Clear your temp file folder.* The installation program may not like remnants of prior installations being left in this folder.

- *Disable your antivirus program.* Disabling the real-time scanning of your antivirus software may help in installing stubborn software.

WARNING! Be sure to turn real-time scanning back on after the install completes. Not doing so can leave your system vulnerable to viruses.

- *Install the software using Safe mode.* There is a known issue in Windows XP with installing software from CD-ROM. You may get an error message or a blue screen. Try installing the software in Safe mode.

- *Update your computer.* Updating Windows may help in solving installation problems. See the section titled "Updating Software" for more information. This section can be found later in this chapter.

- *Reinstall Internet Explorer.* Reinstalling Internet Explorer may possibly repair or reinstall critically damaged or missing system files.

- *Try some prerequisites.* Some software will not install itself unless a certain set of conditions are met. These conditions can include having certain versions of operating system service packs, Internet Explorer, and others. Check the software's documentation for complete details.

How Can I Uninstall Software?

As crazy as this may sound, uninstalling software sometimes can be harder than installing it. Some programs can be very tricky to completely remove from your PC. Why? Some software developers cut corners and don't provide proper features for uninstalling software. Here are some techniques you can try, but keep in mind that these techniques may not always completely remove some software packages from your PC:

- *Use the Add/Remove Programs feature.* Add/Remove Programs can be found in Windows Control Panel. This method is the preferred method of uninstalling software on the Windows operating system.

- *Use the Program files menu.* Find the program in the program files menu. There may be an uninstall option such as the one shown in Figure 3.4. Here is how you can find this:
  1. Click Start.
  2. Hover the mouse over Programs or All Programs. This will vary depending on which version of the Start Menu you are using (Classic or Windows XP).

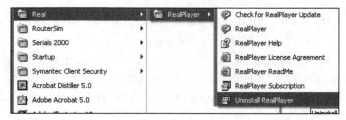

Figure 3.4
Using the uninstall option.

3. Find the program you want to uninstall and hover the mouse over it.

4. Click the uninstall option.

NOTE: *Not all applications offer this method as a means of uninstallation.*

- *Use an uninstall file.* Some programs can be removed by running an uninstall file. These files can usually be found in the software's folder in the Program Files folder. The file is usually named uninstall.exe or uninstall.bat.

- *Contact the software company.* When in doubt as to the best way to uninstall a particular piece of software, you should contact the software vendor directly.

What Can I Do If My Uninstall Fails?

The uninstall process can be as prone to failure as the install process. Here are a few steps you can take if your uninstall fails:

- *Reboot.* Try rebooting and running the uninstall process again. Some of the files being removed may be in use, even if the program is closed.

- *Clear your temp files folder.* When a program installs or uninstalls, it may use your temp files folder to unpack (uncompress) its files and do other file operations. If this folder is full of files or contains files that are preventing an install/uninstall from completing, you need to delete them. You can access your temp files folder by clicking Start | Run, typing **%TEMP%**, and then clicking OK.

- *Use Safe mode.* Try the uninstall process while in Safe mode.

- *Contact the software company.* They should be able to provide you with very specific uninstall instructions.

How Can I Repair a Damaged Software Installation?

Software installations can be very fragile, especially if the program is used frequently. The more a program is used, the more its components are swapped between your hard drive and system memory. This constant swapping can lead to data corruption. Here are some tips on how to get things back to normal:

- *Reinstall the software.* Reinstalling the software will usually replace any critical files that may have been damaged.

- *Use a built-in repair feature.* Some programs have a built-in repair feature. These usually scan all of the critical program files and repair or reinstall them.

- *Uninstall and reinstall.* Try uninstalling the software and then reinstalling.

What If I Can't Remember or Have Lost My Product Key?

Practically all copyrighted software comes with some sort of product license and or activation key that is required to install, activate, and use the software. This key can usually be found on an emblem on the box, on the CD sleeve, or on a certificate inside the box. Your best bet in situations such as these is to contact the manufacturer. If you can provide them with a valid proof of purchase, they should be able to assist you.

PREVENTIVE MEASURE: Keep all your product keys in a central place. We prefer to record them all in one spreadsheet, where we can easily look them up when we need to install. If you do this, make sure you password-protect the spreadsheet file.

How Can I Activate My Software If I Have No Internet Connection?

More and more software companies are requiring an Internet connection to activate their software. This can be a real problem if you don't have an Internet connection, but fortunately software companies have already thought about this issue. The alternative is usually phone activation. When the activation process detects that there is no Internet connection, you are presented with a serial number and a phone number. Once you call and provide your serial number, they will give you an unlock code to enter, and voila— activation with no Internet connection.

Updating Software

- Learn how to update Windows.
- Learn how to update Office.

How Can I Update Windows?

Keeping Windows 2000 and XP current on patches is a snap. You have two options—you can manually update or use Automatic Updates. To manually update, go to the Windows Update website. There are several ways to do this:

- Click Start, then Run, type in wupdmgr.exe, and click OK.
- Click Start and then click Windows Update.
- Go to **http://windowsupdate.microsoft.com.**

Once you are there, you may be prompted to install the latest version of the software. The box may look like the image shown in Figure 3.5.

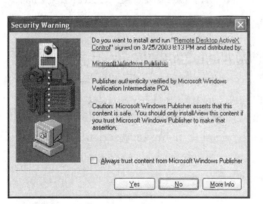

Figure 3.5

Windows Update security warning.

Be sure that the window is truly from Microsoft and click OK. This will install a piece of software on your computer that allows you to utilize the Windows Update site. Once the software is installed, click Scan for Updates. During the next few moments your computer will be scanned for any appropriate updates. Keep in mind that this may take substantially longer when using a dial-up Internet connection.

Once the scan is complete you will be able to choose which updates you want to install. Updates come in several different types:

- *Critical Updates:* These are extremely important security updates that Microsoft releases in response to vulnerabilities in its Windows operating systems. If you do nothing else, you must install these on a regular basis. We cannot stress this enough.

- *Recommended Updates:* These consist of regularly released updates to Windows, Internet Explorer, and other Microsoft products. They can include service packs and other important updates.

- *Windows Tools:* These are utilities and other tools offered by Microsoft for use by system administrators.

- *Internet and Multimedia Updates:* These are the latest versions of Internet Explorer, Windows Media Player, and other Microsoft software.

- *Additional Windows Downloads:* These are miscellaneous updates for desktop settings and other Windows features.

- *Multi-Language Features:* The name says it all.

Click Review and Install Updates and select the ones you want to install. Then just click Install Now. The download will begin. After installation, you may be required to reboot the machine.

How Can I Have Windows Updated Automatically?

If you are like us and you don't like to do anything manually, then Automatic Updates is the way to go. Automatic Updates let you specify when and how your updates are installed. Both Windows 2000 and XP support this neat feature. Automatic Updates can be accessed in Windows XP by doing the following:

1. Right-click My Computer.

2. Click Properties.

3. Click the Automatic Updates tab.

Accessing Automatic Updates in Windows 2000 can be done by taking these steps:

1. Click Start.

2. Point to Settings.

3. Click Control Panel.

4. Double-click the Automatic Updates applet.

You will now see a window similar to Figure 3.6.

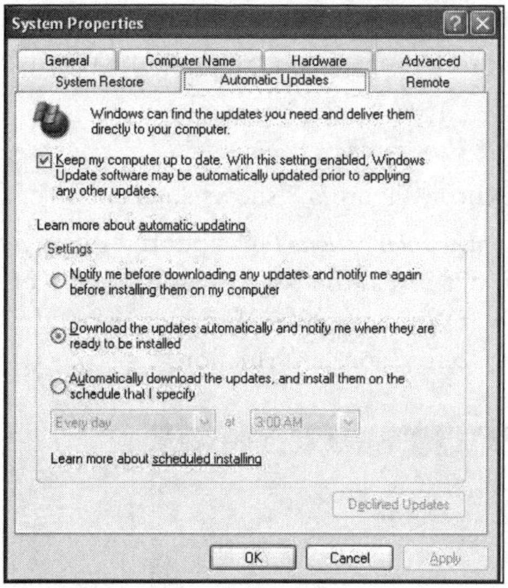

Figure 3.6
Automatic Updates.

Select the check box labeled "Keep my computer up to date." In the set-tings box, you will see three radio buttons. They control how updates are installed on your PC. The middle option is the most commonly used instal-lation method. It downloads updates automatically and then prompts you for permission to install. This allows you to see what updates are being installed.

What Can I Do If a Windows Update Has Harmed My PC?

Believe it or not, Microsoft occasionally releases an update that may cause a problem with your PC hardware or software. Just a little advice here: suing Bill Gates will not work (even the U.S. government can't seem to touch him). There are a few alternatives though:

- *Use System Restore.* Windows XP and ME come shipped with the System Restore utility. It allows you to roll back major system changes and keep personal data files. See Chapter 13, "Backup and Recovery," for more information on using System Restore.

- *Use Add/Remove Programs to uninstall.* You can also use the Add/Remove Programs feature in Control Panel to remove installed hotfixes. The only trick is determining which hotfix caused your problem. You can access this by following these instructions:

1. Click Start.

2. Click Control Panel or point to settings if you are using the Classic Start Menu.

3. Double-click Add or Remove Programs.

4. Find the hotfix and click Remove. Figure 3.7 shows an example of this.

• *Use the Last Known Good Configuration option.* This option restores your computer to the configuration it had at the last successful startup of Windows. It is only available in Windows 2000, Windows XP, and Windows 2003. See Chapter 13 for more information.

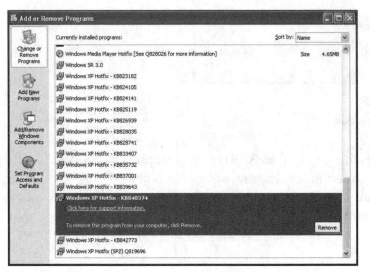

Figure 3.7
Hotfix Removal.

Why Can't I Install Windows Updates on My PC?

Sometimes, you will not be able to install Windows updates on your PC. Usually the reasons are similar to the reasons you can't install software at all:

• *Make sure you have Administrative privileges on your computer.*

• *Make sure you have a valid product key installed.* A bootleg copy of Windows XP will not be allowed to scan for updates or install Windows XP Service Pack 1.

How Can I Update Microsoft Office?

Microsoft Office started out as a nice little suite of programs to do simple computing tasks such as word processing, using spreadsheets, and creating small databases. It has now grown into a monster of a program that does just about everything. Keeping it up-to-date is a snap thanks to Microsoft.

Take the following steps to update Office 2003:

1. Open up any of the Office suite of programs. This can include Outlook, Word, Excel, and so on.
2. Click Help on the top toolbar.
3. Click Check for Updates. You will be magically whisked away to the Office Update site.
4. Click Scan for Updates.
5. Click Start Installation.

Office Update will begin the process of downloading and updating your Office installation.

Follow these steps to update Office 2000 and XP:

1. Open up any of the Office suite of programs. This can include Outlook, Word, Excel, etc.
2. Click Help on the top toolbar.
3. Click Office on the Web.
4. Select your country.
5. On the next page, click Scan for Updates in the upper-right corner.
6. Click Start Installation.

Office Update will begin the process of downloading and updating your Office installation. You may be required to reboot your computer once the installation is complete.

How Can I Update Other Software?

Symantec and McAfee products both come with a built-in mechanism for downloading and installing updates. The only thing necessary is an Internet connection and verification that the update feature is turned on. Check your documentation for specific details.

If you have software from another company, visit the manufacturer's website. You should be able to determine what the latest revision of your software is and download updates if necessary. You can also try using this handy web tool: **www.versiontracker.com.**

How Do I Update My Software If I Don't Have an Internet Connection?

This can be a problem for some people. Some people do not have an Internet connection at home or at work. There are some ways to get around this:

- *Request an update via mail.* Call the software company and ask for an update to be sent via mail. They may charge you a nominal fee for this service, but you will have the most current updates.

- *Download updates at a friend's house.* Visit a friend who has an Internet connection and download it, copy it to a CD, and bring it back home.

- *Bring your computer to a friend.* Bring your computer to a friend's house and connect to the Internet. This can be tedious if you don't have a laptop. I would not want to make a habit of carrying a desktop PC around just to download updates.

- *Bring your PC to a computer shop.* Go to any local computer repair shop and ask them to download the update for you. If they know their business, they should be more than happy to help you out.

New Operating System, Old Software Issues

- Learn about application compatibility.
- Learn how to determine if your software is compatible with Windows.

Why Do I Run into Problems when Trying to Run Old Software?

The problem of running old software on a newer operating system is a recurring one in technology. Operating system companies release a new version and subsequently software companies scramble to make their product compatible. The process is renewed when the operating system company releases a newer version.

Running your old software on a newer operating system can be a crapshoot. You never know if (or how long), it will work. Sometimes, the only way to know for sure is to install it and see what happens. Some of the common problems are listed here:

- *Performance:* Your computer's speed can be severely degraded by installing and running old software.

- *System files:* By installing older software on your PC, you may be overwriting important files with older versions.

- *Memory leaks:* Old software can potentially be a source of memory leaks. This in turn can cause your computer to crash intermittently.

How Will I Know If My Software Will Run on Windows XP?

Microsoft goes to great lengths to do the work of finding compatible software for its operating systems. It then offers this information free of charge to the public. You can access this information at the Windows catalog website at **www.microsoft.com/Windows/catalog/**.

How Can I Make My Old Applications Work on a Newer Operating System?

Microsoft recognized the need for backward compatibility when it introduced Windows XP. A neat new feature called the Program Compatibility Wizard was added. Using this wizard, you can easily make any program written for earlier versions of Windows run on XP. You can also manually configure application compatibility settings using the compatibility mode tab found in the properties of a program's executable or launch file. Figure 3.8 shows this tab in all its glory. However, it is much easier to do it through the wizard. Here is how:

1. Click Start.

2. Point to All Programs or Programs if you are using the classic Start Menu.

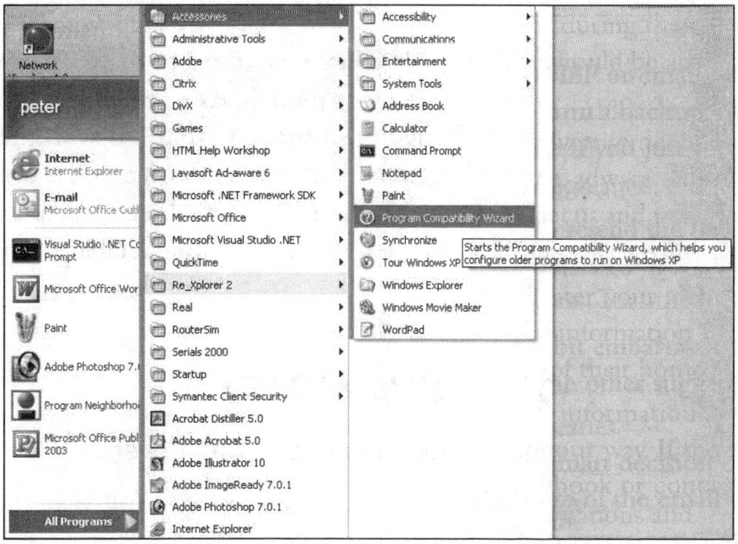

Figure 3.8

The Program Compatibility Wizard.

3. Point to Accessories.

4. Click Program Compatibility Wizard. Figure 3.8 shows where this can be found.

5. Click Next on the intro screen.

6. Pick your poison on the selection method. Selecting from a list is the easiest. Click Next.

7. Windows will scan your computer for installed programs. Select the program you want to use and click Next.

8. Select the operating system you think will best suit the program and click Next.

9. Select the display settings. These usually apply to old games and educational programs, so no settings change is usually necessary. Click Next.

10. The program will now open and you will be allowed to test the settings. Go ahead and use the program and then close it.

11. If the settings work fine, let the wizard know by selecting Yes and clicking Next. If not, try other settings by No, or try different compatibility settings.

12. After successfully selecting settings you will be prompted to share this information with Microsoft. This is completely up to you. Click Next.

13. Click Finish.

Why Do My Old Applications Run More Slowly on My New Operating System?

Older applications are just that: older. They were meant to run on old machines with far less resources than current models. As a result, they will not run as fast as newer software. The reasons usually have to do with the way the programs were written. Most older software is known as 16-bit software. They were written for use on DOS or Windows-based machines and ran on 16-bit processors. They can be extremely unpredictable when run on a newer 32-bit machine.

Software for Hardware

- Learn how to determine if you require updated drivers.
- Learn how to install drivers.
- Learn how to roll back drivers.

You may be asking yourself, "Why are these idiots talking about hardware in a chapter devoted to software?" Well, the explanation is simple. In order for your computer to be able to communicate with hardware, it must use some piece of software. This software is called a *device driver*. Without the correct driver installed, your hardware simply will not work. Windows XP comes preloaded with thousands of drivers at its disposal. However, you may at times need to install, update, or roll back a driver for various reasons. This section deals with these issues.

How Do I Know If My Device Needs New Drivers?

Hardware drivers get updated by manufacturers constantly. Bugs are discovered in the current version, security vulnerabilities are fixed, and support is needed for newer operating systems. Unfortunately for you, hardware manufacturers do not make much of an effort to alert people about these new drivers. Here are the tell-tale signs that it may be time for a driver update:

- *Is your computer old?* Drivers will be updated several times during the lives of most hardware. If your computer is more than one year old, chances are the drivers have been updated.

- *Did you upgrade your operating system?* If you update your operating system, you will most likely have to install new drivers.

- *Check with the manufacturer.* Your PC's manufacturer should be able to tell you if your current drivers are the most recent versions.

Where Can I Find Updated Drivers for My Device?

Finding updated drivers is not a big deal if you know where to look and what to look for. You need to know what operating system is loaded on your computer and the model name or number of the piece of hardware you are using. Here are some ways to track down drivers:

- *Go to the manufacturer's website.* This should be your first stop for an updated device driver. They should have the most recent driver available for your particular piece of hardware and the OS it runs on.

- *Go to Windows Update.* See the section on updating Windows for more info.

- *Check the Web.* Sites like **www.DriverGuide.com** and **www.WinFiles.com** have tons of drivers available for download.

What Can I Do If I Can't Tell Who Made a Particular Piece of Hardware?

Finding drivers for a piece of hardware that you do not know the manufacturer of can seem like an impossible task. However, there are still ways to find drivers. The Federal Communications Commision (FCC) must license every piece of hardware that is installed in computers and other devices. When this happens the device gets a unique number assigned to it. By law, this number must be recorded somewhere on the hardware. It can be found imprinted on the board or on a label that is affixed to the hardware. Once you get this identification number, you can look it up in the FCC database. It can be found at **www.fcc.gov/oet/fccid**.

This search will more than likely give you some information with which to find yourself a driver. Some pieces of information you will need include the manufacturer, model number, and revision number.

What If My Hardware's Manufacturer Went Out of Business or No Longer Offers Drivers?

Most companies will stop making drivers after a certain period. They may eventually even pull them off their website. It's also possible that the company that made your hardware was bought out or went out of business. Here are some things you can do to locate a driver:

- *Check the Web.* Again, check sites like **www.DriverGuide.com** and **www.WinFiles.com**. If the hardware has a strong following, you may also find a driver that someone has authored on their own.

- *Check online auctions.* You may be able to purchase a driver disk or, better yet, another piece of hardware identical to yours.

- *Try a driver for a different operating system.* This option may work in a pinch. You can try installing a Windows 2000 driver on XP and vice versa. Keep in mind that this may do more harm than good and should be used as a last resort.

- *Try a driver from a similar product.* You may be able to use a driver from a similar product from the same manufacturer. A classic example of this is HP's line of DeskJet and LaserJet printers. The driver for an HP LaserJet 4 plus will work for a LaserJet 4000.

- *Try a generic driver.* Windows comes with some generic drivers that may be able to get you going. This usually works with modems. Keep in mind that these drivers most likely won't give you access to all of the device's features.

What Should I Do Before Updating Drivers?

After you have been installing hardware drivers for as long as we have, you quickly learn what can go wrong. Part of this process is anticipating failures and planning for them. Here is a list of things to watch out for:

- *Note the name of the device and where it is under the device manager tree.* Knowing the status of a piece of hardware before updating its driver is very important. If you update its driver, it may become unstable or unknown to the operating system

- *Note the driver name and version.* This will allow you to roll back the driver if necessary.
- *Note the specific device settings (for example, DMA).* Updating the driver may change the settings and cause conflicts with other hardware.

How Can I Install Updated Drivers?

Windows has come a long way in terms of hardware support. Installing new drivers in Windows 95 could quickly become a nightmare. Windows XP solves many of the problems in older versions of Windows by offering the following:

- *Installing new drivers in Windows 2000 and XP is a breeze.* It can be done from the Device Manager using the Hardware Update Wizard. You can open the Device Manager by right-clicking My Computer, clicking Properties, selecting the Hardware tab, and clicking Device Manager.
- *If it's an INF file, you can right-click on it and choose Install.* INF files contain all of the necessary information to install a driver for a particular piece of hardware.
- *Most drivers come packaged into an installer program.* See the section titled "How Do I Start a Software Install?" for more information.

Why Can't I Install/Update Drivers?

Installing and updating drivers involves many of the same obstacles as installing software. There are several prerequisites that must be met:

- *Got permissions?* You must be a member of the Administrators or Power Users security groups on your computer to install software.
- *Are you in terminal services?* If you are in Terminal Services, you probably will not be able to update any drivers.
- *Is your system affected by Group Policy?* Group Policy consists of sets of rules that system administrators can impose on users. They can control your default home page for Internet Explorer, remove the Run option from the Start menu, and perform a ton of other nifty things. A thorough discussion of Group Policy is beyond the scope of this book. Just keep in mind that your computer at work may be affected by these.
- *Is the system locked down by an administrator?* System administrators can also lock down systems without using Group Policy. Again, if this computer is in a work environment, chances are that it has been locked down by technical staff.

What Can I Do If a Driver Update Ruined My Computer?

This is an all too familiar scenario. You just downloaded an updated driver and installed it perfectly. You reboot the computer and are greeted by a blue screen and an error report saying something about hardware failure. Here's what you can do:

- *Roll back the driver.* See the next section for more information.

- *Boot in Safe mode.* Booting Windows in Safe mode should allow you to be able to get to the Windows desktop. Once there, you can roll back the newly installed driver. See Chapter 13 for more information.

- *Disable the device.* If the computer boots but acts weird, try disabling the device. This can be done in Device Manager. Just right-click the device and select Disable.

- *Use the last known good configuration.* You can do this by pressing F8 when the Windows splash screen shows during booting.

- *Use System Restore.* You can also roll back settings in Windows XP by using System Restore.

- *Restore from original disks.* Running the Windows setup will remove all hardware drivers and reinstall them.

How Can I Rollback a Driver?

There may come a time when you install a driver update and decide it is not for you. You may have lost functionality or the update may have completely disabled the device. Whatever the reason, you will still be able to revert to the last driver that was installed. Follow these simple instructions:

1. Open Device Manager. You should be an expert in this by now.
2. Right-click the device in question.
3. Click Properties.
4. Click the Driver tab. Figure 3.9 shows this tab.
5. Click Roll Back Driver.

What Are Signed Drivers and Why Should I Care about Them?

Driver signing is Microsoft's way of giving its stamp of approval on a device driver. Microsoft introduced driver signing with Windows ME and has continued to use the system ever since. The purpose of driver signing is to let users know that a hardware driver is compatible with Windows.

Figure 3.9
Driver Roll Back.

Any time you see a "Designed for Windows" logo on something, it has undergone testing by Microsoft to determine that it is fully compatible. This means that when you install it, the chance of harm being done to your system is greatly reduced. Most of the danger of installing new software lies in current files being overwritten by a different version. Other pitfalls include improperly written or corrupt software causing program errors or memory corruption or introducing viruses to your system.

Here is a list of things to keep in mind with driver signing:

- Windows by default will warn you when you try to install an unsigned driver.
- Even though a driver is unsigned, it may still work great.

Windows Optional Components

- Learn what optional components are available in Windows and how to access them.

What Optional Windows Components Are Available in XP?

Microsoft decided to leave some parts of Windows XP uninstalled by default. In our opinion, they happen to be some of the most useful. Here is a list of some of the hidden goodies in Windows XP:

- *IIS:* Internet Information Services allows you to run a website from your computer. Although this may be overkill for the majority of the readers of this book, it may prove useful in some situations, such as in a small to medium office. You can share information with co-workers using an intranet website. Setting it up and posting web pages is beyond the scope of this book. However, there are a ton of resources available on the Internet.

- *Fax Services:* Windows Fax Services allows you to send and receive faxes via your PC without the use of third-party software such as WinFax. Best of all, this faxing capability is free of charge.

How Can I Install Windows Optional Components?

Installing these missing pieces in Windows is easy. All you need is a few minutes and your Windows disk. Follow these simple instructions:

1. Open the Windows Control Panel.
2. Double-click Add or Remove Programs.
3. Click Add/Remove Windows Components.
4. Check off any components you want to install (or uninstall) and click Next.

NOTE: *You will need your Windows XP disk in order to install these optional components.*

Critical System Files

- Learn how to prevent yourself from deleting critical system files.

What Can I Do After I Delete or Replace a Critical System File?

Deleting system files is easier to do than you think. You may have been "cleaning house" on your computer or you might have possibly deleted an entire system folder by accident. In reality, curiosity usually kills the cat, but computers are different. They tend to be a little more forgiving. If you find yourself in this predicament, take these steps to fix it:

- *Check the Recycle Bin.* If you have not rebooted yet, you may be able to retrieve the file out of the Recycle Bin.

- *Use the System File Checker (SFC) utility.* The System File Checker is a utility that can detect and restore corrupt, replaced, or missing critical system files. To run the SFC, click Start|Run, type **SFC /SCANNOW**, and then click OK.

NOTE: *You will need your Windows XP disk when running this utility.*

- *Use System Restore.* A system restore may be able to help you, depending on what file was deleted.

- *Install the latest service pack.* A service pack is a collection of system files that are used to replace existing system files to solve existing issues. Installing the latest service pack will usually reinstall any missing or corrupt system files.

- *Use Windows Update.* The file you deleted may be part of a Windows hotfix or critical update.

How Can I Prevent Myself from Deleting Critical System Files?

Windows by default hides all critical files from users. However, at some point you or someone else may have revealed these files. Hiding them again is a simple matter. Just follow these instructions:

1. Right-click Start.
2. Click Explore.
3. Click Tools in the upper menu.
4. Click Folder Options.
5. Check "Hide protected operating system files."
6. Check "Do not show hidden files and folders."
7. Uncheck "Display the contents of system folders."
8. Click OK.

Summary

In this chapter, you learned about all of the things that can go wrong with software. Software can fail on many levels. Everything from the operating system to individual programs falls under the scope of software. Just like hardware, software can fail in many ways. Things like improper installation, incompatibilities, viruses, and user error can wreak havoc with software.

When you run into a software problem, use this chapter as a foundation to determine what went wrong. We have covered many of the most common problems that we encounter on a day-to-day basis in our jobs. Our goal was to save you time and aggravation by pointing you in the right direction.

Networking Disasters and Mishaps

4

Disasters to avoid:

- Having multiple devices with identical names on your network.
- Losing your Internet connection.
- Having your network come to a standstill.

Mishaps and blunders to run from:

- Using the wrong cables for your network.
- Unintentionally causing network problems yourself.

Unless you've been living in a cave, you are already familiar with the world's largest network—the Internet. The Internet is a global network that connects many smaller networks (.com, .edu, .gov, and so on), but what exactly is a network anyway? It's a group of interconnected devices (usually computers) that have a common mission—sharing data.

In the evolution of PCs, networking is a relatively new thing. In the first 10 years after the PC's introduction, few users had any experience with networking. It's hard to remember this, especially since networking has become so pervasive over the past 5 years. We do everything now with our PCs through networking—share our favorite music, install software, book our vacations, and even find a date for Saturday night.

Connecting up a bunch of computers is a good way to share data and expand our horizons, but it also can create a myriad of problems. And the more dependent we become on using networks to share information, the bigger the disasters and mishaps can be when our networks fail.

In this chapter, we'll start by quickly discussing some basics about networks so that we can make sure we're all speaking the same language. Then we'll dig in and look at the types of disasters and mishaps that surround hardwired networks—the kind of networks that need lots of cables or wires to operate. In the next chapter, we'll look at wireless networking. For this chapter, we've divided up our discussion of problems into different types of networks, including high-speed wired networks, dial-up networks, X10, and other networks. You'll learn what you can do if your network is not set up properly and what you can do if your network fails.

Understanding Network Speak

- Learn about network cabling.
- Learn how to update your networking equipment.

To deal with the types of network disasters and mishaps you might encounter, you'll need to get a crash course in the types of networks that are in use and the terminology that is used. The two type of networks are local area networks (LANs) and wide area networks (WANs). A LAN is a network that covers a single location. If you have a network at home, it would be called a LAN. A network that covers more than a single location is a WAN. Typically, a WAN is an interconnection of LANs. So, when an office in Los

Angeles is connected to an office in New York, a WAN is formed. The Internet is the world's largest WAN.

For devices to connect to one another and form a network, they must all speak the same language. In "geek speak," this is known as a protocol. A protocol describes how to form the data, compress it, and handle errors. While there are many types of protocols (IPX/SPX, NetBUI, and the recently deceased Banyan Vines), TCP/IP is the most commonly used protocol for the home, office, and Internet. OK, we lied. TCP/IP is not a protocol; it's actually a suite of protocols (Transmission Control Protocol and Internet Protocol). Now that we've regained your trust, we can tell you that TCP/IP is widely used because of its ability to recover lost or corrupted data. It works behind the scenes to make sure that you don't lose valuable information. So just think about all of the disasters that could occur if you didn't have TCP/IP working for you! Just imagine trying to read this book with every other word missing.

Understanding Networking Equipment

In the early days of computer networks, computers were connected directly to each other like a tin can and string telephone system (ever seen *The Little Rascals?*). Obviously, this type of system had some drawbacks. Today, most businesses have all sorts of fancy networking equipment, ranging in price from a few dollars to thousands of dollars. The home network is evolving to support wireless networking, network printing, and more. Here is a list of some of the key networking devices that are commonly used in the home or office:

- *Firewall:* A firewall is a software program or a hardware device that prevents unauthorized entry into a network. Think of a firewall as a brick wall. There is fire on one side and you are on the other. The "fire wall" protects you from danger. This is an absolute must for any network.

- *Hub:* A hub is a device that connects multiple network devices together. On a hub, only one device can talk at a time. When one connected device sends data to another, that data is actually sent to all connected devices. The intended recipient accepts the data and all the other devices simply ignore it. Think of this type of communication as yelling in a crowded room. While you may eventually get your point across, you will also unnecessarily distract and occupy the time of others. Hubs are an older technology and they are being replaced by switches, where appropriate.

- *Router:* A router is a device that forwards data using the best path to another router or network device. Think of a router as a smart traffic management system. It knows that transmitting your data to the left would take 2 seconds but transmitting it to the right takes 1 second, so it transmits it to the right (or so we hope).

- *Switch:* A switch is a "smart" hub that allows multiple devices to talk at the same time and directly communicate with a connected device (as opposed to the yelling). When you need to connect multiple, nonwireless, computers together, a switch is the way to go.

- *Wireless access point:* A wireless access point (WAP) is a device that authenticates and connects wireless devices to a network. Think of an access point as the maître d' at a reservation-only restaurant; it greets you, verifies who you are, and shows you to your destination—a table by the window if you're really lucky. This is the most commonly used device in a wireless network.

- *Wireless repeater:* A wireless repeater (a.k.a. range extender) is a device used to extend the range of a wireless signal. Every access point has a maximum range that a signal can reach (typically 100 to 150 feet). That range easily diminishes due to interference and attenuation (more about this later in this chapter). A wireless repeater can take a dying signal, reconstruct it, and rebroadcast it.

What Kind of Cables Should I Use?

If you have ever tried to purchase network cables, you have seen all the different types out there. Usually, the packaging on the cable is about as helpful as the people selling it. Purchasing and using the wrong cable will cause poor performance, cost more, or simply not work. Here's a list of the more popular types of network cables:

- *Cat3:* An old standard originally intended for telephone connectivity, Cat3 can handle speeds up to 10 megabits per second (Ethernet). We recommend not purchasing cables that are Cat3. Try to use a minimum of Cat5, for both computers and telephones.

- *Cat5:* Now being phased out by Cat5E, Cat5 is a cable standard that can handle speeds up to 100 megabits per second (Fast Ethernet).

- *Cat5E:* This cable standard is an enhanced (hence the *E*) version of Cat5, offering complete backward capability with Cat5. It can handle speeds up to 1 gigabit per second (Gigabit Ethernet).

- *Crossover cable:* Also known as a *null-modem cable,* this special-use cable is intended for direct device-to-device connections (PC to PC, switch to switch, and so on). On network devices, the special port this cable connects to is called an uplink port. Again, this is a special-purpose cable and should only be purchased and used if you know exactly how to use it.

How Can I Keep My Networking Equipment Up-to-Date?

You buy, you install, you use. This seems to be the logical pattern, and should be most of the time. But, you also need to maintain. Networking equipment updates may bring you things like improved speed, less battery consumption, additional features, and error fixes. The following list describes a few ways to keep your networking equipment up-to-date:

- *Update the firmware.* Firmware consists of tiny software programs that reside in a memory chip inside a device and control everything the device does. Think of it as the operating system for devices. Almost all tech devices run off of updateable firmware: PVRs, Video cards, motherboards, CD/DVD-ROM drives, and yes, even networking equipment. Visit your device manufacturer's website to obtain the latest firmware

- *Update the drivers.* A driver is a piece of software that installs on your computer and helps your computer interact with your device. Think of it as an interpreter that translates device language into computer language and computer language into device language. While your driver may be available through Windows Update (see Chapter 3 for more information), you should always obtain your drivers from your device manufacturer to avoid complications.

- *Use your device's update tool.* Some devices (like Microsoft's Broadband Networking equipment) include software that installs on your computer to interact with the networking equipment. That software may contain a mechanism to obtain and install or automatically update your firmware. See your owner's manual for more information.

What Is X10 Networking?

You have probably seen the sexy Internet X10 ads from X10.com, selling wireless cameras. X10 is a communication protocol that transmits and receives over the electrical lines in your home. X10 creates a network for most of your electronic devices. All you need to do is plug an X10 remote control receiver into some outlet and then connect a lamp to an X10 transmitter plugged into another outlet and voila—you can remotely turn on, off, and even dim the lamp with a wired or wireless remote control.

With advanced X10 controllers, you can set schedules and turn on and off your house lights, sprinklers, radios, coffee makers, and basically anything that turns on via a switch. X10 will work with any device that turns on when it's plugged in. For example, modern televisions do not work with X10 because they usually don't turn on automatically when plugged in; you must press the power button. Lamps and lights are perfect for X10 because you can leave them switched on, remove power, reconnect power, and they go back on.

In addition to turning devices on or off and dimming them, you can perform even more advanced tasks with X10:

- Report which devices in your home are on or off.
- Control house temperature with an X10 thermostat.
- Control sprinkler systems.
- Control X10 devices from a wired or wireless controller.
- Unlock, lock, open, and close doors and garage doors.
- Control your X10 from your PC.
- Call your home and perform any of the tasks in this list.

Major Network Failures

- Learn how to analyze your network's performance.
- Learn how to get your network to work when it isn't.
- Learn how to resolve various networking issues.

What Are the Signs of a Sick Network?

Some people may have a sick network and not have even realize it because they don't know what to look for. Before you can even begin to fix your network, you must realize that you have a problem. You may have had some of the following things happen for quite some time and just blamed it on your computer:

- *Poor performance when printing to a network printer*
- *Errors when using email programs such as Outlook or Eudora*
- *Errors when browsing the Internet*
- *Slow performance or errors when opening files on other computers*

What Can I Do If My Network Is Slow or Is Down?

There is nothing worse than a slow network. It can really put a quick end to your day. A slow network can manifest itself in many ways. You may have trouble sending email, opening files from a file server, printing when using a network printer, or browsing the Internet. With all of these problems, it's sometimes difficult to figure out exactly what is going on. In order to effectively diagnose a slowdown, you need to have a little background on networks. Networks consist of nodes (computers, printers, PDAs, and so on), switches or hubs, and routers. The nodes produce network traffic and the switches, routers, and hubs transmit this traffic. This is a pretty simple concept to understand. With this information, you can now begin to troubleshoot a sick network as follows.

Are you experiencing the problem at all of the computers on your network? This is an important thing to determine early on in your diagnosis. Go to each of your computers and do some normal routine tasks like browse the local network or send a print job to a network printer. Did all of the computers seem slow? If this is the case, you may have a networking problem. If not, your problem is probably not network related. Things to look at include general system performance and the presence of a virus and junkware.

To troubleshoot the slowness any further, you will need the IP address from every network-connected device (computers, printers, routers, WAPs) on your network. You will also need to know the default gateway. This is usually the private IP address of your router. Here is how you can find this information:

- *Computer:* Click Start|Run. Type **Command** and click OK. You will now be at the command prompt. Type **IPCONFIG** and press Enter. The IP address will be listed in the information that follows. Figure 4.1 shows an example of this. As you can see, this device is connected to the network via a wireless Ethernet adapter and its IP address is 192.168.1.2.

- *Printer:* You can usually determine your printer's IP address by printing a configuration page. This can be done on most printers by holding down the power button while the printer is on. External print servers usually have a button on them that prints a configuration page. Check your print server's documentation for the final word on how to do this.

- *Router or WAP:* You can determine the IP address of these devices through their configuration utility. Check your manual for specific instructions.

Figure 4.1

Getting the IP information.

One of the most important tools you have in your troubleshooting arsenal is the Ping tool. If you have ever overheard two network engineers talking, you probably heard them mention the word *ping*. Well, now you will know what they are talking about. A ping is a sequence of packets that are sent to a particular network device to test connections. What we are looking for here is the successful delivery of all packets and the amount of time it takes. You can use the Ping tool by doing the following:

1. Click Start.

2. Click Run.

3. Type **Command** and click OK. This will open the command prompt.

4. Type **Ping** followed by the IP address of the device for which you wish to test connectivity. Figure 4.2 shows what the output looks like if you have a problem. Figure 4.3 shows a perfect set of results.

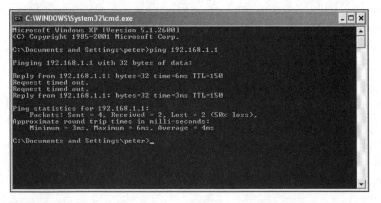

Figure 4.2

Bad ping results.

Figure 4.3
Good ping results.

If you do not receive any results, such as shown in Figure 4.4, then you really have a problem.

Figure 4.4
No ping results.

Once you have determined that you actually have a problem, you need to figure out what is causing the problem. Here is a list of things to be on the lookout for:

- *Length and type of cable:* If you have a Cat5E cable that is longer than 329 feet you may have already found your culprit. Anything longer than this and you will lose signal due to attenuation. Signs of this would be loss of pings. Also, keep in mind that those Cat3 cables someone gave you just do not cut it anymore. Get rid of them and invest in some good Cat5E patch cables.

- *Link light:* Most Ethernet adapters have a link light that shows their link status. If you have the Ethernet cable plugged into your device and into a switch, the link light should be lit. If it is not, you have a problem. Try using a different cable or plugging into a different port of your switch. You may also have a bad Ethernet adapter or one that has been disabled in the system BIOS.

- *No IP information:* When checking your IP information as shown previously, you may have found that none had been assigned. This can happen for one of two reasons: the device may not have been able to contact a DHCP server or there may be a problem with the device itself. If your IP address reads something like 169.254.0.1, the device assigned itself an IP address because it could not contact a DHCP server. If it reads 0.0.0.0, the Ethernet cable may not be plugged in. Make sure that all of your devices have valid IP information.

- *All components powered up:* A switch or router will not work if it is not turned on. Make sure it is turned on and that the indicator lights are on.

- *Duplicate IP information:* The nature of networks prohibits the existence of two machines with the same IP address. Make sure all of your devices have a unique IP address.

- *Duplicate hostname:* Another important thing to look for is that each computer on your network has a unique host name. Duplicate names will cause nothing but trouble. You can check this in Windows 2000 and XP by doing the following:

  1. Click Start.
  2. Click Run.
  3. Type **Command** and click OK.
  4. Type **Hostname** and press Enter.

HORROR STORY! A friend of ours recently bought three new identical laptops from a major computer company. He quickly broke them out of their boxes and got them up and running on his network. Within minutes, he began to have major problems. After spending some time on the phone with tech support, he discovered that all of the computers were named Laptop. Changing the names to something unique fixed the problem.

What Can I Do If My Networking Equipment Won't Work after Updating?

You never realize how much you need your network until it's unavailable. Whether it's printing, getting your email, or surfing the Web, a bad update on your networking equipment can prevent you and everyone else from using the network. The following list outlines the steps you should take if your networking equipment won't work after an update:

- *Check the usual suspects.* Before assuming that a device is corrupted from a bad update, you should check all the usual suspects: device is off, power cord is disconnected, dead battery, and so on. See Chapter 2 for more information.

- *Make sure you have the correct update.* Applying an update from one type of machine to another or applying an older update to a device that has a newer update may cause problems. Confirm you have the latest update for your specific device before installing.

- *Soft-reset your device.* Most networking equipment comes with a button to reset the configuration to the factory defaults. Typically, there is a pinhole where you insert a paper clip and hold for 10 seconds to reset. Consult your owner's manual for more information.

- *Reimage.* Some PDAs require updates to be applied in a specific order. If they are not applied in this order, the networking functionality will be rendered useless and you will have to reimage the device and apply the updates in the correct order. You may also have to reimage if you applied the wrong update. Always read the prerequisites of any install and read the messages that are displayed to you during the install to avoid having to reimage.

- *Contact your device's manufacturer.* If these suggestions did not work, you may have to contact your device's tech support for assistance.

Network Security

- Make your network a hard target for hackers.
- Prevent a hacker from stealing your files or personal information.

How Can I Prevent Hackers from Getting into My Network?

Nothing has gotten as much press lately as the topic of Internet hackers. Stories of hackers turning PCs into zombies to do their evil bidding have become the norm. The thing that makes it so easy for a hacker these days is that everything is so wide open. Starting from the PC all the way up to the router (you do have a router, don't you?) that connects you to the Internet. Everything is designed to work as easily as possible right out of the box. Unfortunately, this makes it a piece of cake for a hacker to gain access to your network. To better protect yourself, you need to learn how to "harden" your computer equipment, as we'll discuss in the sections that follow.

How Can I Harden My Computer?

An air-tight computer is a hacker's worst nightmare. Once they realize they are up against a secure computer, they usually move on to their next target. It is usually not worth their time to try to break into yours if it is going to give them trouble. Here's how you can lock yours down like Fort Knox:

- *Update, update, update!!!!!!!!!!!!!!* No matter what operating system you use, make sure you update your operating system and all installed software. Not updating will leave you open to vulnerabilities that hackers will be sure to exploit.

- *Use antivirus software.* Do not leave this to chance. Always have fully updated antivirus software working for you.

- *Be wary of email attachments.* Do not open any email attachments you receive from unknown senders. It could very well be a hacker trying to get into your computer.

- *Turn your computer off when not in use.* A very good way of thwarting a hacker attack is to make your computer inaccessible. We can't think of anything better than turning it off.

- *Remove unnecessary Windows components.* There are certain features in Windows that are particularly interesting to hackers. Internet Information Services (IIS) is one of them. To make matters worse, Microsoft decided to install this feature by default in Windows 2000. If you are not making use of this feature or any other features in Windows, you should remove them. See Chapter 3 for more information on adding and removing Windows components.

- *Use a firewall software program.* Software firewalls are a great line of defense against hackers. Windows XP comes with a built-in firewall, or you can use a third-party program like ZoneAlarm. You can get ZoneAlarm from **www.zonelabs.com**.

- *Use strong passwords.* Set a strong password on all user accounts on your computer. Most people make the mistake of using no password at all. Talk about putting out the red carpet.

- *Use a router.* One common mistake people make is connecting their computer directly to the Internet using a broadband connection. You might as well set up a desk out on the street and invite people over to use your computer. Get yourself a router to connect yourself to the Internet. This will provide you with some protection from the evils of Internet hackers.

How Can I Harden My Networking Components?

Computers are not the only thing that can attract a hacker. They can also hack into your networking components and cause you all sorts of problems. Here are some ways that you can prevent this from happening to you:

- *Router:* Make sure you have the latest updates applied to your router. These devices operate on little mini operating systems that can be as prone to hackers as Windows.

- *Switches and hubs:* These devices usually do not require much attention. There are some cases in which this can change. If your switch or hub is manageable through a Web interface or other software, you will want to set a password or change the default password.

- *Wireless:* See Chapter 5 for full details on how to harden your wireless network.

Dialup Networking

- Learn how you can solve dial-up connection problems.

What Should I Do when I Can't Connect with a Dial-Up Connection?

Whether at home or in some hotel (hopefully some place nice) on a road trip, you may use a modem to dial in and connect to the Internet or remote network. Many stars need to be aligned to connect properly using a dial-up connection. The following tips will help you troubleshoot when you can't connect via a dial-up connection:

- *Check for a dial tone.* This should be the first thing you check. Checking for dial tone will tell you if the line is working and if someone else is using the line.

- *Make sure you are dialing the correct number.* If you are visiting an area but your device is configured to dial up a number local to your main area, you may be dialing the wrong number. Contact your ISP for a number local to your current area or for a 1-800 number.

- *Make sure the number isn't busy.* Most ISPs provide multiple numbers for you to try if one is busy. Contact your ISP to obtain these phone numbers.

- *Dial 9.* When at a hotel or a place of business, you may have to dial 9 or some other prefix before making an outside call. If you are not in a location that requires a prefix, make sure your connection is not using one.

- *Make sure you're using an analog phone line.* Your modem needs a working analog phone line in order to connect properly. Some offices and hotels have digital phone lines and may burn out your modem when you connect to them. See the following section for more information. Also, just because it looks like a phone jack doesn't mean it is one. You may be plugging your modem into a network jack. When in doubt, ask for help from the local tech support personnel.

- *Check the quality of the phone line.* The phone line may be so low in quality that your dial-up connection is slow or unusable. This is especially true when visiting countries or areas with older phone systems. Unfortunately, if this is the case, there is not much you can do.

- *Check the cord.* The cord may be chewed (hopefully not by you), stretched, or damaged just enough to prevent a connection. If so, switch the cord and try again.

How Can I Prevent My Telephone Modem from Being Damaged?

Using telephone modems was one of the first popular methods to network a PC and laptop. A telephone modem allows you to send and receive faxes, voice calls, and data over an everyday phone line. The typical use for a telephone modem is to dial in to your Internet service provider (AOL, MSN, and so on). While it's common to find telephone modems in your PC or laptop, you can also find them in any device that dials in for service (DVR, satellite receiver). Modems are sensitive devices and become easily damaged. You may be able to replace a bad modem in your PC, but replacing it in devices like a laptop and DVR where the modem is built in will require that you send your device in for repair. Here are some ways you can prevent your modem from being damaged:

- *Know what you are connecting to.* Many businesses and hotels use digital phone lines for ease of management and to use advanced phone features such as name display and digital recording. These are high-current phone lines, and they will burn out (fry) your analog modem when you connect to them. Most manufacturers are including smart circuits to protect against damage from connecting your analog modem to a digital phone line, but this is no reason to connect blindly. Always ask what type of line it is before connecting. If you have an older modem that does not include digital frying prevention, consider purchasing a new one or purchasing a digital-to-analog converter (discussed next).

- *Use a DAC.* To use a digital phone line with your analog modem (properly, without the frying), you will need a digital-to-analog converter

(DAC). A digital-to-analog takes a digital signal and translates it into an analog signal.

- *Use a surge protector.* Modems are extremely sensitive to power surges from "dirty power," lightning storms, or noises from electrical devices (washing machines, microwave ovens, hair dryers, etc.). Always use a surge protector to clean noise from the line and prevent surges from damaging your modem.

X10 and Other Networking

- Learn how to solve networking problems with X10 networks.

What Should I Do If My X10 Network Is Not Working?

Depending on how big your house is, how your house is wired, and what's connected, X10 can be an easy or difficult thing to set up. The following list will help you troubleshoot X10 connectivity issues:

- *Does your X10 work in parts of your home but not all?* This occurs if your home is wired as a two-phase system, where two separate 110-volt circuit power feeds connect to the breaker box. Since the feeds are separate, the power in your home is also separate and the X10 signal cannot jump from one feed to the next. To bridge these feeds, you must purchase and install a signal bridge (also known as a phase coupler or coupling capacitor).

- *Are devices turning on by themselves?* If you have an X10 wireless controller, perhaps a neighbor also has one and your receiver if picking up their signal.

- *Do your have a power line filter for your house?* X10 works by transmitting data in unused areas of electrical signals. If you have a power line filter for your home (a device that cleans and removes unknown electrical signals), it may be stripping out the X10 data.

- *Do you have other devices transmitting on the power line?* Devices like wireless intercoms, wireless telephone jacks, wireless cable jacks, and wireless networking jacks transmit their information over your electrical line to send the signal (voice, telephone, data, etc.) from the source to the receiver. Unfortunately, these devices are using the same area in the electrical signal that X10 uses. Try disconnecting these devices to see if your problem goes away.

- *Check for interference.* Like wireless networks, X10 is also prone to interference from other devices. Usually major appliances like a washing machine or air conditioner can cause just enough interference to disrupt an X10 signal. You can purchase and install a noise filter to prevent interference from these devices.

- *Do you have a big home?* If your home is over 4,000 square feet, chances are you need an X10 amplifier to cover the distance.

What Can I Do when My DVR Networking Is Not Working?

Networking a digital video recorder (DVR) allows you to receive system updates through the Internet, transfer data between DVRs, program your DVR over the Internet, and more. The following list will help you troubleshoot when your DVR networking is not working:

- *Reboot.* Ah, the magic fix. Rebooting is a common fix for most devices because it clears out memory and reinitializes the device.

- *Boot your DHCP server first.* A DHCP server (computer, router) assigns IP addresses to connected devices that request it. If you boot your DVR first, its request for an IP address will fail and it won't be able to connect to the network. When in doubt and your DHCP server is up and running, reboot to obtain an IP address.

- *Specify/verify your network Info.* Besides dynamically obtaining an IP address from a DHCP server, some DVRs allow you to specify an IP address in the device's configuration menu. If you already specified an IP address, you should verify that the IP address, gateway, and subnet mask are correct.

- *Make sure you are using the correct networking adapters.* While some DVRs come with network cards built in, others allow you to install or connect your own adapters. Make sure you purchase and use supported adapters. Contact the manufacturer for more information.

- *Make sure you are using the right cables.* When connecting DVRs to certain network devices such as a bridge, you may have to use a crossover cable. Consult your owner's manual for more information.

How Can I Network My Gaming Device?

We can remember the days of our youth, inviting friends over to play Ikari Warriors and Mario Brothers. Unfortunately, now it is impossible to schedule and find friends to come over and play games. Fortunately, most gaming devices come with or support network capability, allowing you to play with or against others in your neighborhood, on the other side of the country, or across the globe. Here are some ways you can network your gaming devices:

- *Buy and install the adapter.* While some game consoles come with networking capability built in (Xbox, NGage, and so on), others, such as the PlayStation 2 and the GameCube, require purchasing and installing specific network adapters.

- *Sign up for service.* The Xbox and PlayStation 2 both offer services that allow you to play against other Internet opponents for a small subscription fee. GameCube only allows playing against others on your immediate network and does not offer a service to play against others on the Internet (unless you use an add-on, as described next).

- *Install custom add-ons.* While the Xbox and PlayStation 2 allow you to play against others on the Internet, the GameCube only allows you to play against others on your immediate network. You can install and use custom add-ons like Warp Pipe (**www.warppipe.com)** to play others on the Internet with having to pay for the add-on or for the service.

How Can I Network My MP3 Player?

While some MP3 players may require a little more work than others, chances are you can set up your MP3 player to be part of your network and access it remotely. Here are some tips to help you connect your MP3 player to a network and share your music files:

- *Use included software.* Your device may come with software that allows you to share your music on a network.

- *Share it.* If your MP3 player allows Windows to access it as if it were another drive, you can easily network your MP3 player. First, you can simply share the drive letter that is assigned to the MP3 player.

- *Use Redchairsoftware.com.* Here you will find software to manage and network your Creative Labs, Apple, Dell, RIO, or iRiver MP3 player. When the software is installed and the player connected, others can simply go to a web page served from the computer and browse and play your music and playlists.

- *Use Dot Pod.* Dot Pod (**www.dotpod.net**) is a free utility for the Mac that allows you to share the music on your Apple iPod through the utility's built-in web server. When the software is installed and the player is connected, others can simply go to a web page served from the computer and browse and play your music and playlists.

WARNING! Remember, sharing your music on a network for your own personal use is OK, but sharing copyrighted music with others without permission from the copyright holder is called piracy and is against the law. See Chapter 15 for more information.

How Can I Network My Printers?

If you have a desktop computer with a connected printer, you are probably happy with having everything in one place. But what if you have a laptop? Are you happy with carrying a printer around the house where it is needed? We would think not. Whether you have a wired or wireless network, you can take advantage of network printing. Network printing allows you to place a printer in a central location and use it from different points in your home or office. Here is a list of different ways to accomplish this:

- *Built-in Ethernet adapter:* Some printers come with a built-in Ethernet adapter for network printing. All you need to do is just plug it in at some point in your network.

- *External print server:* An external print server allows you to network any printer. It plugs into the parallel or USB port of your printer and then has an Ethernet jack that plugs into your network.

- *Internal print server:* Some printers do not have built-in Ethernet capabilities but allow you to install an add-on card in order to network them.

- *Wireless print server:* These are the ultimate in network printing. With one of these gadgets, you can put your printer practically anywhere in your house or office as long as you have a wireless signal.

Summary

This chapter should have given you a bird's eye view of the problems you can run into with your home or small office network. No one said it was going to be easy, but we sure hope we have given you some confidence to deal with these problems. Eventually, wired networking will be replaced with wireless. But until it is, you need to be prepared to deal with the bad things that can happen.

Wireless Networking

Disasters to avoid:

- Having a hacker break into your wireless network because It Is not secure.

- Having thieves steal important data because you are working on an unsecured public network (hotspot).

- Not being able to connect to your wireless network to send or receive important emails.

Mishaps and blunders to run from:

- Combining different Wi-Fi network standards (Wireless-G and Wireless-B) and having your network slow down as a result.

- Not being able to configure your access point because you lose your WEP security code.

Portability is king these days. But what good is it to have a portable laptop or PDA and then have to plug it into a network jack so that you can go online or share files? That's where wireless networking comes in. You don't need to be stuck at your desk anymore eating Oreos and surfing the Web. You can do that in bed, on the couch, or in the kitchen, where you probably should be eating cookies in the first place.

Wireless networking is really catching on now. Most new laptops come with built-in wireless cards, and you can easily add a wireless card to your older laptop or desktop PC. And if you have one of the newer PDAs, it's likely that you are already enjoying the benefits of wireless communications. But as wireless networking grows and as more devices get connected, more problems are surfacing. One of the biggest problems facing wireless communications is security. Many wireless users simply connect up and forget to turn on their security features, which can lead to real disasters.

Understanding Wireless Network Speak

Just as hardwired networks have their own standards and jargon, so do wireless networks. Here's a crash course for you so that you can better understand how wireless networks operate. This discussion will help you follow the disasters and mishaps that we'll be presenting in this chapter.

Types of Wireless Networks

Two types of wireless networks are in use today: ad-hoc and infrastructure. The *ad-hoc network* involves connecting to a computer directly to access the network (or another computer connects to you). The benefit of this approach is that you don't need what is called an *access point*. Ad-hoc networks can get complicated and can be difficult to secure. The second type, *infrastructure wireless network,* involves connecting to a wireless access point to access the network. This is the most common type of wireless network. To use this type of network, you'll need to purchase an access point. Access points used to be a big deal, but now they are very inexpensive. We've even seen them for sale at outlets like Home Depot for less than $50. We'll mainly focus on infrastructure networks in this chapter.

Understanding the Confusing Standards

If you've been shopping for wireless devices, you've probably seen the term *802.11*. 802.11 is the networking standard for today's most popular wireless devices. It defines how wireless devices communicate. Part of that specification is power management, error handling, and speed management. Today's wireless devices come in three different and delicious 802.11 flavors: A, B, and G (as if things weren't confusing enough). You should be familiar with the differences between these standards so you can avoid the frustration and mishaps of buying the wrong product and wasting your money. Who needs that?

What Is 802.11a?

802.11a is an older network standard (created in 1999) that supports a transfer speed of 54 Mbps. It is more than sufficient for Internet activity because most of today's broadband Internet connections only allow for a maximum speed of 3 Mbps. Its speed makes it a good choice for intense file operations (moving large files) and high-quality video and music streaming.

802.11a has fewer interference problems compared to 802.11b and 802.11g due to usage of the regulated 5 GHz frequency. Because it uses a different frequency range than the other two standards, 802.11a products are incompatible with 802.11b and 802.11g products that use the unlicensed 2.4 GHz frequency range.

Because 802.11a products tend to cost more, they are typically used in business environments. In addition to each component costing more, 802.11a has a shorter range than 802.11b and 802.11g because of its higher frequency, which means you need to purchase more access points to cover the same area.

Due to microchip manufacturing difficulties supporting the 5 GHz frequency, 802.11a products didn't begin to arrive on the market until 2001, allowing 802.11b to get the jump start it needed to become the most widely adopted standard to date.

What Is 802.11b?

Also created in 1999, 802.11b supports a transfer speed up to 11 Mbps. 802.11b might be sufficient for Internet connectivity, but it may be too slow for intense file operations (moving large files) and high-quality video and music streaming.

802.11b communicates using an unlicensed frequency at 2.4 GHz. For manufacturers, that means lower production costs since they do not have to pay licensing fees. For the consumer, that usually means lower product costs but higher chances of interference. Because the 2.4 GHz frequency is unlicensed, this frequency is already crowded by many types of devices, which ultimately leads to interference when they are used simultaneously and or near each other. Some other devices that use the 2.4 GHz frequency are 802.11g wireless access points, cordless telephones, wireless game controllers, and even microwaves. Later in this chapter we will discuss the possible causes of interference and how to prevent it.

While 802.11b has lower power consumption needs than the other two standards, it actually consumes more power while transmitting and receiving due to its slower transmission speed. Imagine copying a 500 MB file using an 802.11b access point. Although the 802.11b standard moves bits at 11 megabits per second, a large chunk of that bandwidth is overhead. The actual throughput (in other words, the rate that data files move across the wireless link) is much less, typically 5 megabits per second. Moving a 500 MB file would take about 13 minutes: (500 Mb ★ 8 megabits) / 5 Mbps = 800 seconds.

Now, if you copy that same file using an 802.11a or 802.11g access point, it should take you only 3.3 minutes. As with 802.11b, the data throughput of a and g wireless devices is much less than the stated maximum bit rate of 54 Mbps—typically, 20 Mbps is the best you will see. The calculation is thus (500 Mb ★ 8 megabits) / 20 Mbps = 200 seconds. So, even though 802.11b draws less power, it actually ends draining more power because data operations take longer. What does all this fancy math mean to you? If your device is on battery (PDA, laptop, and so on), it means a shortening of your device's battery life—which is never good.

Finally, What Is 802.11g?

Created in 2003 as an extension to 802.11b, 802.11g is a standard that combines the speed of 802.11a with the range and compatibility of 802.11b. Like 802.11a, 802.11g supports data rates of up to 54 Mbps, with throughput of up to 20 Mbps, which makes it ideal for intense wireless video, audio, and data operations. Instead of using the regulated 5 GHz frequency range, 802.11g uses the same 2.4 GHz frequency range 802.11b uses, making 802.11g devices backward compatible with 802.11b devices. For example, an 802.11g access point can host 802.11g clients and 802.11b clients simultaneously. The only issue with this configuration is that the 802.11g access point would step down its speed to 11 Mbps to support the 802.11b clients. That ultimately results in 802.11g clients expecting data rates at 54 Mbps being stepped down to 11 Mbps.

HORROR STORY!

We had a friend who did some consulting for a company that wanted to expand its wireless network. The company had an 802.11b system installed and wanted to add 802.11g devices and access points to take advantage of the newer technologies and speed enhancements. The company representatives decided not to upgrade their current 802.11b devices because they figured the two would be compatible. After they spent a bit of time and money installing the new devices, they were really disappointed with the performance of the system. Moral: Don't mix 802.11b and 802.11g in the same network!

802.11g has the same interference issues that affect 802.11b because they use the same unlicensed 2.4 GHz frequency. In terms of range, 802.11g has better coverage when compared to 802.11b and extremely better coverage when compared to 802.11a.

Which Is the Best Standard for My Needs?

We've included Table 5.1 to help you determine which standard would be best for your own situation.

Table 5.1   The Benefits and Trade-Offs of the Three Wireless Standards

	802.11a	802.11b	802.11g
Compatible Standards	None (Bad)	None (Bad)	802.11b (Good)
Cost	Expensive (Bad)	Cheap (Good)	Moderate (OK)
Interference Issues	Minimal (Good)	Some (Bad)	Some (Bad)
Power Consumption	Low (Good)	High (Bad)	Low (Good)
Range	Poor (Bad)	Average (OK)	Excellent (Good)
Signal Blockage	High (Bad)	Low (Good)	Low (Good)
Speed	Fast (Good)	Slow (Bad)	Fast (Good)
TOTAL	4 Bads, 3 Goods	4 Bads, 1 OK, 2 Goods	1 Bad, 1 OK, 5 Goods

As you can see, the results favor 802.11g. There are some hybrid wireless access points on the market that combine A/B and A/G. These devices are typically more expensive than an 802.11g access point, but if you have the money and are determined, the A/G covers you on all standards.

Wireless Security Issues

- Learn how to secure your wireless network and devices.
- Learn how to detect if someone is trying to access your wireless network.
- Learn how to be more secure when you connect to a public hotspot.

How Can I Secure My Wireless Network?

Wireless networking provides lots of convenience for the home and office user, but it can also provide an open door into your network for any hacker with a Pringles can, a laptop, and a network sniffer (a program that can capture transmitted data). (Believe it or not, hackers still use Pringles cans as antennas to locate wireless networks, but the smart hackers have figured out that Pringles cans don't really work that well.) While almost all wireless access points include functionality to secure your wireless network, by default the security is disabled or easily bypassed. Here's how you can quickly secure your wireless network:

- *Change the default password.* See the section "Enabling Wireless Security" later in this chapter for more information.

- *Disable web configuration.* See the section "Enabling Wireless Security" for more information.

- *Change the default SSID and don't broadcast it.* See the section "Enabling Wireless Security" for more information about how to set and use the service set identifier (SSID). We recommend that you change the default SSID on a frequent basis. This is necessary just in case someone figures it out.

- *Use Wireless Security.* See the section "Enabling Wireless Security" for more information.

- *Eliminate your outdoor signal.* If your signal is strong enough to reach the outside of your home or business, hackers can just sit outside your location, trying to break in. Moving your access point to the center of your home or business, lowering your antennas, or doing anything else that will prevent your signal from reaching outside of your location is the most effective way to secure your wireless network. If a hacker cannot obtain your wireless signal, they cannot break in.

- *Use Media Access Control (MAC) filtering.* See the section "Enabling Wireless Security" for more information.

- *Unplug it when not in use.* This is one of the best defenses against hackers. Turn the damn thing off. Keep it on only when you need to use it.

- *Turn off Dynamic Host Configuration Protocol (DHCP).* See the section "Enabling Wireless Security" for more information.

- *Enable the access log on your router.* See the section "Enabling Wireless Security" for more information.

- *Keep the firmware on your router or WAP up-to-date.* As mentioned in Chapters 2 and 3, manufacturers are constantly updating the software for their devices. This also applies to wireless appliances. Firmware updates are released in response to security vulnerabilities and usability issues and for other reasons. Make sure you update yours accordingly.

How Can I Determine If Someone Is Using My Wireless Network?

If you suspect that someone is hijacking your wireless access point, you should be able to detect their presence fairly easily. Here's the strategy you can use to smoke them out:

- *Turn off all of your computers and listen.* This reminds us of submarine movies like *The Hunt for Red October.* After shutting off all of your computers and other wireless devices, check the wide area network (WAN) activity light on your wireless access point (WAP). This light will show any traffic being passed to the Internet. Is it still flashing like crazy? If it is, chances are you have an intruder using your network. If you have a stand-alone WAP, try unplugging it from your network. Did the activity light stop blinking? If so, you have an intruder.

- *Check your DHCP log.* If your intruder relied on DHCP to provide them with IP information, this will be reflected in the log. Log into your router or WAP and check this log. Figure 5.1 shows an entry from a Linksys BEFW11S4 router/WAP. Your log may or may not look like this one does. Here we see that there are three devices connected to our network.

TIP: You may be tempted to check the box and click Delete in order to revoke your intruder's wireless access. Unfortunately, this will not help you. You will be revoking only the lease of the IP information. It does not strip it away from the device that is currently holding it or prevent them from getting another one.

- *Check your ARP cache.* My what cache?!?!?!?? Every time your computer communicates with a network device (router, WAP, other PC, and so on),

Figure 5.1

Viewing the DHCP log.

an entry gets made in the Address Resolution Protocol (ARP) cache. This is a good place to look for more intruder information. Figure 5.2 shows some of the same devices we saw in our DHCP log.

Figure 5.2

Viewing the ARP cache.

They are on this list because they either communicated with our PC or vice versa. Again, turn off all of your devices and do the following:

1. Click Start.

2. Click Run.

3. Type in **CMD**.

4. Click OK.

5. Type in **Ping x.x.x.x** (where x.x.x.x is any of the IP addresses shown on this list).

6. If you get a reply as shown in Figure 5.3, then you have yourself an intruder.

7. You will now be able to block that particular device by blocking its MAC address in your router or WAP. See the section on enabling wireless security.

Figure 5.3
Checking Ping results.

NOTE: *The computer you are working on will not show up on its own ARP cache.*

• *Check your router's access log.* If someone has connected to your network, chances are they are accessing the Internet on your dime. By checking your router's access log, you can quickly tell if someone is intruding. Figure 5.4 shows our friend at 192.168.1.4 visiting a website titled **www.jesseweb.com**. We're sure that this website must be a hacker hideout of some sort.

How Can I Securely Connect to a Public Wireless Network?

Wireless hotspots are getting much more popular. They represent locations where you can connect to a public access point to get a fast Internet connection. Many hotels, airports, and stores like Starbucks and McDonald's provide hotspots. Most public hotspots and wireless access points don't require passwords and don't use encryption. This means your data is unencrypted and easily available to a reasonably knowledgeable hacker. Whether you are connecting to a wireless access point at a friend's or neighbor's house, a business location, or just a wireless hotspot, you should

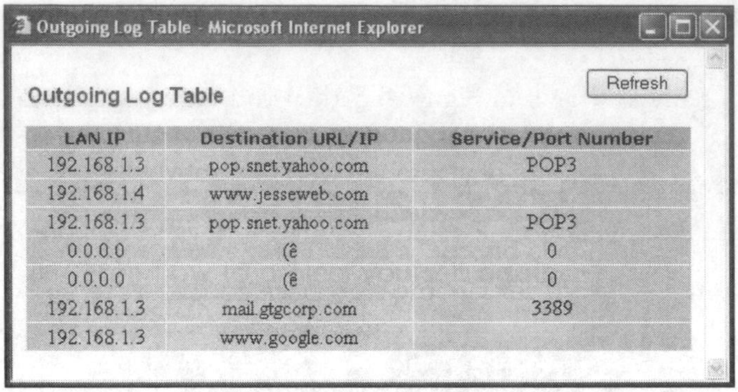

LAN IP	Destination URL/IP	Service/Port Number
192.168.1.3	pop.snet.yahoo.com	POP3
192.168.1.4	www.jesseweb.com	
192.168.1.3	pop.snet.yahoo.com	POP3
0.0.0.0	(ê	0
0.0.0.0	(ê	0
192.168.1.3	mail.gtgcorp.com	3389
192.168.1.3	www.google.com	

Figure 5.4
Router access log.

always take precautions because you never know who else is on the network and what they are doing. Here are a few ways you can protect your data and your PC while connecting to a public wireless network:

- *Stay up-to-date.* Before connecting to a wireless hotspot, make sure your operating system, antivirus software, and firewall have all the latest updates applied.
- *Use a firewall.* A firewall will prevent others from connecting to your device when they are connecting to a wireless hotspot. If you are using Windows XP, turn on Personal Firewall.
- *Use encryption.* When you're connected to a hotspot, anyone can be "sniffing" the traffic, ultimately reading the emails you send and receive, knowing what websites you visited, and worse, seeing your passwords and confidential information. You should never send confidential information or perform any activity (such as typing in a password, viewing your online bank statement, and so on) when connected to a hotspot. If you must send email, use email encryption such as PGP.
- *Be cautious of rogue access points.* Just because you are at a trusted location (let's say your favorite major fast food chain) and you use its access point, don't think that you are actually using a safe access point (or the correct one). Any hacker near that location can set up an access point and hope people accidentally connect to their access point as opposed to the location's access point. Be sure to ask what the SSID name is of the hotspot and connect only when the name matches exactly.

HORROR STORY! A few years ago some clever thieves set up phony ATM machines in different cities around the country. Customers who thought the machines were safe to use would put in their bank cards and passwords and then the machine would keep the cards and passwords and not dispense any cash. The thieves then used the cards and passwords to raise some quick cash. We always thought that this was really sneaky because a tactic like this could easily fool customers. Recently, thieves have used similar tactics in cities such as New York, but this time they are doing it with wireless networks instead of ATM machines. One enterprising thief we heard about set up phony hotspots next to Starbucks locations. Customers would come in to have their morning coffee and surf the Web and send out emails only to find out later that their credit card numbers were being stolen. Because the crime was so hidden, it took detectives quite a few months to figure it out.

What Can I Do If I Lose My WEP Key?

WEP (Wired Equivalent Privacy) is an encryption scheme supported by most access points. You can use WEP to keep wireless neighbors out and keep you and your friends and family in. Just as when you lose your car keys, losing a WEP key will lock you out of your wireless access point. Without the key, you will be able to see the wireless access if it is set to broadcast its SSID, but you will not be able to connect to it. Here are some things you can do to regain access to your wireless access point:

- *Retrieve your WEP key.* If you have another computer that can connect to the access point, or if your access point has a built-in switch that you can connect to, you may be able to retrieve the key from the access point. To do this, you will need to enter the access point's Web-based management utility. Consult your owner's manual for instructions on how to do this. Once connected, you may be able to retrieve the key or at least reset it.

- *Reset it.* See the section "How Can I Reset My Wireless Access Point?" for more information.

What Can I Do If I Lose My Wireless Access Point's Password?

Wireless access points are protected with an administrator password. Without a password, anyone with a wireless card and some spare time can take control of your access point and use your network and computers as they wish. If you lost or forgot this password, the access point must be reset. Resetting the access point will return the password to its default setting. See the section "How Can I Reset My Wireless Access Point?" for more information on how to do this. Once it's reset, consult your owner's manual for the default password, log in, and set it to a different password for added security.

How Can I Secure My Wireless Phone Conversations?

Phone conversations have been prone to eavesdropping since the invention of the phone. To eavesdrop on a corded phone, you simply need a splitter and an extra phone. Eavesdropping on a wireless phone is a little more complicated, but it can be done by simply turning on a baby monitor. Here's how you can secure your wireless phone conversations:

- *Use included security.* Your phone may have additional security features that may encrypt the transmission. This feature may require your provider to support it, your provider to enable it for your account, and or the party you are talking with to have the same type of security. Consult your provider and owner's manual for more information.

- *Buy a phone that uses DSS technology.* Sometimes referred to as frequency hopping, digital spread spectrum (DSS) was invented during World War II to guide and prevent unauthorized redirection of American torpedoes. Whether used in torpedo guidance or cordless phones, the technology is the same: rapidly and randomly switch frequencies during communication to make it impossible for others to intercept or jam communication. DSS will prevent the classic "baby monitor" eavesdropping approach.

- *Get rid of your analog cell phone.* An analog cell phone simply transmits your conversation as is, and anyone with a scanner can possibly intercept the signal and just listen in with no additional work required. Digital phones transmit your conversation digitally, requiring the hacker to decode an intercepted signal.

- *Know your service.* CDMA, PCS, GSM, TDMA, or whatever type of digital service you have will provide a different level of protection. Some scramble while others encrypt. Talk to your service provider for more information.

Enabling Wireless Security

- Learn how to turn on your wireless security features.

Everyone likes to tell you to turn on your wireless security, but few actually show you how to do it. Fortunately, it isn't difficult, but it does require following a few steps. In this section we'll provide you with some specific instructions. Keep in mind that the instructions are based on a Linksys BEFW11S4 router/WAP. We chose Linksys because they are probably the most popular and widely used wireless networking products for home and small office use. If you don't have a Linksys product, you will at least learn the basics for enabling security. As always, go to the manufacturer's website for the latest and greatest instructions and tips.

As a final note, if you are thinking that we are going overboard with this security stuff, keep the following fact in mind. All of the screenshots and examples in the following section were taken on a neighbor's wireless access point. The security threats we bring up are all real and should be heeded.

How Can I Change My Default Password?

Almost every wireless access point has a username and password to change its settings. The username is usually admin, administrator, or blank, and the password is usually the same. If someone else has the same wireless access point you have, then they obviously know the password and can change your settings if connected to it. If not, this information is readily available on the Web. Change your password as soon as you can and change it to something that cannot be easily guessed. Here is how to do it:

1. Access your router's configuration interface through your web browser. You can do this by typing **192.168.1.1** in the address bar and clicking Go.

2. Leave the username blank and type **admin** in the password box as shown in Figure 5.5. Click OK to log into your router.

3. Click the Administration tab. You will now be in the management subsection.

4. Type your new password in the Router Password box and confirm in the Re-enter to confirm box. You can see this in Figure 5.6.

5. Click Save Settings.

NOTE: *You will now be required to log back in to the router using the new password.*

How Can I Disable My Access Point's Web Configuration Utility?

Some higher-end combination router/WAP devices can be configured from the Internet. This is definitely a feature that you should disable as soon as

Figure 5.5

Linksys router login window.

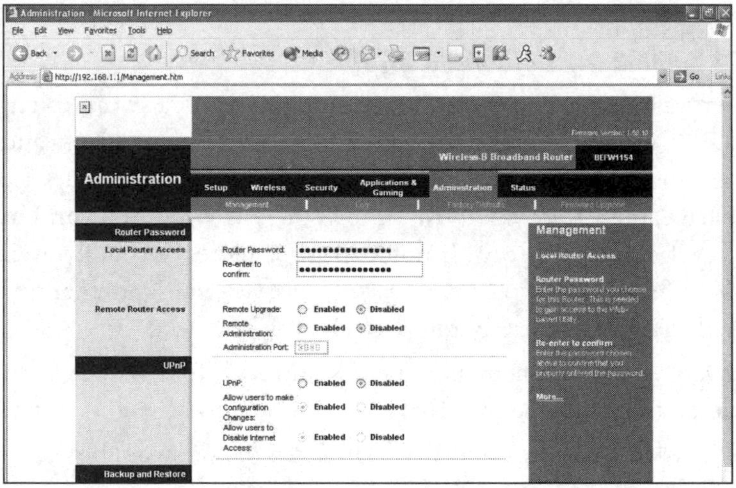

Figure 5.6

Password Change and Remote Administration Disable.

possible. This is especially true if you have not changed the default password or if you've set a weak password in the router. Follow these instructions to disable this feature:

1. Access your router's configuration interface through your web browser. You can do this by typing **192.168.1.1** in the address bar and clicking Go.

2. Type in your new router password. (You did read the previous section, didn't you?) Click OK to log in.

3. Click the Administration tab. You will now be in the management subsection.

4. Make sure the Remote Upgrade and Remote Administration radio buttons are set to disabled as shown in Figure 5.6.

5. Click Save Settings.

NOTE: This feature is usually disabled by default. However, it is good practice to make sure it is disabled.

How Can I Change My Default SSID?

The service set identifier (SSID) is the name that identifies your wireless network. When others try to connect to your wireless network, they must know the SSID. Just as with the default password discussed earlier, most wireless access points have default SSIDs; usually *wireless* or the name of the manufacturer, or some combination thereof (e.g., *dellwireless, linksys*). Change your SSID as soon as you can and change it to something that cannot be easily guessed (e.g., *SSID, accesspoint,* and so on). You can change it by doing the following:

1. Access your router's configuration interface through your web browser. You can do this by typing **192.168.1.1** in the address bar and clicking Go.

2. Type in your router password and click OK.

3. Click Wireless. You should now be in the Basic Wireless Settings subsection.

4. The Wireless Network Name(SSID) box should contain the word *linksys*. Go ahead and change this to whatever you want. We chose bigalsnetwork. This is shown in Figure 5.7.

5. Click Save Settings.

How Can I Disable SSID Broadcast?

By default, most wireless access points broadcast their SSIDs to anyone listening. Since others need to know the SSID of your wireless network to connect, you can make things a little more difficult for the novice hacker by not broadcasting your SSID. Here is how you can do this:

1. Access your router's configuration interface through your web browser. You can do this by typing **192.168.1.1** in the address bar and clicking Go.

2. Type in your router password and click OK.

3. Click Wireless. You should now be in the Basic Wireless Settings subsection.

4. Click the Disabled radio button. This can be seen in Figure 5.8.

5. Click Save Settings.

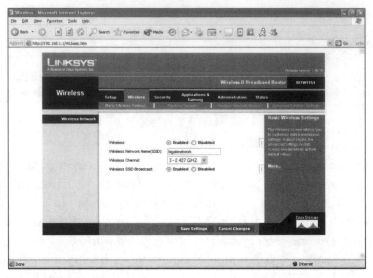

Figure 5.7

Changing the default SSID.

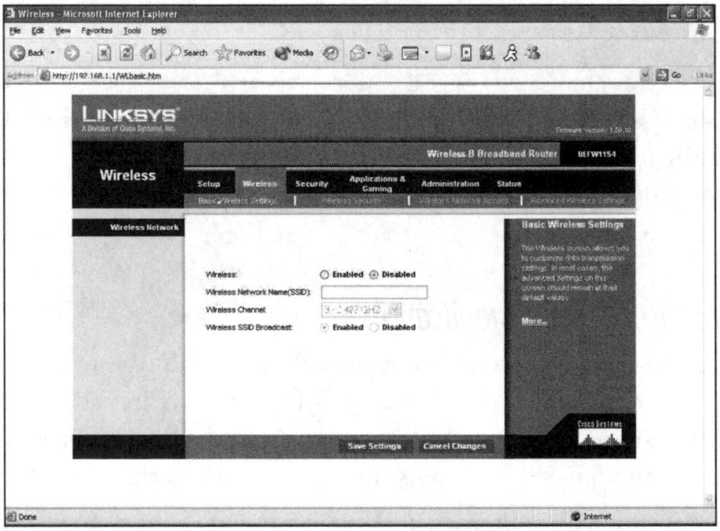

Figure 5.8

Disabling the SSID.

WARNING! Make sure you note your SSID before taking these steps. You will need it to connect to your WAP.

How Can I Enable WEP?

By default, wireless access points are set with no security. That means that all a hacker needs is the SSID to connect to your wireless network. When you enable Wired Equivalent Privacy (WEP), others need to know your WEP key (access code) in order to connect. Also, all data transmitted between your wireless device and wireless access point will be encrypted (scrambled to a listening hacker) when you use WEP, whereas by default your transmission is not encrypted. To enable WEP. take the following steps:

1. Access your router's configuration interface through your web browser. You can do this by typing **192.168.1.1** in the address bar and clicking Go.

2. Type in your router password and click OK.

3. Click Wireless. You should now be in the Basic Wireless Settings subsection.

4. Click Wireless Security.

5. Click the radio button next to Wireless Security.

6. Select WEP in the Security Mode drop-down box.

7. Select the Wireless Encryption Level. The more the merrier here. Note that 128 bit WEP is not a standard and may not work with all types if wireless products.

8. Type in a pass phrase of your choosing and click Generate. (We chose *bigal.*)

9. Record the keys that are generated. You will need them in order to connect to your wireless network.

10. Figure 5.9 shows all of these settings. Click Save Settings.

How Can I Enable Mac Filtering?

If your WAP supports MAC filtering, you should use it as an added security measure. By using MAC filtering, you will be able to restrict access to your wireless network to devices that you specify. You can enable MAC filtering by following these steps:

1. Access your router's configuration interface through your web browser. You can do this by typing **192.168.1.1** in the address bar and clicking Go.

2. Type in your router password and click OK.

3. Click Wireless. You should now be in the Basic Wireless Settings subsection.

4. Click Wireless Network Access.

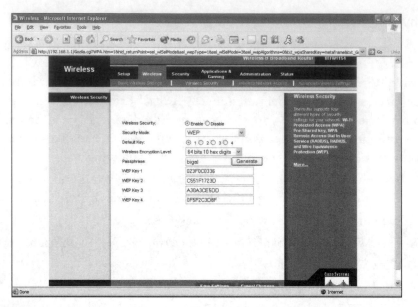

Figure 5.9
Enabling WEP.

5. Click the Wireless Client MAC List button. You will see a window
    similar to the window in Figure 5.10. This list shows all devices currently
    connected to your wireless network. Find your device on this list (and
    any others you wish to allow access) and note the MAC address. Close
    this window.

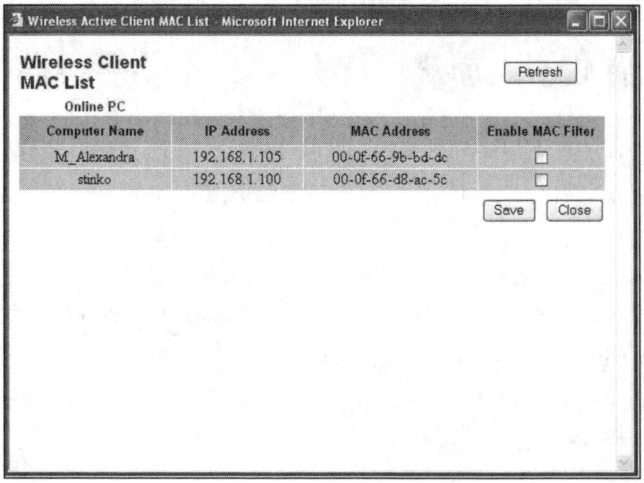

Figure 5.10
Wireless MAC list.

6. Back in the Wireless Network Access subsection, click the Restrict Access radio button.

7. Enter the MAC addresses you previously noted in the Access List section. This is shown in Figure 5.11.

8. Click Save Settings.

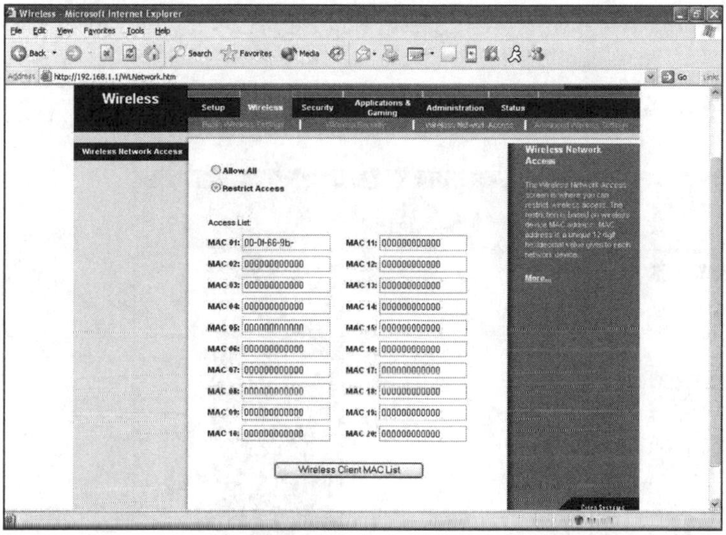

Figure 5.11
MAC access list.

HORROR STORY! A previous co-worker of ours had MAC filtering set up on his home wireless network. His laptop's wireless card broke one day, so he had to replace it. He went to the store, bought a new card, returned home, and installed the card in his laptop. He then could not connect to his wireless network no matter what he tried. He called me in a panic and asked what to do. I told him that his new wireless card had a different MAC address than the one he had before. He would need to add this card to the WAP's MAC address list. After he did this, he was able to connect.

How Can I Disable DHCP?

Dynamic Host Configuration Protocol (DHCP) is what provides your computer with the essential IP information it needs to access your local area network (LAN) and the Internet. DHCP provides an IP address, subnet information, default gateway, name servers (DNS), and other information. Turning this service off and providing this information to your computers manually is a good idea. Here is how you can disable DHCP on your router and assign static IP information to your Windows 2000 and XP computers:

1. Access your router's configuration interface through your web browser. You can do this by typing **192.168.1.1** in the address bar and clicking Go.

2. Type in your router password and click OK.

3. You should now be in the Basic Setup screen. Check the Disable radio button next to Local DHCP Server. Figure 5.12 shows an example of this.

4. Click Save Settings.

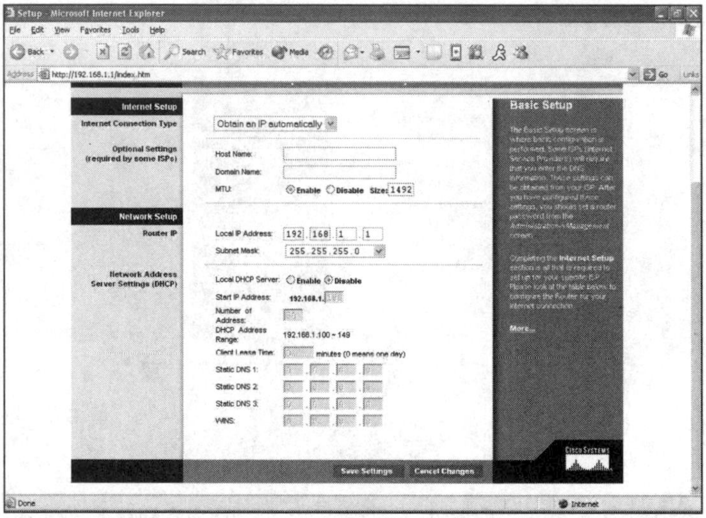

Figure 5.12
Disabling DHCP.

Your wireless router will no longer provide DHCP information to devices that request it. In order for your computers to be able to access the network, you will have to assign it yourself. Here is how you can do that in Windows 2000 and XP:

1. Click Start.

2. Windows XP users click Control Panel. Windows 2000 users hover the mouse over Settings and then click Control Panel.

3. Double-click Network Connections.

4. Find your wireless connection. Right-click it and select Properties.

5. A window similar to the one shown in Figure 5.13 opens.

Figure 5.13
Wireless connection properties.

6. In the section "This Connection Uses the Following items," scroll down until you see Internet Protocol (TCP/IP). Click this and then click the Properties button.

7. A window similar to the one shown in Figure 5.14 opens. There are a few things that you need to do in this window.

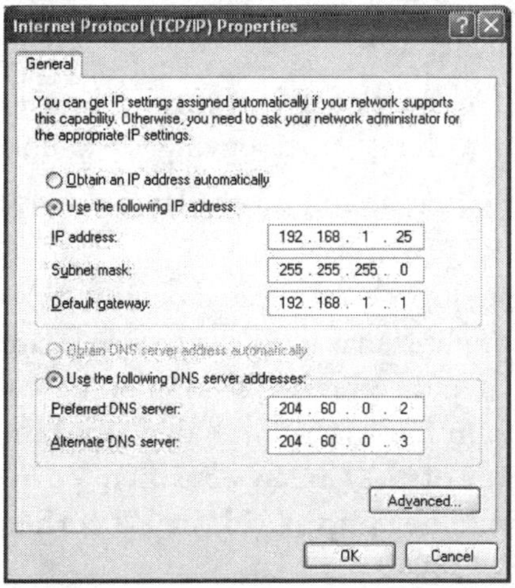

Figure 5.14
TCP/IP Properties.

8. Click the "Use the following IP address" radio button.

9. Enter the IP address you want to assign. Addresses in the range 192.168.1.1 through 192.168.1.255 are the default on the Linksys routers. The first IP address (192.168.1.1) is usually taken up by the router itself, so go ahead and choose any other one in that range. Remember, the first three sets of numbers (192.168.1) will not change in this scenario. Only the last set will change. In Figure 5.12, you can see that we chose 192.168.1.25.

10. Enter the subnet mask. In this case it will be 255.255.255.0.

11. Enter the default gateway. In this case it will be 192.168.1.1.

12. Click the "Use the following DNS servers" radio button.

13. Enter the DNS servers assigned to you by your ISP.

14. Click OK to close this window.

15. Click OK to close the previous window. You're all done now!

How Can I Enable the Access Log on My Router?

The access log will give you a detailed analysis of all of the traffic going out of and coming into your network. This log will aid you in determining if you have an intruder and may possibly help you find out who it may be. You need to turn this feature on to be able to use it. Follow these instructions in order to turn it on:

1. Access your router's configuration interface through your web browser. You can do this by typing **192.168.1.1** in the address bar and clicking Go.

2. Type in your router password and click OK.

3. Click the radio button next to Yes and click Save Settings as shown in Figure 5.15. This will provide you with real-time logging capabilities.

4. Click either the Incoming or Outgoing button for the latest activity.

TIP: You also have the option of saving logs to a dedicated computer. You will need a few things to do this: a computer that is on all the time, static IP information assigned to this machine (see the previous section on how to do this), and the log file viewing utility from Linksys. You can download the log file viewer at the following Web address: **http://linksys.custhelp.com/cgi-bin/linksys.cfg/php/enduser fattach_get.php?p_sid=nqZKccrh&p_tbl=10&p_id=644&p_created=1086138099**

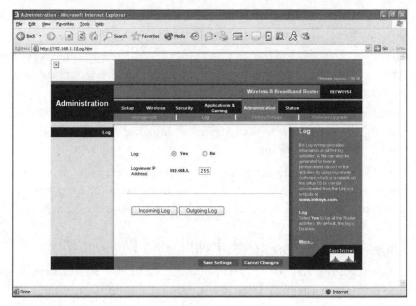

Figure 5.15
Enabling the access log.

Wireless Connectivity Issues

- Learn where to place your access point to get better wireless connectivity.
- Learn how to detect and prevent interference and signal loss.
- Learn how to troubleshoot wireless connectivity and hardware issues.

Where Should I Place My Wireless Access Point?

Most people just place their wireless access point right next to their source of Internet connectivity (i.e., next to their cable or DSL modem). Usually this isn't the best spot, especially if your connection is not in the middle of your home or office. You need to find the best location so that you can minimize interference and get the widest possible range. If you live in a house that has more than one floor, you'll also need to be careful where you place your access point. Here are a few tips on finding the best location for your access point:

- *Start with the center.* Place the access point in the central location of the area you wish to cover

- *Raise it.* The higher the access point, the less likely that the signals will be obstructed by objects placed in front of it.

- *Avoid interference.* Read the section "How Can I Prevent Interference on My Wireless Devices?" to learn how to avoid signal interference and where not to place your wireless access point.

- *Avoid signal attenuation.* Read the section "What Can Degrade Wireless Signals?" to learn how to avoid signal attenuation and where not to place your wireless access point.

- *Avoid heat and water.* Don't place your wireless access point where it can get wet or overheated. Areas like an attic or a basement are prone to heat and humidity problems and are not ideal locations for your access point.

Do I Have to Position My Access Point Near a Wall Outlet?

Most experts agree that your access point should be placed in a central location in your home or office. They also say that it should be mounted high up on a wall for best coverage. The only problem with this is that most of us do not have a wall outlet handy near our ceilings. So we just place them on a desk or table and suffer the consequences. There are some tricks for getting the best of both worlds though. Here are a few ideas you should try:

- *Install an outlet.* Have a qualified electrician install a wall outlet exactly where you want it. This will allow you to position an access point optimally for best coverage. The cost of having the work done should not be too high and will result in greater coverage.

- *Use a Power over Ethernet (PoE) adapter.* Companies such as Linksys and Orinoco make Ethernet adapters that can supply power to your access point. Basically, you plug the adapter into a wall outlet or power strip, run an Ethernet cable from your router to the adapter, and then run another Ethernet cable to your access point.

What Should I Do when I Can't Connect to an Access Point?

Whether it's in the home, at work, at a friend's house, or at a hotel, you're bound to have problems connecting to a wireless access point. Don't give up just yet. Here's what you can do:

- *Make sure the access point is turned on.* You also need to make sure that your PDA or laptop is hardware-activated to use its wireless feature. (Some PDAs and laptops have buttons to turn their wireless adapter on and off to save battery usage. If your battery is low, you may have to wait until you have a decent charge.) Make sure your cable/DSL modem is also turned on. Remember that your access point is just a transmitter/ receiver, and without an active cable modem or DSL modem, you won't have anywhere to send your signals.

- *Make sure your wireless device is enabled.* For PDAs, you may have to enable your wireless adapter through your device's operating system. On Windows XP, you can go to Start|Settings|Network Connections to view your available network connections. You can right-click on a connection and select Enable or Disable.

- *Make sure the wireless adapter is looking for the right SSID.* A wireless adapter can be set to connect to a specific access point by entering the access point's SSID value into either the adapter's client manager utility or (for Windows XP) in the wireless networking property page. If you have the wireless adapter set to an SSID other than the one you're trying to connect to, the connection won't happen.

- *Use your indicators.* You may have a built-in indicator that can help you troubleshoot connectivity issues. On your device (commonly found on PDAs and laptops), you may have a light that indicates if wireless is on and or connected. On computers running Windows XP and 2003, you can use the Network Connection Status icon in your system tray (the area in the bottom right next to the clock). Looking at the icon alone will show you if you are connected or not, but double-clicking it will bring up the wireless connection status page. From here, you should check the following:

  - *Status:* Tells you if you are connected or not.

  - *Signal strength:* Shows you a graph of how strong a signal you are receiving.

  - *IP address:* On the Support tab, you can see if you were assigned an IP address by the network's DHCP server. Without the proper IP address, you will not be able to connect. Clicking the Details button will show you if you were properly assigned an IP address and when it expires.

- *Make sure you are connecting to the correct access point.* If you are in an area where there are multiple wireless access points, it's easy to accidentally connect to the wrong one, especially if you haven't entered the SSID of the intended access point into your PC's wireless adapter. In fact, if you don't specify the SSID of the access point that you want, the operating system on your device may just pick one for you—and it may not be the one you intend. (In fact, connecting to an access point without permission, even if your PC does it accidentally, is illegal.) Always make sure you are connected to the right access point, not only for connectivity but for security as well.

- *Make sure you have the correct encryption key and type.* If a wireless network uses a wireless encryption scheme (for example, WEP), you will need to use the same type of encryption with the correct encryption key. Also, if a wireless network is not using a wireless encryption scheme, you must make sure you are not using a wireless encryption scheme when connecting to it.

- *Check to see if your location uses a proxy.* If you can connect to the wireless access point and cannot use the Internet, an Internet proxy may be preventing you from going out on the Internet. An Internet proxy is a software program loaded on a server that manages Internet activity, controlling which sites are allowed, logging who's going where, setting how fast you can connect, and so on. Whenever you connect to a new network, you should ask if they use a proxy and how to configure your computer to use it. Also, don't forget to remove proxy settings when you connect to a network that does not use a proxy (most likely your home).

- *Use IPConfig.* IPConfig is a command-line utility that shows and manages your IP information. To run it, select Start | Run and type **CMD**. Click OK and when the command window appears, type **IPCONFIG /ALL** and press Enter. From here, you can see the IP information for all of your network adapters (wired and wireless). If you see "Media disconnected" on the adapter you are using, chances are your wireless adapter is off. If your IP address is 169.254.x.x, then you either cannot completely connect to the network or simply have not been assigned a proper address. To force an IP address assignment, type **IPCONFIG /RENEW ALL** and then type **IPCONFIG /ALL** to see if you have a new address.

- *Reboot your access point.* If you still cannot connect to your access point, the problem may lie at your wireless access point. Try unplugging the access point, leaving it unplugged for 10 seconds, and then plugging it back in and powering on.

HORROR STORY!
We knew someone who, while traveling, was staying at a really nice hotel for a convention. The hotel offered wireless service in its rooms. Our friend had a few very important emails to send out so he decided to use the wireless Internet connection. Of course, after trying many times he couldn't connect to the access point. So he called the tech support department for the hotel and spent over an hour on the phone trying to get the wireless connection to work. After wasting all of this

time, he simply plugged his laptop into the phone line and used his dial-up modem to send his emails, which only took a few minutes. The lesson here is that wireless connections don't always work as advertised, and if you find you are wasting valuable time trying to get a connection, don't forget about the old reliable dial-up modem.

Can I Use Someone Else's Access Point?

Sure you can (if you want the Feds knocking on your door one day). In some cities, houses are really close together and you might be able to connect up to your neighbor's access point, especially if your neighbor doesn't know how to secure their network. This is, however, basically stealing, and it's not a good practice to get into.

HORROR STORY!

We have a friend who has a summer cabin in the mountains that doesn't have a phone line hooked up. He took his wireless laptop once and realized that his neighbor was broadcasting a nice wireless signal from his access point. So our friend hooked up and starting enjoying the free ride. One weekend he went up to the cabin expecting to get some really important work done online. The neighbor caught on to his antics and secured the access point and our friend blew the entire weekend because he couldn't get his work done. The moral: If you need a reliable connection, don't be cheap!

How Can I Reset My Wireless Access Point?

Resetting an access point means returning all its internal values back to those it had when it came from the factory. This is usually done as a last resort when your wireless access point stops responding, you lose your WEP key, you lose the administrator password, or you want a quick way to reset the access point. Take caution, because this will reset your SSID, username, password, WEP key, DHCP, and anything else you can think of back to their defaults. Typically, access points have a very small and usually recessed button labeled "reset" (most of the time this is a pin-sized hole you can access with a paper clip). Disconnect power from the access point, press and hold this reset button for 10 seconds, and then reconnect power and turn the access point on.

Why Is My Wireless Connection So Slow?

Once you pay top dollar for a wireless device (laptop, PDA, desktop PC), a wireless access point, and a broadband Internet connection, you don't want to experience a slow wireless connection. Here's what you can do if your wireless connection is not working as fast as you think it should:

- *Check for signal loss.* When you have a poor signal, your connection speed will be reduced. See the section "What Can Degrade Wireless Signals?" presented later in this chapter.

- *Upgrade your wireless standard.* If you have 802.11b devices connecting to an 802.11g access point, the access point will drop the connection rates from 54 Mbps to 11 Mbps. If this is the case, we recommend upgrading your B devices or purchasing an 8.0211b access point for your B devices to use. Remember, most PDAs that have wireless capabilities are 8.0211b devices.

- *Make sure other users aren't sucking the bandwidth.* Are there a lot of people using your access point? Is there someone else on your network doing some heavy downloading? Both of these things can slow your network down. Also, Internet access through a cable modem may slow down depending on the number of neighbors who are online and how they are using it. DSL does not have this problem. If someone if hogging all the bandwidth, go have a nice chat with them and ask them to slow down.

- *Check for a broken antenna.* A broken antenna (either at the access point or at the connected device) may cause signal degradation or prevention. See the section "I Just Broke the Antenna on My Wireless Device, Is That OK?" later in this chapter.

- *Check your expectations.* Wireless services on cell phones and PDAs are noticeably slower than on a traditional computer. If this is your first time using this service, you may need to lower your expectations (for now anyway).

How Can I Prevent Interference on My Wireless Devices?

Interference is a big issue. You probably have more wireless devices in your home or office to consider before you hook up your PC or PDA than you realize: cordless phones, cell phones, pagers, wireless cameras, remote control toys, home alarm systems, wireless speakers, and even baby monitors. When you connect your PC, interference can make your network service slow, interrupt it, or even prevent it from working. Here are a few methods you can use to prevent interference on wireless devices:

- *Avoid frequency overlap.* Wireless devices that have the same or overlapping frequencies can cause interference to one another. You can avoid this type of interference by buying products at different frequencies. For example, consider a baby monitor at 900 MHz, a wireless access point at 2.4 GHz, and cordless phones at 5.8 GHz.

- *Keep your wireless devices as far apart as practical, especially if they operate on the same frequency band.* The distance between them may be enough to avoid interference.

- *Change the channel.* Most wireless devices allow you to switch channels. Some devices have physical DIP switches, others a button, and others (for example, wireless access points) have software to change the channel. Consult your owner's manual for more information.

- *Keep away from major appliances.* Appliances such as refrigerators, microwave ovens, and even televisions may cause interference with wireless equipment. Microwave ovens may cause interference on networks that use the 2.4 GHz range because this is the same frequency they use to heat food. To determine if an appliance is the cause of interference, unplug each appliance to see if the interference goes away. If you conclude that an appliance is in fact causing the interference, simply try moving the wireless devices to see if the interference is eliminated or lessened (before using this as an excuse to toss your old TV and buy a new 60-inch plasma TV).

- *Keep away from major electrical equipment.* Electrical closets, large fans, motors, and generators can cause a huge amount of interference not only on wireless devices, but other electrical devices as well. The motors in elevators can cripple both a wired and wireless network. Try keeping your wireless devices as far away as possible from these electrical sources. If you are trying to catch up on your email while you are in an elevator, you'll probably look a little strange to the other passengers anyway.

How Can I Find the Source of Interference on My Wireless Devices?

Interference can disrupt your phone conversations, terminate your wireless connection, and even deafen you with loud screeches. Once you notice the interference, it can annoy you to death. Here are the steps to help you determine the cause of the interference:

- *Determine the root device you wish to remove interference from (for example, cordless phone).*

- *Determine if you have low or no signal.* It's easy to mistake interference from another device with interference from signal loss. Check your signal strength and move to an area where you normally have a strong signal.

- *Make sure you have a decent battery charge.* It's easy to mistake interference from low batteries causing the signal to become distorted (especially on wireless headphones/headsets).

- *Try gently moving all connecting lines (phone, cable, Ethernet, and so on) to see if the problem is a loose connection or bad connector.* If the interference worsens, chances are this is the reason.

- *Determine if you have DSL Internet service.* If you have a DSL modem, you need to install a digital line filter on *all* phone lines to prevent interference.

- *Turn off and unplug all wireless devices except for the root device.* If you still have interference at this point, you may have missed a wireless device. Make sure that you review all of the wireless devices that you have in your home or office. Don't forget the wireless baby monitor!

What Can Degrade Wireless Signals?

Your wireless devices communicate through radio waves. These radio waves can be blocked or absorbed by another object. This is known as *attenuation*. Simply put, attenuation is what happens when a signal reduces in strength between the transmitter and the receiver. This is not to be confused with interference, which is something that mixes with your signal, causing it to be corrupted. Here are some of the common causes of a degraded wireless signal:

- *Distance*: All wireless devices have a maximum transmission range they reach before the signal drops down. Once you exceed or approach this range, your signal will begin to reduce because the radio wave is almost out of energy. Have you ever jumped into a pool to splash someone (CANNONBALL!)? You have to be close to be effective because the strength of the wave can reach only so far. Same goes for wireless devices.

- *Solid surfaces:* Solid surfaces like concrete, brick, and even books will block radio waves to a certain degree. Metal objects and (interestingly enough) water-filled objects like aquariums, fountains, and even houseplants and trees block microwave-frequency energy even more. Have you ever placed your hand over a phone so the other person couldn't hear you (perhaps because you wanted to take that opportunity to yell at a little one who is about to write on a wall you just painted last week)? By placing your hand over the phone, you are blocking any audio signal from reaching the recipient. Same goes for wireless devices. Of course, this only affects you if these objects are in-between the transmitter and receiver.

- *Reflective surfaces:* Reflective surfaces such as windows, mirrors, water, and metal can cause radio waves to deflect and decrease in intensity. When a signal is deflected away from the receiver, the receiver will pick up a weaker signal. Of course, this only affects you if these objects are in between the transmitter and receiver.

- *Weather:* Clouds, storms, rain, snow, and so on can cause signal degradation for many reasons. Weather can absorb, block, and deflect signals, ultimately causing you to receive a poor signal or no signal. This is a problem that plagues satellite service providers (TV, radio, Internet).

- *The great outdoors:* Trees, bushes, and other types of foliage absorb radio signals. Of course, this only affects you if these objects are in between the transmitter and receiver.

HORROR STORY!

My (Peter's) in-laws had quite the experience with satellite television over the last year. They called and ordered the service last winter and set up an install date. The technician arrived and took one look, and quickly told them that it was not possible. My mother-in-law (God bless her) was more than happy to send the technician on his merry way, but my father-in-law was not satisfied. He quickly called the provider and requested a second opinion from another technician. The next day someone was dispatched to their home to take another look. This poor soul spent the better part of two days trying to get a good enough signal to appease my father-in-law's lust for live sports. After the dish was mounted on a 10-foot extender on the roof, they finally had enough signal to watch TV. Everything was great for about six months. Then one day early in the baseball season all hell broke loose. As my father-in-law sat down to watch the Yankees, the screen went fuzzy and would not return to its original glory. Several phone calls to the provider resulted in a technician visit. The technician (coincidentally, the one who originally said it was not possible) quickly concluded that the vegetation that had grown on the trees had blocked the signal for the satellite. Short of cutting down a dozen trees that did not belong to them, there was nothing that could be done. So, after all of that fuss, they are stuck with a 10-foot tower on their roof and no satellite service.

How Can I Extend the Range of My Wireless Devices?

As you learned from the previous section, wireless signals can degrade for many reasons. When your wireless signal degrades, you may see anything from slower transfer speeds to complete signal dropouts. Even without signal degradation, you may just want to extend the coverage of your existing wireless network. Here's how you can extend the range of your wireless signal:

- *Raise your antennas.* Many wireless devices have movable antennas (access points, cell phones, cordless phones, and so on). Raising and positioning your antenna may cause better transmission and reception, effectively extending the range of your wireless device.

- *Change your antennas.* You may be able to purchase a stronger antenna from your device manufacturer or from a third party. This is especially true of Wi-Fi wireless networking devices. You may also be able to purchase an extra external antenna to increase the range.

WARNING! Cell phone antenna boosters may cause damage to your phone. They do not boost your signal enough for you to notice, and they may void your warranty and or insurance. Stay away.

- *Add another wireless access point.* By adding another wireless access point, you can effectively double the range of your existing wireless network.

- *Add a wireless repeater.* A wireless repeater does exactly what its name states: it repeats wireless signals (both incoming and outgoing). By placing this device in an area where the signal is weak, you will get strong wireless reception and almost double the range of your existing wireless network. Adding a wireless repeater is an easier and possibly cheaper option than adding another wireless access point because a repeater requires less setup and only performs the sole operation of repeating signals.

- *Move your access point.* See the section, "Where Should I Place My Wireless Access Point?" for tips on optimal placement.

I Just Broke the Antenna on My Wireless Device, Is That OK?

Broken hearts, broken promises, broken antennas—no matter what it is, broken is never OK. Depending on how your access point is designed, a broken antenna can produce different results but usually does not result in making the device inoperable. Here are the effects caused by a broken antenna:

- *If your access point has two antennas, it may be using each antenna separately so it can have a better chance of picking up your signal and can cover more area.* The two antennas work together to form what is called a "diversity antenna system." The access point's firmware will determine which antenna has a stronger signal and will use that one to communicate. If you notice your range has decreased, the broken antenna combined with a "diversity antenna system" is probably the reason. If your speed has decreased, but increases to normal when you are near the access point, this may also be the reason.

- *If your access point has two antennas, it may be aggregating the signals between the antennas to obtain faster speeds.* For example, 11 Mbps on one antenna and 11 Mbps on another results in 22 Mbps total. If your speed has decreased and does not increase back to normal when you are near the access point, this may be the reason.

- *If your access point has one antenna, chances are the device has been crippled to slow (or no) connections.* An access point with a single antenna is known as an omni-directional antenna system. Since this antenna is the primary source of the signal, breaking it may render it useless.

- *If your antenna broke off your laptop's wireless card, it definitely needs immediate replacement and should not be used.* While most access points allow their antennas to be unscrewed, detached, and replaced, a laptop wireless card usually does not. Laptop cards (PCMCIA) are extremely sensitive devices, and the slightest damage may cause it to short out (spark) and not only damage the card, but possibly damage your laptop as well.

TIP: You may be able to replace your broken antenna for a new one. Contact your device's manufacturer for more information. It may be as simple as buying a new antenna, unscrewing the broken one, and screwing on a new one.

What Should I Do when My Wireless PDA Is Not Working?

For the home user, it may simply be disappointing to not be able to get an instant message or the latest movie show times, but for the business user, it can be devastating not being able to get email or the latest stock quotes. Here are some tips to help you resolve your PDA wireless problems:

- *Make sure you have a signal.* Is your wireless signal low or absent? Try moving to a location where you know you should have signal. If your device has a movable antenna, make sure it is in the raised position.

- *Check the connection.* Have you correctly set up the connection (SSID, WEP key, phone number, and so on)? Do you have an IP address and all correct network addresses (subnet mask, gateway, DNS, etc.). Verify all these settings and retry.

- *Make sure the wireless adapter is turned on.* Some PDAs allow you to turn the wireless adapter on or off to save battery life. There may even be an indicator light to let you know the wireless is on or off. Consult your owner's manual for more information.

- *Check the battery level.* Some PDAs will turn off the wireless adapter when the battery is low. Make sure you have a full or decent charge before trying to use the wireless adapter.

- *Try to remove all peripherals (connected memory cards, expansion packs, and so on) and even the battery.* With peripherals and power disconnected, press the reset button on your PDA. Reconnect the battery and power and try your wireless adapter.

- *Did it stop working after you installed something?* When some PDA applications are installed, they may overwrite important wireless driver files, causing the wireless adapter to fail. When this happens, you will have to revert to the last system backup you have.

- *Is your PDA broken?* After trying everything else, your PDA may need to be repaired. Consult your device's manufacturer for more information.

Why Is My Satellite Service Not Working?

Satellite television, radio, and Internet are great ways to get digital picture, sound, and data into your home. Despite which service or services you have, they all work the same way: there is a receiver with an antenna that picks up signals from a satellite in outer space. The following list will help you determine why your satellite service is not working and how you can or can't correct it:

- *Did you just sign up?* You may have to wait until you get a signal and your receiver has downloaded the initial authorization code from your provider.

- *Check the access card.* Television satellite receivers use access cards to basically give you the channels you paid for. Check if this card is fully inserted, inserted properly, and so on.

- *Got signal?* All satellite equipment requires a signal from the satellite to work. Satellite radios require that their antennas are near a window to successfully pick up the satellite signal. All television satellite receivers require a disk placed high on your home or business and also pointed in an exact direction to receive a signal. If you have already installed your dish, it may have been moved during heavy weather (wind, snow, rain, and so on).

- *Did you paint your dish or antenna?* Some people paint their satellite dishes to match their home or business. The problem is that the paint will prevent your dish from properly receiving a signal and may void your warranty. If someone painted your dish, you may try to remove the paint with a solvent, but it may just be easier to obtain a new dish.

- *Are there leaves, snow, or ice on your satellite dish?* Weather may be blocking your dish from successfully receiving a signal. When clearing these items from your dish, ensure that you first take the necessary safety precautions not to slip and fall, and then ensure that you do not move the dish when cleaning. Moving the dish will definitely disrupt your service, and it will need to be repointed to the correct satellite.

- *How's the weather?* Bad weather is something that plagues satellite service. Unfortunately, there is not much you can do about controlling the weather (or can you?).

- *Reboot.* Known as the "magic fix," rebooting your device may clear any error you are having.

Summary

The next time you are sitting at your local Starbucks hangout and you are able to surf the Web, check your email, and drink your coffee all at the same place, you can thank the wireless gods. When wireless networking operates as it should, it's simply the best thing that has come along in decades. But when it doesn't work, your wireless devices can leave you feeling really stupid and helpless.

In this chapter you learned how to keep your wireless devices up and running and what you can do when disaster strikes. Whether you are having trouble getting the access point in your home or office to work, or you are having trouble connecting to the Internet using a public hotspot, there are steps you can take help you stay connected.

6

Internet Fraud

Disasters to avoid:

- Unscrupulous spammers and criminals who use the Internet to steal your credit card information and your identity.
- Paying for a broken, old, or simply wrong product and not having a way to get your money back.
- Selling an item and never receiving the money for it.

Mishaps and blunders to run from:

- Spammers who try to run con games to rip you off as they offer everything from get-rich schemes to health and diet scams.
- Online vendors who trick you by using bait and switch tactics, peddle gray market merchandise, and overcharge you for shipping.

Everywhere you turn, everyone is telling you about the vast dangers of using the Internet and technologies like your cell phone. Whether it's a humorous credit card commercial about identity theft or a local news story about how the "Jeffersons" were scammed out of their piece of the pie (and were then evicted from their deluxe apartment), the hype is all around us. Hype aside, the risks and dangers are real. Most of us have a close friend or family member who has become the victim of a scam. Think about it: If the credit card companies weren't losing a lot of money because of identity theft, they certainly wouldn't be running commercials on prime-time TV.

If you think that fraud or identity theft on the Internet is something that would never happen to you, think again! The Internet and technology make so many things easier (research, communication, entertainment, productivity), and it makes fraud and theft easier as well.

When we were growing up, thieves had to be strong enough and close enough to beat up a victim and steal their wallet. Now your entire life savings can be taken faster than you can blink, and by a clever teenager living 12,000 miles away. Or even worse, an impossible-to-track-down thief hiding out in a country like Zimbabwe can clean out your bank account one morning before you finish your cup of coffee. And who is going to catch them and get your money back? There are also plenty of local thieves ready to rack up hours of long distance charges the second you lose your cell phone.

In this chapter, we'll help you avoid the disasters, mishaps, and blunders that relate to Internet fraud for both shoppers and retailers. As you'll learn in this chapter, there is no reason to feel helpless because there are many things that you can do. Of course, buying this book is a great first step. If the stuff in this chapter doesn't help you, you can at least whack 'em with the book.

Internet Sales Fraud

- Learn how criminals try to trick you out of your money.
- Learn how you can be scammed by emails and phishing.
- Learn how Internet vendors use techniques like bait and switch tactics, displaying misleading photos, omitting important information, and selling older models than they advertise.

What Exactly Is Internet Fraud?

Fraud is when someone deceives you to obtain some sort of gain illegally. In this section, we'll focus on Internet sales fraud—people who try to rip you off when you buy products and services online. Shopping online can be a scary thing. It's a new concept and one that is quite different from what we are used to. When buying online, you can't see or touch the item (or service) you're buying. In fact, you can't even see the merchant or the store. You pay on good faith that the correct item (if any item) will be delivered to you. Not only do you hope that the merchant doesn't rip you off, you also hope that hackers don't steal your credit card information and rip you off. These things are happening more often because of the growth of the Internet. But the more you are conscious and educated about these things, the less likely that others will be able to take advantage of you.

What Do I Need to Watch Out For?

Most of us have to purchase our own tech toys, books, CDs, clothes, and other goodies. While the Internet is a great place to find a good deal, it's an even better place for con artists and shady businesses to easily trick you out of your money. The Internet allows them to operate almost anonymously, from anywhere. In the majority of cases, you never see or speak to any of the people you are dealing with. All of this can increase the chances that you'll get ripped off.

As you shop online, you'll discover that there are different degrees of fraud that can occur. In some cases, criminals set up shop with the sole purpose of trying to steal your money. These are the really bad rip-offs you need to avoid because they can result in a financial disaster. The other type of fraud is more subtle and involves online retailers doing bad things such as over-charging you for services, using bait and switch tactics, and selling you re-conditioned products as new. Not all of these tactics are technically illegal, but the end result is that you get ripped off. In our book, fraud is fraud.

How Can I Be Scammed by Emails?

Email scams occur when a crook sends you an enticing email in hopes of obtaining your money. These emails are usually disguised as legitimate business opportunities or offers for free goods, and they almost always require you to send your hard-earned money before you reap any of the "rewards."

The target audience for these scams usually consists of the elderly, stay-at-home mothers, low-income families, the disabled, people with less than stellar credit, and those with limited education.

One quick thing to look for in these emails is poor grammar and punctuation. Most of the time this happens because the people that send this stuff do not have a good grasp of the English language—the exception being when words are misspelled on purpose in order to bypass spam filters (e.g., Re&finance, Vlagra, St0ck, and so on).

Here are some examples of email scams to watch out for:

- *Business opportunities:* You've likely received emails that have subject lines like "Work at home," "Make money online," and "Have your computer make money for you." Regardless of what the premise or the promise is, the purpose of this scam is to convince you that you can start your own business with a small initial investment, work very little, and make a ton of cash—the American Dream! These opportunities can include stuffing envelopes, processing medical bills, legal typing, and more. Remember, with legitimate opportunities, you may be required to pay for materials, but you will never be required to pay "to get started," pay "for more information," or call 1-900 numbers "to learn more." When you get emails like this, delete them as fast as you can!

- *Chain letters:* Receiving a chain letter in the mail was bad enough; now we have to deal with them clogging up our email boxes. The delivery method may have changed but the scam is still the same— to part you from your money. Steer clear of these types of emails no matter how pathetic or legitimate they might seem.

- *Health and diet scams:* We all know that it's impossible to lose 100 pounds in a month just by taking a pill and sitting on a couch eating cheesy poofs. Often these products are described as "breakthroughs" or "the secrets of Hollywood." These products can also be very dangerous, if not deadly, to your health. Always consult your doctor before even thinking about trying these products. Better yet, don't even let yourself be tempted.

- *Free income:* This is one of our favorites. These emails promise that you can learn to generate thousands in income overnight. They try to sell you a business plan to accomplish this. Trust us on this: it takes hard work and some luck to make money. After spending your money and time on these products, you'll ultimately realize that the quickest way to make money (fraudulently) is to sell phony business plans to unsuspecting victims on how to generate thousands in income. Nothing in life is free.

- *Free goods:* These promise you free computers, electronics, long-distance phone cards, and other similar items. The truth is that they are covering up a pyramid scheme. Read the fine print. Nothing in life is free.

- *Plans and kits:* These scams try to get you to buy plans or kits to build your own crafts, dolls, cable descramblers, or whatever. For products you keep, they usually don't work or are of poor quality. For products you assemble for a company in exchange for payment, the scam involves you paying for a kit, assembling the product, mailing it to the company, and waiting for your check, only to have the company send the product back, saying it was assembled incorrectly. The scam is this: The company doesn't care about the product. Their profit comes from the kit payment you sent, so they will always say you assembled it incorrectly to avoid having to pay you.

How Can I Be Scammed by Phishing?

We briefly introduced phishing (pronounced like and derived from the word *fishing*) in Chapter 1 when we discussed the disasters and mishaps surrounding data loss and theft. Phishing (also known as brand spoofing and carding) is a very devious scam that has emerged recently. With phishing, someone sets up a website to look like the website of a popular company (Citibank, Charles Schwab, Amazon.com, AOL, Best Buy, eBay, and so on) in order to trick users into entering their usernames, credit card numbers, passwords, social security numbers, and other critical information. Financial institutions, Internet service providers, and even government agencies have all been targets of recent phishing scams.

Victims are usually sent an email from a fake, spoofed, or hacked address asking them to visit the site, click on a link, and confirm their user information. These emails and websites may look very official and almost identical to the real website. Figure 6.1 shows an actual phishing email that is trying to trick you into thinking it was sent by Citibank.

If you click on the link in the email, you will be taken to the attacker's website, which is set up to look exactly like the Citibank website, as shown in Figure 6.2.

Notice how good the fake website looks. If you didn't know any better, you could really be taken in with a scam like this.

Remember, any respectable company will never (or should never) call or email you to confirm your private information. When in doubt, get the official phone number or email address and ask.

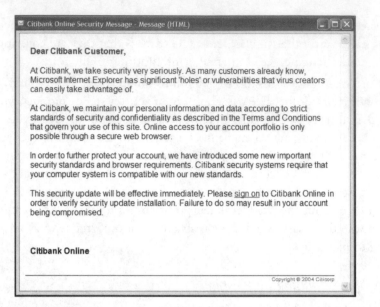

Figure 6.1

Citibank phishing email.

Figure 6.2

CitiBank phishing website.

Here is a list of common traits associated with phishing that you should watch out for:

- *Scare tactics:* The email or letter stresses urgency and states that your account will be suspended or closed if you do not fill out or reconfirm your information (as in the email example just shown). This is designed to scare you so that you don't think, and you do what they want. Sneaky, right?

- *Wacky URLs:* The fraudulent website address contains part of (or a variation of) the web address of the legitimate website. Some examples might include AOLMemberUpdates.com, eBayBilling.com, and SchwabInvestments.com.

- *Misspelling:* The fraudulent website address is a misspelling of the real site they are trying to copy.

WARNING! After you click on a link in a phishing email, the URL address in your web browser may display as that of a legitimate website (for example, **http://www.citibank.com**) while you are actually displaying a page from the phisher's website (**http://www.phisherhomepage.com**). How do they do that? There is a bug in Internet Explorer that allows one URL to be displayed in the address bar while actually directing you to another. To protect yourself from this bug, keep your system up to-date with the latest patches. See Chapter 3 for more information.

HORROR STORY! We have a fried who is an active eBay PowerSeller. He recently received an email that he thought was from eBay telling him that he would lose his standing with eBay unless he went to a specified website and entered in some of his account information. He followed the instructions and he even put in his main credit card number that he used for purchasing products on eBay. He thought the whole thing was a bit unusual, but then he forgot about it. A few weeks later, he got a call from his credit card company telling him that someone had been purchasing a lot of products on the Internet using his credit card number. At that point, he was just feeling lucky that he didn't enter his social security number on the bogus eBay site.

How Can I Be Scammed by Bait and Switch Tactics?

This deception is one of the most widely used tricks by crooked merchants. The "bait" is a lower-priced item, special, or sale item that lures you to the seller's store or website. The "switch" occurs when the salesperson tells you that the item is not available (back-ordered, out of stock, already sold) but (wouldn't you know) a more expensive item is immediately available for purchase. If you encounter a salesperson or a website using this tactic, you are better off doing your business elsewhere.

How Can I Be Scammed by Incorrect, Blurry, or Missing Photos?

Assume you see the perfect computer system on sale for $499 and you rush to order it before the sale ends. You feel pretty good about the deal you just got and await the delivery. When the box arrives, you notice that the printer is missing, the monitor is different, and the computer is a different model. Either you just fell victim to a scam related to having been presented with a image that misrepresented what you just purchased or you were simply ripped off unknowingly by a vendor. Here are some things to look out for:

- *Pictures that show peripherals that are not included:* Popular missing peripherals are monitors, docking stations, and printers. Figure 6.3 shows and example of this popular scam.

MONITOR SOLD SEPARATELY

Figure 6.3
The "monitor not included" scam.

- *Pictures that include the wrong peripherals:* An example is an ad showing a desktop with a flat-panel monitor. Examining the fine print, you may discover that the system comes with an old CRT monitor and that the flat-panel cost hundreds of dollars more. This is becoming extremely common, so be warned.

- *Blurry pictures that hide the model number or other important info about the model shown*

NOTE: *While it is not fraud for a company to advertise items in a picture and include fine print indicating that some are not included, it is deceptive. Most vendors have adopted this practice, so get used to it and make sure you read and fully understand the fine print.*

Can I Be Scammed by a Vender Pushing Last Year's Models?

Another unscrupulous practice of the fraudulent retailer is trying to pass off previous models as new. The retailer may need to sell leftover stock to make room for newer models. Buying an older model isn't such a bad deal as long as you know it beforehand and the price is reasonable (in fact, you may save a lot of money this way). Model numbers are often of no use. They usually do not reflect the model year, but the uniqueness of the device and the features it offers. Before purchasing a product, get the latest model number directly from the manufacturer, not from the retailer.

WARNING! Be careful about buying products from Internet sites that specialize in selling overstock items, such as overstock.com. Of course, there is nothing wrong with doing business with the more reputable companies; however, keep in mind that these businesses are typically selling older model products. It's easy to fall into the trap of thinking that you are getting a really good deal because you may be comparing the price of the older model with a newer model. In some cases, you can actually purchase the new model from a discount vendor for less than you'll pay for the older model.

Can I Be Scammed by Gray Market Products?

Manufacturers often sell discounted, sometimes "modified" versions of their local (domestic) products to foreign distributors authorized for overseas (international) sale only. This can include products with expired/limited/no warranty, manuals in different languages, cheaper components, missing accessories, missing or modified features, and less-restrictive safety requirements. A shady foreign distributor will buy these products and import them back into the U.S. for sale. This is known as the *gray market*. It is illegal to sell, buy, or own black market products, but it is not illegal for you to buy or own gray market products. Buying these products should save you some money because they are usually discounted considerably from their domestic counterparts. You should be able to distinguish between a domestic and international item by the model number (for example, Zd7020US vs. ZD7020). Before purchasing, you should be well aware of all the differences between the domestic and international versions.

How Can I Avoid the Back-Ordered/Out-of-Stock Scam?

If you're like us, when you order something on the Internet, you want it immediately. We don't care what it takes after we dish out our hard-earned cash to buy something. We want instant gratification.

Most retail outlets strive to keep a good supply of items in stock. The bigger outlets can stock most models of the key brands. At least that is what they say in their sales pitches. Another advantage retail outlets have is that it is fairly easy for you to see if they have something in stock. Just look for it, and if you don't see what you are looking for, you can move on to the next store.

Ordering online is a completely different ball game. Online vendors usually do not have large storage facilities, if any facilities at all. The reason is pure economics. Storage facilities can cost big bucks and add another level of complexity to their operation. This cuts into the company's bottom line and its ability to compete with other online vendors. When shopping online, keep the following in mind:

- *Contact info:* Look for a customer service number (preferably toll free) where you can call and inquire about stocking status. If you cannot find this information, something may be wrong.

- *Call to verify:* Just because the website says an item is in stock does not mean it really is. Depending on the vendor, a website can be out of sync (from a few minutes to a few days) with an actual inventory count. Call the company and verify that it has the actual item in stock before ordering. Take the time to verify the model number. Also, double-check the price and shipping info.

- *Ask about policies:* Find out what the company's policy is on back-ordered and out-of-stock items. Some companies charge your credit card in advance, even when the item is not available. Then when you decide to cancel because your order is taking too long, you may need to fight with them to process the refund to your credit card.

- *Post order status:* Make sure the company has a way for you to check order status after you have placed your order. Not having this valuable feature can leave you in the dark after you have made the purchase.

- *Alternative offers:* Some companies will offer an alternative item in place of the out-of-stock item. Although this usually benefits the consumer, you should always fully research what they are offering. This may be a classic bait and switch maneuver.

- *Additional charges:* Some shady vendors may add on extra charges for back-ordered items. They may try to charge you the shipping that they paid to get the item, plus the shipping costs involved in getting the item to you.

How Can I Avoid Excessive Shipping and Handling Charges?

The shipping and handling charges are an often-overlooked aspect of any transaction. Typically, a buyer looks for the best price and assumes the retailer will charge a fair shipping rate. Unfortunately, this is not always the case. The crooked merchant will lower the price of the item slightly while raising the shipping rate dramatically. Sometimes the merchant may even charge you for "handling," which is simply ridiculous (of course they have to handle what they sell). You should be well aware of all these inflated charges and calculate them into the total cost of the item before purchasing. Here are a few links to help you calculate your shipping costs:

- U.S. Postal Service: **http://postcalc.usps.gov/**
- UPS: **http://wwwapps.ups.com/QCCWebApp/request**
- FedEx: **http://jcapps.dmz.fedex.com/ratefinder/home?cc=US&language=en**
- DHL: **www.dhl-usa.com/ratecalculator/HandlerServlet?client=RATE_DISPLAY**

Can I Be Scammed by Important Details That Are Hidden in the Fine Print?

Everybody knows "Nobody reads the fine print," especially deceptive salespeople. An unscrupulous salesperson will take full advantage of minor details that can be imposed using fine print. If you look, you will find all sorts of goodies buried in the fine print (hidden charges, product condition, cancellation procedures, restocking fees, and so on). The best advice here is to read. As boring as it can be reading all of that stuff, it is a very important part of being an educated consumer.

Can I Be Scammed by Misrepresented OEM Products?

Manufacturers often sell discounted, sometimes "modified" versions of their products to PC makers, known as original equipment manufacturer (OEM) parts. These can include products with limited/no warranty, cheaper components, missing accessories, missing or modified features, modified driver disks, and so on. There is nothing wrong with selling and or purchasing OEM parts, provided you are well aware of the differences between the retail and OEM versions before purchasing.

HORROR STORY! A few years ago, I (Jesse) saw a company advertising an expensive sound card for half price. The advertisement included a picture of the boxed sound card. When I went to pay for the product, they handed me three floppy disks and the sound card in a bag. I figured, "OK, that's why it's cheaper—no box." After fighting to install the card, I called tech support who told me that I bought an OEM card—custom install disks without their full software suite, and the card was missing the core sound chip (which was the reason for my purchase). After several hours of threatening to go to the police (since their newspaper advertisement showed a boxed sound card), refusing to pay their "re-stocking fee," insisting on a cash refund, and insisting on an immediate refund, I got my money back.

Do I Need to Watch Out for Missing Accessories?

"Hey, the charger and extra battery are missing!" Have you ever purchased an item and noticed that some of the accessories were missing? The retailer that sold you the item may have intentionally withheld them. Most of the time, your missing accessories are sold as replacements to other people. You may even run into a retailer who tries to sell you the items that should have been included with your order. Talk about adding insult to injury!

Can I Be Scammed by Rebates?

Offering rebates is an attractive method of luring consumers to products. A company announces that its $500 product is now $300 with mail-in rebate. Why the rebates and why the mail-in versus instant rebate? First, rebates give the manufacturer a way to place its product "on sale" without having a sale. Second, rebates are commonly used to push closeout products. Third, mail-in rebates allow the manufacturer to get a free short-term loan from the consumers. Let's look at an example: Assume a manufacturer sells 50,000 units of a product that include $200 rebates. The company just floated a loan for $10 million (50,000 purchases $\star$ $200 rebate). That's why some rebates say, "Please allow four weeks for processing." Imagine receiving a free $10 million loan, investing it for four weeks at a mere 2 percent interest gain. You'd make a profit of $200,000. Last, shady companies may offer rebates and take off with the money and then declare bankruptcy. Trust me, we know about this personally. Shady companies will file bankruptcy, the customers file a class action lawsuit, and six months later you receive a $5 check for the $500 in rebates you were owed.

Despite the negatives, rebates can be a good way to save on your favorite product. Before purchasing, you should be aware of the following:

- *Rebate method:* Unless the rebate is instant, you pay the entire cost up front, mail in the rebate, and then receive a rebate check.

- *Sales taxes:* You pay tax on the total cost of the item, not on the cost of the item minus the rebate.

- *Do the math:* Some rebates require you to sign up with some sort of service (Internet, cable, cellular, and so on). This is usually associated with laptops and desktops. Before purchasing, calculate the total cost of commitment (monthly fees * months obligated) and find out if there is a fee for early termination.

- *Duration:* Is there a time limit associated with the rebate? Has the time limit passed already?

- *Ease of use:* How complicated is the rebate process? Some rebates require you to fill out a form, send two photocopies of the original receipt, cut out the UPC code from the original box, write the product serial number on the outside of the envelope, and so on.

Most important, though, is to ask yourself whether you really need the product. Don't buy things you don't need. Rebates are attractive, but unless the rebate makes the product free, save your money.

HORROR STORY! A friend of ours visited a major computer store and stood in line to purchase some computers that came with a few hundred dollars back in rebates. While the cashier was ringing up the computers, the cashier was also taking the UPC codes, rebates, and a copy of the receipt in his pocket (allegedly to send in the rebate himself and keep the money). Luckily our friend spotted this and questioned him. The cashier stated that he could not let our friend have the UPC codes unless he bought their extended warranty. Our friend demanded to see the manager, got his receipt, UPC codes, and rebates, and left the store in disgust. Make sure you have all the items you need for the rebate before you leave the store.

Can I Be Scammed by Refurbished, Reconditioned, and Remanufactured Products?

These terms are often used interchangeably because they describe a product that has been returned, repaired, and or rebuilt by the manufacturer due to some defect (such as a broken button, bad power supply, dim display, scratched case, and so on). These products are sold in perfect working order, may have limited or full warranty, and are usually in perfect to near-perfect cosmetic condition. Buying refurbished products can save you some money because they are usually discounted considerably below their brand-new counterparts. You should be well aware of the differences between the new and refurbished versions before purchasing a product.

WARNING! Some major retailers are starting to sell refurbished items in their stores. The items are mixed with non-refurbished items and have abbreviated descriptions (i.e., refur).

Can I Be Scammed by Sneaky Typos?

Everybody makes mistakes, but some people make them way too often. A misplaced decimal point combined with an incorrectly listed model number may trick you into paying top dollar for bottom-of-the-line technology. Some companies even state that they are not responsible for typos on their websites or in their catalogs. You should be aware of the company's policy before purchasing a product. Besides, do you really want to buy something from someone that doesn't know how to spell?

HORROR STORY!   A friend of ours was shopping online for a DVR when he found a website selling a 140-hour DVR for $200. This was great news since this DVR normally sells for $400. He purchased it, waited patiently for it to arrive, and was shocked when it did. The DVR was only a 40-hour device. Extremely angered, he checked the website and the emails confirming his purchase. He thought the listing stated that the product was a 140-hour DVR, but the actual listing was for one 40-hour DVR (i.e., "1 40 hour DVR," not "140 hour DVR"). While this obviously was a deceptive practice by the seller, it was arguably legal. Moral of the story: Always confirm and spell out the specifics to the seller before purchasing. For example, ask the vender, "You are selling a one hundred and forty hour DVR?" You can also check the model numbers to confirm that you get exactly what you intended to get.

Internet Fraud Prevention

- Learn what to watch out for before you buy something online.
- Learn how you can distinguish between a good deal and a scam.

What Should I Do before Buying Online?

You found something you want to buy online, so now what? Do as much research as possible when buying stuff online. A little legwork can and will save you an incredible amount of time and money in the long run. Plus, who wants to waste their time chasing down crooked online merchants when you could be playing with your new toys? Here are some guidelines to help you before you make any online purchases:

- *Determine your limits and needs.* You need to figure out what your finances will allow you to buy and what you can handle in terms of horsepower. Don't buy the most expensive and feature-filled model unless you are willing to learn about it and use all of its capabilities. Doing otherwise is just a waste of money.

- *Do your product research.* This is an important step in purchasing new tech toys. See what other people are saying about the product you are looking to purchase. If a large percentage of people don't like it or are experiencing troubles, then you will probably have the same results.

- *Print out item info as given by the manufacturer.* The best place to get this info is at the manufacturer's website. You need this info to do a side-by-side comparison of potential candidates. Some of the things you should be looking at are features, MSRP (Manufacturer's Suggested Retail Price), battery life, weight, footprint size, and so on. If an item does not meet your criteria, remove it from the list and move on. When you have ruled out all of the unlikely candidates, you should be left with about two or three possible choices.

- *Use Internet search engines and price guides.* These resources should give you the largest pool of potential vendors to buy your item from. You can literally find a hundred places to purchase from by using just a few keywords.

- *Research the vendor.* Ask your friends, family, and colleagues if they have ever done business with any of the vendors you are considering. Word of mouth is usually the best way to see if the vendor will provide you with sufficient service and not rip you off. Other resources at your disposal include the Better Business Bureau and the Internet.

- *Be wary of places with little or no contact info.* This should definitely be a red light for you. There's most likely a reason behind a vendor not wanting to be reached.

- *Know the retailer's polices.* Vendors can have some pretty crazy policies regarding damaged items, lost items, restocking fees, and so on. Make sure you know how they play ball before laying out any cash. If their policies seem too harsh, it's best to pass. It is not worth the aggravation of dealing with their rules just to save a few bucks.

- *Don't get caught up in the hype.* Somewhere along the line, you will see a deal that seems like a winner, but there may be some catches. Be wary of auctions and sales that are ending soon. They may just be a honey pot set up to lure unsuspecting buyers into sending money. This is also another good time to read fine print. In a rush to complete a transaction, you may miss the line saying that you owe them your firstborn.

- *Buy software from authorized dealers only.* Fraudulent vendors may sell you copies of "not for resale" versions (NFR versions), academic versions represented as retail, OEM versions meant to be bundled with new PCs, and blatant unauthorized copies (also called backup copies). Steer clear of any of these scenarios. If you are caught trying to purchase any of these, you may be opening yourself to prosecution, fines, and possible jail time. See Chapter 15 for more information.

- *Know your acronyms and abbreviations.* For example, there are huge differences between XGA, SXGA, UXGA, SVGA, and VGA monitors. By passing over words you don't know, you may sacrifice quality and price. If anything looks amiss, call the vendor and ask for verification of what the specific features are.

- *Print out your order form before submitting your order, and print your receipt after placing your order.* You will need this information in case you need to pursue the vendor for ripping you off.

- *Watch out for second chances.* Some auction sites allow the seller to offer you a second chance to purchase an item if the winning bidder backs out. Some con artists will send out fake "second chance" notices, trying to get you to send them your money. If you decide to take advantage of the second chance, ensure that you are sending your money to the original seller.

How Can I Distinguish between a Good Deal and a Scam?

Whether you're shopping for a digital camera or thinking about making money online, it's hard to tell what a good deal is and what a scam is. The following is a list of some tell-tale signs of a scam:

- *Too good to be true:* The selling price is significantly lower than it is at most retailers. You can expect to see a slight difference in retail prices for a particular item. If the price difference is over 30 percent, you should proceed with caution.

- *Accepted payment methods:* The retailer does not offer payment by credit card or allows payment only through nonstandard channels (money orders, PayPal, check, cash). Retailers that deal in cash might be on the run.

- *Unsolicited offer (phone call, email, flyer):* Hang up, delete the message, and tear up the flyer. You are more than likely about to be ripped off.

- *Pushy sales people:* Don't get railroaded into making a purchase you might regret.

- *Extremely complicated deal:* If you have to jump through hoops to get a good deal, then just forget about it. The end result of deals like these is that you do what they want but don't get what you want.

- *No risk:* The deal is advertised as "no risk."

- *Requires money:* The deal involves you sending someone money in exchange for more money.

HORROR STORY! On the local news recently, we heard a story that will likely send chills down your spine if you are an avid eBay shopper. A family just moved across the country to Arizona. As they were moving into their new house over a two-day period, some thieves broke into their garage and stole a number of cartons containing their belongings. The family likely thought their stuff was safe because no one would steal basic items such as dishes, bath towels, books, clothes, and other items. A few days later one of the family members was scanning auctions on eBay and came across many of the items that were stolen from their garage. How stupid is that? The moral of the story is online services such as eBay have opened up many new channels for fencing goods. Watch your stuff closely. Internet fraud is not limited to thieves who operate only online.

How Should I Pay when Buying Online?

When buying online, you may be presented with all sorts of options (some you've never even heard of). Traditionally, payment has been cash, check (money order), or charge. The Internet complicates this tradition by adding payment services like PayPal and CyberCash. These are services that allow you to pay for items through an intermediary. You are required to create an account with the service and are then allowed to deposit, withdraw, and send money. Here is a list of the types of payment methods you can use when shopping online and why you would use them:

- *Use a credit card.* This is the safest way to pay for something online. If you become a victim of online fraud, you will be protected by the Fair Credit Billing Act, a federal law that limits your responsibility to only the first $50 in charges.

- *Use a real credit card.* Obviously, using a fake credit card is against the law, but that's not the point we're trying to make here. A popular option for bank savings cards is to include a credit card account. This is known as a debit card or check card and allows you to make credit card charges but have the money taken straight out of your bank account. Because this card is a bank card first and a credit card second, it may not be protected under the law to the same extent a credit card is. Also, using your bank card exposes your bank account. You probably won't shed a tear if a criminal takes $5,000 from your credit card company and you have to pay $50, but you likely will if they take $5,000 or drain your bank account.

- *Don't use checks or cash.* You won't get any fraud protection for using cash and checks. Additionally, using a check exposes your checking account.

- *Never email your credit card information.* Email is not a secure medium. It can be easily intercepted and forged. If the vendor requires your credit card information again, you should enter the information on the site directly or call the vendor (using the official number).

- *Purchase from sites that use secure pages.* A secure web page encrypts (scrambles) the data to prevent others from reading it. This is especially important when buying online and entering credit card information. You can easily recognize a secure web page when you visit one. The URL of the web page starts with "https" (Secure HTTP) and causes a little yellow lock icon to be displayed in the lower-right corner of your web browser.

How Can I Avoid Overpaying when Buying Online?

We've started to notice some scary trends growing among the major Internet retailers. Instead of giving you the best price, the retailer will bury the best price on its site and if you click the wrong link, it can mean the difference between paying 50 to 100 percent of the cost. The other trend is "the coupon code." If you have one, you can save over 50 percent of the cost (or even get the item for free), get free shipping, or receive other promotional items, but if you don't, you're stuck overpaying. You can keep from overpaying by visiting sites such as these:

- *Coupon code list sites:* These are sites devoted to showing you the best deal and providing you with the coupon codes and instructions on how to avoid overpaying. Here are the more popular sites:
  - **http://slickdeals.net**
  - **http://techbargains.com**
  - **http://dealcatcher.com**
  - **http://www.shopping-bargains.com**
- *Dell.com:* When buying from Dell.com, you have the option of entering the "Home and Office," "Small Business," or other portals of the site. Most people click on "Home and Office," but you may end up getting better prices and more choices if you use the "Small Business" portal (don't worry if you're not a small business because Dell doesn't care). The *biggest* money saver is hidden in the "Small Business" portal. Once you are in, there is a link on the page labeled "Outrageous Deals." These deals can change daily, and you can save over 50 percent. Dell also sells its refurbished computers for considerably less than retail, and it offers the same warranty it provides for new computers. You can see the list of available systems at **http://dell.com/outlet**. Don't forget to use the Coupon Code List Sites to see if there are any Dell coupon codes you can use to save even more money.

What Should I Do after Ordering and Never Receiving the Product?

Ahh, the fresh smell of a cardboard box, Styrofoam, and Bubble Wrap. Waiting for a package to arrive is exciting, kind of like Christmas Eve, except it can happen as often as you can afford. Here's what you can do after waiting, waiting, waiting, and still no package:

- *Use the tracking information.* Unless your package is coming by pony express, you should have been given a tracking number. Use this tracking number to locate your package. The shipping company should be able to give you details such as when it was shipped, all of the stops it has made on its journey, and an estimated delivery date.
- *It could be "foul play."* Verify that your wife, offspring, or co-workers aren't playing games. Search all of the usual places like closets, the basement, and the attic.
- *Don't jump to conclusions.* Follow up with the retailer.

- *Allow enough time for your order to arrive.* By law, the retailer has 30 days to deliver your package or inform you of the delay.

- *Search your property.* Sometimes the delivery person places the package in locations that are hidden or overlooked. This is commonly known as the "stop, drop, and run" policy. Take a quick stroll around your house to see if it was placed around back. Also, ask your neighbors if they have seen a delivery person at your house. Sometimes, nosy neighbors are a good thing.

- *You've been ripped off.* If the retailer is not cooperative, contact the proper channels to report the fraud. An extensive list can be found at **www.cybercrime.gov/reporting.htm**.

WARNING! Shipping insurance doesn't ensure your protection. If an item is lost, stolen, or damaged during shipping, the sender is responsible for filing a claim with the delivery service (FedEx, UPS, and so on). While the claim can be transferred to you, it is ultimately up to the sender to initiate the transfer. Also, most shippers will not honor the warranty unless the item is shipped in its original packaging.

Safety Checklist for Online Shopping

With the knowledge you've gained in this section, you are many steps ahead of the average online consumer (and even retailer). You know how retailers and others will try to take advantage of you and how to avoid it. You know how to get exactly what you want, for the price you want. You know how to protect yourself from all sides and what to do if things don't go your way. Congratulations. The following list provides a quick checklist you can review when buying online:

- *Know the product.* Model numbers, features, costs, rebates, condition (new, refurbished, and so on).

- *Know the retailer.* Reputation, return policies, accepted payment types, contact numbers.

- *Use the safest payment method.* Always use your credit card.

- *Receipt and tracking:* Print original ad or listing, online receipt, and tracking number.

Internet Vendor Fraud

- Learn how to best protect yourself if you are selling products online.

Because all of us are consumers in one way or another, we tend to think of Internet fraud as something that can only happen to us as consumers. But the reality is that there are many petty thieves and criminals who target online businesses, especially businesses that are inexperienced and more trusting than they should be. This is becoming a bigger problem as more individuals are using services such as eBay to sell their products.

Online thieves who target business can be tricky to catch because they are so transparent. They can easily hide and they can be out there operating 24 hours a day, 7 days a week. They are experienced at using stolen credit cards, stolen identities, and tactics that can cause real disasters for any online vendor unless you know how to protect yourself.

What to Watch Out For

The Internet can be a great place to sell things. After all, you can reach millions and millions of people for practically nothing and little work. But for every few potential buyers, there may be that one criminal trying to rip you off. The following list reviews a few of the common scams targeted toward sellers:

- *Bid, block, and run:* Imagine you are selling an item at an auction site (estimated value $100). A thief will use one account to bid low (for example, $5) and then immediately use another account to bid ridiculously high (say, $500). When other bidders see that the bidding is extremely high, they won't even bother to bid. Right before the auction ends, the thief retracts the high bid ($500) and ends up getting the item for the low bid ($5). Always set a reserve price or start the bidding at the lowest price you are willing to accept for the product.

- *Fake escrow services:* An escrow service is something that is supposed to protect the buyer and the seller, but it's also the best place for a criminal to strike. Not only does the criminal get the money from the buyer, but they also get the product from the seller. Always use a well-known, reputable escrow service (even if it costs a little more).

- *Fake payment emails:* A fraudulent buyer may send you a fake email stating that they have paid. If you receive a payment email, always confirm that the funds have been delivered before sending out the product.

- *Fake payments:* A fraudulent buyer may send you a fake payment (money order, wire notice, check, stolen credit card number, and so on). Always ensure that the money has cleared through a bank before sending out the product.

- *Back-out bidders:* A bidder wins the auction and is then supposed to send payment. Unfortunately, a growing trend is for winning bidders to back out and never be heard from again. Why? Perhaps they found a better deal, made a mistake, no longer have the money to pay, or just place fake-bids for kicks. In any case, you are stuck with a product you needed to sell and have wasted valuable time. If this happens, see if your auction service allows you to send a "second chance" to the runner-up, giving them a chance to buy the product for their final bid.

How to Best Protect Yourself

Criminals are constantly coming up with new ways to rip you off. While it's almost impossible to detect every scam that comes your way, you can implement a few practices to protect yourself:

- *Payment first, product second.* We've all heard the phrase "the check's in the mail," and most of the time it translates to "you've been ripped off." Never send the item to the buyer until you have received payment.

- *Use an escrow service.* An escrow service helps the seller get the money they expect and helps the buyer get the product they expect. For the seller, escrow services not only ensure that you get the money you expect, but they also help you escape from the headaches of dealing with troublesome buyers.

- *Insure the product.* There's nothing worse than selling an item, receiving the money, and then having to refund it because the item was damaged on the way to the sender. Now, not only do you not have the money, but you have a broken item. While dealing with insurance and claims can become a nightmare, at least it provides you with some extra protection from becoming a two-time loser.

What Can I Do when the Buyer Doesn't Pay?

Depending on your line of business, there can be some pretty big repercussions for someone who doesn't pay on time. Before sending out your "Uncle Tony" to "collect," try the following:

- *Patience, grasshopper.* If you are having trouble contacting the buyer, don't assume you've been ripped off. The buyer may have stepped out of town or is simply having computer/email troubles. Give the buyer sufficient time (about 10 days) to make payment before taking any action.

- *Request the buyer's contact info.* If you are selling through an auction site, the site may allow you to request the buyer's contact information. You can then call and even visit the buyer to settle the score (I mean, collect the payment). You can request an eBay buyer's contact info at **http:// cgi3.ebay.com/aw-cgi/eBayISAPI.dll?UserInformationRequest**.

- *Relist your item.* After trying to work things out with the buyer, inform your auction site and it may allow you to relist your item for free (and they may even refund any fees).

Safety Checklist for Online Vendors

This section has provided you with information on how to protect yourself when selling online. Finding buyers is hard enough without having to worry about scams and con artists. The following list provides a quick checklist you can review before selling online:

- Payment first.
- Verify payment.
- Use a reputable escrow service.
- Buy the insurance.

Summary

The Internet is becoming an open playground for thieves and con artists. The thieves can reach more victims faster, and they can easily hide their tracks. But the Internet is also a virtual super Wal-Mart, allowing you to buy just about anything for less than you might pay at your local mall. With both of those points in mind, this chapter has helped prepare you to become a better, smarter, and safer online shopper. You learned about how to recognize and how to avoid the various tricks and scams thieves may use to rip you off. You also learned how not to overpay and to get exactly what you want for the best possible price. You learned that criminals try to rip you off not only when you buy something, but also when you sell something. Finally, you learned how to deal with and recover from fraud in case it does happen.

7

Spam

Disasters to avoid:

- Getting ripped off by spammers who promise you the "deal of a lifetime."
- Having important email you send out get marked as spam and thus get overlooked.
- Letting your email program send information about you to spammers.

Mishaps and blunders to run from:

- Wasting valuable time by spending hours trying to sort through all the spam you receive.
- Accidentally deleting important emails because you think they are spam.
- Sending out messages that are themselves spam or contain hidden viruses.

We're all really sick of all those things we don't ask for that waste our time or clutter up our lives—annoying phone calls from telemarketers, mall surveys, flyers under our windshields, and those never-ending Pottery Barn catalogs. It's like having a persistent car salesperson leave you Post-it® Notes all over your house. If these marketing interruptions weren't enough to drive you crazy, you now have to wade through tons of junk on your computer, in the form of spam, each time you check your email.

We all find spam annoying, intrusive, and most of the time outright offensive, so why does it continue to exist? Evidently, it works. Aggressive spammers have learned how to reach a lot of people without spending much money. This is a direct marketer's dream. Once a spammer has a list of email addresses, a computer, and an Internet connection; they can send out millions of email messages to recipients all around the world. Spammers may only convince a very small percentage of the people they target to actually buy something, but each time they sell their junk, they make big profits. The stuff they sell is cheap and certainly isn't worth what you pay for it. They look for products that people are embarrassed to buy in stores and those that have an extremely high profit margin.

Spam has rapidly become the top problem facing email administrators and anyone who receives email. Spam messages are usually sent in bulk to many email recipients simultaneously. This can be done manually, but it's usually done using a software program or spamming service. The person sending you the spam is called a *spammer* (although you may call them worse names) and can be anyone from a work-at-home mom to a con artist; it can even be a virus.

In this chapter, we'll first help you deal with the key hazards of spam. You'll learn why receiving so much spam can be a disaster, and you'll learn why and how spammers are getting so devious. In the second part of the chapter, we'll focus on things you can do to prevent and block spam so that your email doesn't get out of control. Finally, in the last part of the chapter, we'll show you how you can fight back.

Hazards of Spam

- Learn why spammers have become so devious and why this is a disaster waiting to happen for you.

- Learn the smartest things you can do when you receive spam.
- Learn what you can do if you accidentally delete a non-spam message.

Why Am I Receiving So Much Spam?

Despite how careful you are on the Internet (not clicking on pop-ups, not clicking on things you're not supposed to, visiting only PG-13-rated websites), you will inevitably get spam. Here are some reasons you are likely getting way too much of it now:

- *Spammers harvest your address.* Spammers use software programs called *bots* to scan the Internet and record any email address they find. This is similar to how a search engine indexes web pages on the Internet. Email addresses can be found on personal websites, newsgroup postings, and sites from which you bought something. Having your email address on a web page in a searchable text format is a really bad idea, so before you do anything else, take your email address off your website! In the section "How Can I Tell If My Email Address Is Posted on the Internet?" we'll show you how to determine if you are vulnerable.

- *Your address is part of a list that's sold.* E-mail list brokers are companies that maintain databases of email addresses that they sell to spammers. Once your email address makes its way into one of these databases, chances are it will be there forever. If your email address gets into too many databases, sometimes your best recourse is to simply start using a new email address.

- *You signed up for something.* Sometimes you sign up for things and later, the moment you are bombarded with emails, you realize what a bad idea it was. Be very careful about using your active email address to sign up for future offers, newsletters, and so on.

- *You clicked on something without realizing the danger.* Spammers sometimes include a "click here to remove me from this list" option. That's like a thief asking to hold your wallet for safekeeping. Never click on these links, even if the email comes from a reputable site (Sears.com, Amazon.com, and so on).

- *You use a simple email address.* If your email address is easy to guess, chances are you'll be sent spam by a program designed to guess email addresses. While these types of programs may start out with a simple guess routine (**a@example.com**, **aa@example.com**, **aaa@example.com**, and so on), the routine usually involves dictionary words, including names. The rule of thumb you should follow: If your email address is easy to remember, it will also be easy to guess.

- *You registered for a domain.* If you have your own domain (**www.example.com**), your ownership information is publicly available for the world to see. Not only does this include your email address, but your home address and phone number as well. To check what information your domain registration is displaying, go to **www.whois.net** and search for your domain name.

DID YOU KNOW Bill Gates gets over 4 million emails a day, with the majority of it being spam? In fact, he receives so much spam that there are special systems and an entire department dedicated to removing the spam from his inbox. It's true! Check out: **http://abcnews.go.com/US/ wireStory?id=262568**.

HORROR STORY!
If you think you are receiving too much spam, keep in mind that there are always other people out there who are receiving much more than you can even imagine. Consider Jonathan Land who recently wrote the popular book, *The Spam Letters* (No Starch Press, ISBN: 1-59327-032-1). In his book, Jonathan published many of the spam letters he received along with his witty responses to try to keep the spammers off guard. On a typical day, Jonathan claims that he receives 400 pieces of spam (**www.nostarch.com/spamletters**).

Why Are Spammers So Aggressive about Spamming?

If people find spam annoying, intrusive, and most of the time outright offensive, then why does it continue to exist? Simple—because it works. Here are the reasons spam works, continues to exist, and will continue to exist for some time to come:

- *Cost, reach, and volume:* Traditionally, people who wanted to send out a high volume of advertisements had to pay a high price. If it costs $.80 cents to send out a business reply post card, it would cost $8,000 for 10,000 cards. Once a spammer has a list of email addresses, a computer, and an Internet connection, they can send out millions of email messages to recipients all around the world for free.

- *Profitability:* If you sell an item for $100 and it costs you only $50, you make $50 for each item sold (we know this is easy math, but just bear with us). If you send out 1 million email messages and only 1 percent of people buy an item, you'd make half a million dollars (that's $500,000). Let's be clear: this is not an endorsement for spam, so don't quit your day job.

- *Anonymity:* Using a technique called spoofing, spammers can forge the inner contents of an email message to hide their identity and make it look like the email is coming from someone else. In addition, spammers can switch email providers or use various free email services to also hide their true identity. So even if you have 10 spam emails from 10 different email addresses, they may all be coming from the same spammer.

- *Ease:* Most spammers use mass email programs or services to send out their messages. They simply choose what advertisement to send and what email address to spoof and off go one million emails with the click of a button.

What Are Some of the Tricks Spammers Use?

Spammers have gotten much more devious over the past few years because people are getting more cautious and software for blocking spam is getting better. Here are some of the sneaky things you should be on the lookout for:

- *Spoofing:* Spammers can forge the inner contents of an email message (a special area called the header) to hide their identity and make it look like the email is coming from someone else. This technique is called spoofing. Toward the end of this chapter, you will learn more about spoofing, how to detect it, and even how to trace the spam back to its true sender.

- *Using mass email techniques:* Most spammers use mass email programs or services to send out their messages. They simply choose what advertisement to send and what email address to spoof and off go one million emails with the click of a button.

- *Message beaconing:* Ever notice how most spam messages have pictures in them? It's not for good looks. They are using a technique called *message beaconing.* When you view a message, any included images get downloaded from the spammer's web server and displayed. The spammer can then check the server logs to see which images have been downloaded. So how do they know it was you? The spammer usually names each image uniquely for every spam message they send out (for example, 1001.jpg for spam message number 1001). They can just match the name of the image downloaded with the spam message ID (1001.jpg = spam message 1001 = **johndoe@example.com**). The best way to prevent sending a message beacon is to either not view the message, turn off the preview pane, or use a product like Outlook 2003 which blocks message beacons (see Figure 7.1).

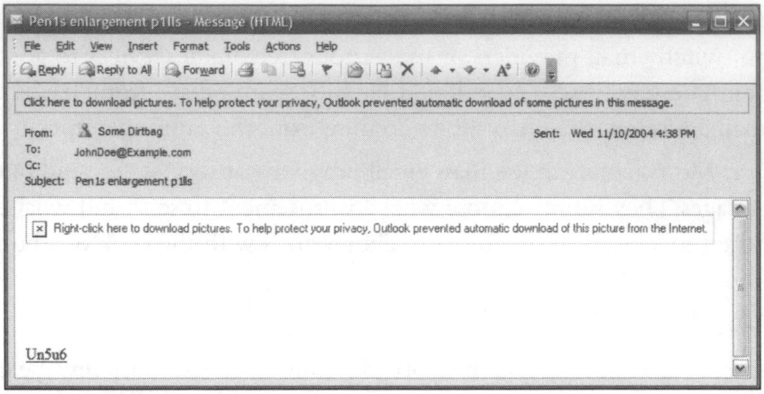

Figure 7.1

Spam message beaconing prevented by Microsoft Outlook 2003.

- *Spim:* Spim is spam sent through an instant messenger program (AIM, Windows Messenger, Yahoo Messenger, and so on), and it's on the rise. You could be online chatting with a friend and then *bam*—you get an instant message from someone you don't know trying to sell you Viagra. While a spammer could log on and send these messages by hand, most of the time they use a bot program to create a randomly named instant messenger account. The bot can log on to the instant messenger network pretending to be a real person and then send its messages to a list of screen names. The best way to avoid spim is to not answer instant messages unless you really know the person sending the message.

What Should I Do when I Receive Spam?

Once spam arrives in your inbox, the steps you take can mean the difference between stopping the spam and getting tons more. Spammers usually work with other spammers, reporting to each other who has viewed or replied to their messages, which in the spammer world is effectively engraving your email address in stone. Here is what you should do once a spam message arrives in your inbox:

- *Don't view it.* Even if displayed in a preview pane, viewing a spam message may send data back to the spammer, letting them know your email address is active.

- *Don't take action.* Even if the spam message claims that clicking on a link or replying to the message will remove you from their spam list, chances are that it won't and you are just letting the spammer know your email address is active. If you really want to fight back, see the section "Fighting Back," presented later in this chapter.

- *Delete it.* Spam messages may include viruses and other dangerous items that should be removed from your system as soon as possible. The only exception to this rule is if you plan on reporting the spammer to someone. You may want to hold on to the message as evidence. For more information on reporting spammers, see the section "Fighting Back" presented later in this chapter.

Can I Really Lose a Lot of Money when Dealing with Spammers?

"It's just a few emails. What harm can it do?" When we hear someone say that, we want to sign them up for every piece of spam available to teach them a lesson. Here are some ways spam can cost you money, resources, and aggravation:

- *Lost productivity:* The average person spends 15 minutes a day sifting through spam. For a work week, that's 1 hour and 15 minutes that you could have spent on more productive things (like reading this book). You may also accidentally delete emails that you wanted to keep.

- *Hard cash:* Spam is an abuse that everybody pays for. Because of the extra volume of email spam adds, you and/or your ISP may have to pay for additional bandwidth, for additional storage, for antispam software/hardware, and sometimes even for each individual message (especially on a cell phone). It may really cost you if you are scammed by one of these deceptive or scam spam messages.

- *Speed:* Spam is the hair clog in the Internet sink. While you may only get a few spam messages per day, these messages can really add up when you consider all of the people using the Internet on a daily basis. Your ISP's mail server and your email client may respond more slowly because they have to process, inspect, detect, or remove spam messages.

- *Inappropriate material:* Being sent vulgar or pornographic material you didn't ask for may offend you and place you in an awkward situation. (Your boss might be walking by!) It may also be illegal. See the section "How Can I Fight Back?" later in this chapter for more information.

- *Safety:* Spam may contain viruses and or junkware that can expose your personal information and your computer. Additionally, since spam is usually sent out by shady individuals, the products they sell may not work, may not be what they advertised, or may never show up at all. Finally, con artists have found spam to be an effective way to reach millions with their scams. What may look like a low interest mortgage may end up costing you a fortune.

HORROR STORY! This is something that has probably happened to every person reading this book. You are looking through your email and open one up that is sent from a spammer, just as your child or spouse is walking by. Unfortunately, the email is loaded with porn-related images that just don't fit in with family life. Now, try explaining this one to your spouse. If you want to see a short, funny, and (best of all) free movie about such a disaster from 20th Century Fox, go to **www.foxsearchlight.com/lab/shorts/farmsluts/quicktime.html**

Should I Ever Buy or Take Part in Anything Presented in a Spam Message?

Most of the spam you'll get is really dumb. After all, how many mortgages or "pen1s p1lls" do you really need? But some spam messages are enticing. You might stop and think, "This looks like a really good offer. How can I turn it down?" First, remember that the spammer is more clever than you are at making things sound like an incredible offer. Our feeling is that you should never buy something from an unsolicited email (unless you really like playing with fire!). Here are three rules your parents taught you that actually work when it comes to spam:

- *Never talk to strangers.* Spammers are vampires, draining you of your patience and your cash. They also are draining the Internet of its speed and flexibility. By refusing to respond or buy products advertised through spam, you are sending a clear message to the sender that this type of marketing is not welcome. When the spammers stop receiving profits, they will stop sending out spam.

- *Don't take candy from strangers.* Purchasing and consuming pharmaceutical, herbal, or diet products from a spammer may be dangerous or deadly to your health. Spam emails may also distribute a virus, Trojan horse, spyware, or some other sort of malicious software. They may be a danger to your computer's health if you are not really careful.

- *Don't trust strangers.* Most spam emails are actually scams. The scam might be as trivial as selling a cheap product at a high price or as damaging as scamming you out of your life savings. The fact is, if it were truly an amazing deal, it would be in the public eye, not in a spam email.

HORROR STORY! A friend of ours received a spam offer for what sounded like a great vacation package. For $495, he could take his entire family on a seven-day, all-expenses-paid cruise vacation in the Caribbean. To a guy who sat in front of his computer all day, this sounded like a much-needed break. So he sent in his money and took the vacation six months later, only to discover that the offer was too good to be true and that the $495 didn't cover much of the trip. So much for "all expenses paid"!

What Should I Do If I Accidentally Delete a Non-Spam Message?

While trying to get rid of the spam that clutters your inbox, you may accidentally select and delete a legitimate message. This can turn out to be a real mishap, especially if you delete an important message. Before you start panicking, here's what you can do:

- *Check your Deleted Items folder.* Most email programs move all deleted email to a Deleted Items folder unless you permanently delete the email (hold down the Shift key while pressing Delete) or your email administrator has overridden the default settings. The important thing is that you'll need to do this quickly after you first accidentally delete an email. If your deleted items are not in your Deleted Items folder, you may still be able to recover them (read on).

- *Recover your deleted items.* In a corporate environment that uses Outlook, your email administrator may have turned on the option for you to recover deleted items even after they have been removed from your Deleted Items folder. To recover deleted items in Microsoft Outlook, view your Deleted Items folder by double-clicking it. From the Tools menu, select Recover Deleted Items.

- *Restore your deleted items using a backup.* Your ISP or email administrator may be able to restore your deleted items from a backup. This is usually an involved process and may not be possible if you just received and deleted the email. It never hurts to ask, though.

- *Get a copy.* Rather than asking the sender to resend the deleted message (which can be embarrassing), have a friend or a co-worker forward you a copy of the email if they also received it.

- *Ask the sender to resend.* While it might be a bit embarrassing, asking the sender to resend is truly your last resort if the other suggestions haven't helped.

- *Deny you even received it.* This may not be a smart decision because most email servers can track every detail of the life of the email (even who received it and when an email was deleted).

A friend of ours came into work one morning to find his mailbox filled with spam. He quickly selected the spam messages and then pressed SHIFT+DELETE. Unfortunately, not only did he delete the spam messages, but also every other email in his inbox. He couldn't recover his deleted items because he permanently deleted them (SHIFT+DELETE instead of just DELETE). He also had no luck convincing the IT department to restore his email. The moral of the story is – don't delete in anger.

Spam Prevention

- Learn why you are receiving so much spam.
- Learn how to prevent and quarantine spam on your desktop, laptop, PDA, and cell phone—with or without spending money.
- Learn how to prevent the emails you send from being marked as spam.

Why Is It So Difficult to Fight Spam?

Fighting spam is a never-ending battle. The enemies are many, and they are constantly moving and evolving. They are really good at hiding their tracks. They are also good at disguising their spam as legitimate emails. Your job is to avoid spam and eliminate it or to identify legitimate email and eliminate what remains.

After avoiding, detecting, and preventing, how many spam messages can enter your inbox and still be considered a victory? Not one. We have implemented a zero tolerance policy against spam, and so should you. Spam is a drain and danger to you and everyone you know. Do not rest until you have finely tuned your antispam methods to remove every last piece of spam from your inbox. In the following sections, we'll show you our effective attack plan, which works extremely well in the battle against spam (we're about 99.9 percent spam-free).

How Can I Keep Spammers from Sending Me Their Junk in the First Place?

The first step in spam prevention is to not get spam in the first place. This is becoming more difficult as spammers are becoming more sophisticated at finding new ways to discover your email address. Here are some steps you can take to keep the spammers at bay:

- *Never reply.* Replying to spam (whether replying to be removed from a spam list or to give them a piece of your mind) tells the spammer that your email address is valid. Once they know about you, your email address is almost guaranteed to end up on a few spam lists. Sometimes spammers even provide phone numbers you can call to be removed from their list. Unfortunately, calling these phone numbers usually results in charges of a few dollars to your phone bill, and they likely won't remove you from their list. Never reply and never call.

- *Never click a link you don't trust.* Whether it's a link to be removed from the spam list or a link to a website, clicking it will let the spammer know that your email address is valid.

- *Never sign up at a no-spam site.* As this book went to press, there was no government sponsored no-spam list or website where you can submit your email address. Any site that speaks of such a list may actually sell your address to spammers. This is a con game you don't need.

- *Read all online forms you fill out carefully.* If you've been online for a while, chances are you've filled out an online form or two. This is usually required when you buy something online, but you may have also filled out a form to sign up for a service, pay bills, or answer a survey. Most of these forms have check boxes that, if left at their default values, will authorize the site owner to send you spam and or sell your email address to others. Make sure you read the form in its entirety before submitting.

- *Use a public and private email address.* Using a public and private email address is one technique to divert spam. Your private email address can be given to your friends, family, and coworkers, while your public address can be used for online shopping and posting.

- *Use a hard-to-guess email address.* Spammers use dictionary and name lists to send out emails. Email addresses like **JohnDoe@Example.com** or **YourFriend@Example.com** are easy to guess and will receive more spam than **JohnDoe2004AD@Example.com** or **YourFriend2CU@ Example.com**.

- *Stop forwarding humorous emails.* Don't forward unsolicited emails, even if they are funny. You may spread a virus or pass on a scam.

- *Always use blind carbon copy (BCC) when emailing a large group of people.* By using BCC for each individual email address, as opposed to simply putting each address in the To field, you prevent each recipient from seeing each other's email address and accidentally or intentionally sending it to a spammer.

- *Don't write your email address in public address books.* Wherever you go, merchants will put out address/comment books for people to sign, and they often ask for your email addresses. If you want to give your email address to someone, hand them your business card in private. Don't write it down for the rest of the world to see.

How Can I Prevent Spam Once It Has Been Sent to Me?

So now you're under attack and need to play defense. Fortunately, there are many weapons readily available to combat spam. Some you may have to purchase. Some you may already have and not even know it. Others may be freely available services and all you have to do is ask. Here are a few of the better ways to prevent spam once the spammers have caught on to your email address:

- *Block it before you get it.* Your ISP may provide tools to prevent spam from arriving in your inbox. Contact your ISP to see what it can offer you. But always be mindful that blocking spam at the server level could keep you from receiving important email that gets misclassified as spam.

- *Set up your email client for spam blocking.* While the features may be limited, most email clients include ways to block or filter spam. You should examine these features first before purchasing any additional software to prevent spam. See the next section for tips on how to block spam.

- *Use antivirus software.* Although spam is not a virus, it can contain virus-infected attachments or malicious embedded HTML code that antivirus software can detect, prevent, and delete. There are even viruses that can turn your computer into a spamming machine, as you'll learn later in this chapter.

- *Consider using antispam software.* Similar to antivirus software, which is solely designed to detect, block, and remove viruses, antispam software is solely designed to detect, block, quarantine, and delete spam. You'll learn more about today's antispam software later in this chapter.

- *Use a antispam service.* Some sites (**www.PostINI.com**, **www.spamsoap.com**, and **www.0spam.com**) provide services to constantly scan and remove spam from your mailbox before you view it.

- *Set up a spam firewall.* These are physical hardware devices designed to detect, block, quarantine, and delete spam. Spam firewalls are usually expensive, rack-mounted hardware designed for use by small to large companies.

What Are Some Common Ways to Block Spam on My PC?

Since no one has created the perfect way to block spam without blocking legitimate email, you need to choose a solution that utilizes the best approach for your situation. Here are a few ways you can set up your email client or use a service to block spam:

- *Scan for keywords and phrases.* One of the original ways to stop spam, this technique works by searching incoming emails and blocking them when certain words or phrases are found. For example, the spam filter may contain the word *Viagra,* scan all incoming email for the word, and block any email that contains the word. The problem with this technique is that there are hundreds of ways to misspell and disguise a word but still have it be readable. Visit **http://cockeyed.com/lessons/viagra/ viagra.html** to see the many ways to spell Viagra. Bottom line: this is a very weak method and should not be used if more advanced methods are available.

- *Set up a blacklist.* This is a list of email addresses, email servers, or email domains that you wish to block. For example, if you are getting annoying email from **JohnDoe@Example.com**, you can add this email address to your blacklist and future emails from this address will be blocked. The problem with this method is spammers can constantly forge and change their email address. Bottom line: this is a very weak method and should not be used if more advanced methods are available.

- *Set up a whitelist.* A whitelist is a list of email addresses or email domains that you wish not to block. An all-whitelist system will block all email except for those found on the whitelist. While this may sound foolproof, spammers get around whitelists by spoofing their email address with yours or that of a popular trusted company (Microsoft, Amazon.com, Apple). Bottom line: this method is a necessity to ensure that emails you want do not get blocked.

- *Use Bayesian filtering.* If I know what spam looks like, why can't someone create something that recognizes it? That's the exact reason Bayesian filtering was developed. It works by watching your decision on whether something is spam or not, and then it builds a rule set that mimics your decision process. The more you manage your email, the smarter the Bayesian filter gets until eventually it can pick out spam messages better that you can. Bottom line: this method is a must and works as your own personal email manager.

How Can I Configure My Email Client to Block Spam?

Why go through the trouble of manually blocking spam or buying a program to block spam when your current email program probably has some features to block junk mail. Here's how you can access the junk email features of today's more popular email programs:

- In Microsoft Outlook 2003

    1. Start Outlook.

    2. From the File menu, choose Tools | Options.

    3. Click the Junk E-mail button.

- In Microsoft Outlook Express

    1. Start Outlook Express.

    2. From the File menu, choose Tools | Messages Rules.

    3. Choose Blocked Senders.

- AOL

    1. Start AOL and sign in as a master screen name.

    2. From the toolbar, click Mail | Block Unwanted Mail.

- Eudora (if you are using the paid version of Eudora, you can use SpamWatch to detect and block spam):

    1. Start Eudora.

    2. From the File menu, choose Tools | Options.

    3. Click on the Junk Mail category.

    4. Minimally, ensure that "Automatically place junk in the Junk mailbox" is checked.

- Netscape/Mozilla

    1. Start Netscape/Mozilla.

    2. From the file menu, choose Tools | Junk Mail Controls.

    3. Minimally, ensure that "Enable junk mail controls" is checked.

- Hotmail

    1. Log on to Hotmail and go to your Hotmail inbox.

    2. Click Options | Junk Email Protection | Junk Email Filter.

How Can I Secure My Email Client from Spam?

While your email client may include methods to block spam, it may not be secured to stop spam messages from collecting information about you. Here's how you can configure your email client to stop sending information to spammers:

- *Turn off the preview pane.* By leaving the preview pane on, you let spammers know exactly when you view their messages. When you view or even preview a message, any included images get downloaded from the spammer's web server and displayed. The spammer can then check the server logs to see which images have been downloaded. So how do they know it was you? The spammer usually names each image uniquely for every spam message they send out (for example, 1001.jpg for spam message number 1001). They can just match the name of the image downloaded with the spam message ID (1001.jpg = spam message 1001 = **johndoe@example.com**).

- *Change your email format to text.* By switching to text format, you'll ensure that malicious HTML embedded scripts can't attack your system when you receive email and can't attack a remote system when you send email. Text format also prevents message beaconing and is the preferred format for PDAs.

- *Turn off automatic confirmation.* Spammers can send you an email with the "Request Read Receipt" option turned on. If you have automatic confirmation turned on, your email client will automatically send the spammer an email confirming that you have opened and viewed their email.

- *Turn off automatic replies.* Most email programs provide a way to automatically respond to incoming emails if you are on vacation, out sick, or simply away from your email. The email usually says, "I am out of the office and will return on …" Unfortunately, these types of replies also tell spammers that your email address is valid. If you must use this automatic reply method, you should also set up a rule to send the replies only to people on your whitelist or to co-workers.

What Programs Can Help Block Spam on My PC?

Fighting spam is tough when you're doing it alone. Spammers are constantly coming up with new ways to get your email address, sneak spam into your inbox, and trick you into viewing or clicking on a message. Your email program might include a few antispam features, but it probably doesn't include the more advanced features of a program solely dedicated to blocking spam. Here's a quick set of reviews of the more popular antispam programs:

- *Norton AntiSpam:* This product (also included in the Norton Internet Security Suite) is a spam prevention program that can block or flag spam based on whitelists, blacklists, and filtering. It also contains advanced features such as automatic updates, and it blocks ads and pop-ups when you're surfing the Web. It works as a plug-in for Microsoft Outlook, Outlook Express, and Eudora but can work with any POP3 email account. For more information, visit **www.symantec.com**.

- *McAfee SpamKiller:* This is a spam prevention program that can block or flag spam based on whitelists, blacklists, content filtering, and Bayesian filtering. It also contains advanced features like automatic updates, allowing for custom filters, blocking virus hoaxes, and automatically learning what you consider to be spam. It works as a plug-in for Microsoft Outlook and Outlook Express but can work with any POP3 email account. For more information, visit **http://us.mcafee.com**.

What Can I Do If My PC Is Spamming People?

A spammer's dream would be to not only send spam to every email address they know, but to have each they sent spam to send the spam to every email address they know, and so on. Eventually, that spam could reach every email address on the Internet. The dream has become a reality. While illegal, more and more spammers are writing, or paying hackers to write, viruses to send out their spam. The process works like this:

1. Your machine becomes infected (you opened a virus-infected attachment, or you download and ran a program).

2. The virus scans your computer for an email client.

3. The virus obtains email addresses from your address book, email addresses you have sent mail to, and email addresses from which you have received mail.

4. The virus starts emailing spam to the obtained addresses.

TIP: See Chapter 8 to learn how to detect, prevent, and remove viruses.

How Can I Protect My Email Address when Posting on the Internet?

As discussed previously, spammers use programs called bots to scan the Internet and record any email address found. At one time or another, you may have to post your email address on the Internet (newsgroups, personal website, company website, and so on). Here's how you can post your email address and avoid spam:

- *Use an alternate address.* Using an address dedicated for spam is a surefire way to keep your regular inbox spam free. You can then create a link with a specific subject (for example, **<a href="mailto:mytempaddress@ example.com?subject=My Specific Subject">Email Me</a>**), use a rule to check for that subject, and forward the email to your regular email address.

- *Disguise your address.* Email addresses have a standard format (**emailname@provider.xxx**). This is a format that computers understand. By placing your address in a format that only humans understand, you can prevent a bot from grabbing it. Here are some examples of disguising (or "munging") your email address:

  - johndoe(at)example(dot)com

  - johndoe(insert an @ symbol here)example(insert a . here)com

- *Obfuscate your address.* This changes the address from its standard format (**emailname@provider.xxx**), to a format that is obscured but understood and translated by a web browser:

```
<ahref='&#109;&#97;&#105;&#108;&#116;&#111;&#58;&#101;&#109;
&#97;&#105;&#108;&#110;&#97;&#109;&#101;&#64;&#112;&#114;
&#111;&#118;&#105;&#100;&#101;&#114;&#46;&#120;&#120;
&#120;'>&#101;&#109;&#97;&#105;&#108;&#110;&#97;&#109;
&#101;&#64;&#112;&#114;&#111;&#118;&#105;&#100;&#101;&#114;
&#46;&#120;&#120;&#120;;</a>
```

While the obfuscated email address looks like gibberish, it will be in clear text when viewed by your web browser. This method is becoming less effective as spammers are aware of this technique and they have figured out ways around it. A free online obfuscation tool can be found at **www.fingerlakesbmw.org/main/flobfuscate.php**.

- *Use a script.* Instead of placing a direct link to your email address (**<a href=mailto:johndoe@example.com>Email Me<.a>**), you can use JavaScript to provide the same functionality without having your email address in plain sight:

```
<a style="cursor:hand; text-decoration: underline; color:blue"
onclick="javascript: location='m' + 'ai' + 'lto:' + 'john' + 'doe'
+ '@' + 'example' + '.' + 'com';">Email Me</a>
```

- *Use an image.* More and more websites are utilizing this technique. While bots are smart enough to scan text, they are not smart enough to interpret an email address from an image (such as a JPG, bitmap, or GIF).

- *Don't post your email address.* If you run your own website, you can have others email you through a web form. This prevents bots from retrieving your email address while providing a simple way for your website visitors to still contact you.

How Can I Tell If My Email Address Is Posted on the Internet?

At one point or another, your email address will end up on the Internet. You could have posted a message in a newsgroup, responded to a message in a message board, wrote a product review on Amazon, sold something on eBay®, or even just signed up for something and didn't realize your address would be posted on the Internet. Here's how you can determine if and where your email address if posted on the Internet:

1. Go to **www.google.com**.
2. Enter your email address in the text box and click the Google Search button.
3. If your email address is listed on any Internet web page, it should be displayed to you now.

If you find your email address listed on a web page, you should contact the webmaster of the website and demand they remove it immediately.

You can also search the newsgroups to see if your email address is posted there:

1. Go to **www.google.com** and click on the Groups link on the top of the page.
2. Enter your email address in the text box and click the Google Search button.
3. If your email address is listed in any newsgroup posting, it should be displayed to you now.

Unfortunately, you cannot have your email address removed from a newsgroup posting. These postings do not reside on one server; they are replicated to every news server the moment they are posted. Once the message has been posted, the server does not allow updates to the posting.

What Should I Do If I Need to Give My Email Address to a Source I Don't Fully Trust?

Whether you are purchasing a product or simply want to read an article online, everyone seems to require your email address first. While giving your email address to a respectable website (such as Amazon.com) is not an issue, you may be concerned about giving your email address to a website you don't fully know or trust. Here are a few ways to avoid giving your email address to an unknown source but still be allowed to purchase a product or view a service:

- *Use a public email address.* Free email services such as Hotmail and Yahoo Mail allow you to sign up for a new email address that you can use online.

- *Use Mailinantor.com.* This is a free service that allows you to use throwaway email addresses for websites that require an email address. All you have to do is enter **<whateveryouwant>@mailiniator.com** and your emails will be sent to that address. Then you go to Mailinator.com, enter the email address you made up, and you can read the emails sent to that address. Pretty cool.

How Can I Prevent Spam on My PDA?

Email on a PDA has its own set of problems—retrieval is slow, storage is limited, and viewing is odd due to the PDA's small screen and or lack of support for HTML-formatted email messages. You don't need spam adding to the mix. Here's how you can help prevent and combat spam on your PDA:

- *Pocket SpamFilter:* This is the first antispam software for the Pocket PC. Some of its advanced features include whitelists, blacklists, and custom filters. You can order or find out more information about Pocket SpamFilter at **www.pocketpcsoft.com**.

- *Client-side software:* Use client-side software such as Outlook and leave your mail on the server for a few days.

How Can I Prevent Spam on My Cell Phone?

Cell phone spam, or spim, is a new annoyance that can cause you extreme aggravation and money. While most methods to prevent spam on a computer are used while the email is being delivered, you want to stop the spam before it hits your cell phone so you aren't charged for airtime or email/text messaging fees and so you're not bothered while you're out and about. Most cell phone providers supply options to prevent text messages originating from the Web or email or allow text messages to come only from other phones. Contact your cell phone provider for more information.

How Can I Prevent Spim through Windows Messenger?

Windows Messenger Service is not an instant messaging program, but rather a service used by the operating system, programs, and administrators to send simple pop-up messages to remote users (see Figure 7.2). Spammers can also send these pop-ups to your computer if your computer is not properly secured by a firewall. Here are some ways to prevent Windows messenger spam:

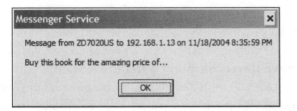

Figure 7.2

Windows Messenger spam.

- *Use a firewall.* A properly configured firewall will allow communication on only trusted ports (windows to the outside world) and prevent communication on nontrusted ports (Windows Messenger ports).

- *Disable Windows Messenger Service:*
  1. Click Start | Run, type **services.msc**, and click OK.
  2. Right-click on the messenger service and select Properties.
  3. Change the startup type to Disabled and click OK.

NOTE: *Windows Messenger Service is disabled by default on Windows XP Service Pack 2 and Windows 2003 machines.*

WARNING! If you are receiving Windows Messenger spim, either you do not have a firewall or it is not properly configured. This should be a bigger concern than the spim because a missing or improperly configured firewall will allow hackers to steal your files, crash your computer, and basically do whatever they want.

How Can I Prevent Spam Messages from Myself?

One tactic spammers use is to spoof your email address and send emails using your address. When this happens, most antispam methods are fooled into allowing the message to go straight through to your inbox. Why? Because it's you! If you're like most people, you don't often send yourself email. To prevent all emails from your email address from arriving in your inbox using Microsoft Outlook, do the following:

1. Start Outlook. From the file menu, select Tools and then Rules and Alerts.

2. Click "Create a new rule," and under Step 1, leave the default selection "move messages from someone to a folder."

3. Under Step 2, click "people or distribution list."

4. In the From field, type your email address and click OK.

5. Under Step 2, click on "specified."

6. Select the Junk-Email folder and click OK.

7. Click Finish.

8. When returned back to the Rules and Alerts dialog, click OK.

You can test your new rule by sending yourself an email and watching it go straight to the Junk-Email folder.

HORROR STORY! Despite what your local gossip column tells you, the King is dead and he's not coming back. So how could you receive a spam from yourself and Elvis? Spammers use a technique called *spoofing* to hide their true email address and replace it with a fake one. By modifying the message header, they can make it appear like the email came from Elvis, the pope, and even you. To see who the message really came from, see the section "How Can I Trace Spam to its True Sender?" later in this chapter.

What Is the Best Spam Attack Plan I Can Use?

We wish we had a foolproof plan to prevent spam in the first place, but we have learned that this will never happen. So the best you can do is to divert the spam away from your inbox (quarantine it, if you will). With our inbox free of spam, we can leisurely and safely check our Spam folder for any messages we would like to keep. So, what's our secret? We don't use antipam software or hardware. We simply use Microsoft Outlook 2003 and follow these guidelines:

- *Change to "safe lists only."* "With this option turned on, only emails from a safe sender or emails simultaneously sent to you and a safe recipient are allowed to enter your inbox and all other email addresses are already treated as a blocked sender and is routed to your Junk-E-mail folder. To set this option, follow these steps:

1. Start Outlook.

2. From the File menu, select Tools and then Options.

3. Click the Junk E-mail button.

4. From the Options tab, select Safe Lists Only and click OK.

- *Specify your "safe senders."* Any email sent from an address listed in your safe senders list is automatically allowed to go into your inbox. This is your whitelist. You can add an entire email address (**johndoe@example.com**) or an entire domain (**@example.com**). You can add a safe sender by following these steps:

  1. Start Outlook

  2. From the File menu, select Tools and then Options.

  3. Click the Junk E-mail button.

  4. From the Safe Senders tab, you can add, edit, export, import, or remove safe senders.

  You can also add a safe sender quickly by clicking the Not Junk button when viewing messages in your Junk E-mail folder.

- *Specify your "safe recipients."* Any email sent to you and someone else's email address that are in your safe recipients list are automatically allowed to go into your inbox. For example, if an email is sent to you and your boss, you can assume that you're both on the same spam list or, more likely, that you can automatically trust that email because chances are it's business related. Same goes for emails sent to you and a family member, you and a close friend, or you and anyone you trust. This is your smart whitelist. You can add an entire email address (**johndoe@example.com**) or an entire domain (**@example.com**). You can add a safe recipient by following these steps:

  1. Start Outlook

  2. From the File menu, select Tools and then Options.

  3. Click the Junk E-mail button.

  4. From the Safe Recipients tab, you can add, edit, export, import, or remove safe recipients.

You can also add a safe sender quickly by clicking on the Not Junk button when viewing messages in your Junk E-mail folder. When the Mark as Not Junk dialog box appears, check the specific email address listed under "Always trust e-mail sent to the following addresses."

- *Do not bother specifying "blocked senders."* Since only emails from a safe sender or emails simultaneously sent to a safe recipient are allowed to enter your inbox, all other email addresses are already treated as a blocked sender and are routed to your Junk E-mail folder.

- Follow the instructions listed in the section "How Can I Prevent Spam Messages from Myself?" earlier in this chapter.

Can I Have Spam Automatically Deleted Instead of Just Moving It?

Automatically deleting anything is a bad idea. Imagine automatically shredding every piece of mail that was delivered to your home that you didn't recognize. You might destroy something you didn't expect, like a rebate check, a bill, or a letter from a long-lost friend. The same goes for email. By moving it out of your inbox and into another folder, you get the manageable inbox you deserve and you can safely filter through the rest at your leisure.

How Can I Prevent My Emails from Being Flagged as Spam?

With antispam and antivirus programs intercepting messages, you can no longer assume that your email will reach its recipient, especially when sending email to people you've never emailed before. The following list explains a few steps you can take to help prevent your email from being flagged as spam:

- *Always use a subject.* Most antispam routines and some email recipients flag messages without subjects as spam. After all, if the point of an email is described in the Subject field and that field is blank, that indicates to the recipient that there is no point to the email, so they might as well just trash it.

- *Be careful what you put in the subject line.* Avoid using phrases that might get caught by a spam filer, such as "Here's a money-making opportunity you can't ignore," "Get a better rate on your mortgage now," or "Please your girlfriend all night long." Subject lines are examined closely by spam filters and then by anyone who scans their emails.

- *Only send attachments when necessary.* Most antispam and antivirus programs prevent certain (if not all) types of attachments from being delivered to recipients.

- *Always zip your attachments.* Some antispam and antivirus programs will block certain types of attachments (such as EXE, BAT, CMD, PIF files). This is to protect the user from blindly opening an attachment. Zipping an attachment will not only decrease the chance of your email being mistaken for spam, it will also reduce its size, which benefits everyone (it's faster and requires less storage space).

NOTE: *Most antispam and antivirus programs are smart enough to search within ZIP files for the specific file types they wish to block. Always ask the recipient about their ability to receive attachments before sending one.*

- *Always send follow-up emails when you send emails with attachments.* Since more and more antispam and antivirus programs are quarantining attachments (even if they are "safe"), you can no longer assume that the recipient received your message.

- *Do not to use public email providers.* Free email providers like Hotmail.com provide spammers with an unlimited number of email accounts to spam from. These email servers may be blocked by most businesses and a few ISPs.

- *Avoid sending emails to a large number of users at the same time.* Most antispam software will consider email sent to a large number of users as spam. While there may be times you need to send the same message to a large audience, you should send the emails in small groups, if not individually. The individual email adds a personal touch that most people appreciate anyway.

- *Use plain-text format.* HTML format may allow you to send prettier emails, but it also allows spammers and hackers to embed malicious code. Some antivirus and antispam software may block your email even if one HTML tag is malformed. Besides being blocked, most PDAs (Pocket PC, BlackBerry®, and so on) cannot properly view HTML-formatted emails.

- *Don't use profanity.* Even if you didn't intentionally swear, abbreviations and others words out of context mat be interpreted as a swear word. For example, the phrase "I will have my business ass. take a look at it" could be flagged because the wrong abbreviation for the word *associate* was used (the correct abbreviation is *assoc.*).

- *Ask the recipient to add you to their whitelist.* Whitelists provide a way for the recipient to always trust email from your specific address.

- *Always inform recipients of email address changes.* If you are going to change your email address (new ISP, domain, job, and so on), inform your recipients of your new address prior to using it. The recipient may have to put your new address on and take your old address off a whitelist (or inform their email administrator to do so).

I've Tried Everything to Stop Spam, so Now What?

If you've tried everything but can't seem to stop the spam, your best recourse is to start over with a new email address and follow the recommendations listed earlier to prevent this new address from being listed in a spammer database. While this method is effective, it's not always convenient. Maybe you like your email address, maybe it would be difficult to let everyone know your email address is changing, or maybe you just feel like you are throwing in the towel by changing your email address to stop the spam. We agree with all these concerns, but if the spam you receive has gotten out of control, don't waste your time fighting a losing battle.

If you need to get a new email address, here are some smart tips to follow:

- *Make a good transition plan.* Once you decide that you really need a new address, plan out your process for letting everyone you communicate with know. Don't just switch over to a new address and tell everyone later. Secure your new address and then select a date in the future when you plan to start using it. Let everyone know at least a month in advance. Compile a list of everyone you work with or socialize with and let them know about your transition.

- *Don't retire your old address too quickly.* Keep your old address active as you try to let everyone know about your new address. Each time you get email at your old address, send a reminder about your address change.

- *Don't sign up for anything on the Web for a while.* Don't even sign up for newsletters at trusted sites. Keep your new email clean and clutter free as long as you can so that you can focus on receiving important emails that are sent by people you work with or socialize with. This will help you determine if everyone who needs to be communicating with you is sending email to your new address.

Fighting Back

- Learn how to determine the sender of a spam message.
- Learn how to fight back against spam by fooling their collection methods and reporting them to an ISP or the authorities.

Defense, defense, defense. When can we take a position of offense with spammers? Spammers are a new kind of scum, thinking they can do whatever they want to whomever they want. Well, they were wrong. This section will teach you how to obtain the true identity of the spammer and how to properly let them know that spam is not something you will tolerate.

How Can I Trace Spam to Its True Sender?

Most spammers use various tactics to forge the From and Reply To email address as well as falsify the delivery information in the message header. They do this to avoid being reported to their email provider, avoid listening to your complaints, bypass your antispam methods, or pretend to be someone else in order to defraud you. To view where the spammer wants all replies sent, follow the instructions outlined in the next section, "How Can I View an Email Message Header?" Once you have the header, it may look like this (extra information omitted):

```
Return-Path: <joespammer@example.com>
Reply-To: <joespammer@example.com>
From: "Bill Gates" <billgates@microsoft.com>
```

As you can see, the spammer wants you to think the email is coming from Bill Gates, when in fact all replies will be sent to **joespammer@example.com**.

NOTE: *This method works only if the spammer wants to receive email replies.*

How Can I View an Email Message Header?

Here's how you can display the message header with some of the more popular email clients:

- In Hotmail:
    1. Log on and click the Options tab.
    2. Click the Mail Display Settings link.
    3. Set the Message Headers option to Fill and click the OK button.

- In Yahoo Mail:
    1. Log on and click the Mail tab and then choose Options.
    2. Click General Preferences.
    3. Under Headers, select to show all headers and then click the Save button.

- In Microsoft Outlook 2003:
    1. Right-click on the email message and select Options.
    2. The header will be displayed in the Internet Headers text box.

- In Microsoft Outlook Express:
    1. Right-click on the email message and select Properties.
    2. Click the details tab to see the header.

- In Netscape: Depending on your version, you can either:
  - Click Options | Show Headers | All.
  - Click View | Headers | All

TIP: For a complete list, go to **www.haltabuse.org/help/headers/**.

How Can I Fight Back against Spam?

Fighting back against spammers can be an all day, every day event. While you might not find the need or the time to fight back against every spammer, there will always be that one spammer that annoys you enough to force you into action. Here are a few techniques you can follow to fight back against spam:

- *Use Poison.* OK, poisoning the actual spammer is illegal, but poisoning their bot program is not. WPoison is a free CGI script that detects when a bot is trying to scan your website and dynamically writes tons of fake email addresses and links. You can find more information about WPoison at **www.monkeys.com/wpoison/**.

- *Report the spammer to the authorities.* Pornography, racism, and sexual harassment by email is a punishable crime. If you receive any of these types of email, do not delete the message and contact the FBI.

- *Report the spammer to your ISP.* The best way to fight a spammer is to report them to your ISP, demand that the ISP take action, and follow up to see what happened.

Summary

If you've been fighting spam alone, it can sometimes feel like you're drowning in a sea of unwanted emails. It's not an easy battle and it's only going to get worse. This chapter has taught you how to deal with all kinds of spam disasters and mishaps. Your ISP and IT staff may be able to help you combat spam, if you only ask. You can take matters into your own hands by using antispam software to automatically keep your inbox clean. Besides purchasing antispam software, you can use features of your existing email software to keep spam out. You need to focus not only on protecting your inbox, but on protecting your email address as well. We taught you our personal spam fighting techniques in the hopes that you can use them to keep your inbox spam free (well, almost). Finally, you learned how to trace the true sender of these spam messages and report them to the proper authorities.

8

Surviving Viruses

Disasters to avoid:

- Getting a virus that can keep your PC from booting up.
- Catching a bad virus because you forgot to activate your antivirus software.

Mishaps and blunders to run from:

- Losing your antivirus protection because your software has expired.
- Accidentally sending a virus to your friends and co-workers.

Viruses are the biggest threat to digital network devices. At the rate things are going, it's only a matter of time until your PC gets a virus that corrupts your data, your MP3 player gets a virus that erases all your music, or your cell phone gets a virus that makes prank calls to all of your saved phone numbers. Once you get your first virus, your entire attitude toward virus protection changes.

Viruses are mysterious creatures. On one hand, we are angered by their damaging effects when they cause us to lose work, waste time, and crash our PCs. On the other hand, we are amazed by how quickly they spread and how damaging and how devious they can be.

This chapter will tell you what you really need to know about viruses. It will help you prevent viruses from attacking your equipment and show you how to get rid of a virus quickly if one unexpectedly gets you. Viruses can be really tricky, so there's a lot of ground to cover. Our goal is to make sure that you are really prepared so that you can greatly minimize the potential disasters and mishaps that can be caused by viruses.

Virus Hazards

- Learn what viruses can do.
- Learn how you can get a virus.
- Learn how virus hoaxes can cause real disasters.
- Learn how you can get a virus on your PDA or cell phone.

What Do I Really Need to Know about Viruses?

A virus is basically a computer program, but not a good one by any means. They can be small or large, simple or complex, written in any kind of language (batch, script, compiled, and so on). The one design feature that all viruses have in common is that they must be able to replicate. Unlike most biological viruses, technical viruses do not occur naturally; they have to be created by someone. A technical virus infects a host (computer, phone, PDA), spreads infection rapidly, and can move to other hosts just as quickly. Once a device is infected, its files and even hardware are susceptible to damage.

There are many myths that have been spread about viruses, so let's dispel them first:

- *Virus-writing is complicated.* Although some complex viruses have been written, most are very simple programs. Virus writers are usually people interested in and just starting programming, so the simplicity of these programs is no surprise.

- *Virus writers are all teenagers.* This is a very commonly-believed myth. We realize how easy it is to associate viruses with vandalism and blame it all on the youth. The average virus writer is someone who just completed college or is just starting their first real job as opposed to someone in high school.

- *All viruses are damaging.* While this may be true for the most part, not all viruses do harm. Some are designed to spread a message, give a greeting on a certain date, fight other viruses, or be just plain annoying.

- *Running antivirus software will always protect you.* This is a trap that can cost you. Using antivirus software is a good start, but there are many reasons why merely having it installed is just not enough. Antivirus software must be running, have the latest engine and signatures, have a valid subscription, and be properly configured. See the section on using antivirus software later in this chapter.

- *Viruses infect only programs and Office documents.* While viruses typically infect programs and Office documents, some viruses target pictures, music, emails, and movie files.

- *Viruses can harm only software.* This is often the case, but viruses can also be damaging to your hardware. There are several ways a virus can cause hardware damage:

  - Overclock a CPU, causing it to overheat
  - Turn off system fans, causing your CPU, hard drive, or other components to overheat
  - Change resolution and refresh rates, causing damage to your monitor or video card
  - Drain battery life with extra processing

HORROR STORY! I (Jesse) can still remember our first virus attack. It was the summer of '94. While sitting indoors booting up the computer to play a new game, *Leisure Suit Larry 6,* the worst happened. The PC was attacked by a boot virus and the computer would not boot up. Apparently, the virus had been on the system for months, infecting the computer and every floppy disk that touched it. Angrily, I raced to the local computer store and bought antivirus software. A few hours, a few dollars, and 200 hundred wasted floppies later, the computer was back but all of the data was lost.

What Types of Viruses Do I Need to Watch Out For?

Most people place all viruses into two categories—the bad and the ugly. Actually, there are many types of viruses, depending on how and where they attack. Here are the types of viruses that can cause you problems:

- *Retro:* These viruses are designed to attack antivirus software. They can circumvent or disable antivirus software and then do their real damage without you being notified.

- *Boot sector:* These viruses are designed to attack the first sector of bootable media, known as the boot sector. The boot sector instructs the media how to load. On your computer's main hard drive, the boot sector is what actually starts your operating system (Windows, Linux, and so on). Once the boot sector becomes infected, it will infect any other boot sectors it can touch (hard drives, floppy disks, Zip drives) and will render the media unbootable.

- *BIOS:* The BIOS (basic input/output system) is an area of memory in your computer that controls everything (keyboard, mouse, hard drives, CD-ROMs, video cards, and so on). Once a virus infects your BIOS, it can render your system completely useless, even requiring you to send your computer in for repair.

- *File:* File viruses are the most common types of viruses. They infect existing files (sometimes replacing them), causing the virus to load into memory whenever you execute an infected file.

- *Macros:* Macros are code embedded in Office documents (Excel, Word, Access) to automate certain tasks. Virus writers place their malicious code inside these macros, where they have the capability to spread to other documents.

- *Worms:* While regular viruses spread on the local device, worms are viruses that spread quickly and infect other systems through existing networks (the Internet, home networks, work networks).

- *Trojan horses:* These are viruses pretending to be normal applications, while performing their destructive behavior behind the scenes. For example, the trojan horse may be a game that deletes your files while you play. Not very fun, is it?

What Can a Virus Do to Me If I'm Not Careful?

Ultimately, it can do anything a mean person could do:

- *Attack files:* Viruses can delete or corrupt existing files. They can also fill up your computer with worthless files.

- *Attack email:* Viruses can read your email, email from anyone and everyone (both people you know and people you don't), and even turn your computer into a post office, allowing the virus writer to send mail through your computer (relaying).

- *Damage hardware:* Viruses can damage your hardware and any device connected.

- *Steal personal data:* Viruses can steal your personal data and information (including passwords and credit card numbers). See the sections on identity theft in Chapter 1.

- *Kill relationships:* A virus can send itself to anyone from your PC (sometimes even including your name in the email or message). Sending virus-infected files to friends and associates can be harmful to your relationship.

- *Annoy the heck out of you:* Viruses may cause your system to reboot continuously, cause it to not boot up at all, display rude or annoying messages, and much more.

How Do I Know if I Have a Virus or I'm Just a Victim of a Virus Hoax?

A virus hoax is exactly what it sounds like: a rumor about a virus that does not exist. Most virus hoaxes are spread via email, but they can also be spread by word of mouth. The email usually describes the virus, the damage it does, and the action you must immediately take to prevent it. So why would someone send you a fake virus alert? It's a prank. The alert describes some terrible virus (the scare tactic) and asks you to take action. The action can be anything from deleting system files to downloading virus-infected files. The alert is sent to cause you and those you know to damage your computers (just as a virus would, but without the effort of writing one).

HORROR STORY! We had a friend who was concerned he had a virus because his computer had been running slowly. He had recently installed new software, which had likely done some things to his computer to slow it done, but he didn't know that. Somehow he convinced himself that he had a virus lurking on his computer. So when he received an email alert a few days later about a nasty virus that was being circulated, he took the hoax way too seriously. He followed the instructions in the hoax email he received and he ended up deleting files on his computer that would later keep the computer from booting. The sad thing is that he also told a few of his friends who ended up following his advice and doing the same thing. The lesson: Don't become an easy victim of a hoax and don't spread virus warnings unless you receive one from a very trusted source.

How Can I Get Infected by a Virus?

Despite how careful you are (visiting safe websites, not giving out your email address, downloading files from a trusted source, and so on), one day you will get a virus. In fact, it's more likely that you will get a virus a couple times a year (we do). Here are the common ways you can get a virus:

- *Bad neighbors:* If your PC is connected to a network (the Internet, home network, work network), another computer can send you a virus (intentionally or unintentionally).

- *Exposed vulnerabilities:* Software companies (like Microsoft) release patches regularly to fix recently discovered issues. Sometimes the issue can be as simple as a misspelled word in a help file, but most times it's to fix a security issue that makes your system vulnerable to viruses and hacker attacks.

- *File transfers:* Since viruses can attach themselves to files, you can get a virus on any file you touch. Downloading files from questionable websites is a common way to get a virus, but you can also get viruses from installation media, files emailed from friends, newly-installed applications, and removable media (floppies, CDs, and so on).

- *Email:* Email is a very common way for virus writers to spread their viruses to others. While the virus writer could spread these viruses manually by sending a virus-infected email to everyone they know, it is more common for the virus writer to infect systems so that they automatically send out infected emails.

- *P2P programs:* P2P programs allow a way for virus writers to easily spread their viruses around the world. Virus writers will name their viruses with the same names as today's most popular downloads (newsong.mp3.vbs, newmovie.avi.com, newprogram.exe.bat), share them, and then wait for someone looking for their favorite song, movie, or program to download and run their virus. See Chapter 15 for more information on this topic.

- *Freeware, shareware, and pirated software:* Always be cautious when someone gives you something for free. Although most freeware and shareware are virus free, some are purposely designed to give you the functionality you desire while installing a virus or Trojan horse in the background (Back Orifice being the most popular). People who contribute to piracy by sharing pirated software have no quarrels about including viruses in the software. See Chapter 15 for more information on this topic.

Can I Get a Virus on My Cell Phone?

Email is a common communication method that allows virus writers to spread their creations with multiple users quickly. It only makes sense that the next target would be the cell phone. The Cabir virus is the first virus for the cell phone. It works by scanning for other Bluetooth-enabled devices and replicating itself to any device in range. It's only a matter of time until more viruses follow.

Can I Get a Virus on My PDA or PDA-Enabled Cell Phone?

If you own a PDA or PDA-enabled cell phone (smart phone, Pocket PC, Palm, BlackBerry, and so on), then you are just as vulnerable to viruses as with a computer. The Duts virus (WinCE4.Duts) is the first Pocket PC virus that infects devices with the ARM processor. The Palm.Liberty.A is the first virus for the Palm OS and works by deleting installed applications. Since most people use their PDAs as a digital wallet, you can assume that more and more virus writers will be targeting PDAs.

TIP: A hard reset should clear your PDA of any viruses, but by then the damage is done.

Help, I'm Infected

- Learn how to tell if you really have a virus.
- Learn how to quickly remove a basic virus.
- Learn how to remove nasty viruses such as boot sector viruses.

How Can I Tell If I Really Have a Virus?

When you catch a biological virus, you show symptoms (coughing, sneezing). When your PC gets a virus, you'll likely encounter symptoms like these:

- *Your antivirus software won't work.* This software will likely not start or stay running. We'll look at antivirus software in more detail in the next section.
- *Your computer is running extremely slower than usual.*
- *You'll experience boot-up problems.* Your computer refuses to boot or takes a long time to start up.

- *Your PC is much busier than usual.*

- *You receive strange errors from your system or antivirus software.*

- *Your PC freezes unexpectedly.* Your system or programs that normally ran fine now have periods when they do not respond (freeze).

- *Your computer reboots for no reason.*

- *You receive an email attachment that has a double extension (mypicture.jpg.exe).*

- *Mysterious emails are received.* Your friends, co-workers, or families inform you that they have received an email virus or strange email from you and you did not send it.

HORROR STORY! While there are no official records of a computer virus being a direct cause of death, it's not unreasonable to think that a tech virus can kill you. In August 2003, the Yorkhill Hospital in Glaskow was hit with the Nachi worm, affecting about 1,000 network devices. While the virus damage did not affect any patients, it could have easily affected life support systems, incubators, and other systems critical to the survival of patients. In May 2004, British Airways had to delay 20 flights due to the Sasser virus interfering with its flight map software. Although the flights were delayed before the damage would affect in-air flights, the virus could have easily caused issues with take-off, landing, traffic control, or in-flight navigation. Sadly, it's only a matter of time until the first virus-related death is officially recorded.

How Can I Quickly Remove a Virus from My PC?

OK, don't panic. If you quickly take the correct steps now, you'll stop further infection dead in its tracks. You'll also keep the virus from spreading to others. Here is the smart action plan to avoid any further disaster:

1. *Make sure your antivirus software is running.* If you don't have antivirus software, make sure you carefully read the section "General PC Virus Prevention—Using Antivirus Software." Antivirus software is easy to get, install, and use, so what are you waiting for? If you're really tight on cash, you can obtain free or trial software.

2. *Listen to what your antivirus software is telling you.* If your antivirus software informed you that a virus has been detected, you should be in good hands. Follow the instructions your antivirus software gives you rather than performing the remaining steps in this section.

3. *Check your network situation.* If your computer is part of a work or school network, inform your local tech support department *Then disconnect from the network as soon as you can.* Listen and perform the steps the tech

support people want you to perform rather than performing the remaining steps in this section.

4. *Disconnect from your network.* If the virus is a worm, the best way to stop it from spreading to other computers is to disconnect your PC from the network (that includes wireless networks as well).

5. *Run a full antivirus scan.* If you have antivirus software installed and up-to-date, run a complete virus scan on all your drives.

6. *Get rid of the infected file or email.* If you know which file or email is distributing the virus, delete it immediately. Don't forget to empty the Recycle Bin.

How Can I Remove a Boot Sector Virus?

Up until now we've been focusing on common viruses that are typically distributed through file transfers and emails. These are the types of viruses that impact your data files and operating system files. You can also get more deadly types of viruses known as boot sector viruses that can affect your PC at a very low level. Once your PC is infected with a boot sector virus, your system will be unusable until you rewrite the infected boot sector. Here are several techniques you can use to recover your system from a boot sector virus. Keep in mind that solving a problem like this can get a little tricky, so it's a good idea to get someone who has lots of technical knowledge to help you (unless you are already an expert):

- *Use your antivirus software.* Your antivirus software CD may be bootable and allow you to remove boot sector viruses. Consult your software documentation or manufacturer for more information.

- *Use FDISK /MBR.* If you can obtain a boot disk for your operating system, you can use it to rewrite the infected master boot record. Write-protect the boot disk, set the computer to boot from a floppy, and then boot from the disk. When you get to a point when you can enter a command, run the command FDISK /MBR.

- *Use the recovery console.* If your computer is running Windows 2000 and up (XP, 2003, and so on), you'll have access to the recovery console, a mechanism for recovering critical system failures. For Windows 2000, boot from your Windows 2000 installation CD and choose "Repair a Windows 2000 installation" and then "…repair…using the recovery console." For Windows XP, boot from your Windows XP CD and choose "…repair…using the recovery console." Once you are in the recovery console, run the command FIXMBR.

WARNING! Fooling around with your master boot code can make your drive inaccessible. You should always use an antivirus program first and the fixes mentioned in this section as a last resort.

What Should I Do If a Virus Has Damaged My PC?

As careful as you might be, a virus may still slip through the cracks and damage your files or system. If you take the correct steps, you may be able to fix corruption and get your system back to normal. Here's how you can quickly recover from virus damage:

- *Use your antivirus software.* By the end of this chapter, we'll probably sound like a broken record when it comes to using antivirus software, but that's because this software is so important. Your antivirus software may be able to fix the damage caused by viruses. This applies to both system files and your personal data files. Always use this as your first avenue of recovery.

- *Visit your antivirus software vendor's website.* You antivirus software vendor may provide additional tools for removing or recovering from the offending virus. See their website for more information.

- *Run Windows System Restore.* If the virus has only attacked system files, you may able to undo the damage by performing a system restore. See Chapter 13 for more information.

- *Restore from backup.* This should be your last point of recovery after trying everything else. Only restore from backup once your system is virus free. Restoring when a virus is still present on your system may cause your restored files to become infected.

General PC Virus Prevention—Using Antivirus Software

- Learn about antivirus software.
- Learn how antivirus software works.
- Learn how to ensure that your antivirus software is protecting you.

How Can I Protect Myself from General PC Viruses?

Virus writers are getting smarter and viruses are getting more difficult to detect. Fortunately, companies have gotten really good at creating effective antivirus software (and keeping it updated) that you can use on a regular basis to keep viruses from infecting your PC. Using the latest antivirus software is always going to be your best prevention method.

Most antivirus programs work silently in the background and receive updates automatically. They provide a scan engine that uses virus definitions to examine files and determine if they are infected by a virus. The scan engine can also determine if your PC or a specific program is showing signs of infection. The virus definitions are the key to identifying known viruses. They contain information on what viruses, running processes, and infected files look like.

Antivirus software typically detects viruses by either examining file headers or reading data inside files. Today's viruses dynamically change their headers and encrypt this data, which makes detection extremely difficult if not impossible. They also alter their behavior (mutate) and attack critical system processes, making detection and removal even more difficult. While antivirus software vendors scramble to release a virus definition when a new virus comes out, your system remains vulnerable to attack. This is the main reason you should always use antivirus software that updates itself frequently.

What Does Antivirus Software Protect?

In order to be effective, antivirus software must be able to protect every method by which a virus can enter your system. Some of these entry points can include:

- *Files:* Your files will be scanned on demand or automatically scanned as they are being accessed. Automatically scanning files is called *real-time scanning* or *auto-protection* and should always be enabled.

- *Email:* Your emails will be scanned as they are being sent and received. This means that you are not only protected from viruses being sent to you, but also from sending viruses to others. (Your friends and family will thank you!).

- *Removable media:* Your removable media will be scanned when accessed. This is extremely important if you use floppies, CDs, and so on that have been in or have files from other systems.

- *Macros in Microsoft Office documents:* When opening an office document that contains macros, the macros will be scanned for viruses and malicious code. While you may not think it, macro viruses can be very destructive (since they can contain all sorts of code).

What Are the Limitations of Antivirus Software?

Antivirus software has its share of problems (just like any other software):

- *Constant updates:* Antivirus software is only as good as its last update. Updates ensure that the software is able to prevent, detect, and remove known viruses and virus-like processes.

- *False positives:* Occasionally, antivirus software will incorrectly flag clean files as viruses.

- *Software installation:* Installing software may cause many changes to your system in a short amount of time. Antivirus software may accidentally see this activity, determine it's a virus, and block or corrupt the installation.

WARNING! Many software installations instruct you to disable your antivirus software before installing the software. Take strong caution before disabling your antivirus software because it leaves you wide open to infection.

What Are the Most Popular Antivirus Products?

With viruses plaguing our systems, it's no wonder that there is also a sea of available antivirus products. Before purchasing any antivirus software product, you should check the levels of protection offered, the ease of use, what others think of it, the resources it takes (how much slower it will make your system), and of course, the price. Here are our choices of the most popular antivirus products:

- *Norton AntiVirus:* The captain of reliability. It offers protection against viruses, spyware, and keyloggers, as well as automatic updating. Price: $49.95. For more info, visit **www.symantec.com**.

- *McAfee VirusScan:* The second most popular antivirus product. Some of the features included are protection against viruses, spyware, and keyloggers and automatic updating. Price: $34.95. For more info, visit **http://us.mcafee.com/**.

- *PC-cillin Internet Security:* A software suite that includes a firewall and acts as an antispam and antivirus program. Some of the antivirus features included are protection against viruses, spyware, keyloggers and automatic updating; it also offers PDA virus protection. Price: $49.95. For more info, visit **www.trendmicro.com**.

Should I Use the Antivirus Software That Came with My PC?

Most computer manufacturers bundle antivirus software with a computer. Unfortunately, most bundle versions are only trial versions that expire in 60 to 90 days. Most people aren't even aware of this and just assume they are protected. Always check if your version is about to expire. You may be able to renew your antivirus software without uninstalling existing software or installing new software.

How Can I Tell If My Antivirus Definitions Are Up-to-Date?

Your antivirus software needs to continually obtain the latest virus definition to be able to detect and remove today's virus threats. If your virus definitions are a month old, then you are not protected against any virus that came out in the last month. Here's how to see if your antivirus software has obtained the latest virus definitions:

- Norton AntiVirus

  1. Start Norton AntiVirus.

  2. By default, Norton AntiVirus displays the status page at startup. You should see the date of the installed virus definitions from here. Figure 8.1 shows an example.

- McAfee VirusScan

  1. Right-click the McAfee system tray icon.

  2. Choose VirusScan Professional and then About.

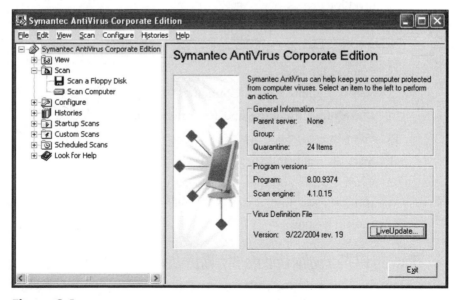

Figure 8.1

Virus definition file date.

3. The definition date is listed as the DAT file creation date.

- PC-cillin Internet Security
    1. Start PC-cillin Internet Security.
    2. Click on the Update tab.
    3. Click the Manual update link.
    4. You should now see the last update date of the antivirus component.

NOTE: *Antivirus software manufacturers release their virus definitions at different intervals. Sometimes they do it every few hours and other times they do it every few days. If your definitions are over a few days old, you should be concerned and either automatically or manually update your virus definitions (as described in the next two sections).*

How Can I Enable Automatic Update for My Virus Definitions?

To enable, verify, or modify your antivirus software's update settings, follow one of these sets of instructions:

- Norton AntiVirus

    By default, Norton AntiVirus automatically updates virus definitions through your Internet connection. To modify this feature from Control Panel (Start | Settings | Control Panel), double-click Symantec LiveUpdate.

- McAfee VirusScan
    1. Right-click the McAfee system tray icon.
    2. Choose Updates.
    3. When prompted, click Configure.
    4. Make sure "Install the updates automatically" is selected.

- PC-cillin Internet Security
    1. Start PC-cillin Internet Security.
    2. Click Update and then Update Setting.
    3. If the Enable Intelligent Update check box is not checked, select it and click Apply.

How Can I Manually Update My Virus Definitions?

Although your antivirus software may automatically update itself, it does that on a set schedule. If a new virus just came out, it may be hours or days before your receive the virus definition to defeat it. Here's how you can manually update your virus definitions:

- Norton AntiVirus
    1. Start Norton AntiVirus.
    2. Click the Live Update button.
    3. Follow the instructions given to update your Symantec products (including virus definitions).
- McAfee VirusScan
    1. Right-click the icon in the system tray and choose Updates.
    2. Click Check Now when prompted.
    3. Click Update if there is a new update for you to install.
- PC-cillin Internet Security
    1. Start PC-cillin Internet Security.
    2. Click Update Now.

How Can I Verify That My Antivirus Is Working?

Once antivirus software is installed, most people forget it even exists. This is great for productivity, but it's really bad for security. While most antivirus software will attempt to notify you if it is not working properly, you must be able to recognize the signs when it happens. Here's what you should be on the lookout for:

- Norton AntiVirus
    - You should see the program icon in the system tray.
    - The program icon in the system tray should not have a red x on it.
    - You can also start the program and see the status of each component.
- McAfee VirusScan
    - You should see the program icon in the system tray.
    - The icon should be red; it should never be black.
    - You can also start the McAfee SecurityCenter and then click the antivirus icon.
- PC-cillin Internet Security
    - You should see the program icon in the system tray.
    - The icon should have a lightning bolt that is red in the middle, not white.

- You can also start the program, click on the status tab, and then click the antivirus status icon.

Why Won't My Antivirus Software Work?

If your system's antivirus software isn't working, it's just like having no antivirus protection at all. Until you get your antivirus program operational again, your system is susceptible to all viruses. Here's how you can quickly troubleshoot why your antivirus software is not working:

- *Is this thing on?* Oops! Try to start the program and see if you get any error messages that provide more information. See the previous section to determine if your antivirus program is working.

- *Are your running a trial version?* If you bought a new PC and it came with antivirus software or you downloaded a trial version, then you must purchase the full version of the software to be completely protected. After the trial period has ended (normally 60 to 90 days), the product may stop updating or working at all. Consult the program manufacturer for instructions on how to upgrade to the full version.

- *Did you activate or register it?* Even if you purchased the full version of the product, you may still have to register or activate it. Products that require activation/registration are similar to trial version software in that updates, features, or the full product may stop working. Consult the program manufacturer for instructions on how to activate/register the software.

- *Did your subscription expire?* Most antivirus software works on a subscription basis (normally 1 year). Once the subscription has expired, the software will act like trial version software; updates, features, or the full product may stop working. Consult the program manufacturer for instructions on how to renew your subscription.

- *Do you have the latest definitions?* Without the latest virus definitions, your antivirus software will not be able to correctly identify new viruses. See the section "How Can I Tell If My Antivirus Definitions Are Up-to-Date?" earlier in this chapter.

- *Did you install something?* Installing most software should not interfere with your antivirus software, but there is always the chance that the install replaced a critical file needed by your antivirus software to operate correctly. If you are using Windows XP or higher, you can perform a system restore to roll back the changes to your system.

- *Do you need to reinstall your antivirus software?* This is a last-ditch effort. If you've tried everything else, it may just be quicker and easier to reinstall your software. Before reinstalling, you may also be able to perform an install repair. See "How Can I Repair a Damaged Software Installation?" in Chapter 3 for more information.

Where Can I Obtain Free Antivirus Software?

Some ask, "Why pay for it when it's free?" Others say, "You get what you pay for." Who do you believe when deciding whether to use free or commercial antivirus software? The choice is simple: try the free version first. Free antivirus software may provide the protection and features you need without having to shell out any money. The following list describes a few free antivirus products:

- *AntiVir Free Edition:* AntiVir Free Edition is a limited version of AntiVir Professional Edition offered free of charge for home users only. It contains many of the features of the professional edition (automatic updates, email scanning, real-time protection). For more info, visit **http://free.grisoft.com**.

- *avast! 4 Home Edition:* This product provides a complete antivirus software solution offered free of charge for home users who do not use their computer for profit. It contains the features you would expect from the more popular antivirus products (automatic updates, Outlook plug in, and real-time protection). For more info, visit **www.avast.com**.

WARNING! Be cautious when using free antivirus software not on this list because it may contain viruses or spyware. Do your research before doing the installing.

Can You Suggest an Antivirus Checklist?

Here's a good checklist you should follow for keeping viruses off of your PC:

- *Install antivirus from a trusted source.* Files downloaded from the Internet are more likely to have viruses than files on a CD purchased from your local retailer. Install only antivirus software (or any software) obtained from a trusted source.

- *Enable real-time scanning.* The only way to effectively protect your computer is to have your antivirus product automatically scan files and emails.

- *Enable automatic updates.* Your antivirus software is only as good as its last update. Make sure automatic updates are enabled.

- *Make sure your antivirus software is working.* Once your antivirus software stops working, your system is left vulnerable to virus attacks. Make sure your software is working.

Specialty Virus Prevention

- Learn how to protect yourself against email and boot sector viruses.
- Learn how to protect yourself against viruses that can attack your cell phone or PDA.

How Can I Protect against Email Viruses?

Sending viruses through email is a common, quick, and easy way for virus writers to spread their viruses around the world. Email viruses will also spread themselves to strangers and people you know, using your computer and email address. Here's how you can protect yourself from email viruses:

- *Turn off the preview pane.* Depending on the version of Outlook you use, leaving the preview pane on may activate a virus sent to you via an email message (even if there was no attachment). Unless your version of Outlook is Outlook 2000 Service Pack 1a or higher, turn off your preview pan immediately.

- *Change your email format to text.* This ensures that malicious HTML-embedded scripts cannot attack your system when you receive email and they cannot attack a remote system when you send email. Text format is the preferred format for PDAs.

- *Use Outlook 2003 to prevent unsafe scripting.*

- *Don't open attachments even if they come from someone you know.*

How Can I Protect against Boot Sector Viruses?

As we stated earlier, boot sector viruses can render your computer and re-movable media useless. Here's how you can protect your computer from boot sector viruses:

- *Remove floppies before booting up.* If your system is configured to boot from a floppy (most are by default), then your system can easily become infected if you boot up with an infected floppy in the floppy drive. Make sure you remove any floppy disks before booting up your PC.

- *Stop your PC from booting from floppies.* Be default, most systems are configured to boot from floppy disks. Most people will never need to boot from a floppy disk. Configure your system to stop booting from floppy disks. Consult your owner's manual for more information.

- *Write-protect your removable media.* Always write-protect any removable media that does not need to be written to. This is especially true when inserting your media into an untrusted computer. Write-protecting your media can be as simple as sliding a tab and is the most effective way to prevent boot sector viruses on removable media.

How Can I Prevent Viruses on My Cell Phone?

Today's cell phones allow you to play games, receive email and text messages, surf the Web, and more. Even if your cell phone does not have an integrated PDA (Palm, Pocket PC, BlackBerry), it may still run the same operating system as one of them. Your cell phone is more advanced than you know, and all that advancement requires security. Here are a few ways to protect your cell phone from viruses:

- *Turn off Bluetooth.* If your phone has Bluetooth capability (consult your owner's manual), you should turn it off when not needed. Not only does it drain your battery, but it also broadcasts a way into your cell phone to any viruses and hackers nearby.

- *Password protect your Bluetooth connection.* If you leave your Bluetooth connection on all the time (perhaps to connect a Bluetooth wireless headset, GPS, etc.), you should password-protect it. If you don't password-protect your Bluetooth connection, you will be broadcasting an open door for viruses and hackers. Consult your owner's manual or cell phone provider for information on how to secure your Bluetooth connection.

How Can I Prevent Viruses on My PDA or PDA-Enabled Cell Phone?

If a PDA is a mini computer, then it's no surprise that it is just as susceptible to viruses. The first virus for the Pocket PC has been released, and it's only a matter of time until there are viruses for all PDAs. Here's how you can prevent viruses on your PDA or PDA-enabled cell phone:

- *Follow the two procedures in the preceding section for protecting standard cell phones.*

- *Install antivirus software.* While there are only a few viruses created for PDAs, installing antivirus software is the best way to protect against future threats. Here are a few available products for PDA antivirus protection:

  - *avast! 4 PDA Edition:* Protects PDAs running the Pocket PC or Palm OS. For more info, visit **www.avast.com**.

- *Symantec AntiVirus for Handhelds:* Protects PDAs running the Pocket PC or Palm OS. For more information, visit **www.symantec.com**.

- *Back up your data:* A good (and recent) backup will help you get back up and running after a vicious virus attack.

Viruses: What You Want to Know but Were Afraid to Ask

- Learn why people are writing viruses.
- Learn how virus writers get caught.
- Learn why viruses get weird names.

Why Are People Writing Viruses?

Writing a virus is not a smart idea. They cause damage, waste time, and cost everyone money. Penalties for writing viruses can be fines, jail time, and even death. So why would anyone write a virus? Here's why:

- *Curiosity:* Writing a virus can be an educational experience to the aspiring programmer. It involves learning a programming language and learning how to interact with the device's operating system, how to control the installed software, how to work with the existing file system, how to identify security weaknesses, and how to circumvent security.

- *Boredom:* Writing a virus can be a challenge, an antidote to boredom for some virus writers. Making a virus smaller, more efficient, undetectable, and easily spread are a few of the challenges virus writers face (besides fines, jail time, and death).

- *Protesting:* Some virus spreaders find viruses to be an effective mechanism to get their point across. Examples of such viruses are the mawanella (conflict in Sri Lanka), Code Red (U.S. government), Zafi-B virus (help the homeless and implement the death penalty in Hungary), and the Noped (child pornography) virus.

- *Wanting to be helpful:* Some viruses are designed to protect against and remove other viruses and security holes. Example of such viruses are the cheese worm (fixed security holes on Linux) and the Welchi worm (removes the Blaster worm and patches security holes).

- *Rebellion:* Young people have lots of energy, and sabotage is a very attractive way to release it. When we were growing up, TP'ing (throwing rolls of toilet paper), prank calling, and doing donuts (driving in circles to cause skid marks) in the mall parking lot were the ways to rebel. Today, kids do much crazier things, including writing viruses.

- *Feelings of being powerless:* Many virus writers write viruses because they feel insignificant. They may be lonely, struggling to be noticed, or merely outcast because of their intelligence and love for technology.

- *Vengeance:* Scorned lovers, disgruntled employees, and vindictive students are a few of the people who write viruses in order to enact revenge.

- *Fighting:* At times, virus writers declare war against other virus writers. While they would have released these viruses anyway, a virus writer might include in the virus source code a typically misspelled message to another virus writer. Examples of such viruses are the Bagel.J and K, Netsky.F, and the MyDoom.G.

- *Greed:* Some virus writers are motivated by making a little illegal cash. Examples of such viruses are the Downloader-GN Trojan horse and the Backdoor.AXJ, both which steal logins, passwords, and or credit card information.

Isn't Writing a Virus Illegal?

Believe it or not, writing a virus is not illegal in the United States and in some other countries. Simply writing a virus (or as we stated earlier, a program) is not (and in our opinion should not be) illegal. Only when the virus enters a system without permission or is used with malicious intent is the virus considered illegal. Common penalties for virus-writing include fines, jail time, and court orders to stay away from computers and technological devices. Other countries (China, for example) even implement the death penalty.

How Do Virus Writers Get Caught?

Virus writers use various techniques to cover their tracks. They use public computers (available at libraries, universities, and so on) and they target networks that do not log activity. They bounce their viruses through networks all around the world before finally making that initial infection. But they do get caught, and here's how:

- *Code Analysis:* When you write a program, extra information is buried into the program (operating system, compiler used, country). Organizations like the FBI have experts that can disassemble and analyze a virus to determine its source.

- *Logging:* Most ISPs log every detail when a computer connects to its network. Some of this information includes the IP addresses assigned and the MAC address of the computer's network card. Once an organization has your MAC address, it can determine what type of network card it is. It can then contact the manufacturer, determine if it was sold individually or as part of a computer system, and ultimately locate the person who purchased it.

- *Bragging:* Apparently (for some reason we can't seem to understand), dumb criminals love to brag about their illegal activities, and virus writers are no exception. Virus writers boast about their conquests to online newsgroups or bulletin boards. How smart is that?

Why Do Viruses Get Weird Names?

Just like real viruses, computer viruses have both a common and an official name. The virus naming convention differs from vendor to vendor, but most antivirus software vendors follow a three-part naming convention:

- *Prefix:* This indicates the operating system or program that the virus affects. It can also indicate the language the virus was written in or the virus type. Examples of prefixes used are Win32 (Windows/Linux), WM (Word Macro), AOL, VBS (VBScript), or OM (Office Macro).

- *Name:* The virus name is usually embedded in the virus itself (given by its creator).

- *Suffix:* This piece is optional. If a virus mutates (changes on its own, or someone else modifies the virus and rereleases it), the piece includes a number or letter to distinguish between variants. The suffix can also be used to describe the virus type. Examples of suffixes are A, B, 1, 2, @M (attaches itself to email you send), @MM (sends itself via email), or Worm.

Summary

Viruses have plagued (no pun intended) computers for years and are now starting to make their way onto your PDAs and cell phones. As you learned in this chapter, viruses can not only destroy your files, they can destroy your hardware as well. Fortunately, there are many methods and tools (some even free) to prevent, detect, and remove viruses. You learned how to use these tools, keep them up-to-date, recognize when they aren't working, and get them back up and running. Overall, you learned how to protect yourself and minimize risk, recognize problems, and recover from the viruses that may slip by.

Junkware: Malware, Adware, and Spyware

Disasters to avoid:

- Having junkware installed on your PC that spies on you and steals your valuable data.
- Having junkware eat up valuable resources on your PC.
- Having spyware that puts your credit card or other personal data in the wrong hands.

Mishaps and blunders to run from:

- Distributing software to your friends or co-workers that contains junkware.
- Software that causes annoying ads to pop up when you use your PC.
- Getting junkware that modifies your PC and browser settings.

Many people are getting really frustrated with their PCs and the Internet because of the ever-increasing annoyance factor. Growing up, we can remember our dads running around with a hanger and a pair of pliers to get better reception on our TVs (which were black and white). Today, the frustrations we experience are considerably more complex. We've already seen how spam and viruses can really cause a lot of problems and waste valuable time, but there are other big annoyances—in the form of junkware—you need to protect yourself from.

Junkware is essentially a term for software programs installed on your PC without your consent or knowledge. Unfortunately, they do all sorts of bad things. Junkware is a new threat that has caught most home users and software developers off guard. Once junkware has invaded your system, it can display advertisement pop-ups, record your Internet activity, and steal your personal information and send it to a third party (who usually sells it to anyone who pays for it). As you'll learn in this chapter, junkware comes in three flavors: malware, adware, and spyware.

We'll now show you how to avoid the disasters and mishaps that can be caused by the three types of junkware. We'll first look at what exactly junkware is and how it can invade your privacy, and then we'll help you protect yourself from different types of problems that can occur with malware, adware, and spyware.

Junkware and Privacy

- Learn about malware, adware, and spyware and their damaging effects.
- Learn how all forms of junkware are an invasion of your privacy.

Malware (malicious software) is installed on your PC with the sole purpose of doing very bad things. This software can crash your PC, delete your data, and even open your PC for a hackers' BBQ. Viruses are actually one type of malware. Since we have already showed you how to deal with viruses in the previous chapter, in this chapter we'll show you how to protect yourself against other forms of malware.

Adware (advertising software) is software that displays advertisements on your PC. It's bad enough that we can't go to the movies without seeing commercials; now we have software that forces advertisements to be displayed on our PCs. They may be in the form of annoying pop-ups or inside applications. They might even erase the advertisements on the web page you are viewing and replace them with their own advertisements.

Spyware (spy software) is software that secretly collects personal information from your PC and sends it to remote sites. This can include things like the websites you visit, your passwords, and your credit card numbers. This probably sounds a lot like identity theft, and spyware can be used for identity theft, although it isn't the tactic most identity thieves commonly use.

Why Does Junkware Exist?

Junkware is a new phenomenon plaguing PC users. Here are a few reasons junkware exists today:

*   *Privacy and security:* Privacy, as well as security, is usually an afterthought for most software developers. Developers are typically focused on providing certain features and getting their products out before their competitors do. Fortunately, privacy and security have become big topics in recent years. Software developers are now being forced to address these issues even before their software is released.

TIP: You should always keep your software up-to-date. Software updates may strengthen privacy and security (if not eliminate them), as well as fix current bugs and add new features. See Chapter 3 for more information about updating your operating system and software applications.

---

*   *Marketing statistics and demographics:* By collecting information about you, the sites you visit, the purchases you make, and so on, a marketing team can see what products would appeal to you. These guys can be really devious about finding ways to get you to spend your money.

*   *Direct marketing:* Adware can become smart and start showing you ads that apply to your interests. For example, you may visit Amazon.com intending to buy a book and see a pop-up ad telling you how you can save up to 30 percent just by clicking on the Save button. Don't be fooled by these tactics (more on this later in the chapter).

*   *Protect and prevent:* Parents and bosses often install spyware programs to find out more about their children's or employees' Internet activities and to prevent them from visiting certain sites. This type of spyware is commonly referred to as spy software.

- *Distrust:* Someone you know may install spyware to literally spy on you. They may be a fearful employer, distrusting spouse, scorned lover, crazy roommate, or even a government.

- *Identity theft:* Since your computer can tell a thief everything about you, identity thieves use spyware to do their dirty work for them. This not only makes it easier for the thief, it allows them to steal the identity of millions of users.

- *Lack of laws:* Currently, laws involving junkware are scarce. Just like laws preventing spam, it will be many years before we see the enforcement of laws causing a reduction in junkware.

Is Your Privacy at Risk?

Technology makes it far too easy to inform manufacturers, marketing departments, and even hackers of our every move. You go to the ATM, buy gas for your car, rent a movie, and then buy some popcorn; by the time you pick up the cell phone to call your family to tell them you're on your way home, they might already know where you've been and what you've been doing, perhaps even what song you were listening to on the radio (well that might be stretching it a bit).

The point is, with advancements in technology comes the need for protection of privacy, especially when it comes to your PC. Email addresses, phone numbers, credit card numbers, usernames, and passwords —these are just a few pieces of personal information your PC may store. By inspecting someone's computer, you can find everything you could ever need to know about them (name, age, address, ethnicity, sex, marital status, likes, dislikes, financial status, and so on). This is exactly what makes junkware so popular and so dangerous.

Junkware Hazards

- Learn about the information that junkware collects.
- Learn how junkware can harm your PC.
- Learn about the most common junkware and junkware bundling applications.
- Learn how antijunkware software can help you combat junkware.

What Type of Information Does Junkware Collect?

Once junkware is on your PC, it can collect any information it wants. Some junkware developers may state that they collect only one type of information. The truth is that they can collect anything, from your surfing habits to your credit card numbers. Here are a few pieces of information a junkware program might be capable of collecting:

- *Email addresses:* Email addresses are usually collected to sell to spammers.

- *Usernames and passwords:* Collecting usernames and passwords is a tactic of identity thieves. Once the thief has your username and password, they can log on to your financial websites and drain your accounts. If they access usernames and passwords to retail sites (Amazon.com, Best Buy, and so on), the thief can use the account information to make purchases. See Chapter 6 for more information.

- *Credit card numbers:* Stolen credit card numbers are used to make numerous purchases until your card is maxed out and you are in deeply in debt.

- *Internet activity:* Junkware developers can sell information about which websites you visit, how long you stay, and the items you purchase to marketing and research companies. They can also display advertisement pop-ups that are relevant to the current site you are viewing. For example, you may be visiting Blockbuster.com and a pop-up advertisement for an online DVD rental company may appear.

- *Application information:* Junkware can collect information about what applications you have installed and send it to marketing companies.

- *Files on your PC:* Junkware may be used to steal or delete files from your system. There is a well-publicized case of junkware being used to steal files from AOL in 1999.

- *Type of computer and connected peripherals:* Again, by collecting information about your PC and peripherals, marketing companies can see which computers and devices are more popular and try to spot purchasing trends.

HORROR STORY! A friend of ours who works in the computer industry recently ran into some trouble with his finances. He noticed several charges that he did not make appearing on his credit card. The funny thing was that the credit card to which the charges were made had been used only once. Yup, you guessed it: he used it on the Internet. After a little investigation, he noticed a strange program silently running on his home PC, the same computer he used to make the credit card purchase. The program was a spyware program that was sending anything typed into an Internet form to a remote server. The lesson here is that anyone is susceptible to these types of exploits—even experienced computer users.

What Else Can Junkware Do?

Most junkware programs operate in stealth mode, completely silent and hidden from the user. Other junkware programs aren't so subtle and can become very disruptive in addition to invading your privacy. Here are a few of the things junkware can do to your PC:

- *Modify your web browser:* Junkware can do anything from changing your home page and search page to adding favorites and toolbars.

- *Modify web pages:* Junkware can inject links on any web page you visit, tricking you to click and redirect to the site of their choosing.

- *Hijack websites:* Hijacking a website simply means that the contents of the page you intended to view are modified by junkware before you view it. Junkware can hijack a website to include its own links and advertisements or to completely redirect you to another site. The ultimate goal is to force you into seeing their advertisements and visiting their links, all without you knowing.

TIP: When a site that looks like, for example, a banking, credit card, or investment site is used to defraud you and steal your money, it's called *phishing.* See Chapter 6 for more information.

- *Pop-ups:* Pop-ups are little windows that display on your PC. You've probably seen pop-ups that tell you when an error has occurred on your system, and if you've ever surfed the Web, you've most likely seen a pop-up or two trying to sell you something. Adware uses pop-ups to display advertisements to you.

- *Video/Audio recordings:* Junkware can record a video of everything you do on your computer as well as turn on microphones and web cameras to record you and send the file to the junkware developer.

How Can I Be Harmed by Junkware?

Junkware might seem like the new kid on the block who just wants to be accepted and loved. After all, all it does is collect a little information about you so it can try to save you money while helping companies manufacture and promote products that appeal to you. Think again. Junkware is not your friend. Here's why:

- *Violation of privacy:* Junkware treats your computer as its own Willy Wonka Chocolate Factory, running around, grabbing, and consuming any goodies it can find. Some junkware programs limit what kind of information they take and from where, while others don't. Regardless, junkware is rummaging through your personal information and sending it to others.

- *Scams:* Adware may appear to be helpful by showing you a discount coupon when you visit a retail website. But taking advice from adware is like taking advice from the stranger who broke into your house, peers over your shoulder all day, and lives in your basement.

- *Sucks up memory resources:* While a junkware program is busy searching your PC, collecting information, and reporting it back over the Internet, your available computer resources will diminish.

- *Sucks up your bandwidth:* Some junkware is constantly sending your private information and receiving advertisements and various other updates from their creator. This extra activity can really slow down your Internet connection speeds, especially if you use a dial-up connection. If you are on an Internet plan where you pay for your bandwidth usage, this extra activity can start to add up.

- *Crashes:* Junkware digs deep to get information and might dig into places your system may not like. Junkware may interfere with your PC's operating system or other programs, causing your programs to freeze up or crash. Poorly coded junkware can cause these problems from the moment they are installed. Freezing and crashing will ultimately lead to data loss and corruption.

- *Annoyances:* While some advertisements are entertaining and informative, most of us can live without them (unless it's during the Super Bowl). This especially holds true for activities that should be advertisement-free, such as using your PC.

- *Disruptive behavior:* Being forced to watch advertisements is not only annoying, it's disruptive, such as, for example, adware displaying pop-ups while you're working, causing you to lose focus and make errors.

- *Identity theft:* As you learned in Chapter 1, identity thieves will do anything to steal your personal information and then later, your identity. Junkware is an easy tool for them to use to steal personal information from millions of people without having to leave the comfort of their home.

- *Spam:* Once junkware has collected enough information about you, expect a heavier amount of spam to come your way. If the junkware has collected email addresses from your address book or contact list, your friends and family can also expect more spam.

- *Deceptive practices:* From installing even after you clicked No several times to burying a "right to do whatever we choose to your system" clause in a lengthy and confusing license agreement, junkware creators implement some pretty deceptive practices to get their software on your system. Always read the full license agreement for software that looks suspicious.

- *Obscene content:* Some junkware may display or redirect you to sites containing obscene or inappropriate material, including pornographic text, pictures, audio, video, and offers to illegally sell pharmaceutical drugs like Viagra.

What Are Some Popular Software Applications with Spyware Bundled?

While junkware can find its way to your system from many different avenues, a common method is to bundle it with another application, which is usually given away for free and which secretly installs the junkware. Here are some of the more popular software applications that bundle junkware into their installer (we don't recommend that you visit any of these sites but have included some of the Web addresses in case you're curious):

- *Weatherbug:* This application provides weather temperatures and forecasts in your system tray. While Weatherbug claims to be junkware free (and is), it does come bundled with MySearch bar (previously Gator and SaveNow), which is known junkware. In addition, the end user agreement box is extremely small (3 lines high) and you have to scroll 283 lines down until you see what the bundled software can do to your system. Weatherbug can be found at **www.weatherbug.com**.

- *Bonzi Buddy:* Bonzi Buddy is a program that displays a cartoon purple monkey on your desktop. He does all sorts of things, including talking, juggling, and telling you jokes. He also displays advertisements, changes your home page, and even collects and reports on your Internet activity. Bonzi Buddy can be found at **www.bonzi.com/bonzibuddy/ bonzibuddyfreehom.asp**.

- *Hotbar:* Hotbar is a program that allows you to customize Internet Explorer and Outlook by adding coloring and skinning (changing the look). Unfortunately, Hotbar is more than just a friendly customization software. It displays pop-ups and monitors your Internet usage and then sends this information to its servers. Hotbar is also know to slow down your PC, if not crash it. Hotbar can be found at **http://hotbar.com**.

- *Gator:* Gator is a utility that can automatically enter usernames, passwords, credit card numbers, and other information on web forms and websites. The company that designed Gator also created GAIN (the Gator Advertising Information Network). GAIN, which comes bundled with Gator, displays pop-up advertisements and reports every website you visit back to the manufacturer's servers.

- *P2P applications:* Bearshare, Kazaa, Limewire, and Morpehus are peer-to-peer file sharing applications that all include adware or spyware with their free versions. See Chapter 15 for more information about P2P applications.

What Are Some Popular Junkware Applications?

Here are the applications you want to avoid. They display pop-ups, record your Internet activity, or collect other types of information:

- *SaveNow:* Bundled with Bearshare and other applications, SaveNow is an adware application that displays advertisements and coupons in pop-ups based on the websites you visit.

- *eZula:* Bundled with Kazaa and other applications, eZula is an adware application that hijacks the web pages you view by injecting extra words and links.

- *CoolWebSearch:* CoolWebSearch actually refers to a variety of website hijacker applications. These applications can change your home page and search engine, redirect you to various websites when you're surfing the Web, and display pornographic material. It is usually installed via an Internet Explorer exploit when you visit certain pornography sites.

What Is Antijunkware Software?

Antijunkware software is to junkware what antivirus software is to viruses. Typically, antijunkware software can detect and remove junkware installed on your PC. Advanced antijunkware software can even detect junkware threats in real time before junkware gets installed on your PC. Antijunkware software is a must-have application because it is impossible to manually prevent, detect, and remove all junkware attacks.

What Antijunkware Software Should I Use?

While some antijunkware products require a purchase, most are currently free and provide even better detection and removal than their retail competitors. Of course it's only a matter of time until they all have a price, but enjoy the free ones while you can:

- *Ad-Aware:* This is the most popular antijunkware software on the market. It can protect against a wide variety of junkware, including Trojan horses and software designed to shut Ad-Aware down. Just like antivirus software, Ad-aware receives new junkware signature files when needed, protecting your PC from the latest threats. It's fast, easy to use, and best of all, it's free. An enhanced version, offered for $26.95, provides real-time protection, quarantining, and silent removal. You can get more info at **www.lavasoftusa.com**.

- *Spybot:* This is a free antijunkware software program that provides an extremely easy-to-use interface and support for 25 languages. Spybot blocks a wide variety of junkware, including usage trackers, keyloggers, Trojan horses, and even malicious downloads through Internet Explorer. It even creates a backup of all files and settings changed just in case you need to roll back the change. You can get more info at **www.safer-networking.org**.

- *Spy Sweeper:* This is *PC Magazine*'s Editor's Choice for antijunkware software. Spy Sweeper receives new junkware signature files when needed (protecting your PC from the latest threats) and offers real-time protection, quarantining, and more. Spy Sweeper is available at $29.95 for a one-year subscription. You can get more info at **www.webroot.com**.

- *PestPatrol:* PestPatrol offers a user-friendly interface as well as an easy-to-understand explanation of each threat. It can protect against a wide variety of junkware, including Trojan horses, keyloggers, and denial of service attacks (an attack to prevent you from accessing the Internet). PestPatrol is available at $39.95. You can get more info at **www.pestpatrol.com**.

TIP: While some antivirus software or Internet security suites include antijunkware protection, they currently do not provide the same level of protection as a product solely dedicated to preventing, detecting, and removing junkware.

When Junkware Attacks

- Learn how to tell if junkware is installed on your system.
- Learn how to spot and avoid common junkware tricks.
- Learn how to protect yourself from various junkware attacks.

How Can I Tell If My PC Has Junkware Installed?

The past four computers that we have worked on have all had junkware installed on them (some even with 300+ items). Unfortunately, junkware is not always easy to detect. There are, however, some symptoms that you can look for to better detect it:

- *Offline pop-ups:* When you are not connected to the Internet, do pop-up advertisements appear? If so, this is a sure sign of junkware.

- *Specific pop-ups:* When you visit certain websites, do you receive pop-ups that are related to the site you are visiting? Do you get "Save 50% off" coupons. Unless you are sure the pop-up is coming from the site you are visiting, this could be a sign of some junkware.

- *New home page or search engine:* Has your home page (the default page that displays when you start your web browser) changed from what it normally is? Has you default web browser search engine (Google, Yahoo) changed? These are typical tactics of junkware.

- *New toolbars:* Do you have toolbars in your web browser or other programs that you have never seen before? Junkware often adds toolbars to existing applications to trick users into clicking on them. They also use them to actually control the application itself.

- *New shortcuts:* Do you have new shortcuts on your desktop or Start menu? Without clicking on the shortcuts, see if you recognize the name. If it's not something that should be on your computer, chances are it's junkware.

- *New favorites:* Do you have new website favorites in your web browser? Junkware will sometimes insert favorites to redirect you to their site or the site of one of their affiliates.

- *New icons in your system tray:* Do you see new icons in your system tray that weren't there before? This indicates a new process was started and could have possibly been installed. Hover your mouse over the icon to see the name of the program. If it is not something you recognize, chances are it's junkware.

- *Antijunkware or antivirus software not working:* Did your antijunkware or antivirus software stop working? If so, you can follow the steps in Chapter 8 to help troubleshoot your antivirus software. If your antivirus or antijunkware software is still not working, chances are your system has junkware installed or, worse, a virus.

- *Screen flickering:* Does your screen suddenly start flickering? If so, follow the steps in Chapter 2 to help troubleshoot your display problem. If the problem persists, you may have junkware installed. Junkware programs may be taking screen shots (pictures of your screen) to send to their remote servers, hoping they caught a username, password, credit card number, or some other piece of information.

- *Strange errors:* Are you starting to see more or strange error messages? Junkware may be poorly coded or performing a disallowed function that causes other programs to produce errors.

- *Slowness:* Is your computer or Internet connection becoming slower than usual? Junkware may be poorly coded or require additional resources to scan, collect, and report all your personal information to its final destination.

- *Nothing:* Does your computer not show any of these symptoms? If so, you may have junkware installed on your computer anyway. Like a virus, well-written junkware is designed to be silent and undetected by the user. It may display no symptoms, and yet it could be stealing and reporting your private information.

WARNING! Don't take junkware lightly. If the only sign you see is that junkware changed your default home page, you may be inclined to change it back and do nothing else about it. A changed home page or search engine may seem trivial, but it's what's happening behind the scenes that can really be damaging.

How Did Junkware Get on My PC?

Ah, the million dollar question. Like any true spy, junkware can infiltrate your PC in many ways. It can take the back door (piggybacking with another program you installed), the front door (tricking you into installing it), or the side entrance. Here are a few ways junkware can get on your PC:

- *Viruses:* Viruses can carry spyware to your system or open back doors for other viruses, spyware, and hackers to enter and treat your PC as their own personal playground. See Chapter 8 for more information about how to protect yourself from viruses.

- *Good catch phrases:* Junkware usually has good catch phrases to pull people in. "Surf faster," "Kill pop-ups," "Stop spam," "Speed up your computer," and so on. In the excitement to find a product that can solve problems, the average user ends up clicking on the notice only to have the newly installed software (junkware) do more harm than good.

- *Adware:* Adware is advertiser-supported software. These programs are given away for free but include advertisements. Sometimes you can have advertisements removed in exchange for purchasing the program.

- *License agreement:* People who want junkware installed on your PC rely on the fact that most users breeze through software installs by clicking Next, Next, Next. We all know license agreements are boring. But if you don't read it, you may be consenting to having junkware installed.

- *Fake user interfaces:* Fake user interfaces (FUI) are screens that look exactly like or closely resemble Windows system messages, alerts, or screens. FUIs can also mimic your antivirus, antijunkware, or any other software you have installed. The goal is to trick you into clicking. Once you click, you may be redirected to a website or begin installing junkware or other type of malicious software.

- *Greeting cards:* Did someone send you an electronic greeting card in an email? Junkware developers are using electronic greeting cards to spread their junkware. Be wary of such cards.

- *Browser security settings:* Your browser's default security settings may have been altered to allow software to automatically install. See the section "How Can I Configure My Web Browser to Stop Junkware from Installing?" presented later in this chapter.

- *Bundled with your new PC:* While not common with the mainstream computer retailers, some retailers install additional free programs to make the computer purchase more enticing. This may be a photo editor, a pop-up blocker, or even a diagnostic program. Unfortunately, to cut costs and appear more attractive, they may have compromised your PC's security by installing junkware.

- *Letting others use your PC:* If others use your PC (kids, friends, co-workers), they may have fallen into any of the traps described in this list.

How Can I Remove Junkware from My System?

Removing junkware can be an extremely complicated process. Some can be removed by simply uninstalling them, but most bury their way deep inside your PC and would rather kill your PC than be removed (sort of like those "ear worms" from *Star Trek: The Wrath of Khan*). Here are a few ways you can remove junkware from your system:

- *Use the Add or Remove Programs feature.* If you are lucky, you may be able to remove the junkware the same way you remove any other piece of software. See Chapter 3 for more information about uninstalling software.

- *Use the System Configuration utility.* The System Configuration utility (MSConfig.exe) is a Windows utility that allows you complete control of what applications, drivers, and services run at startup. Through this utility, you can see if there are any suspicious-looking applications set to start when you boot up, and you can remove them. You can start MSConfig by clicking Start | Run and then typing **msconfig**.

WARNING! Incorrectly removing an application, driver, or server from startup may cause some of your applications to fail, errors to pop-up, and may even kill your Internet connection. Be very careful when using MSConfig.

- *Use antijunkware software:* Antijunkware software can be used to not only remove junkware, but also to prevent it from entering your system. Refer to the list of suggested anijunkware software programs presented earlier in this chapter

HORROR STORY! One of our relatives came home one day to discover that her son had accidentally installed junkware (or maybe she did it and was too embarrassed to admit it). It was a mess. Her home page kept changing to inappropriate websites, ads popped up everywhere, and her system slowed to a crawl. She called the PC manufacturer, who quickly convinced her to perform a system restore (not the friendly Windows restore, but the manufacturer restore which restored her computer to the state it was in when she bought it). Sure, this got rid of the junkware; but it also got rid of all her files, settings, and drivers for all new hardware she added after she bought the computer. Just remember: As fast as you want to get rid of the junkware, the PC manufacturer help desk wants to get rid of you when you call. Before performing a manufacturer restore, make sure you have everything backed up.

How Can I Get the Most out of Antijunkware Protection?

Unlike antivirus companies, antijunkware companies have yet to come together to share the information about threats and how to stop them. This is why you can scan your system with one antijunkware and find five junkware threats and then scan with another and find five more. To get the most out of antijunkware, use one that offers real-time protection and automatic updates. In addition, run at least two different types of antijunkware software. You'd be surprised at what one scanner can miss and what the other can find.

How Can I Tell a Fake User Interface from a Real One?

Fake user interfaces (FUI) are getting more difficult to detect. While the Internet is providing richer experiences, blurring the line between desktop applications and Internet applications, the creators of FUIs are using this to their advantage to fool you into installing some software. Here are a few ways you can distinguish an FUI from a real message displayed from your computer:

- *Web browser header:* When you're surfing the Internet with Microsoft Internet Explorer, the title bar should show the name of the site and then the name of the web browser. For example, if you go to Google.com, the title bar will say "Google – Microsoft Internet Explorer" or something similar (because your PC manufacturer and other programs can modify this). Windows messages never display titles like this, so that should be a dead giveaway. Figure 9.1 illustrates this point.

- *It just looks wrong:* Does the message look weird or not like a normal message? Windows messages have a standard look and feel. With an FUI, there may be an attempt to mimic this look, but they may not always get it right. See Figure 9.2 for an example.

Figure 9.1

FUI with web browser header.

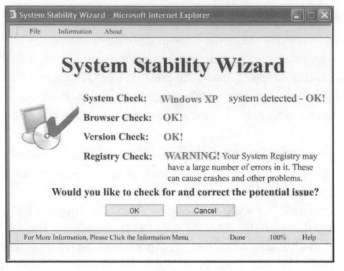

Figure 9.2
FUI with abnormal look.

- *Messages inside your web browser:* Can you tell that the message is inside your web browser? Do you see your web browser toolbar? Real message are presented outside the web browser.

- *Menu:* Do you see a menu at the top of the FUI (File, Edit, View and so on)? Real messages do not have menus.

- *Scrollbars:* Does the interface have a scrollbar at the right and or the bottom? This is typically a sign that the interface is a web interface and not an actual Windows interface.

- *Typos and grammar:* Official messages are usually spell-checked and include proper grammar. Fake user interfaces may be developed by someone with poor grammar or spelling skills. The language used may not be the developer's first language, so there might be a lot of typos and grammar mistakes.

- *Disclaimer:* Some of the more honest junkware (isn't that an oxymoron) will include tiny messages ("Advertisement," "Ad," "Sponsored Message") to let you know the interface is fake. Why would they do this if the point is to trick you into clicking? The message is small, in an odd-colored font, and in a location away from the central reading point. Make sure you read all text on all areas of the message. Figure 9.3 shows a fake user interface that contains a disclaimer.

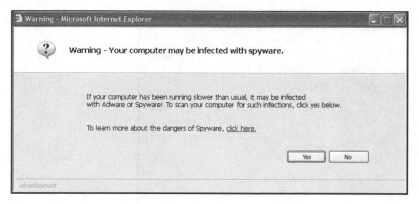

Figure 9.3
FUI with a disclaimer (bottom left).

How Can I Protect Myself against Fake User Interfaces?

Here are various ways to help prevent being tricked by fake user interfaces:

- *Use a pop-up blocker.* A pop-up blocker will prevent pop-ups from appearing in the first place, thus preventing fake user interfaces.

- *Don't just say no.* You may be tempted to just click the No button if a pop-up prompts you install something, run a scan, and so on. The problem with a fake user interface is that everything is fake, including the No button. To remove the pop-up, click the close button in the upper-right corner; never click anything else.

- *Use the information in the preceding section to help spot FUIs.* There may be an obvious sign that the message is fake.

Have Can I Tell If I've Been a Victim of a Drive-By Download?

A drive-by download is a program install that occurs when you visit a website or read an email message. If your web browser's security settings are set at a low level, the junkware can automatically install without warning. If your web browser's Internet security settings are set at a higher level, a security message titled "Security Warning" will appear. It's now up to you whether you click Yes to install, No to not install, or the X in the upper right also to not install. Figure 9.4 shows a typical security warning dialog.

How Can I Configure My Web Browser to Stop Junkware from Installing?

By default, the security settings in your web browser should be at a level to protect your PC from a drive-by download. If the security setting is too low, your web browser may be allowing junkware to install itself while you are

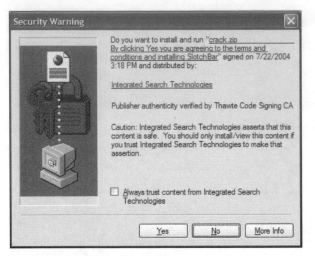

Figure 9.4
Security warning dialog box.

viewing a web page or reading an email. It also may leave you open to other threats, including viruses and Trojan horses. Here's how you can reset your web browser to its default settings:

- *Avant browser and Internet Explorer:* Because Avant browser works on top of Internet Explorer, modifying security settings for one affects the other. Here's how to reset your security settings back to their defaults:

   1. Start your browser.
   2. Choose Tools | Internet Options.
   3. Choose the Security tab, click the Internet icon, and then click the Default Level button.

- *Firefox:* Firefox is extremely secure by default and cannot be reset.

WARNING! The downside to Firefox's security is that it won't allow you to properly visit websites that use ActiveX controls (which is common).

Why Doesn't My Software Work After I Remove Junkware?

After finally getting the junkware off of your system, you may discover that another software program refuses to work properly. Here are a few of the reasons a software program would stop working after junkware is removed:

- *Adware protection:* Ad-supported software may become inoperable after removing its associated junkware/adware. Developers of ad-supported software get their money from ad sponsors. If you have removed the adware from their product, the product may detect it and refuse to work.

- *Oops:* Your antijunkware software may have falsely identified a legitimate file as junkware and removed it from your system. If your antijunkware product uses quarantine, you may be able to have your antijunkware software reverse the changes it made.

- *Operating system:* Some types of junkware replace key Windows files with similar versions. When you run antispyware, these files are mistaken for junkware and are quarantined or deleted. The problem here is that now there may be critical Windows system files missing. The most common result is losing your ability to surf the web. The bottom line here is to be very careful when running antispyware programs.

Junkware Protection

- Learn how to best protect yourself against future junkware attacks.
- Learn how to set up your Web browser to protect against junkware.

How Can I Protect against Junkware?

Antivirus software not only protects the files currently on your computer, it also needs to integrate with your email to stop viruses as they come from the Internet. Junkware protection works in the same manner, protecting your system from junkware and also integrating with your web browser to prevent adware. Here are a few ways you can protect your system against junkware:

- *Browser toolbars:* A toolbar is simply a row of buttons and or menu items. If you start your web browser, you will see buttons that allow you to go back, go forward, stop, refresh the current page, and go to your home page. These buttons are on a toolbar. A toolbar to prevent adware looks for pop-ups and stops them from displaying.

- *Enhanced web browsers:* Believe it or not, Internet Explorer is not the only web browser in the world. Some enhanced browsers have junkware protection built in, allowing you to stop certain types of adware that the typical browser toolbar can't handle.

- *Antijunkware software:* Antijunkware software is similar to antivirus software in that it can detect and remove threats quickly, quietly, and safely. Antijunkware software is a new market, so it may not have all the bells and whistles of typical antivirus software.

- *Software firewalls:* A software firewall will monitor the activity of your computer and the programs on it and prevent programs from performing acts that compromise your security and privacy. This is similar to how antivirus software detects new viruses.

- *Keeping your system up-to-date:* A common tactic for creators of viruses and junkware is to use an unpatched weakness on your system to gain entrance and do damage. By keeping your system up-to-date, you'll protect against these kinds of threats, and patches can bring improved performance, add new features, and fix existing errors. See Chapter 3 for more information.

- *Securing your network:* Another way viruses, hackers, and junkware can infiltrate your system is through an insecure network. Your network should be protected by a firewall (software or hardware) and your access point should be secured with wireless encryption to help keep intruders out. See Chapters 4 and 5 for more information.

How Can My Web Browser Help Protect against Junkware?

An enhanced web browser not only includes the standard functionality of a basic web browser, it also includes a variety of enhancements, such as automatic updates, tabbed browsing, pop-up blocking, and more. Here is a list of the most popular enhanced web browsers to help protect your PC against junkware:

- *Avant browser:* This is a free, enhanced web browser that works on top of Internet Explorer, allowing for complete backward compatibility. The browser includes antijunkware features like pop-up blocking, flash animation blocking (which is a very common type of adware), and ad blocking. It also includes the ability to block ActiveX controls and other security-related features in addition to tabbed browsing, Yahoo/Google search, and automatic updates. You can get more info at **www.avantbrowser.com/**.

- *Firefox:* This is the latest web browser from Mozilla. It is a free, enhanced web browser that includes antijunkware features such as pop-up blocking, prevention of loading images that do not originate from the site you are visiting, and the complete prevention of ActiveX controls. The browser also includes tabbed browsing, Google search, and automatic updates. You can get more info at **www.mozilla.org/products/ firefox/**.

- *Internet Explorer:* This is the default web browser for Microsoft operating systems. While it may not feature all the enhancements of other web browsers; if you have Windows XP, Windows XP Service Pack 2 adds an integrated pop-up blocker into Internet Explorer 6. Internet Explorer 6 also adds the ability to block ActiveX controls and other security-related features. You can get more info at **www.microsoft.com/windows/ie/ default.mspx**.

What Are Today's Most Popular Browser Toolbars?

Although a browser toolbar may be capable of stopping adware pop-ups, that's typically not its sole purpose. Most include tools to make surfing the Internet a little easier (and safer). Here are a few of today's more popular browser toolbars and their features:

- *Google Toolbar:* This toolbar can prevent adware pop-up advertisements and can even display a counter to show you how many pop-ups have been blocked. It also includes a quick "search the web" feature, an automatic form filler so you don't have to constantly type your information on every form you come across, automatic updates, and more. You can get info at **http://toolbar.google.com/**.

- *Yahoo! Toolbar:* This toolbar also prevents adware pop-up advertisements and displays a counter to show you how many pop-ups have been blocked. It also includes antijunkware software (the only toolbar currently with this capability) and places a button on the toolbar so you can quickly scan your system when you choose (currently there is no support for automatic scans). It also includes a quick "search the web" feature, quick access to Yahoo email, finance, entertainment, and more. You get more info at **http://companion.yahoo.com/**.

- *MSN Toolbar:* This toolbar can prevent adware pop-up advertisements, display a counter to show you how many pop-ups have been blocked, and allows you to turn off pop-up blocking for your local intranet (really useful if your company's website uses pop-ups that were being blocked by other browser toolbars). It also includes a quick "search the web" feature, access to Hotmail, MSN Messenger, and more. You can get more info at **http://toolbar.msn.com/**.

- *EarthLink Toolbar:* This toolbar can prevent adware pop-up advertisements and Windows Messenger advertisements and even allows you to view a quick preview of the pop-up before it's blocked. The toolbar includes a feature called ScamBuster, which protects you from known scam websites and phishing attacks (see Chapter 6 for more information on phishing). It also includes a link to an online spyware checker that can detect and report junkware, but it will only remove it for EarthLink members. There is even a quick "search the web" feature powered by

Google. You can get more info at"**www.earthlink.net/home/soft-ware/toolbar/**.

How Can I Keep from Blocking the Wrong Pop-Ups?

Not all pop-ups are adware advertisements. Some sites use pop-ups to display their own advertisements, while others uses pop-ups to display forms and other types of information. If you are visiting a site that should never have pop-ups blocked (company intranet, Amazon.com), you should configure your browser to always allow pop-ups from the site.

- *Avant browser:* To add a site to the pop-up block exception list, choose Tools | Avant Browser Options | Popup Blocker, click the Exception list tab, and then add the site.

- *Firefox:* To add a site to the pop-up block exception list, choose Tools | Options | Web Features, and then click the Allowed Sites button (next to Block Popup Windows) to add the site.

- *Internet Explorer:* If you are running Windows XP with at least Service Pack 2, you can ensure pop-ups never get blocked from a specific site. To add a site to the pop-up block exception list, choose Tools | Popup Blocker | Popup Blocker Settings and then add the site.

Prevention Checklist

This checklist will help you protect your system, privacy, security, and identity from junkware:

- Take the time to read license agreements or messages on the screen.

- Check your web browser's security settings to prevent drive-by downloads.

- Only install software from trusted sites.

- Use junkware detection and removal software.

- Install a web browser toolbar or an enhanced web browser to seamlessly prevent junkware while surfing the Internet.

- Keep your system and software up-to-date.

- Never install software just because you are prompted to do so. If you are visiting a site that prompts you to install software, make sure the site is trusted (a site like Amazon.com as opposed to Joe's Hacker Heaven) before installing the software.

- Install Windows XP Service Pack 2. This service pack includes a software firewall, a pop-up blocker integrated into Internet Explorer, and other security enhancement as well as numerous system fixes.

Summary

Just when we are starting to get a handle on spam and viruses, a new menace rears its ugly head: junkware. This makes you wonder what will be next. Although junkware is a new menace, there are plenty of tools and methods to remove and prevent junkware from affecting your systems. In this chapter, you learned about the various types of junkware and how they can make their way onto your system. You learned how not to be fooled by fake user interfaces and deceptive pop-ups, and you even learned how to prevent them. As you saw, there are various tools and settings you can use. Junkware spreads quickly and can be quite damaging, but you now have the knowledge to remove it, detect it, and even prevent it before it starts.

10

Email and Other Internet Hazards

Disasters to avoid:

- Losing your job because you sent an inappropriate email message to a co-worker.
- Revealing too much information to an online friend and losing the friendship.

Mishaps and blunders to run from:

- Meeting Mr. or Miss Wrong online.
- Getting taken by unscrupulous online dating websites.

I (Peter) received a very strange email one evening a few years ago. It said something like, "Were you the Peter that was at this bar the other night with your friend Kevin?" For some reason, I sent the following message back to this crazy person: "I was not at the bar but I do have a friend named Kevin and I can be whoever you want me to be...." Fast-forward four years: that crazy emailer is now my wife and we have two beautiful boys. All this is the result of an email.

At the same time, we know a lot of people who have really been burned by email. We've had friends who have been fired, been in the doghouse with their spouses, and have lost friends because they had bad email or instant messaging habits. In Chapters 7 through 9, you learned about the disasters and mishaps of spam, viruses, and junkware. In this chapter, we'll focus on other disasters that can occur when using email and the Internet and engaging in activities such as meeting people online and online dating. The Internet has rapidly become a way to communicate and meet people without ever leaving the comfort of your home. Because these methods are so new, many of us simply jump in and end up making a lot of blunders.

Email and Instant Messaging Hazards

- Learn how to communicate properly at work and keep your job.
- Learn how to avoid getting a virus while using instant messaging.
- Learn how to stop someone from pestering you.

Email and instant messaging have become the tools of choice for business and personal communications. Just imagine how difficult your life would be if you had to give up your email. But as popular as email and instant messaging are, they also can be a minefield if you are not careful. There are tons of ways that you can make big blunders with your electronic communications. Since we use email and instant messaging so much, we are likely to mess up at some point. Mishaps and blunders can be made by sending inappropriate emails at work, by revealing too much information to an online friend, or by simply sending an email to people on a company address list. In the following sections, we'll show you some very common mistakes you can make with email and instant messaging, how to avoid them in the first place, and how to recover if you do mess up and get caught.

Can I Get in Trouble Sending Personal Emails at Work?

Yes. We are continually amazed by the stories we hear from people who get fired or get into a lot of trouble because of their email habits at work. At most businesses, everything you send out and receive is recorded and saved. Someone might not be reading the emails that you are sending or receiving on a regular basis, but if some issue arises at work, your employer might start reading everything you've ever written or received using the company's email address. Not only could you get in trouble, this could be really embarrassing.

We recommend that you review your company's policies for sending and receiving emails and make sure you follow them. This could save your job at some point. If you need to send or receive personal emails while at work, you should use a separate email address, and don't save your emails on your PC at work.

HORROR STORY! Do you remember the company Enron, which got into a lot of trouble because of its really bad business dealings? You probably didn't hear about all of the employees who also got into trouble because of their email practices. During the investigation of Enron, the government collected employees' personal email and eventually this email went on public display. Everything from employee romances and affairs to personal business dealings were displayed for the world to see.

Can My Employer or Internet Service Provider Read Emails I Have Sent?

Of course they can. They only need to have the proper systems set in place. Your employer may be legally obligated to archive email and your ISP may be subpoenaed in a lawsuit to divulge your email communications. Here are some ways in which you can communicate using email and not reveal anything you don't want to reveal:

- *Password-protected archive*: Compress your document in an archive and password-protect the archive.

- *Encryption*: Use an email encryption program to keep people from reading your emails. One of our favorites is a program called ShyFile. It allows you to enter data into a text file, encrypt it, attach it to an email, and send it. The recipient simply enters a predetermined pass phrase and has access to the contents. It can be found at **www.shyfile.net**.

NOTE: Some corporate email systems prohibit the sending of encrypted emails.

HORROR STORY! A client recently asked that all incoming and outgoing emails be archived for various purposes. They were not looking for anything in particular but were alarmed at some of the things they found, such as employees emailing company data to competitors and love letters being sent to and from other employees. Needless to say, the senders of these messages were politely let go.

TIP: Always lock your computers desktop or log off when leaving your computer. A nasty co-worker can just walk up to your PC and send an email that may get you fired.

Can I Stop an Email That Might Get Me in Trouble from Being Delivered?

This can be a most compromising situation. You just sent an email that, for whatever reason, can get your goose cooked. It might have been an email to a coworker that contained something that violates company policy. Maybe it was an email to a friend that revealed your true feelings for them. Whatever the case, you wish that you could travel back in time a few minutes to reel it back in.

Well, we have both good news and bad news. The good news first: there are ways to give yourself some options when sending these emails. The bad news is that none of these will help you with something you have already sent. Also, keep in mind that many of these settings are only available in stand-alone email software programs such as Outlook and Eudora. If you send and receive email through AOL or Hotmail, you are out of luck. Here are some techniques you can use to protect yourself:

- *Automatic send/receive:* Your email software probably has options that control when it actually sends out new email. You can either turn off the automatic send/receive or set it to do it less frequently. This way, your email will hang out in your outbox until you are ready to send it. This will give you the opportunity to delete it if you change your mind.

- *Deferred delivery:* This is another option available in most email software programs. It allows you to specify exactly when an email will be sent by your software. This way, you can delete an email from your outbox if you decide that it should not be sent.

- *Save as a draft:* If you have an email that is not ready to send or you are not sure it should be sent, you should first save it as a draft. You can later review it and send it when you really need to.

Is It Safe to Respond to All Emails That I Receive?

These days you have to be really careful who you respond to. Hopefully we've convinced you of this because of all of the spam and virus senders who have gotten out of control. It's really wise to adopt a policy of not responding to emails or downloading attachments unless you know the sender. You also need to be careful about how you respond to messages that you receive. When dealing with email, keep the following points in mind:

- *Just because an email appears to have come from a friend, do not assume this to be the case.* It may have been sent by a virus or by a hacker that is trying to ensnare you in their web.

- *Be very careful about emails that appear to be from financial institutions or other large companies.* The truth is that a good number of these emails have been sent by hackers in an attempt to steal your personal information.

- *When responding to an email, be very sure of what you are trying to say.* Once you click the Send button, there is no surefire way to magically stop your message from being delivered.

- *Be careful when replying to or forwarding emails.* Double-check to make sure that you are sending the email to the intended recipients.

- *Remember that just because you deleted an email, it does not necessarily mean that it is gone.* It is probably still lurking in your deleted items folder. Be sure to clear this out on a regular basis.

- *Be careful of your email signatures.* When emailing some people, your email signature may be giving away too much personal information, such as your address and home phone number.

HORROR STORY! We recently heard a story about a woman who had a close friend who moved to Japan. She received an email that her friend sent to a wide group of people. She responded to the email by telling her friend (in a rather crude way) about her really hot new boyfriend. Unfortunately, she responded using the Reply to All feature and her rather personal message was broadcast all around the world, even to her friend's very conservative parents. The moral: treat the Reply to All feature as you would a loaded gun.

How Can I Stop Someone I Don't Like from Sending Me Emails?

Even though this email may be considered unsolicited, it's not quite spam. An old boyfriend or girlfriend may be trying to rekindle an old romance or an annoying friend might be sending you emails as a practical joke. Whatever the problem, there are some things you can do:

- *Set up a rule to auto-reply.* If you are using Outlook or a similar email client, set up a rule to reply to their emails. You can even add some choice words. Hopefully, they will eventually get the point and leave you alone.

- *Add them to your junk email list:* Have your email software automatically send their emails to your junk mail folder. You'll still receive the emails, but it will make you feel good that they are being directly sent into your junk email folder.

- *Add them to your blacklist.* If you are on a corporate network, have your administrator blacklist the email address of the person that is annoying you. Any subsequent emails from this individual will be blocked even before it reaches your mailbox.

TIP: Administrators can also whitelist an individual's email address. This would prevent any emails they send to you from being blocked by antispam software.

- *Change your email address.* Obviously, this is a last resort. Not everyone wants to go through the hassle of changing their email address because of some fool, but sometimes this is your best option.

Why Does My Full Name Appear when I Email People?

When you send an email to someone, the email arrives in their inbox and your name is listed as the sender. You may be a little confused about this because your email address is luvbug@hotmail.com. Shouldn't your email address be listed as the sender? Rather than using your email address, your display name is shown as the sender. This can be a big problem if you are trying to reveal a minimal amount of information about yourself to the people you are emailing.

The way to fix this small problem depends on how you send emails. Here is how it is done:

- *Email software:* If you are using an email client program such as Outlook or Eudora, you need to change your email display name. This can usually be done in your account settings. Figure 10.1 shows the display name setting in Outlook. It can be found in the box labeled Your Name.

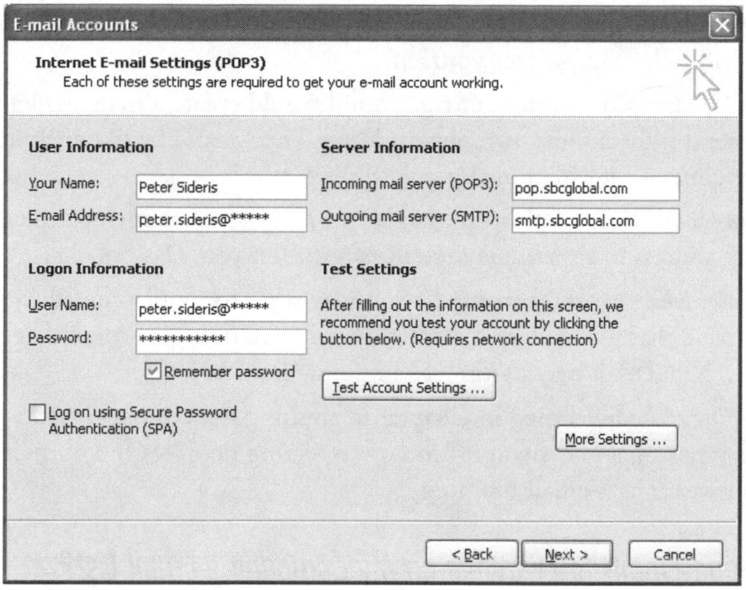

Figure 10.1
Display name setting in Outlook.

NOTE: If you are on a corporate network, you will likely not be able to change your display name. It will have to be done by an administrator. They will probably not change it to anything other than your real name.

- *Internet email:* If you have a Hotmail, Yahoo, AOL, or another similar email account, you probably send and check your email on the Web. Changing your display name is done at the same place you access your email. Look for a preferences page where you can change this information.

HORROR STORY! A girl we know had gone to great lengths to hide her personal information from the fellow she was dating online. She followed all of the most important rules but still managed to goof this up. How did she do it? She used a signature in her email program that revealed her telephone number, address, and fax number. It was all there!

Can People Send Me Emails That Look Like They Came from Someone Else?

You bet they can! This is called *email spoofing*. Of course, the average person will have no idea how to do this. There are many reasons someone would want to spoof an email address. You are probably wondering how people are able to do it. The truth is that we would love to tell you. However, by doing so, we could run into trouble. But knowing why someone would want to do this will help you protect yourself:

- *Virus sender:* No one in their right mind would create a mass-mailer virus and send it from their own email address. That would be like including your contact information along with the virus.

- *Spam sender:* Ditto with spam. No spammer is going to include their email address in a spam message that they send you.

- *Practical joker:* An enterprising person may want to send an email to someone that looked like it came from a friend or a government agency. If this happens, it may be time to find new friends.

- *Phishing:* As you learned in Chapter 6, phishing is a common tactic used to pry personal information from unsuspecting people. One of their main weapons is email spoofing.

Can I Send Emails to Everyone on My Company's Email List?

Most medium to large companies host their email systems on internal servers. This makes it easier for their tech staff to administer the company email at a lower cost. The advanced systems they use usually have what is called a global address list, which consists of every mailbox on their system. In some large companies, it can easily contain thousands of email addresses.

It can be very tempting to send an email to every person on this list. Perhaps your daughter is selling Girl Scout cookies or you are having a company keg party for Labor Day. Whatever the case, using this list can sure get the word out quickly. Before you send out your email, please do yourself a favor and wait a day or so. Sending emails to the entire list is a considered a big blunder in most companies. You might even make a blunder that you could lose your job over. Think about what you would need to say at your next job interview: "Well, I got fired because I sent out this really stupid email to everyone who worked at the company, even members of the board of directors...."

HORROR STORY! I (Peter) once worked at a company that had a very strict policy concerning the global email address lists in Outlook. The policy stated that no one, under any circumstance, was to use these lists without approval from management. One poor soul decided to not heed the warning and sent an email anyway. They sent a joke to everyone on the list. Needless to say that was the last email they sent.

Is It Safe to Use Instant Messaging (IM)?

The popularity of instant messaging has been downright ridiculous. Everyone from little children to the old lady down the street is using IM to communicate with friends, family, and co-workers. Using IM, you can communicate with people around the globe with just a few mouse clicks and a few keystrokes. The most appealing thing about IM is the complete anonymity it provides. With a screen name like Bigmama or Slickryder, you can say whatever you want to whomever you want to say it to. But is this really safe?

The problem is that you can get into a lot of trouble with IM if you aren't careful. Here are some tips to help you stay safe:

- *Make sure you know who you are talking to.* People use clever IM names these days and it is easy to get your friends mixed up. Don't fall into the trap of sending a message to the wrong friend.

- *Be careful when communicating with friends or family who share a PC.* You might think that you are exchanging messages with a friend or co-worker only to later find out that someone else is using your friend's or co-worker's PC and IM account. It's always a good idea to exchange some "safe" messages first to ensure that you are communicating with the right person.

- *Watch what you type, especially if you are communicating with co-workers.* Instant messaging is fun because you can really express yourself and speak what is on your mind. But if you are communicating with co-workers, be careful. The person who you are communicating with might be saving the messages that you are sending. The message that you send about the boss looking really fat in her new dress might just make it to the boss when you least expect. (Imagine having to explain that blunder!)

- *Keep an eye out for devious spammers.* Rogue spammers love to use IM to get you to visit porn sites and connect up with other desirables. If you get a message from someone you don't recognize and the message is something like "Hi I've been trying to reach you because I think you are really hot and I want you to visit my site," don't respond.

- *Be wary of viruses.* Viruses can be transmitted through IM, so be careful (see the following section, "Can I Get a Virus through IM?").

Can I Get a Virus through IM?

Instant messaging presents a whole new world of opportunity for virus writers. Having grown tired of spreading them through email, they have now turned to this new medium. Here's how they operate: Someone you don't know IMs you and they start transferring a file to you. If you accept the transfer and download the file and then you open it, you'll get the virus. Here's how you can protect yourself:

- *Reject file transfers.* Do not accept a file transfer from anyone you do not know.

- *Don't click IM hyperlinks.* Another way in which you can get a virus is by clicking a hyperlink that directs you to a site containing malicious content.

How Can I Stop Someone from Pestering Me with IM?

This can be a very frustrating situation, especially if someone is constantly harassing you through IM. They know when you are on and pounce on you as soon as you log in. It is almost as if they have a camera mounted near your PC and can actually watch you as you cringe in disgust when they IM you. So who are these Internet predators? Nobody really knows for sure. They could be bored teenagers, sexual predators, ill-behaving business associates, or old ladies with nothing better to do. Whatever the case, here are some steps you can take to thwart these annoying Internet losers:

- *Block them.* Most IM software used today has some mechanism by which you can reject IMs from particular people. You can also specify that you would only like to receive IMs from particular people.

- *Report them.* Most IM software allows you to report people who are behaving indecently or may be breaking the law. The only problem with this method is that the culprit can just create another account and continue to bother you.

- *Change your screen name.* This is a surefire way to get someone to leave you alone. It is kind of like an online witness protection plan. Just be sure to tell the people you trust that you have a new screen name.

HORROR STORY! Our publisher told us a story about an author who was using IM to harass everyone about his recently published book. The author would monitor the activity of all of the editors in the company and then send IMs (as many as 20 to 30 a day) to check on how his book was selling, what everyone was doing to market his book, why he was getting poor reviews on Amazon, and when he would receive his royalty check. The author created so much bad will that no one wanted to sell his book and the book ended up being a big flop.

Will My Employer Know That I'm Chatting while at Work?

In times past, most employers did not even realize that this technology even existed. They were to busy trying to block you from going to certain websites. This meant you were pretty much free to chat away as much as you wanted to. Now that IM has become more mainstream, employers are watching. Companies now go to great lengths to monitor or even block chat sessions. The best advice we can give here is to not use these programs at work for personal communications.

How Much Personal Information Is Safe to Reveal to a Chat Friend?

We'll answer this question with another question: How much information would you reveal to a complete stranger on the street? You should never, under any circumstances, reveal any personal information, to an online friend until you have passed some very important hurdles. Here is a list of that personal information, in case you are wondering:

- *Name:* This includes first, last, middle, maiden, or any combination. An Internet savvy person could Google your name and potentially get some vital information.

- *Address:* If you provide this, you might as well provide the keys to your house.

- *City/state:* Be very careful about providing this information. Used in conjunction with some of the other items on this list, this information would allow someone to find out more than you want them to know.

- *Names of friends or family:* You shouldn't provide your name, so why provide the name of someone you know?

How Can I Determine the True Sex of an Online Friend?

As you sit there chatting with online friends until the wee hours of the morning, you may be thinking to yourself, "How do I know if this person is male or female?" We agree that this is indeed a very important question. The funny thing is that the person on the other end may be thinking the same thing about you. Determining this through chatting itself might not be possible. Here are a few tips to help you figure this out:

- *IM font:* If they use plain font with no color, chances are it's a guy. Only a female would take the time to use a fancy font and add color. Guys just don't care about this sort of stuff.

- *Avatar:* The avatar is the picture that the user has added to their IM profile. Again, most guys would not even bother to add one. If they do, it is usually something very manly like motorcycles or guns.

- *Picture:* Have them send you a picture via email. Just to be sure they are actually the person in the picture; ask to see more than one picture. Chances are they will not have numerous pictures of someone else.

TIP: Remember to use an anonymous email address when communicating with online friends.

- *Speak to them:* Try speaking to them using your IM program if it supports that feature. You should be able to get a good idea by listening to their voice.

HORROR STORY! A friend of a friend once met a person in an online chat room. Her screen name was bettieboop54. They chatted for several weeks and then decided to meet each other. Well, unfortunately for our friend, bettieboop54 ended up being another guy. So the moral of the story is to not assume important things like this by just looking at the person's screen name.

How Can I Prevent My IM Program from Starting when My PC Starts Up?

One thing that annoys us about instant messaging programs is that they all start up when Windows starts. This means that you are logged on automatically and everyone on your buddy list sees that you are online. If someone is monitoring your activities, they can easily tell when you are starting up your PC and shutting it down. It's not that we're antisocial, but when we log on to our PCs, we frantically have to close the instant messaging program or someone is bound to start a conversation. It does not have to be this way, though. Somewhere in the IM program's menus you will find an option that prevents it from starting automatically. You can also remove it from your PC's startup items using MSConfig. See Chapter 3 for information on how to do this.

HORROR STORY! A good friend of ours recently got into some trouble with his wife because of instant messaging programs. He said that he was going to be working late and would be home after she was asleep. Instead, he went down to the nearest internet café and logged onto AIM. Little did he know that his wife was logged on at the time. We're sure you can figure out the rest of this story on your own.

Can I Install More Than One IM Program on My PC?

Yes, you can have more than one IM program installed on your PC. Go ahead and install all of them if you want. I bet you are now wondering if you can use them all at the same time. Will the programs get confused and send the wrong message to the wrong person? Fortunately for you, the companies that make these programs have all of these details worked out. Go ahead and use as many as you want. Here are the programs that we recommend:

- *AIM:* This is America Online's extremely popular IM software. AOL subscribers get access to tons of different chat rooms covering a broad range of interests. Nonsubscribers can still use it, but they have access to a limited number of chat rooms. It is installed along with the AOL software or can be downloaded from **www.aol.com**.

- *Windows Messenger:* This IM software comes with Windows XP. You will probably notice it very shortly after you boot up your new computer for the first time. Look for the annoying icon in the taskbar asking you if you want to add your .NET passport to Windows.

- *MSN Messenger:* This is an upgraded version of Windows Messenger. It adds features such as news, sports scores, and stock information. You can download it at **www.msn.com** You can also download a version of this for use on your Pocket PC.

- *ICQ:* A favorite among more advanced computer users. It offers all of the features of AIM and its counterparts and boasts a large international user base. It can be downloaded at **www.icq.com**.

- *Yahoo Messenger:* This is Yahoo's offering for the IM community. It can be downloaded at **www.messenger.yahoo.com**.

NOTE: You won't be able to chat with people using the IM software that's different than the software you are using. We foresee this changing at some point, once all of the different companies figure out that we want this functionality.

If I Get a New PC, Will My IM Contacts Still Be Available?

If you have been using IM programs for any length of time, you probably have a long list of contacts. Like most people, you probably would not remember all of them if your life depended on it. This scenario would normally be cause for concern, except for the fact that this information is not stored on your computer. The fine folks that make these programs decided to store all of the people in your buddy list on their servers and not on your PC. This means that the same list of buddies will show up no matter what PC you happen to be using.

Online Socializing and Dating Hazards

- Learn how to post online ads without getting ripped off.
- Learn how to dump someone that you meet online and don't really like.

If you think that communicating with your business associates, friends, and family by writing or visiting them is old-fashioned, just wait until you see how the rules of meeting people and dating are changing. Meeting new friends in person or by placing ads in the local paper seems to be old news. Unless you live in a big city like New York or Chicago, your options are limited.

You can now use the Internet to meet someone who lives halfway around the globe just as easily as you can call your friend in town. Online relationships are a major aspect of sites such as AOL, MSN, Yahoo, and others. There are also sites dedicated solely to helping people meet each other. But meeting people online comes with its own set of risks and dangers, as you'll learn in the sections that follow.

What Are the Big Risks of Meeting People Online?

Outside of the obvious problem of meeting people you don't like and then having to get rid of them, you need to be careful about the websites you use to meet people. Although many sites are set up as legitimate websites that actually care about their clients, many of them are looking to rip you off. Before you drop a red cent into any of these sites, do your homework. You will be glad you did. In particular, the sites that offer brides from around the globe should be avoided. See Chapter 1 on ways to avoid being ripped off online.

Is It Worth Paying Money to Post an Online Personal Ad?

There are sites that offer matchmaking and dating services for a price. Many of these are legit, but just as many are not. Finding the good ones can be a challenge. Here is a list of ways to find the good ones:

- *Word of mouth:* This is probably the best way to find a good site. If a friend of yours had a good experience, chances are you will too.

- *Build it yourself:* Some people have gone to extremes to meet new people on the Internet. They have created entire websites to showcase themselves to the world. Although this may sound a little weird, it is effective.

- *Web references:* Sites like **www.msn.com** and **www.yahoo.com** periodically have online articles about online personal ads. They usually highlight a handful of these sites to let you know which ones are worth it.

HORROR STORY! A friend recently signed up for an online matchmaking service. The cost to sign up was $2,000. At this point in the story, most of us would have stepped away and said no way. Unfortunately, this friend decided to go ahead with it. Guess what happened. Nothing good. They sent a few completely incompatible people his way. The sad news was that they had fulfilled their end of the bargain and there was nothing he could do about it.

I Didn't Get a Response with an Ad, So What Went Wrong?

So, you finally got the guts to post an online ad. The next few days can be very nerve-racking for you. You will probably check your email every five minutes for responses. If you don't get a response, here's what you can do:

- *Make sure your ad was put online.* Just because you filled out an online form and clicked submit, there is no guarantee that the personal was posted. Go back to the website and find it yourself to make sure it is there.

- *Add a photo.* Most people will not respond to a personal ad that has no picture. It is kind of like buying a car without ever seeing it.

- *Make sure your contact information is correct.* You may have put in the wrong email address when you posted the personal. Double-check all of this important information.

Is a Photo Necessary to Get Good Response?

People are apprehensive about posting a picture of themselves when posting an online personal ad. They may be worried someone might recognize them, they might not think they are attractive enough to get a response, or they might not have a digital copy of their picture. Whatever your apprehensions about posting a picture, you need to get over them quickly. People just don't respond to ads that are lacking a photo.

Should I Research My Online Friend's Past?

If you were going to purchase a used car, you would likely do a little research first. Follow this same technique and stay safe when you are meeting new people online. You never know what you may come up with. The main objective here is to stay safe and have fun at the same time. Unfortunately, there are all sorts of predators waiting to take advantage of you. Here are some tips to help you do some homework on your online acquaintances:

- *Do a Google search.* This is the quickest way to do a little snooping. Figure 10.2 shows a Google search conducted using one of the author's names.

Figure 10.2

Google search.

- *Check out your state's sexual offenders website.* Most states now have websites where you can look up sexual offenders by city. Make sure your online friend's name does not show up on these lists.

- *Check the FBI list of wanted criminals.* Another scary list to check out.

- *Do an online people search.* Websites like Yahoo and MSN offer free person search utilities. If you do not find them there, you can try a pay site like **www.publicrecordfinder.com**.

Where Should My Online Friend and I Meet in Person?

At some point, you are going to want to meet your online friend in person. This is no time to let down your guard. Communicating using IM, email, and telephone does not mean you are safe. In fact, this is when you are most vulnerable. Here are some ideas on safe ways to meet your online friend:

- *Group date:* This is perhaps the safest way to meet your online friend. Bring a handful of your friends along for the ride. This way you have some backup in case your friend tries any funny stuff.

- *Bar or pub where people know you well:* You should be very comfortable in familiar surroundings, and those that know you will sense if something goes wrong.

- *Bookstore café:* Another good place to meet a new friend.

- *Restaurant:* A restaurant is good, but choose carefully. Do not go somewhere that is noisy and very busy. You may get lost in the shuffle.

TIP: Always let people know you are going to meet someone new. Also, call that person at least once during your date and let them how things are going and where you are.

Where Should I Avoid Meeting My Online Friend in Person?

Just as there are good places to meet your online friend, there are some very bad places. Your online friend may be trying to lure you to a place where you are very vulnerable. Here is a list of places to avoid for a first encounter:

- *Mall:* The local mall is a very bad idea. They are generally too busy for this type of meeting. It would be very easy for an abduction to go unnoticed in the surrounding chaos.

- *Park:* Definitely a bad place.

- *Their house:* Need we say more? If your friend suggests their house, chances are you are being set up for a bad time.

- *Your house:* Although this may seem like a good idea, nothing could be further from the truth. Never let your online friend know where you live until you have met them a number of times in another place. Even then, you must be extremely cautious.

- *A dark alley:* Avoid this like the plague.

What Are the Warning Signs of a Bad Situation?

At least once in your online search for love, you will get into a bad predicament. Of course, this isn't the rule, but you should be expecting it anyway. This is typical when your online friend is expecting much more than you are willing to give. If you see any of the following tell-tale signs, then you should move on:

- *Your online friend is wearing a wedding ring.* A real bad tip-off that something just isn't right. Many people will begin looking online for a new friend way before the divorce is actually final, or maybe even if there is no divorce in the works. Try and steer clear of these situations.

- *They insist on meeting you alone.* This person simply cannot be up to anything good. Why else would they want to meet you alone? Do not give in to this request, and if you do, expect to find yourself in trouble. Don't say we didn't warn you.

- *There are more people there than you bargained for.* If you show up for your date and you find your online friend has brought friends, be cautious.

- *Your online friend is 12.* You may have fallen victim to an FBI sting operation.

- *Your online friend is the same sex as you.* Depending on your sexual orientation, this may not be such a bad thing. However, if your online friend said they were a certain sex and they turn out to be the other, you should leave.

How Can I Quickly Ditch My Online Friend without Much Trouble?

Trying to break up a regular relationship is a very hard thing. You would figure that an online relationship would be a snap. It is possible that you may have never even met them in person or even know what they look like. However, it can sometimes be more difficult than you think. People sometimes reveal a good deal about themselves online and don't expect to be dumped because of it. Here is a list of things to try:

- *Be honest.* Don't beat around the bush. Frankly explain that you are not sure if you are a good match.

- *Change your email address.* If they continually send you emails, just change your address.

- *Change your screen name.* If they are constantly hassling you through IM, change your screen name. Better yet, change the program you are currently using.

- *Change your ISP.* Get a new Internet service provider. This will give you an email address with a new domain and eliminate any way that they can find you.

HORROR STORY! A female friend of ours once found herself in a predicament with online dating. She really did not like the fellow she had met but just didn't know how to let him go easily. Something about the virtual nature of online dating made it a very difficult thing to do. The moral here is that if you just are not interested, let the other person know as soon as possible.

What If My Online Friend Just Doesn't Get the Picture?

If you have been trying to ditch an online friend for quite some time but have not been successful, you may need to resort to drastic measures. Although none of us wants to do something as drastic as we are suggesting, it may be necessary to make sure you stay safe. Something about an online relationship brings out the best and worst in all of us. Rejection may lead to something you did not quite expect from your online friend. If the situation sours quickly, follow these tips on how to deal with it:

- *Notify the authorities.* If you receive threats of any type from your online friend, you should notify the authorities immediately.

- *Switch Internet service providers.* Take this step to sever any method by which your online friend can contact you online.

- *Stay off the Internet.* If you can bear to tear yourself away from your PC, you should do so.

Summary

The online experience has truly revolutionized communications in ways no one could have foreseen even 10 short years ago. Technologies like email and instant messaging have gotten a strong foothold in even the most private parts of our lives. We now reveal some of our most intimate and private secrets with complete strangers on the Internet. The thing that probably makes this possible is the anonymity the Internet offers us. We forget about our inhibitions and let loose.

But we sometimes may go a little too far. We may reveal information that puts us in harm's way, or we may offend someone with an email. Whatever the case, we need to be aware of the implications of using this technology improperly. After all, our jobs and our personal lives may depend on it.

11

Travel Disasters and Mishaps

Disasters to avoid:

- Having your laptop stolen when you are going through the airport.

- Not being able to find a reliable Internet connection while traveling.

Mishaps and blunders to run from:

- Forgetting to bring the proper equipment so that you can connect your laptop to the Internet.

- Having someone who doesn't know what they are doing mess up the settings on your PC.

- Receiving email but not being able to send email.

Connecting back to your home or office to access files or information was almost unheard of 10 years ago. Once you were on a plane, it was pretty much guaranteed you were cut off from home or work. In fact, you weren't even allowed to turn on any type of electrical device. You might as well have been heading to another planet because you definitely had no way of accessing anything.

Times have changed. The most important advance has been in the area of fast, cheap Internet access. Without the blazing speed of today's Internet, trying to connect was a lost cause. Of course, this does not mean that you need broadband access to connect back home. But let's face it, it sure makes things easier.

Unfortunately, one of the things you will become aware of in your travels is the lack of common standards, which can lead to unreliable connections. Whether you are traveling to another state or flying across the Atlantic, you will find that there is no one way of doing things. To make matters worse, everyone thinks that their way is the only way.

In this chapter we'll help you arm yourself with the knowledge that can keep your travel disasters and mishaps to a minimum. We can't guarantee that we can keep you from missing a plane or getting stuck in Chicago because of a snowstorm, but we can help you keep your devices running and help you stay connected to your home or office.

Travel Survival 101

- Learn what to bring when you travel so that you can minimize travel disasters.
- Learn how to keep your equipment safe.
- Learn what to do if your laptop is stolen.

What Do I Need to Bring when Traveling?

Any traveler that depends on technology should be prepared to face any situation they may find themselves in. You might get stranded somewhere for a few days, or you might not be able to connect to the Internet as easily as you anticipated before you left on your trip. This is especially true if you are traveling outside of the United States. Here are a few items you should add to your travel tool belt:

- *Extension cord:* You should have at least one extension cord of a decent length. These can come in handy at hotels, airplanes, and airports.

- *Outlet adapters:* Buy yourself a universal adapter kit. These should come with all of the common adapters that you will need while out of the country. You can purchase them at Radio Shack for about $15. You can also buy individual adapters for a few dollars each.

- *Phone jack adapter kit:* You will need adapters for plugging in your modem to some phone jacks.

- *Acoustic couplers:* These devices were originally used in the dawn of modern computing to connect computers to telephone company equipment to transmit data. They can be used to connect to the Internet anywhere you have a dial tone. Once connected, you can send and receive email and faxes and access online services wherever you are. These can be used, for example, in telephone booths or on hardwired phones that may be found in hotels. A good place to purchase them is **www.extremecomputing.com**.

- *Modem saver:* These handy devices tell you whether a phone jack is safe for your modem. Plugging a modem into a digital phone line can fry your modem instantly. This happens because of increased voltage levels on the digital lines. Some modem-saving devices can also filter out tax impulses, which are used to determine the length of phone calls for billing purposes.

- *Spare modem and Ethernet adapter:* You should always carry a spare modem in your arsenal. You never know when your main one will stop working. Also, if your laptop has a built-in Ethernet adapter, you should bring a spare one in PCMCIA form. You never know when a built-in port will go bad.

- *Extra-long or retractable phone cord:* In some cases, you will not be able to get close enough to a phone jack to use it with a short telephone cable. Make sure you have a longer cable for cases like these.

- *Power strip or surge protector:* This is another must-have for your traveling tech kit, especially if you are traveling in a country like India where the power can go out on you when you least expect.

HORROR STORY! A client of the consulting company I (Peter) work for was heading to Europe for an important business meeting. Upon arriving at the hotel, he wanted to set up his laptop to make sure all of his presentation materials were in order. He powered up his laptop only to find that the battery was completely drained. He reached into his laptop case and quickly reeled in horror. He did not have the power adapter with him. Had he spent the extra time to make sure he had everything he needed, he would not have been in such a predicament.

How Can I Best Keep My Equipment Safe?

The biggest worry that most travelers have is keeping their important devices like laptops and PDAs from being stolen and keeping them in good working order. The place where theft is most likely to occur is an airport, and so we've included some helpful tips on protecting yourself against theft in airports in the next section. Another place to be on the lookout for theft is your hotel. You should always try to keep your important devices with you when you can. If you need to leave a device such as your laptop in your hotel room for a short period of time, put it away so that it is not sitting out in plain view. We also recommend that you carry your laptop in a case that makes it look less obvious that you are carrying around a laptop.

HORROR STORY! We heard a story on NPR recently that will make anyone who travels with their laptop worry more than they should. A frequent business traveler was rushing off to the airport to catch his plane. When the taxi arrived at his house, he rushed out and put his bags in the trunk. He unfortunately forgot to put his laptop in the trunk; he left it on the ground, behind the taxi. When the taxi driver had to back up out of the driveway, he heard a terrible crunch and he knew instantly that his trip was ruined.

How Can I Protect My Devices from Theft at the Airport?

Airports are hotbeds for all types of criminal activity. In particular, theft is highly prevalent in all phases of the airport experience. Thieves know that travelers are most likely carrying expensive goods, are usually running late, and are at their most vulnerable while at the airport. Here are some tips that can help protect you and your belongings from thieves:

- *Use a laptop or luggage alarm.* If you are traveling with a laptop, you should invest in a motion sensing alarm. They usually consist of two parts, one that stays with your bag and another that stays with you. When the transmitters are separated by a predetermined amount of space, an audible alarm rings. This is also handy if you happen to forget your bag somewhere.

- *Mark your bag clearly.* Make sure you mark your bag with your contact information. This way, if you leave it behind you will be able to quickly identify it. In addition, if it is recovered by airport employees or returned by an honest person, you will be able to reclaim it with very little inconvenience to yourself.

- *Use STOP plates.* A company named STOP sells travelers a device and a service that greatly decreases the chance that a device will be stolen and increases the chance it will be recovered if stolen. The system works by affixing to your laptop a metal plate that has tracking numbers stamped on it and that can't be removed. The thinking behind this system is that thieves will be discouraged to steal devices that have tracking plates. You can find more information at **www.stoptheft.com**.

- *Watch the X-ray machine.* Be very careful at these machines. Ask a security person to hand-check your device. Also, do not place anything on the ground while waiting. One final tip is to wait until there is no one ahead of you to place your device on the conveyor. Don't let the security people rush you into putting your laptop through the X-ray machine until you are ready to follow along with it.

- *Be careful at the check-in counter.* Do not put your device on the ground while checking in your luggage. Thieves love to mill around these areas and make off with whatever goodies they can get their hands on.

- *Disguise your laptop.* Do not carry your laptop in one of those expensive leather cases specifically designed for laptops. A saddle bag or book bag works just as well and will not attract any unwanted attention. The point here is to attract as little attention to your device as possible.

TIP: For more information about how to protect yourself from theft, see Chapter 1.

HORROR STORY! We had a friend who traveled across the United States for business on a regular basis. Because he traveled so much with his laptop without any problems, he never really thought anything would happen to him. In other words, he let his guard down. At an airport on the East Coast, he put his laptop through the X-ray machine before he was ready to go through. The person in front of him was carrying a piece of metal in his pocket and set off the scanner. The security checkers ran over to check the person with the metal in his pocket, and in all the commotion, a thief grabbed our friend's laptop and disappeared. It turned out that the person with the metal in his pocket was working with the thief.

What Do I Need to Know to Use Phone Lines Abroad for Modem Communications?

You should always be aware of the differences in standards around the world. The standards for telephone lines are no exception. You will either know the differences and thrive or have something horrible happen to your equipment. The following tips should come in handy when using phones and modems outside of the United States:

- *PBX or analog:* Modems are designed to work on analog phone lines that are usually found in homes and small offices. In your travels, you will most likely run into a private branch exchange (PBX) phone system. PBX systems can be found in hotels, businesses, government offices, and facilities for other medium to large organizations. PBX phone lines are not held to any standards as regular analog phone systems are. This has led to a wide range of operating voltages used on these lines. Some of them can deliver up to an amp of current to specially designed telephones. Plugging your modem into a PBX jack will most certainly destroy your modem. Your computer's modem was simply not designed to handle anything above 120mA. To make matters worse, PBX phone jacks are impossible to distinguish from normal analog phone jacks without help. Using a modem saver device is your best bet. Most modem savers have an indicator that lights if the phone jack voltage is at dangerous levels.

- *Reversed line polarity:* Telephone wiring is made up of four wires. In the United States and in most other countries, the inner wires are used for line 1 and the outer ones are used for line 2 if it is being utilized. Reversed polarity can occur when this wiring gets reversed because of bad wiring or a nonstandard phone extension cord is used. This mismatch in wiring can lead to a very slow modem connection or no connection at all. Trying to diagnose this can be very difficult, if not impossible. Using a modem saver device that has built-in polarity testing is the best way to determine if reversed line polarity is your problem. Most modem saver products have a yellow light that will warn you of mismatched wiring.

- *Pulse or tone dialing:* You need to be aware of whether pulse or tone dialing is being used in the area you are in. Pulse dialing is used with rotary phones, while tone dialing is used with push button models. As crazy as this sounds, there are still areas in the world where pulse dialing is still in use and will continue to be for a long time. See the following sections for information on how to configure your modem properties to get around this problem.

- *Voice mail notification dial tone:* Voice mail systems have a tendency to do strange things to dial tones, such as create longer tones, several short tone bursts, or a delay in the dial tone. They do this in order to notify you that you have voice mail. This change in the dial tone can wreak havoc on your dialing software. Setting your software to ignore dial tones is the best way to combat this. See the following sections for information on how to configure your modem properties to get around this problem.

- *Pulse noise or tax impulse:* These are tones that are inaudible to the human ear and used by phone companies to track the length of a phone call. These tones will prevent your modem from dialing out and making a connection to the Internet. They are commonly used in India, Spain, Switzerland, Austria, Belgium, the Czech Republic, and Germany. Some modem saver devices have built-in filtering for these annoying tones. When buying a modem saver, make sure it includes this important feature. Setting up your modem to ignore dial tones will eliminate this problem as well. See the following sections for information on configuring your modem properties to get around this problem.

Getting Connected

- Learn the best ways to get an Internet connection while you are traveling.
- Learn how use a pay phone to connect to the Internet.
- Learn how to deal with modem problems.

How Can I Best Access the Internet while Staying at Hotels?

The hotel room is one of the best places to get a reliable Internet connection. You will probably end up doing more of your work there than anywhere else. You will also probably need access to the Internet for research purposes and for possibly connecting back to the office. Here are some of the better and more reliable ways you can connect to the Internet at a hotel:

- *Check in advance.* Call ahead and ask whether the room has data ports for either dial-up or broadband Internet access. Most hotel chains offer at least a dial-up line in every room.

- *Use wireless hotspots.* More and more hotels are offering wireless access in their lobbies and other common areas. Call ahead to see if the hotel you are staying at offers this service. Your hotel might also be right down the street from a retail location, such as Starbucks, that offers a free hotspot for Internet access.

- *Look for an Internet café.* There may be an Internet café located in or around the hotel. You can check for Internet café locations at **www.cybercafes.com**. They have an exhaustive database of thousands of Internet café locations around the world. You can also find Internet cafés by searching near universities and colleges.

- *Use a pay phone.* See the next section for tips on how to use a pay phone to connect to the Internet.

HORROR STORY! A friend of ours was traveling in Bangkok several years ago. In his room there was an Internet connection port that would plug into his laptop. He couldn't get it to work right away so he asked for help from the hotel's IT guy. The IT guy came and reconfigured some settings on his laptop. After that, not only could he not connect to the Internet, his laptop became unusable for the rest of the trip and he had to borrow another computer so that he could give an important presentation. The Lesson: Never let anyone touch your computer's settings while you are traveling unless you are certain they know exactly what they are doing.

How Can I Use a Pay Phone to Connect to the Internet?

It is possible to use a pay phone to connect to the Internet, especially if you can't find a connection while traveling. Do you recall that acoustic coupler we asked you to carry with you earlier in the chapter? Well, this is where you will use this little gem. The first thing you want to do is dial the number yourself to verify that the number works. You should hear a modem tone. Once you have verified that you have a valid number, you need to set up your equipment. Here are some tips:

- *Set up the coupler.* Make sure you know which side of your coupler goes to the phone receiver's mouthpiece. Obviously, if you have the coupler backwards, you will not be able to make a connection.

- *Check the distance.* Keep the speaker of the phone receiver centered on the coupler. The goal here is to have a nice loud signal so that the coupler can do its thing.

The actual act of dialing out can be tricky. However, with enough practice, it should be a very easy thing to do. Here are the two options for dialing and connecting up:

- *Manual dialing:* You can dial the number on the keypad yourself. It's a little more difficult than having the computer dial for you, but it's not impossible.

- *Computer dialing:* Place the receiver on the coupler. Get a good dial tone. Then just let your computer do the dialing.

If everything was done correctly, you should hear the usual squawking of the modem and should soon be connected. For best results, you should test these techniques thoroughly before leaving on your trip.

How Can I Set Up My Modem to Ignore the Dial Tone?

Setting up your modem to ignore the dial tone should be one of the first things you do when setting up your PC for international use. This is necessary because of all the extra tones being used for voice mail, tax impulse, and whatever else foreign telephone companies decide to use. Here are the steps to follow to have your modem ignore the dial tone:

1. Click Start | Control Panel.
2. Double-click Phone and Modem Options.
3. Click the Modems tab.
4. Select your modem and click Properties.
5. In the next window, click the Modem tab.
6. Uncheck the box labeled "Wait for dial tone before dialing."
7. Click OK to save your changes.

How Can I Set Up My Modem to Work on a Pulse Dialing System?

In your travels, you are bound to find yourself in an area in which rotary phone technology is still used. Your modem connection on your laptop more than likely will not be configured to dial using rotary phone systems. Here's how to make this change in your dialing properties:

1. Click Start | Control Panel.
2. Double-click Phone and Modem Options.
3. Click Edit.
4. Click the radio button for pulse dialing.
5. Click OK.

Using Remote Access

- Learn how to make sure your remote access works when you need it to.
- Learn how to protect your remote connection from hackers.

What Is the Best Way to Connect to a Remote Computer while Traveling?

If you are traveling with a laptop, you can use it to safely connect to a computer that is at your home or office. This technique is called *remote access* and requires that you have the following:

- A remote access program that will allow you to connect to your home or office computer.

- A good connection to access your home or work network. It is highly recommended that you have a high-speed broadband connection at both ends of the remote connection. At the very least, there should be a high-speed connection at the place you are trying to connect to. Without a high-speed connection, you will find it very difficult to use any sort of remote connection technology.

- You need to set up your hardware so that it can communicate remotely. We'll show you the different ways to do this in the section "How Can I Setup My Hardware for a Remote Connection."

What Remote Access Programs Can I Use?

Here is a list of some of the more popular remote access programs available:

- *Remote Desktop Protocol (RDP):* Remote desktop connection is a nice feature of Windows XP. It allows computers to remotely log into an XP computer that has been configured to accept incoming connections.

- *RealVNC:* This program has one huge advantage over some of its counterparts: it is completely free. One very nice feature of this program is that it is OS independent. You can control a Mac remotely using a PC and vice versa. It is also available for Linux, Solaris 2.5, HP-UX 11, OS/2, and a host of other operating systems. It lacks some of the features offered by pcAnywhere, but who really cares when you look at the price difference. You can find more information and download RealVNC at **http://realvnc.org**.

- *pcAnywhere:* Symantec touts pcAnywhere as "The world's leading remote control solution." Its key features include 13 different authentication methods to choose from, mandatory password protection, a host chat feature, file transfer capabilities, and the ability to hide pcAnywhere connections to protect from hackers. More information can be found at **www.symantec.com**.

- *Citrix (ICA):* Usually only found in business environments, Citrix MetaFrame is the pinnacle of remote access solutions. It also carries a hefty price tag. However, if you are a business owner and have a large traveling workforce, this product simply cannot be beaten. More information can be found at **www.citrix.com**.

- *GoToMyPC:* A product similar to pcAnywhere that touts an impressive list of features and a very nice price tag. This technology was recently purchased by Citrix as a low-cost alternative to MetaFrame. More information can be found at **www.gotomypc.com**.

How Can I Set Up My Hardware for a Remote Connection?

There are a few ways that you can set up your hardware for a remote connection. Here is a breakdown:

- *Virtual private network (VPN):* VPNs offer the highest level of security when making remote connections to home or office local area networks (LANs). They consist of one or more remote sites connected to a central LAN through the Internet. The cost of these components has dropped significantly in recent years, making this approach an attractive option for the mobile worker.

- *Port forwarding:* This method is used when the computer that you wish to connect to is behind a home or corporate firewall and/or router. You connect to the home or office network using one of the programs listed in the preceding section. Virtual ports on the router are forwarded to a computer that is "listening" for connections used by these programs.

- *Direct Internet connection:* This involves having your home or office computer directly connected to the Internet.

TIP: Make sure you have your remote solution working properly before you leave for your trip. It won't do you any good to get to your destination only to find out that you will not be able to connect successfully.

There may also be times when you want someone to be able to connect to your computer remotely. Although you could use pcAnywhere or GoToMyPC, Windows XP has a feature that is tailor-made for this purpose. XP comes with a handy tool called Remote Assistance. Using remote assistance, you can send someone a request for assistance and allow them to access your desktop over the Internet. By default, this feature is disabled as a security measure to prevent unauthorized access. Turning it on is easy. Just follow these steps:

1. Click Start.
2. Right-Click My Computer and select Properties.
3. Click the Remote tab.
4. Check the box labeled "Turn on remote invitations and allow invitations to be sent from this computer."

Once you have enabled this feature, you can send invitations and receive remote assistance.

How Can I Make Sure My Remote Connection Works when I Need It?

Setting up your remote connection system is one thing; making sure it will work when needed is another. There is nothing more frustrating than trying to connect to a remote computer, only to find out that a component in your setup is not working properly. Here's what you can do:

- *Lock your computer.* You can lock the desktop by pressing Ctrl+Alt+Del and selecting Lock Computer on Windows XP and Windows 2000 systems. This will prevent anyone from changing the configuration when you are gone.

- *Use passwords.* Some of the remote access software packages allow you to password-protect the host service. This will prevent anyone from shutting it off or changing any of the settings.

- *Notify people.* Let your co-workers or family members know that they should not touch the computer. Threaten to cut off their fingers just to be completely sure they will leave your computer alone. (We're kidding, of course.)

- *Test it.* Always test your remote connection before you leave on your trip. A few minutes spent testing now will save you aggravation later. Make sure you can connect and disconnect successfully several times before leaving. If anything seems wrong, fix it before you leave. Chances are it will not correct itself.

- *Purchase a dedicated or "business"-class Internet connection.* ISPs often offer upgraded versions of their residential services. These upgraded services offer you greater reliability than is available from normal residential access. They are typically part of more reliable network segments that are monitored and maintained to a higher level. However, they do carry a hefty price tag. Starting prices are usually around $80 per month and rise exponentially from there.

How Can I Access My Home or Office Computer without Using a Static IP Address?

This is usually only an issue when you are trying to connect to a home network remotely. Most businesses purchase Internet access that provides them with a static IP address. This means that the address never changes. Residential customers, on the other hand, do not have this luxury. They are provided with what is called a dynamic IP address. These are addresses that change at intervals that can be hard to predict. You will be unable to connect to your remote host if you do not know the IP address. There are a few ways to get around this, though:

- *Use cable modem instead of DSL.* Cable modem service providers tend to allow their customers to hold onto the same IP address for a long time. Therefore, if it only changes once every few months, you should be good to go. The easiest way to check your IP address is by going to **www.whatismyip.com**. The address will be displayed in big blue numbers at the top of the page. Just record this number and use it when you need to connect remotely.

- *Use dynamic DNS clients.* Another way to obtain your current IP address at home or the office is to use a dynamic Domain Name System (DNS) program. DNS is sort of like an Internet phone book. When you type www.google.com into your web browser, your computer must find the address. DNS servers provide the address to your computer's request. These free DNS programs work using this principle. Popular dynamic DNS programs are available from No-IP.com and dynu.com.

- *Purchase a static IP address.* This is the best way to ensure that your IP address will never change. You should expect to pay a premium for this service.

How Can I Protect My Computer from Being Accessed Remotely?

Being able to connect remotely is great, but it also means that others may be able to connect to your computer. You need to be aware of the possibility of this happening and know how you can protect yourself. Hackers spend countless hours probing the Internet looking for vulnerabilities such as computers that are listening for connections. Once they determine that there is a program listening on a particular port, they will concentrate on breaking into your computer or network through this vulnerability. You can prevent this suspicious activity from happening by taking the following steps:

- *Use strong passwords.* Make sure you password-protect your computer accounts and be sure to use strong passwords. And whatever you do, do not use a blank password or something that is easy to guess.

- *Turn off host software when not in use.* If you are not planning to connect remotely anytime soon, you should disable the software. Turn it on only when you will be away from your home or office for any length of time.

- *Close ports on your router when they are not needed.* Temporarily close or disable the port forwarding on your router. This will effectively keep hackers from discovering any vulnerability in your setup.

- *Keep your computer turned off.* Hackers will not be able to connect to a computer that is not powered up. This is a simple but very effective solution to this problem.

- *Disconnect from the Internet.* Another time-tested solution for keeping people out of your computer.

- *Use a VPN whenever possible.* As we stated previously, VPN connections offer you the greatest level of security when setting up remote connections.

Receiving Email

- Learn how to make your email work better when you travel.

Why Will My Email Client Receive Email but Not Send It?

When you connect to the Internet through a hotel or airline network, chances are it will be with a different ISP than you normally use at home. Everything should go smoothly with one tiny exception. Your email client (Outlook, Outlook Express, Eudora, and so on) may not be able to send emails using your current setup. You will probably also get an error message telling you your email client is unable to relay or cannot contact a Simple Mail Transfer Protocol (SMTP) server. SMTP servers are email servers that handle the sending of your email. When you click the send button in your email client, messages will just sit in your outbox. This is because your ISP's SMTP server will not send emails that originate from another ISP's network. To fix this, you need to change the SMTP server setting in your email client. You should check with the hotel or airline you are flying to determine what setting you should use in your email client settings. Check your email client's help files for instructions on how to change SMTP server settings.

How Can I Check My Email on the Web?

If you typically send email from your email client (Outlook, Outlook Express, Eudora, and so on) you probably are not familiar with using any other methods of checking email. This can be a problem if you do not have access to your device. You may have other options at your disposal, though. Whoever supplies you with email service may also offer web browser access to your mailbox. This means that instead of using your email client, you would be checking your email by using web browser. AOL, SBC, Yahoo, and MSN are just some of the companies that offer this service to their subscribers. To use your ISP's web interface, you need to have some specific information which they should be happy to provide to you. The company you work for may also have some form of web access for email. Contact your email provider or network administrator and find out the following information:

- *URL:* Make sure you know the URL of the email system. It will look something like **www.example.com/exchange**.

- *Username/password:* Without this vital information, you will be locked out of your email. This information should be the same username and password you plug in to your email client to retrieve your email. Make sure you have these if you intend on using a form of web access email.

How Can I Send Email without Using My Computer or PDA?

At times, you may need to send email while away from your laptop or PDA. You may have left these devices at the hotel room, or maybe you did not bring them on your trip at all. As usual, we have some tips on how to send emails without having access to your devices:

- *Internet café:* Internet cafés are great places for doing quick and easy computing. You read about these nifty places at the beginning of the chapter.

- *Email-capable phone booth:* These are the new rage in Europe and Asia. You pop into a phone booth, drop in a few coins, and send an email. How much easier can it get? Verizon is also planning to make phone booths capable of making wireless connections. Just when everyone was tearing these things down, someone has found a new use for them.

- *Public library:* A library is another great place for getting yourself connected to the Internet quickly. Libraries offer quick and easy access to the Internet for free or next to nothing. The only snag can be if the library requires you to live in the city it is located in. If possible, you should check ahead of time for the policy in the city you will be visiting.

- *Cell phone:* The majority of cell phones these days are email-capable. You just have to purchase an email-capable phone and the service from your cellular provider.

HORROR STORY! This is a horror story for one person that turned into a great experience for one of our friends. Our friend was traveling in Italy on a vacation and he stopped in an Internet café that had wireless access. While he was connecting up and checking his email, he noticed a very frazzled woman who was having difficulty getting her laptop to work. He quickly learned that she was desperately trying to get connected so that she could send an email to her employer, Delta Airlines. He took the time to help her out and she rewarded him with an upgrade certificate so that he could fly home in Business Elite class. So while you are on the road, it's always a good idea to take the time to help out others who are struggling to get their devices to work.

Getting Power

- Learn how to conserve precious battery power.
- Learn how to prepare for using your devices on foreign electrical systems.

How Can I Find Outlets in an Airport or on an Airplane?

Keeping your devices charged while on a business trip can be a maddening experience. They always seem to let you down when you need them the most. Trying to keep them charged when you have limited access to outlets is even worse. Since you cannot predict when your next opportunity for charging will be, you need to be prepared to seize any chances you get. Now is definitely not the time to be shy either. You need to learn to schmooze airport employees to get the fix of electricity you need. Here are some sources for the power you'll need:

- *Passenger waiting areas:* These areas offer some of the best choices in electrical outlets. They are loaded with support columns that should have an outlet or two. You may have to stand up or sit on the ground, but we think this is better than having a dead battery.

- *Arrival/departure gate:* Finding an outlet near these gates is usually a sure bet. The staff members that work these gates are usually friendly and may let you use an outlet if you are nice to them. Bribe them with chocolate if you have to.

- *Monitor cleaning crew:* The cleaning crew can quickly provide you with some prime electrical outlets. They use equipment (vacuum cleaners, floor waxing machines, and so on) that require outlets.

- *Airport lounge:* Strike up a conversation with the bartender and tip heavily. Chances are there are outlets behind the bar that you can use. There may also be outlets sprinkled in and around the lounge area.

- *Bathrooms:* Bathrooms can sometimes hold farms of electrical outlets. Look for these both in the airport and on the airplane. Just remember not to forget your device there while charging it. Chances are it will make legs and run before you realize what happened.

- *Airplane seat:* Some airlines now have electrical outlets located right at your seat. After years of only offering an audio outlet, they finally realized what every traveler needs and gave it to them.

- *Floors:* Look for shiny brass rectangular covers in the floor. These are usually used to provide power for vacuums and floor waxing equipment. Make sure you have a large coin handy in order to remove the covers. Using these outlets may draw suspicion from airport staff, so be wary of them.

TIP: Carry an extra-long extension cord in your arsenal. This can be handy both in the airport and on the airplane for charging your device when you cannot actually stand next to the outlet.

WARNING! Be very cautious about using the sources given here overseas. If in doubt about whether to use a particular outlet, you should ask someone. You sure don't want to end up in a foreign jail cell because you needed to charge your device.

How Can I Increase My Battery Life while Traveling?

Making the most of your battery charges is somewhat of an art. The untrained traveler will quickly make mistakes and end up with a dead device. Don't laugh; it happens to even the best of us every once in a while. The thing you need to remember is that batteries hold a finite amount of energy and should be treated as a precious commodity. Don't waste power by keeping your device on longer than you need to, and always charge your battery whenever the opportunity presents itself. Here's what you can do to make the most of your battery charges:

- *Use AC power whenever possible.* Whenever the opportunity presents itself, plug into a wall outlet. When you do this, your laptop does not use the battery and also charges it. Every little bit helps when it comes to conserving power. Do not let these precious opportunities pass you by. You will most certainly regret it later on in your trip.

- *Bring spare batteries.* Purchase at least one high-quality spare battery for your device. Rotate your batteries on a frequent basis to keep them fresh. If you can afford it, think about buying several batteries to use as backups. This will also protect you in case one of your batteries stops working altogether.

- *Use Windows standby power mode.* This feature is a true battery saver. The biggest advantage of using this mode is not having to start your computer from scratch each time you need it. So you benefit twice from using this feature: having faster startups and saving power. What more could you ask from something that comes free with Windows?

- *Turn off any auto-save features.* Some applications have a built-in feature that saves your work automatically. At a predetermined interval, your work is saved in case of power failure or some other bad thing happening. When you are trying to preserve battery life, it is not a good feature to have activated. Every time the auto-save kicks in, your device has to spin up the drive the file is stored on to save it. This wastes valuable energy and can drastically reduce your batteries' run time. Check your software's documentation for instructions on how to disable any auto-save feature it may be using.

- *Turn off your sound card.* Unless you absolutely must have sound capabilities in your device, you should disable it. The sound should be disabled in the device BIOS. Just muting the sound or disabling the card in Device Manager does not truly prohibit it from consuming valuable power. Keep in mind that some device BIOSs do not allow you to disable onboard sound. Check your device's documentation for more info on how to do this.

- *Reduce monitor resolution.* A high monitor resolution can reduce battery run time. Try setting it to a lower resolution to conserve power.

- *Reduce monitor brightness.* You can greatly extend your battery life by reducing the brightness of your device's display. It takes more power to create a higher brightness level. If you absolutely need more light, you should consider investing in a clip-on light that draws its power from batteries. Just be sure to have spares of these batteries on hand for when they go dead.

- *Remove unnecessary PC cards.* Removing PC cards prevents them from robbing power from your device. These cards, when plugged in, still consume electricity even though they may not be currently used. Just keep in mind that you will not be able to remove a modem or network card if you are planning on connecting using these items.

- *Refrain from using drives.* By drives, we are referring to floppy drives, CD/ROM drives, DVD drives, and so on. Playing these auxiliary components can consume an extreme amount of battery power and should be avoided at all costs. If you really have to play that Cher CD or watch *Shrek* for the millionth time, plug into AC power.

- *Test your battery.* A battery that will not hold its charge does you no good. Test it by giving it a full charge, shutting down your computer, removing the battery, and testing it according to your device's manufacturer instructions.

- *Stay offline.* Whenever possible, you should avoid using the Ethernet or modem connections. They consume power and can help drain your battery.

- *Remove USB devices.* These can also drain precious battery power. Disconnect them whenever you are not using AC power.

- *Disable any screen savers.* Set your screen saver to a blank screen. Displaying a fish tank or fireworks is completely unnecessary and will drain your battery faster than just having the blank screen saver. You will not score as high for style, but you'll have power when you need it.

What Can I Do If My Plugs Don't Fit Another Country's Outlets?

Because of a lack of standards, the international traveler needs to know beforehand what to expect. Here is a list of the most common outlet and plug configurations you are likely to run into while overseas on a business trip or vacation:

- *Type 1 (flat blade):* These are the common size plugs found in the United States and many other countries. They usually consist of two equal-sized flat blades. In the United States and Canada, you will find that one of the blades may be larger than the other blade. This is to prevent accidental shock. Most of your devices will have this type of plug. Flat blade plugs are typically used in 110-volt systems but can be found in 220-volt systems as well. Adapters for these plugs are usually included in most universal adapter kits.

- *Type 2 (flat blade with round grounding pin):* These are very common in the United States and other countries. They consist of two vertical blades and a large circular grounding pin. These plugs are typically used in 110-volt systems but can be found in 220-volt systems as well. Adapters for these plugs are usually included in most universal adapter kits.

- *Type 3 (round pin):* These plugs consist of two circular pins set in a round or rectangular plug. Common variations of this plug also include a third circular pin used for grounding purposes. The location of the third pin can vary greatly. They can be found all over the world. They are most likely to be used in 220-volt systems but can sometimes be found supplying 110 volts. Adapters for these plugs are usually included in most universal adapter kits.

- *Type 4 (rectangular blade):* These plugs consist of three rectangular blades on a hexagonal-shaped plug. They can be found in Europe, Africa, the Middle East, and the Far East.

- *Type 5 (oblique flat blades):* These plugs have three flat blades in a triangular shape. The blades at the bottom of the triangle are angled either inward or outward. They can be found in Israel, Gaza, South America, and the Pacific Islands.

NOTE: *The type numbers listed here have been used solely for the purposes of differentiating between the different plugs. They are not based on any standard. In other words, do not go to Radio Shack and ask for an adapter for a type 3 plug. The sales associate will probably look at you as if you have three heads.*

Crossing Borders and Customs

- Learn how to get through customs without being hassled about your equipment.

What Can I Do to Get My Devices through Customs as Quickly as Possible?

Getting through customs can be a harrowing experience, especially with all of the increased security at airports slowing things down even more than usual. This is one part of your airport experience that you want to go as smoothly as possible. The following guidelines should get you through customs as quickly as possible:

- *Keep your device easily accessible.* Make sure that you can whip out your device on a moment's notice. Not only will you speed up the process, but you may also get a free pass from the customs official for being prepared.

- *Keep your laptop in standby mode.* You may be asked to power up your laptop by customs officials. Keeping your laptop in standby mode is a great way to save both time and valuable battery power. Instead of having to go through a full boot-up, your computer will only have to wake itself up from standby.

- *Keep your battery charged.* When asked to boot up your laptop, you do not want to find out that the battery is dead. Customs officials may force you to stay there until you can charge it.

- *Follow instructions.* Listen carefully to what the customs inspector is saying to you. They have a tendency to be moody, especially when someone is not listening to them.

Will the Security Scanners or X-Ray Machines Ruin My Devices?

There seems to be a great deal of confusion on this topic. People seem to think that the X-ray machine will destroy your computer and all of the data you have on it. Well, rest assured that nothing could be further from the truth. The X-ray machine poses no threat to your device or the data stored on it. However, there is a way that these checkpoints can be hazardous to your equipment. The conveyor belt used to transport items through the X-ray machine is a hot target of thieves. You should be extremely wary about putting your device through one. You may even want to have a checkpoint guard hand-check your machine rather than putting it through the conveyor.

How Can I Avoid Paying Duty Fees on My Devices?

International travelers are required to pay duty fees on items that they purchase abroad. Electronics are especially subject to this type of taxing. Unless you can prove that you purchased the device before arriving at your port of departure, you will be required to pay the fee. If you take the time to go about this properly, you should have no problem bypassing these fees. Here are some things you can do to avoid the dreaded duty fee:

- *Passport:* Make sure the device is noted on your passport at the original port of departure. This means that if you leave from New York, make sure that you declare it at that port and have officials stamp your passport. Missing this critical step can mean paying fees upon your return to New York.

- *Export Certificate:* Request an export certificate at the port of departure. An export certificate is another good way to prove that the device was purchased before you left your port of departure.

- *Purchase receipt:* Carry a copy of the original purchase receipt with you when you travel. An original receipt can make it easier to get your passport stamped or to get an export certificate.

- *Letter from employer:* If your employer has given the device to you for business purposes, then you can carry a letter from them stating this. This should sufficiently prove that you did not purchase the computer while out of the country.

Other Travel Hazards and Challenges

- Learn how to protect your privacy when flying.
- Learn how to print documents while you are on the road.
- Learn how to synchronize networks documents that you use while traveling.

How Can I Keep People from Looking at My Laptop Screen While I'm Working on an Airplane?

This is bound to happen to you sooner or later. The person sitting next to you is intent on looking at what is being displayed on your laptop. Not only is this behavior rude, but it can be counterproductive as well. You have a few options here. Some are legal, others are not. Short of punching the person out, here are a few things to keep the peeping at a minimum:

- *Politely ask them to mind their own business.* This is usually sufficient to stop all but the most obnoxious people. In case this tactic fails, read on.

- *Stop working.* If it really is not necessary for you to be working, then just stop. Watch a movie, read, sleep, do whatever is necessary to pass the time.

- *Use a privacy filter.* These are neat contraptions that make it impossible for someone sitting next to you to see what is on the screen. An added benefit is that they protect your screen from scratches.

Where Can I Print While I'm Away from the Office?

Unless you plan on carrying a small inkjet printer with you on your travels, you are probably going to need other options when it comes to printing. You may need to print last-minute revisions to presentations or sales hand-outs, or you may just want to print some of the emails you have received. Here are a few tips:

- *Try stores such as Staples, OfficeMax, and Kinko's.* These chain office stores offer printing services while you wait. Before you embark on your journey, find store locations that are located on your route and at your destination.

- *Try airport printing.* Several companies now offer high-quality printing at major airports. They have been set up with the business traveler in mind and are very easy to access and use. You just go to a designated "laptop lane" in the airport, connect using either a wireless or wired connection, upload your document via a secured site, and within minutes your document is printed.

How Can I Use My Network Files on My Laptop while Traveling and then Merge Them Back into the Originals when I Return?

Microsoft Windows allows you to store files in this manner with a technology called *offline files.* You can automatically copy files from your network and store a copy on your laptop. When you return home or to the office and reconnect to the network, these files will automatically be merged into the originals. The requirements for using this feature are as follows:

- *Microsoft Windows network:* The files need to be stored on a Windows 2000, XP, or Server 2003 computer.

- *Client machine:* The computer requesting the files must be loaded with Windows 2000 Professional or XP.

To go about setting up this useful feature, follow these instructions:

1. Browse through your network to the folders or files you want to make available offline.

2. Right-click the folder or file and select "Make available offline."

The next time you log off the network, the folder will automatically be copied into your offline files folder. While you are away, you can modify these files as many times as you like. When you return from your trip, the files will be merged back into the originals when you log back into the network.

How Can I Store Web Pages on My Computer and View Them Later?

Microsoft introduced a neat new feature in Windows 2000 called Offline Web Browsing. This feature allows you to store web pages in Internet Explorer on your computer for browsing while you are offline. As a seasoned traveler, you will probably find this feature very useful. Here are some cases in which this feature would be useful:

- *Travel info:* You could save pages from travel information websites for viewing at a later time. You may not always have access to the Web in your travels and may need some of this important information.

- *Business presentation:* If you are planning to present material that is available on the Web (such as a company website), you can store this info offline. When it comes time for the presentation, you will have what you need.

So, now that you have a need for offline browsing, you probably want to know how to set it up. It is very easy to do this. Just follow these simple instructions:

1. Open Internet Explorer and browse to the page you wish to store offline.

2. Click Favorites in the top toolbar.

3. Click Add to Favorites.

4. Check the box labeled "Make available offline."

5. Click OK.

Your saved website will now be accessible from the Favorites menu in Internet Explorer.

TIP: You can also select to save pages that link from that particular website. You can do this by clicking the Customize button and selecting the number of pages deep you want to save. Only do this if you have ample hard drive space.

Why Won't the DVD I Bought Abroad Work in My DVD Player Here at Home?

Most people do not quite understand this very common problem. I paid for the DVD, so why won't it play on my DVD player? The answer is a little complicated. In an effort to control how and when a movie is introduced to the public, movie studios have created eight different regions for distributing DVD movies. This allows them to control who can watch a particular DVD release. One example of this is that a movie may be coming out on DVD in the United States and may be simultaneously released in theatres in Europe. In a case like this, someone could buy a boatload of this particular DVD release in the United States, export them to Europe, and sell them. Who would bother going to the movies if you could see it at home?

The system is optional on the part of the disk maker. DVDs lacking this regional lock will play in any DVD player. The regional information consists of one byte of information that is placed at the beginning of the DVD. The regions have been broken down as follows:

• Region 1: United States, Canada, and U.S. territories

• Region 2: Japan, Europe, South Africa, and the Middle East (including Egypt)

- Region 3: Southeast Asia and East Asia
- Region 4: Australia, New Zealand, Pacific Islands, Central America, Mexico, South America, and the Caribbean
- Region 5: Eastern Europe, Indian subcontinent, Africa, North Korea, and Mongolia
- Region 6: China
- Region 7: Reserved
- Region 8: Special international venues (cruise ships, airplanes, etc.)

Another common reason a DVD won't play is because different areas of the world use different broadcasting formats. Not only are the DVDs encoded in different formats, but your DVD player and television may only be able to display the one format for your country. The differences in these formats include picture size, playback speed, resolution, and frequency rates. The following list describes the formats and their assigned areas:

- National Television System Committee (NTSC): America, Canada, North America
- Phase Alternating Line (PAL): Western Europe, Asia, Africa, Australia
- Sequential Couleur Avec Memoire/Sequential Color with Memory (SECAM): Eastern Europe, France

---

TIP: Invest in a "region free" or "code free" DVD player. These DVD players can play back DVDs encoded in any region and in any format. Normally, buying a DVD player for a particular broadcast format requires buying a TV for that same format (i.e., NTSC-NTSC, PAL-PAL). These players include converters that will convert the DVD format to the format of your TV (i.e., NTSC-PAL, PAL-NTSC).

Summary

From the first-time traveler to the seasoned business traveler, everyone will run into a technical mishap sooner or later. It is just bound to happen because of all of the variables involved. This chapter has given you the tools and knowledge to avoid these blunders. We have also shown you ways in which you can increase your productivity by being able to connect to your home or office PC.

There really is no way to making traveling with technology completely fool-proof. However, the tips we gave you should keep you safe and sound for many trips to come.

12

Power Adapters and Batteries

Disasters to avoid:

- Losing a power adapter and not being able to locate a replacement.
- Having a defective battery explode and ruin your device.
- Destroying batteries because you put them in your device incorrectly.

Mishaps and blunders to run from:

- Ruining a power cord that you are trying to repair.
- Having a battery that has a poor battery life.

Power adapters and batteries don't represent the glamorous side of electronics. But without them, the technology we've become hooked on would not be possible.

A power adapter's sole purpose is to convert incoming AC voltage to outgoing voltage. This outgoing voltage can be AC or DC (no, not the rock band). You might be saying to yourself at this point, "Why is this necessary?" Well, imagine if engineers had to use the voltage that came out of your wall to power your devices? Can you imagine a PDA that ran on 120 volts DC? The cost of engineering a device to operate at this higher voltage would be astronomical.

Batteries, on the other hand, are simpler than power adapters. But if you use a device such as a laptop on a regular basis and your battery goes out, you learn really quickly how important your batteries are. Batteries come in all sizes, shapes, and strength levels. You are probably most familiar with the common household types of batteries such as AA, AAA, C, D, and 9-volt batteries.

In this chapter we'll show you how to deal with disasters, mishaps, and even a few blunders that can occur with power adapters and batteries. The tips in this chapter might just save you at a critical time when you lose power and need it the most.

Power Adapter Problems

- Learn what you can do if you lose your power adapter.
- Learn how you can repair a defective power cord.
- Learn what to do if your power adapter overheats.

What Can I Do If I Lose My Power Adapter?

Why does this kind of thing always happen when you are traveling or right before you have to get some important work done or give an important presentation? Don't give up all hope because there are some things you can do to save your butt:

- *If you are using a laptop, make sure you have backed up all the data you'll need.* Assuming that you have some battery life left on your laptop, use the time to make copies of files that you'll need so that, if possible, you can use another computer while you are getting a replacement power adapter.

- *Check with the manufacturer of your device.* Using the Internet is the quickest way to do this. You may be able to order a new power adapter and have it shipped overnight. Make sure that you have the serial and model number of your PC handy and that you order the correct one.

- *Look on eBay.* If you have an older PC, you might be able to find a power adapter on eBay.

What Should I Look for when Buying a Replacement Adapter?

Buying a replacement adapter for your device used to be a big headache. Electronics stores carried a ton of adapters that only worked with specific devices. Trying to find the correct replacement was almost impossible. This problem could then be compounded by sales staff that were inexperienced and unwilling to help you in your quest.

Local electronics stores such as Radio Shack now go to great lengths to make sure replacing an adapter is an easy and smooth process. They now carry a wide selection of adapters in a wide array of output types. Adapters are available in single- or multi-voltage versions. The multi-voltage versions have a switch on them that allows you to change their output voltage. They also have interchangeable connectors that are matched through a numbering system.

Now you have the good news, but there is still some bad news. You still have to know what type of adapter to purchase. Here is a list of things you need to know:

- *Correct connector:* This is imperative. Without the correct connector, you will not be able to plug your adapter into your device. These connectors usually have a male end on them. If you have the original adapter, bring it with you to the store so that a salesperson can match it up for you. If the original is missing, bring the device with you. A good salesperson should be able to determine what connector you need by looking at where it plugs into your device.

- *Proper output voltage:* Another important factor. You need to know if it is AC or DC, and the exact voltage level.

- *Proper output amperage:* Output amperage should be around 50 percent more than the level required by the device.

What Should I Do If I Plug the Wrong Power Adapter into My Device?

We've all done this more than we'd like to admit. It is really an easy thing to do, especially if you're in a rush and just start grabbing wires and plugging things in. Here is a list of problems that will help you identify when this has happened and what to do:

- *There is a burning smell, sparks, and smoke.* An incorrect power adapter may quickly overload itself or your device. This can lead to a burning smell coming from the device, the adapter, or both. Unplug the adapter as quickly as possible.

- *The device will not turn on.* This usually happens when the adapter you used does not have the horsepower to start the device. Ordinarily, this is not a problem, although you should still unplug the incorrect adapter quickly.

- *The adapter or device is hot.* Once again, signs of excessive heat are a bad thing. Quickly unplug the device from the adapter.

- *The device works just fine.* Once in a blue moon, you will find that your device works just fine with a different adapter. Count your blessings; you got very lucky.

HORROR STORY! I (Peter) once went to a friend's house because his scanner stopped working all of a sudden. He said it had been working just fine until he moved his office to a different room. He was not sure if he had plugged it into the correct port on his computer and needed some help. After some quick investigative work on my part, I determined that everything was plugged in and that the problem was not computer-related. It turned out that he had plugged the wrong power adapter into the scanner. This blunder toasted his five-hundred-dollar scanner and could have easily been avoided by properly labeling all of the wires.

What Should I Do If My Power Adapter Gets Hot?

Power adapters tend to generate some heat. How much heat can depend on many things, including the electricity needs of the device, ambient air temperature, and the design of the adapter. If you are concerned about your adapter, here are the conditions to check for:

- *Warm:* A slightly warm adapter is not cause for concern. You can continue to safely use the power adapter.

- *Hot:* A hot adapter may be starting to fail on you. Excessive resistance that builds up in the coils causes the heat. A hot adapter is also a sign of a device that is starting to fail. You should have both items tested.

- *Too hot to touch:* Power adapters should not get to the point where they are too hot to touch. This is usually an indicator of a drastic problem with your device and/or its power supply. These devices should be disconnected immediately and not used further. Also, remove the battery from the device if it has one and have everything tested by a certified repair center.

- *Smoke and melted plastic:* This is definitely cause for concern. Smoke and melted plastic is usually accompanied by a funky smell. Be very careful when trying to disconnect an adapter that has reached this stage. You can be burned or electrocuted.

Can I Fix a Frayed or Broken Adapter or Power Cord?

Fixing a broken power cord or adapter cord can be a tricky proposition. One question you need to ask yourself is whether or not it is worth it. If a replacement cord costs $5, we suggest you buy a new cord rather than fix the old one. On the other hand, if it costs $50 or you might not be able to purchase it at all, you should try to repair it.

The next question that needs to be asked is whether or not you think you are capable of repairing a power cord. If you don't think you are quite up to the task, you should have someone else do it for you. Here are our suggestions for fixing cords:

- *Have the proper tools on hand.* We cannot stress this enough. Some tools that should be on hand include a soldering iron, a wire cutting/stripping tool, and a multimeter for testing the finished product. Other tools that are not necessary but make things easier include a heat gun (for shrinking tubing), a first aid kit (in case you get burned), and a friend to help you out.

- *Make sure you have a proper work environment.* Make sure you have a clear and well-lit workspace and plenty of time. Don't try to do this if you have somewhere to go in 15 minutes. And most importantly, do not attempt this if you are in an agitated state. Believe us; this will only make matters worse.

- *Make sure you have the proper materials.* Make sure you have the parts needed to repair the cord, including extra wire, electrical tape or shrink tubing, and rosin core solder. All of these items can be obtained from your local Radio Shack or home improvement store.

- *Unplug the adapter:* Make sure that you have unplugged the adapter from the wall outlet and device before you begin working on it. Touching an uninsulated wire can lead to electrocution.

HORROR STORY!

The laptop I (Peter) am using to write this section has a power adapter cord that was repaired by yours truly. One day my dog decided he no longer liked the cable and proceeded to mangle it. When he was done, I was left holding the adapter and about 30 pieces of power cord. I checked the manufacturer's website for the price of a new one and was floored. There was no way I was going to shell out a hundred bucks for a new adapter. I grabbed my trusty tool kit and decided I was going to repair it myself. In taking on this project, I pretty much ran into every obstacle I could have possibly run into. Therefore, I feel that I can cover most of the bases when it comes to what to be on the lookout for when trying to repair a power cord.

What Steps Should I Follow to Repair a Cord?

Here are instructions on actually going about fixing the cord:

1. *Determine whether or not you have enough cord left.* If you have plenty of cord, then skip to the next step. If not, you will have to replace the adapter or power cord. Most of these cords are made of very specific types of cables. They are usually made up of an exterior insulation, a layer of copper or aluminum shielding that doubles as a ground, another layer of insulation, and finally, a copper wire that actually carries the electricity. Splicing in a replacement is very difficult for someone who is not experienced with these types of things to do.

2. *Prepare the cord ends.* Strip about three inches of the outer insulation off the cord ends using a suitable wire stripper. Do not try to use your teeth to do this. First of all, this method does not do a good job and looks sloppy, but perhaps more important, you can seriously damage your teeth using this method. You will now probably see the shielding cable we spoke of earlier. Just pull this shielding back. Do not remove it because it will be necessary at a later point. Now you should have one or two wires left. Separate the wires and strip about two inches of insulation off of them.

3. *Use shrink tubing.* If you are planning to use shrink tubing to insulate your repair, now is the time to slip it on. Cut pieces about two inches in length and slip them over each end of your two wires. If you plan on using electrical tape, just skip to the next step.

4. *Connect the wiring.* Take the two ends of your wiring and connect them using a figure-eight pattern. Next, you should apply some rosen flux to both ends of the wire. This will help the solder flow and make a good connection.

5. *Apply the solder.* Warm up your soldering iron for about five minutes. This is important to ensure that it will be hot enough to properly melt the solder and heat the components being soldered. Once it has heated up, apply some solder to the tip of the iron. This is referred to as "tinning" the tip and will help the solder flow around the joint. Next, lightly press the soldering iron onto the joint. Do not press excessively hard because this will only cause the wires to come apart. Once the joint is hot enough, apply some solder to the joint. The important thing to remember here is not to apply the solder to the iron. You want the joint to apply the heat to melt the solder. This will lead to the strongest bond between the solder and wires being soldered. Once a sufficient amount of solder has penetrated the joint, you can allow it to cool.

6. *Apply the shrink tubing or electrical tape.* Once the solder has completely cooled, you can slide one piece of shrink tubing over the soldered joint. Make sure that your tubing covers the entire exposed joint. If any part is left exposed, it may cause a short and subsequent damage to your device. Gently heat the shrink tubing with a heat gun or blow dryer. Make sure that it shrinks evenly and seals up both ends of the joint. Take care not to put the heat gun or blow dryer too close to the tubing because it may melt from the excessive heat. If you have decided to use electrical tape, you can also apply it now. Try to wrap the tape as tightly as possible in a circular pattern. Start on one end of the joint, overlap the original insulation, and make your way toward the other side. One piece of advice we can give you is to not use a new roll of electrical tape. The extra size of the roll will make it difficult to wrap it tight enough.

7. *Connect the shielding.* Now you can connect the shielding that covers the inner wires. You can either just twist them together or solder them. It really doesn't make a difference either way.

8. *Apply the shrink tubing or electrical tape.* Once again, slide a piece of shrink tubing over the shielding and shrink it using a heat gun or blow dryer. If you have decided to use electrical tape, you can also apply it now using the previous instructions.

Once you are done, plug the adapter into a wall outlet and let it sit. You want to do this in case you made a mistake. After you are satisfied that the adapter or cord seems OK, go ahead and plug in your device.

WARNING! Be extremely careful when using a soldering iron. They get extremely hot and can burn your skin badly. Also, make sure you have some sort of stand or holder to put your soldering iron in when it is not in use. Letting one sit on the table is not a good idea. It can easily roll of the table and start a fire if left unattended.

Can I Use a Power Adapter If the Plug Fits?

It always seems that you have more adapters than you have devices to plug them into. This usually happens when you get rid of an old device for a newer model. For one reason or another, human nature prevents us from getting rid of these useless adapters. Unfortunately, these bad habits can lead us into a good deal of trouble. Mistakenly using an improper adapter on a device can destroy it or lead to electrocution or even death. However, that is not to say that you can never use a spare adapter on a device. You can successfully do this if you know what to look for:

- *Input voltage type:* This is always measured in alternating current (AC) voltage because the adapter plugs into your wall outlet, which provides alternating current. The number will typically run from 110 to 127 volts AC. If it reads 210–240 volts AC, it is not meant for use in the U.S. but should be used overseas where 220 volt mains power is common.

- *Output voltage type:* This can be either alternating current (AC) or direct current (DC). Most technology gadgets will use DC current. This value can range anywhere from less than a volt DC to around 15 volts DC for a typical device.

- *Output current:* Output current is usually measured in milliamps (mA). This number can vary greatly from device to device. Typical values range from 300mA to over 1000mA.

Can I Use a Power Adapter with an Amperage Rating Higher than the Device Requires?

Yes—in fact it is recommended to use an adapter with a higher amperage rating than is required. The rule of thumb is to provide at least 50 percent more amperage than is called for on your device's power requirements. For example, if your device calls for 500 milliamps, you should purchase one that supplies 750 milliamps. Here's how you can determine your device's electrical current requirements:

- *Label on the device:* Examine your device for a label that provides power specifications. This same label may have other useful information, such as UL listing information and its FCC ID.

- *Original adapter:* If you have the original adapter, you're in luck. It should have a label or be stamped with power specifications. You may even be lucky enough to find a model number.

- *Device documentation:* Your device's documentation should have a product specification section that will include power requirements.

- *The manufacturer:* Contacting the manufacturer is a surefire way to get power information for your device. Make sure you have the serial number and model number available. This information may be needed in order for you to get the correct specifications.

Why Is My Computer's Power Cord Black and My Monitor's Cord White?

There is no scientific reason why some cables are black and others are white. Power cords actually come in a whole cast of colors (gray, green, white, black, blue, and so on). The more common reason manufacturers use different color cords is so you can easily identify which device is which when trying to connect/disconnect.

WARNING! Just because the color doesn't matter doesn't mean the cord doesn't either. One cable may be thicker (meaning it can handle a heavier load) while another may be thinner. One cable may have three prongs (meaning the connected device needs to be grounded) while the other does not. Always mark your cables so you know which device they go to.

I Mixed Up My Power Adapters; How Do I Know Where They Go?

This is an all too common occurrence these days. With so many electrical devices using adapters, you are bound to mix them up eventually. This is usually done when moving computers to a different room or when storing two devices and their adapters in the same box. Here is how you can determine which adapter goes to what device:

- *Manufacturer:* Some companies manufacture their own power adapters or put their name on an adapter made by another company. This can be an easy tip-off as to where it belongs.
- *Connectors:* Power adapter connectors come in varying sizes, and there are male and female type connectors. Try to match the adapter to the device without plugging in the adapter.
- *Specifications:* Your device should have a label or stamp on it with details about its electrical current needs. Match the adapter to this label by comparing the output voltage and output current numbers.
- *Call to the manufacturer:* Make a call to the device's manufacturer and ask. The manufacturer should be able to provide you with a part number or other information on how to identify which adapter goes with its product.

PREVENTATIVE MAINTENANCE: You can avoid mixing up power cords and adapters by labeling them as soon as you remove them from the box they were shipped in. You can use regular old labels or invest in a high-tech labeling machine. Either way, you are guaranteed this will never happen again.

Battery Problems

- Learn how to protect yourself from exploding batteries.
- Learn how to improve the life of your batteries.
- Learn how to properly charge batteries.

Do I Need to Be Concerned about Exploding Batteries?

Exploding batteries have become almost an urban legend these days. The stories tell of cell phones exploding in people's back pockets or of laptops exploding in people's laps. All of this sounds very dangerous, but do you really need to be worried about exploding batteries? What are the chances of it occurring? Actually, under the right circumstances, the chances of this happening are good. Here is a list of things that can cause an exploding battery:

- *Third-party batteries:* These are batteries that may or may not be made according to the original manufacturers specifications. These batteries usually cost much less than original replacements, but lack the quality of the originals. Things that are skimped on include the casing, proper labeling, and second rate electrolytes.

- *Overcharged batteries:* Overcharging a rechargeable battery or trying to charge a non-rechargeable battery is a surefire way to get it to explode. Batteries build up a great amount of heat when they are charged and even discharged. The faster the charge or discharge, the more heat is generated.

- *Shorted-out batteries:* This is also a quick way to have them explode. Just connecting the two terminals of a battery with a conductor produces heat very quickly. This leads to an almost instantaneous explosion in lithium–ion batteries.

- *Damaged casing:* If you were to slightly crush a battery, you would allow parts that should not come into contact with each other to do exactly that. The result would be a violent explosion.

- *Defective batteries:* A battery that was not manufactured properly can very easily explode. If the battery appears to be damaged in any way; you should not use it.

HORROR STORY! Statistics show that a number of cell phones exploded in 2003. A closer look at the data reveals that many of the phones were manufactured by Nokia. Nokia claims that third-party or counterfeit batteries were to blame. Nokia also found that most explosions were caused by the devices being dropped. The moral of this is that bad batteries and rough activity simply don't mix.

What Should I Do If I Just Purchased a New Device and the Battery Is Dead?

Whenever you purchase a new device that comes with rechargeable batteries, the batteries are packaged in a discharged state (little or no charge). While the battery may have a little charge, you should not use it until you have fully charged it. Consult your owner's manual for the recommended charge time before using the device.

What Can I Do If My Battery Life Stinks?

While batteries have improved over the past few years, there is still a long way to go until we get the kind of battery life we expect. Today's batteries give you enough juice to watch a DVD or use your cell phone for a day, but that's about it. Here are a few tips you can follow to extend the life of your battery:

- *Use power management.* Most devices include power management features to help you get more life from your battery. Power management can provide options to dim the screen, turn off the backlight, and throttle down your CPU. You may also be able to use the hibernate and suspend features included with your operating system. Consult your owner's manual for more information.

- *Mute it.* When your device is muted, the amplifier does not need to draw battery power to play sounds. Your device (like a PDA or cell phone) may even be smart enough to completely turn off power to the amplifier.

- *Eject it.* By removing unneeded CDs, DVDs, memory media, and drives (floppy, CDs, DVDs), you can save battery life by not requiring your device to use power to read these items.

- *Shut it.* Most users have many programs running when their computers start up (most live in the system tray). These programs utilize resources like CPU, memory, and disk access, which ultimately shorten the life of your battery. Close all unused programs to help extend your battery's life.

- *Turn your wireless off.* By turning off your device's wireless capabilities when they're not in use, you can dramatically extend your battery's life.

MYTH BUSTERS: Someone told us that putting batteries in the freezer is good for them. Is this true? The reported purpose of this is that it will make them last longer or may recharge worn-out batteries. Nothing could be further from the truth. Batteries receive no benefit from being exposed to cold. In some cases, it may even help to discharge them quicker.

Why Does My Battery Take a Full Charge, Yet Seems to Be Dead after a Short Amount of Use?

This is commonly referred to as battery "memory" or the "memory effect." Nickel cadmium and nickel metal hydride batteries are especially prone to this effect. The condition can be described as this: when your battery remembers the lowest recharge point and needs a new charge when it reaches that point. This means that if your Ni–Cd battery was only 40 percent used the last time you recharged it; the battery will think it is dead the next time it reaches this 40 percent point. Going through this cycle enough times can irreversibly damage the battery.

TIP: Lithium-ion batteries do not suffer from the "memory effect" and are typically the batteries used in today's laptops, PDAs, and digital cameras. When given the choice, choose the lithium-ion battery until a better technology comes along.

Why Do Dead Batteries Seem to Get Their Charge Back when They Just Sit for a Bit?

This effect is most noticeable in car batteries. You just cranked and cranked your car's starter motor and have completely drained the battery. You leave and come back an hour later and try again. This time the starter motor cranks like a beast. This happens because of products produced by the electrical reaction that takes place in a battery. The reaction products accumulate around the poles of the battery and hinder the reaction. The result is a dead battery. If you wait and let the battery rest, you are allowing these products to disperse.

DID YOU KNOW that the first battery was invented in 1799 by Italian inventor Alessandro Volta? The terms *voltage* and *volts* are derived from his last name. For more information, go to **www.ideafinder.com/history/ inventors/volta.htm**.

Should I Unplug My Device after Charging the Battery?

By leaving your device charging longer than its recommended charge time, you run the risk of overcharging (throw in your own spouse joke here). Overcharging can lead to overheating, which can lead to battery explosion or leakage. Devices that use lithium-ion batteries (most newer laptops, digital cameras, camcorders, etc.) have internal circuitry to prevent overcharging from occurring (that's one reason these batteries are typically more expensive). Check your manual and battery type to avoid overcharging.

Will Putting My Device's Batteries in Backwards Cause Them Harm?

When you place batteries in a device, they must be placed in a certain order (you know, + to +, - to -). Sometimes the symbols are hard to read (other times they are not even present) and you may mistakenly place batteries in backwards. You usually don't notice it until the device doesn't turn on. But will this harm your device or battery? Placing a battery backwards can cause your battery to overheat, leak, or even explode, causing damage to the battery, device, and even you. Always check to see if your device powers on after installing batteries. This will not only tell you if your batteries and device work, but it will also let you know if you installed the batteries correctly.

Will Recharging My Batteries Backwards Cause Them Harm?

As you just learned, placing batteries backwards can cause harm to both the battery and the device that contains it. This is especially true for battery chargers. While some chargers have special checks to prevent charging a backwards battery, others may quickly destroy the battery and the chargers themselves. Check your battery charger indicator lights after placing batteries in the charger. They may indicate if you installed the batteries correctly.

MYTH BUSTERS: Is it true that charging a battery backwards will actually discharge it? While charging batteries backwards can cause some considerable damage, it will not de-charge your batteries.

How Can I Determine What Kinds of Batteries I Need?

You can start by going through the following list:

- *Check the existing battery.* Remove the battery that is in your device now and look for a manufacturer or part number. Also, another good place to look while the battery is out is inside the battery cavity and on the panel or flap that covers the battery cavity. You should be able to find all sorts of info on the battery in these places.

- *Check the device documentation.* The device's instructions should provide you with information on what type of replacement battery to use.

- *Contact the device's manufacturer.* Try searching on the device manufacturer's website. You should be able to find product documentation there.

- *Read the checklist later in this section.*

Can I Use a Different Battery Type in My Device?

While you may use the same battery type from a different manufacturer, you may not be able to use a different battery type even if it comes from the same manufacturer. Different battery types have different charging patterns that may not be compatible with your device and or charge. Consult your owner's manual for compatible battery types.

How Should I Properly Dispose of My Old Batteries?

Old batteries should be disposed of properly. Because some are made from toxic chemicals, they are a threat to the environment. Here is a breakdown, by battery type, on how to dispose of them:

- *Zinc carbon:* These batteries can be disposed of along with household trash. Just do not try to throw them away in large numbers. Old batteries may appear to be dead, but they can still cause problems when they come in contact with each other. Standard methods for disposing of these types of batteries have not yet been adopted. Your local community may offer recycling or collection of these types of batteries if you have a good number of them to dispose of.

- *Lead acid:* Lead acid batteries contain sulfuric acid and must be disposed of properly. When you purchase one of these batteries, you are usually asked to return the old one in exchange. The battery you turn in is then recycled. If you have ended up with one of these in your garage, there are a few things you can do. Check with your local town hall and see if it has a hazardous waste pickup. Also, most local garages should be willing to take them off your hands.

- *Nickel cadmium:* Generally used in rechargeable batteries. All Ni–Cd batteries are identified by the EPA as hazardous waste and must be recycled.

- *Nickel metal hydride:* Commonly used in laptops. They are considered non-hazardous waste, but do contain elements that can be recycled.

- *Lithium:* These batteries most definitely need to be disposed of properly due to lithium's explosive nature when in contact with water.

Checklist for Choosing a Battery

There are many ways to classify batteries. These classifications can be broken down into types and categories. A battery's type refers to the way the battery is constructed and its category refers to how it is used. Here is a breakdown of the various types and categories of batteries:

- *Electrolytic makeup:* This refers to the types of chemicals used to produce the chemical reactions in batteries. They can be acidic, mildly acidic, and alkaline. Acidic electrolytes often use sulfuric acid as their main component. They are typically used in automobile and marine applications. Mildly acidic electrolytes are used in most inexpensive household batteries. Alkaline electrolytes are used in batteries for cellular phones, cameras, laptops, and other similar electronic devices.

- *Wet or dry cell:* Wet cell batteries are ones in which the electrolyte is in liquid form. The electrolyte is allowed to flow around the battery case. Dry cell batteries use a solid or powder-based electrolyte.

Batteries can be made of many different chemicals. Typically, the use of the battery dictates what it is composed of. Here is a list of some types of battery compositions:

- *Zinc carbon (Z-C):* These batteries are the standard run-of-the-mill "cheapos" you buy at the supermarket or local "Battery Shack." They consist of an acidic paste with zinc and carbon electrodes. They are typically not rechargeable and have another very major drawback: sloping discharge curve. This means that the more you use them, the less voltage they can produce. Their cases are made of zinc and actually take part in the chemical reaction that produces the electricity. This can lead to holes forming in the case and the subsequent leakage of a mild acidic electrolyte—very dangerous.

- *Lithium photo:* These batteries are used in cameras because of their ability to provide short bursts or surges of power. This is obviously needed to power the flash in low-light situations. These batteries are expensive and cannot typically be recharged.

- *Lead acid:* Lead acid batteries are used in automobile, marine, and heavy truck applications. They are typically what people mean when they speak of "wet" cell batteries. They are composed of metal plates sitting in an acidic solution encased in plastic.

- *Nickel Cadmium (Ni-Cd):* Nickel Cadmium batteries used to be the de-facto standard for powering mobile electronics such as laptops. They have since been replaced by other types of batteries. Their major downfalls were that they were extremely heavy, were extremely prone to the "memory effect," and contained cadmium, a toxic heavy metal that needs to be recycled properly.

- *Nickel Metal Hydride (Ni-MH):* Nickel metal hydride batteries were introduced as replacements to nickel cadmium batteries. They were highly touted because of their lack of cadmium, being less prone to "memory effect" than nickel cadmium, and offering twice the power output of similarly sized nickel cadmium batteries. They do have their flaws as well. They have difficulty operating in extreme low or high temperatures and are not fully recyclable.

- *Lithium ion (Li-ion):* Lithium ion batteries have become the first choice of device manufacturers for supplying power. They offer the same power output as nickel metal hydride and weigh 20 to 35 percent less. They are fully recyclable but require special handling. Lithium batteries do not require extensive charging when new; one regular charge does the trick. We like this feature because we don't have to wait 24 hours before playing with our new tech toys. Lithium ion does have a few drawbacks. Lithium is a highly volatile substance. This means it can explode when under the right conditions. It is also more expensive than other battery technologies.

- *Lithium ion polymer:* These batteries have never really caught on. Their claim to fame is that they can be produced in very slim profiles. They are also extremely lightweight. This can be accomplished because they do not need a metal casing. They are also safer than traditional lithium ion batteries. There is no chance of overcharging and less chance of electrolyte leakage. When compared to lithium ion batteries, they fall short in that they are more expensive to produce, they do not put out as much power, and there are no standard sizes.

Hazards with Power

- Learn how to protect yourself from power surges and power loss.
- Learn how to obtain and use a surge protector.
- Learn how an uninterruptible power supply (UPS) can protect you from power loss.

Do I Need to Be Concerned about Power Surges?

The electricity that enters your home through your outlets is a very powerful force that can power your devices and kill you at the same time. Actually, in the form of a power surge, the electricity in your home can also kill your devices. Power surges are rapid, sudden increases in electricity, also known as spikes. Spikes can occur miles from your home but can be carried all the way back to your home through electrical, phone, or cable lines. While typical voltage to the American home is 120 volts, a spike can cause the voltage to be raised to 500 volts or more. Lightning is the typical cause of a power surge. Surges can also occur when power is restored from a blackout or downed power line (even if you did not lose power). And they can be caused by hair dryers, elevators, air conditioners, and other large appliances. These surges aren't nearly as powerful as lightning, but they can still damage your devices. If a surge gets high enough above normal levels, it can really do some extensive damage. Even small surges over the course of time can cause damage to your devices.

Do I Need to Be Concerned about Loss of Power?

If you live in a place where you lose power from time to time, you could be at great risk. Here are the two main causes of power loss:

- *Brownouts:* Brownouts (also called sags) occur when there is a dip in power. This usually happens in the summer months when the electric company is overburdened with air conditioner electricity demands. Brownouts do not immediately damage your equipment, but they do cause some devices to work harder and possibly overheat.

- *Blackouts:* A blackout is a complete loss of power due to a problem the electric company must correct (downed power line, bad power line transformer, and so on). When you abruptly lose power, you will also lose any unsaved changes in open files and your equipment can get damaged from not being shut down properly.

How Can I Protect Myself from Power Surges or Power Loss?

The easiest method for protecting against power surges is to use a basic surge protector. You can also use an uninterruptible power supply (UPS) device. We'll cover both in this chapter.

Surge protectors operate by channeling the power from a wall outlet to the various devices that are plugged into it. You hardly even know that they are there. As soon as a power surge hits, they spring into action by redirecting the power to the outlet's grounding plug—the third prong on most common wall outlets. The surge protector does this through some of its internal components. These components sense an over-voltage condition and divert power away from your expensive gear. When the power returns to normal, they stop diverting power away from your devices.

An uninterruptible power supply (UPS) provides smooth, constant power to the devices that are attached to it. It achieves this by using a combination of batteries, line conditioners, and surge suppressors. UPS devices have only recently become popular in small offices and the home as the prices have come down. Getting a UPS is your best insurance for protecting against a power loss.

Do I Need to Have a Surge Protector?

A surge suppressor can generally cost $30 and up. Your tech toys probably cost significantly more. To protect them, you should be willing to spend a few bucks. Here are situations in which you really need the protection:

- *Equipment that is not yours:* If you have borrowed someone else's gadgets, you should definitely protect them accordingly.

- *Older house:* Older electrical systems cannot provide the constant power required by today's tech toys. Remember, when these houses were first built, people had one light and maybe one other appliance such as a radio in a room.

- *New house:* Just because you have a new house with a new and modern electrical system does not mean you are exempt from power surges. In fact, surges may be able to get to your gear easier because of the heftier electrical system.

- *Office or work:* Keeping a work computer running at all times is a must. Having one burn up because of a surge leads to costly tech fees and missed work.

- *Large appliances on the same electrical circuit:* Air conditioners and other large appliances are electricity hogs. They are also very erratic in their need for electricity. This constant change in their demands causes surges in electricity and any other electrical device on the same circuit will experience this voltage change.

- *Electronic rust:* This is a term for damage to equipment that occurs from small, unnoticeable power surges that occur in all homes/buildings. The extent of the damage may not be immediate, but it can shorten the life of your devices.

TIP: Some surge protectors come with built-in line conditioning capabilities. The line conditioners filter out noise caused by tiny fluctuations in the line. The end result is a nice, even stream of electricity going to your devices. Another nifty feature to have in a surge protector is a built-in fuse. Sometimes a surge will come in so fast that the normal protection device will not have time to react. An inline fuse will blow before the surge has any chance of doing damage. Also, a built-in indicator light is another nice feature to have. This way, you will know that your surge protector will work when it is needed.

HORROR STORY! We had a friend who was convinced that a surge protector would guarantee him against damage from electrical storms. Unfortunately, he found out the hard way that he was mistaken. During the summer, a lighting storm struck his neighborhood and he discovered that the sheer power of a lightning strike could overpower any type of surge suppressor or protecting device. Your best bet is to unplug any and all devices from the wall outlet during an electrical storm.

Can I Use a Surge Protector on My Phone Line or Broadband Connection?

Most mid-range and higher-level surge protectors come with additional connectors for Ethernet (RJ45), telephone (RJ11), and cable (coaxial). These are important to have because power surges are very capable of traveling along phone lines, cable lines, and your local area network. These surges can wipe out your dialup modem, broadband modem, switches, routers, and anything else that is connected to them.

Why Does My Adapter or Surge Protector Have Three Prongs and My Wall Outlet Only Two?

This is usually the case if you live in an older house with an outdated electrical system. Older homes were built in an era when most electrical devices you plugged into a wall outlet had wooden exteriors.

Most modern outlets have three prongs: a large vertical one on the left called the *neutral* prong, a smaller vertical one on the right called the *hot* prong, and a large circular prong below these called the *ground*. The ground is what is missing in older outlets in older homes.

WARNING! You could get electrocuted by a device if you cut off the third prong or used an adapter. Under normal conditions, this is not a problem, but if something were to happen with the internals of a device, you could potentially be electrocuted. Always use the third prong whenever possible.

Why Won't My Surge Protector or Power Strip Turn On?

Here is a quick checklist of things to look for:

- *Verify that it is plugged into an outlet.* Also, make sure that the outlet you are using is not controlled by a light switch that may be shut off.

- *Check the fuse.* Most surge protectors have some sort of fuse that protects them. Verify that the fuse is good and replace it if necessary. Most units have a fuse that is accessible without opening it up.

WARNING! Always unplug the surge protector from the wall outlet before trying to replace the fuse.

- *Were there any recent surges?* A recent large power surge may have destroyed your surge protector. This usually happens because of electrical storms. For the best protection, you should always unplug all of your devices in electrical storms.

Which Surge Protector Should I Buy?

Obviously, your budget is the main factor for determining which surge protector to buy. However, don't shortchange yourself by buying something that cannot provide the protection you need. The cost of replacing or repairing damaged equipment is always far greater than the cost of purchasing a decent surge protector. Here is a list of features to look for:

- *Price:* Avoid the $3.99 specials. These "surge protectors" do not offer you any protection at all. Conversely, a high price tag does not necessarily mean the product will protect you.

- *Power adapter slots:* These are specially spaced outlets that allow you to plug in large power adapters without taking up multiple outlets.

- *Fuse:* Make sure the surge protector comes with a fuse that's easily replaceable.

- *Warranty or guarantee against device failure:* Try to get one with a guarantee. The guarantees normally state that the company will reimburse you for damage done to your devices as a result of the surge protector failing.

- *Modem and broadband protection:* Make sure it offers protection for dial-up modems, Ethernet devices, and broadband devices.

- *Indicator light:* This will help you determine when there is a problem with your surge protector.

How Do I Reset My Surge Protector After It Has Been Tripped?

If the breaker in your surge protector has been tripped, you will need to reset it. Typically, you will find a reset switch located somewhere on the surge protector. Flipping the switch will reset the breaker and allow you to continue using it.

Do I Need to Have a UPS?

A UPS will protect your computer and peripherals in the event of a brownout or a total power failure, which can result in lost documents and corrupt data and possibly lead to hardware failure. A UPS will also allow you to continue to work even though your power is out. Here are some scenarios in which a UPS provides needed protection:

- *Power fluctuations:* You would be surprised at how irregular the power coming into your home or workplace is. This constant fluctuation can cause a great amount of damage to your electronic devices.

- *Data corruption:* A UPS will prevent data corruption by keeping your computer on during a power outage.

- *Controlled shutdowns:* Some uninterruptible power supplies can communicate with your computer and do some very neat things. They can save and close open documents, gracefully shut down your computer, and turn it back on when the power returns.

What Are the Different Types of UPS Devices?

There are two types of UPS devices commonly used: standby and continuous. Here is a breakdown of how they operate:

- *Standby:* A standby system runs the devices off of your outlet power until it senses a reduction in electricity. When a reduction is detected, the UPS very quickly switches to battery power. Standby UPS systems tend to cost much less than their continuous counterparts. This makes them appealing for home use and use in small offices.

- *Continuous:* Here the attached devices are powered directly from a battery. The battery in turn is constantly being recharged to maintain a steady power output. The benefit to this system is that there is no switch over time. Continuous UPS systems are typically more expensive than standby systems and are commonly found in server rooms and data centers.

Which UPS Should I Buy?

UPS devices range in price from about $40 for inexpensive models to tens of thousands of dollars for data center units. You can likely get by with a basic model, but here are some features to look for:

- *Maximum surge current:* This refers to the highest electrical hit your unit can protect against. It is normally rated in amps. The greater the number, the better the protection.

- *Surge suppression:* Make sure the UPS has some surge suppression capabilities. This will save you money because you will not have to buy another device to handle this.

- *Suppression response time:* This number refers to the time required by the UPS to react to a surge. The lower the better.

- *Transfer time:* This number refers to the time it takes a UPS to switch from outlet power to battery power. Look for low numbers here.

- *Battery recharge time:* This figure is important after a power outage has completely drained your UPS battery. You do not want a unit that takes a long time to recharge your battery in case the power goes out again. Look for the shortest recharge time possible.

- *Number of outlets:* Make sure the model you are considering has enough outlets for all of the devices you intend to use on it. Keep in mind that not all outlets may provide backup capabilities. Some units have outlets that only provide surge protection capabilities.

- *Replaceable battery:* Make sure the unit has a replaceable battery. You do not want to have to replace your UPS when its battery goes dead.

- *Upgradeable battery:* This is an important feature if you plan to add additional peripherals in the future. The luxury of upgrading or adding additional batteries to your unit will save you in the long run.

How Can I Test My UPS to Ensure That It Will Perform in an Emergency?

There are several ways in which you can go about testing your UPS. You should do this on a regular basis. At least once a month is a good rule of thumb. You want to be sure that your unit will protect you and your data in the event of a power failure. Here are some ways in which you can test your UPS:

- *Pull the plug.* A properly working unit will show you some indication that it has switched to battery power or is running solely on battery power. If your computer instantly dies, you have a problem. Check to make sure your computer is plugged into the UPS outlet that is providing backup capabilities. Most UPS devices have both battery backup outlets and separate surge suppression outlets.

- *Use the built-in-self-test feature.* Most UPS devices have some sort of test feature that is activated by pressing a button on the unit. The results of the test are then shown via an LED or LCD display. Some units even allow you to test them using software that you install on your computer. Check your unit's documentation for specific instructions on how to do this.

- *Have the battery load-tested.* Remove the battery and have it load-tested. Most electronics and computer repair shops should be able to do this for you. By load-testing the battery, you are seeing how it would perform when all of your devices are depending on it.

What Devices Should I Avoid Plugging into My UPS?

Not every piece of electrical equipment you own should be plugged into a UPS because all of these additional items can severely limit the time a UPS battery will last. Here is a list of some particularly power-hungry devices:

- *Printers:* These are at the top of the "Do not plug into a UPS" list. In particular, laser printers draw large amounts of current and can drain a battery in no time.

- *Fax machines:* Most fax machines are glorified laser printers. This also puts them into the "Do not plug into a UPS" category.

- *Monitors:* Unless you need to continue working during a power outage, you should not plug your monitor into a UPS.

- *Large appliances:* You do not want to start plugging in things that really do not need battery backup. These include air conditioners, electric space heaters, small refrigerators, and other large appliances. The reason we bring this up is that we have seen every one of these items plugged into a UPS at one time or another.

Why Is My UPS Beeping at Me?

The beeping means that something is wrong and needs attention. Most UPS devices have LEDs or indicators that tell you exactly what is wrong. Some higher-end units can even have you paged or emailed when something goes wrong. Here's what you need to check for:

- *On battery power:* This indicator means that the UPS is running on battery power. This usually happens when your home or office has lost power.

- *Unit overloaded:* You probably have too many devices plugged into your UPS. Either remove some of them or invest in a larger unit.

- *Replace battery:* This means that you must replace your battery.

- *Battery disconnected:* Somehow, your battery must have become disconnected. Inspect the cable ends and make sure they are plugged in and have not been damaged.

- *Low main power or high main power:* The UPS is compensating as a result of low or excessive power. Try plugging it into a different outlet.

HORROR STORY! One of my (Peter's) clients was having problems with their alarm system (or at least that is what they thought). They called the alarm company out multiple times to have them figure out why it was going off even though it was disarmed. After about a dozen service calls, the alarm company finally gave up. On my next visit, I noticed that their UPS battery was showing low on the indicator and brought it to their attention. It turns out it was actually the UPS that was making the noise that they mistook for their alarm.

What Precautions Do I Need to Take when Replacing Batteries in a UPS?

As simple as changing a battery sounds, you can really screw this up very easily. Here are some precautions:

- *Verify that you have the correct battery.* You do not want to unplug everything, take it apart, and then discover you have the wrong battery.

- *Turn off and unplug all connected devices.* Do not try to replace the battery with everything still plugged into the UPS. Shut everything down and disconnect them from your UPS. This will make things much easier.

- *Unplug the UPS.* Make sure you unplug the UPS from the wall outlet. Leaving it plugged in can lead to electrocution.

- *Do not wear any rings, bracelets, or other jewelry.* Metal jewelry can make contact with the battery terminals and weld to your flesh.

- *Make sure you have whatever tools will be necessary to get the job done.* The UPS manufacturer should have included a tool list in its instructions. Also, be sure that all the tools you will use have insulated handles.

HORROR STORY! I (Peter) used to be employed as an auto mechanic. During that time I replaced my fair share of batteries and only had one little incident. However, I experienced something one day that makes me squeamish to this day. A co-worker was replacing a battery and got his ring finger stuck between the positive terminal of a battery and the body of a car. Ordinarily this would not be much of a big deal. Unfortunately, he was wearing a gold wedding ring. We heard some yelling and screaming and came running to his aid. Within seconds his ring had melted down and burned part of his finger to the bone. So whenever you are working with batteries, or electricity for that matter, always remove any jewelry or other metal items you may be wearing.

Summary

Power is an important topic in technology, a topic that we often take for granted. Whether it's a cordless phone, a laptop, a PDA, or a PC, it wouldn't work without the correct supply of power. In this chapter you learned about the importance of power and what to do when it doesn't work as expected. You also learned how damaging power can be to both technology and people, and how to keep them both free from harm. Finally, you learned how to get the most out of your power supply and help extend the life of both your battery and your device.

13

Backup and Recovery

Disasters to avoid:

- Having your system crash and not having a recent backup.
- Forgetting to do regular backups.
- Not being able to restore data that you've backed up because your backups weren't done properly.

Mishaps and blunders to run from:

- Using software that doesn't back up your data properly.
- Losing your backups because you didn't store them in a safe place.
- Having your system crash and not knowing how to restore it using Windows' built-in features.

In our opinion, data backup has to be one of the most important aspects of computer use. Unfortunately, it is also the most overlooked because most people are unaware of how important it is and how not doing it on a regular basis can affect them. For a moment, imagine that someone snuck into your house and stole your computer or that your hard drive just died. What sort of important data did you just lose forever? Was it last year's tax return, letters of recommendation, your resumé, family photos, banking information? We hope that by now you are starting to get a little nervous.

Once you realize that protecting your data is important, you need to have an understanding of the tools and techniques available, such as backup media, backup strategies, and backup software. These are the components that can save you from having a real disaster and not just a bad hair day.

And if you experience a real disaster, there are tools available that you can use to try to recover. Windows provides features such as System Restore that you can put to work to fix your PC even if something really bad does happen.

In this chapter we'll help you get a plan together to prevent the unthinkable from happening. You will also learn about all of the tools you have at your disposal that are designed to protect your data. And we'll show you how to recover your data the proper way in case you do have a disaster or mishap.

Data Backups 101

- Learn why backups are so damn important even though you hate to do them.
- Learn what backup software is the best for your needs.
- Learn what types of backups are the most effective.

Why Should I Bother with Backing Up My Data?

PC users fail to back up their data because they either get lazy or forget how important their data is. Once you put something on your PC that you don't regularly use, you typically forget all about it. More than likely, though, you have some very important data that you would not be happy to lose. Here are some examples:

- *Legal data:* You may be required to keep some data for a specific length of time to satisfy the legal requirements of the IRS and other groups. If you happen to be unlucky enough to be audited by the IRS, you may be asked to provide tax return data from as long as three years ago. Trust us when we say that the IRS does not care if you claim you lost your tax return info when your computer died.

- *Work-related files:* Your employer may require you to make backups of files that you create while away from the office. In fact, you may even be your own boss. Why would you back up your files at work and not do the same at home?

- *Family photos:* Countless numbers of people now keep their precious family photos in digital format. The decreasing price of digital cameras and hard drives has made this possible. What if you were to lose these because a hard drive crashed? What would you tell your grandchildren?

- *Personal documents:* These can include resumés, letters to friends, saved email attachments, and similar documents. Most of these types of documents should be kept in case you need them in the future.

- *Computer settings:* Internet Explorer Favorites, Microsoft Office preferences, and address book entries are hard to replace if lost. Backing them up on a regular basis will give you assurance in case of a disaster.

- *Financial data:* You may be balancing your finances by using Microsoft Money or Quicken. If so, you need to back this data up or risk losing control of your money. Ask yourself, "How long would it take for me to re-create my financial records after a hard drive failure?" Better yet, ask, "Would I be able to recover if I lost my data?"

HORROR STORY! Imagine if you called your bank one day to get some account balance information and were told that the bank's computer system had died and that all of your account information was gone. What if the bank's representative said, "We experienced a slight technological mishap last night and have lost all of our account data. Additionally, we just realized that our last good data backup was done two months ago. According to our current records, you have five dollars in your account." You'd probably call every lawyer in town and you'd be ready for a big fight. Having a backup plan is important especially when financial or legal data is involved. Fortunately, most financial institutions such as banks and lending agencies have data backup procedures in place. Now, what if you were to have a similar technological mishap at home? Would you be able to restore your data in a reasonable amount of time?

How Can I Lose My Data?

You can lose your data in quite a few ways: system failures, theft, loss, and ignorance, to name a few. Knowing how it can happen can help you determine what you need to do to protect your data. For instance, knowing that you can lose your data from theft may get you to back up your data and keep the backup away from your home. Here is a list of all the ways you can potentially lose your data:

- *Hardware failure:* As presented in Chapter 2, computer hardware failure can happen at a moment's notice. Devices such as hard drives, media cards, and power supplies are subject to data loss. The chances are very high that failures of these types can have an adverse effect on the data stored on a system.

- *Theft:* If your computer is stolen, you can pretty much kiss all of your precious data goodbye. No thieves are going to rip out your hard drive from your computer before they steal it from you. This leaves you wishing you had a backup of all of your data. See Chapter 1 for more on theft.

- *Loss of equipment:* Losing your computer or device is almost as bad as having it stolen from you. Some might consider it even worse than theft because they blame themselves. See Chapter 1 for more information.

TIP: Label or mark your computer. This way, if you lose it, there is a chance that someone may find it and want to return it to you. See Chapter 11 for more info on this topic.

- *Disaster:* Environmental factors such as lightning, fires, and hurricanes can destroy your data in the blink of an eye. Unless you are doing some sort of backup, you will probably be nervous every time the weather turns bad.

- *Viruses and junkware:* In Chapters 8 and 9, you learned about the damage that viruses and junkware can inflict on your system. Some of these programs can wipe your drive clean of all data in the blink of an eye. Arming yourself against these types of attacks will go a long way in preventing this kind of data loss.

- *Operator error:* Have you ever inadvertently deleted a file from a network folder or permanently deleted a very important email? Then you know what the term *operator error* really means. Don't feel bad. It happens more often than you would think.

- *Data corruption:* Sometimes those 1s and 0s that make up data can get jumbled around. There really is no way to predict when this will happen. Your best bet is to have backup copies of your files.

How Can I Back Up My Data?

There are several ways to get your data from your computer to another place. Here is a list of some of the more popular ones:

- *Drive imaging software:* These programs are able to make an image of your entire hard drive in as little as five minutes. They usually consist of a floppy disk or CD that allows you to boot into the program. From there, you can create images, restore images, and perform other tasks.

- *Microsoft Backup:* A free utility that comes bundled with Windows. See the following section on backup software for more information.

- *Third-party backup software:* Programs that you can purchase that allow you to back up and restore data. They range in price from about $20 and can get into the thousands of dollars for the most advanced products.

- *Online backup services:* These services are quickly becoming a popular method of backing up important data. For a fee, you get storage space on a server to which you can upload your data. Once it is there, the online service is responsible for backing it up.

- *CD/DVD recording software:* Most of these types of software allow you to create data disks by creating a selection list and then burning that list of files to disk.

What Backup Software Can I Use?

When it comes to selecting a software package for your backup needs, you have plenty of choices. Data protection has become a hot topic in recent years due to increased activity among hackers. As a result, software companies have made it a priority to get into this market segment and compete for your money. Here are some of our favorites:

- *Microsoft Backup:* Microsoft's backup utility has been a part of Windows for many years. The latest version, which is bundled with Windows XP, is a joint venture between Microsoft and Veritas, the company that brings us Backup Exec and other business continuity products. Using Microsoft Backup is a snap even for the uninitiated. It has a neat wizard that will help you select which files to back up, set backup options, and set a backup schedule.

TIP: Microsoft Backup is not installed by default in Windows XP Home Edition. See **http://support.microsoft.com/default.aspx?scid=kb;EN-US;q302894** for instructions on how to install.

- *Backup Exec:* If you own a small to medium-sized business or are responsible for the data of a business, Backup Exec is the way to go. Veritas Backup Exec is a simple-to-use, high-performance backup solution that includes advanced features like one-button backups, extensive alerting, and even a web browser interface.

- *StompSoft Backup My PC:* This program started out as a desktop version of Backup Exec. It offers many of the features of its higher-priced sibling, but in a small and affordable desktop version.

- *Symantec Ghost:* This program is the godfather of all imaging software. It is used by everyone from home users to large corporations to make images (a one-file backup of everything) of workstation computers.

- *Iomega Automatic Backup:* This software is touted as a one-touch solution for data backup and restore. It will back up to Zip, Jaz, hard drives, network-attached storage, and Iomega DVD drives.

- *Roxio Media Creator:* This program allows you to copy your data onto a CD or DVD for backup purposes.

What Types of Media Are Available for Backups?

Choosing the type of media for your backups can be a daunting task. If you don't believe us, then just go down to your local office supply or electronics store. It will have a selection of media so vast it may take you hours to analyze it all. Here are the most popular types of media available:

- *Floppy disk*: Floppy disks have been around for a very long time. They have come in a host of different sizes, shapes, and capacities. They are also on their way to the great technology junk heap. They have never been a favorite of ours for anything other than quickly transferring small files to a computer or booting a computer up. They should not be used for any sort of long-term backup plan! Their susceptibility to failure makes them bad candidates for backup purposes. Also, they can only hold about 1.4 MB of data. This is hardly enough space to store a handful of digital pictures. You can quickly fill up one hundred of these floppies if you are backing up a significant amount of data.

- *CD/DVD:* Boasting a shelf life of about 100 years, optical media has become a popular option for backing up data. DVD has made this option even more attractive because of the massive amounts of data that can be stored on a single disk and because of the relatively low cost. Keep in mind that although these disks have a long shelf life, they are very prone to failure. A slight scratch or chip in the disk can render it unreadable by your player. See Chapter 14 for more information.

- *Tape:* Backing up to tape was once the standard practice in the business world. However, recent advances in storage technology has changed this. Tape backups need to be monitored and tested very closely. Because of their frail nature, a tape can go bad very quickly. They are sensitive to moisture, temperature, direct sunlight, and a host of other environmental factors.

- *Hard drive:* With the plummeting cost of hard drives recently, they are now a very extremely attractive option for backup purposes. You cannot go wrong with using a 300 GB external hard drive for all of your backup needs.

- *Online backup service:* There are now companies that can store your data for you. You can purchase storage in varying increments. The only catch to this system is the need for an Internet connection.

- *USB key:* Small in size and getting larger by the minute, these devices have become very popular.

- *Zip, Jaz drive:* These types of backup media have been popular for several years now. They offer significantly larger amounts of storage space than floppies. The downside is that you must purchase and install a special drive to use them.

What Types of Backups Do I Need to Be Aware of?

Now that you have hopefully been convinced of why you need to do a backup, we need to discuss all the different types of backups. Each of the following types can be used in particular scenarios to achieve different results. Depending on how much data you plan to backup, how often you plan on backing it up, and how quickly you would need to restore, you have several options. Here they are in detail:

- *Full:* A full backup is exactly that: a complete backup of all of your data. The main benefits of a full backup are that you are ensured that all of your data is backed up and they are the easiest type of backup to restore from.

- *Incremental:* This type of backup involves only files that have changed since the last full backup. Incremental backups are usually the quickest to run because files that have not been modified since the last full backup are not touched. The one drawback is that the restore process takes longer to complete than it does for any other type of backup. You would need to restore the last full backup and then each subsequent incremental backup in order.

- *Differential:* Differential backups are very similar to incremental ones. They consist of files that have changed since the last full backup or last differential backup. They usually take a little more time to complete than incremental backups. Restoring from a differential backup involves restoring the last full backup as well as the last full differential backup.

- *Copy:* This is a backup type that is available in Windows Backup. A copy is similar to a full backup in that it makes a complete backup of all of your data. The difference is that it does not mark your files as having been backed up by setting the archive bit. They are usually used between full and incremental backups.

- *Daily:* This is a backup type that is available in Windows Backup. A daily backup consists of just files that were created or modified on that particular day. Data that was created or modified on a previous day is not backed up. Daily backups should not be used as part of a complete data recovery plan.

How Often Do I Need to Back Up My Data?

Now that we have established the need to back up your data and have an understanding of the tools needed, you must determine when to do it. The method can be as simple as running a full backup every day for the rest of eternity, to something as complex as a multiple media set consisting of hundreds of tapes. Here are three of the most commonly used rotation schemes:

- *Son:* This method is very simple. You need five backup media (CD-R/ DVD-R, tape, and so on). Back up everything (full backup) on a different media each day. This method is ideal for a small business or home users that do not need to back up a large amount of data. The only flaw in this rotation method is that your data is available for only one week. As soon as the media is used for the next week, all of the previous week's data is gone. Table 12.1 outlines the Son backup rotation method.

Table 12.1 Son backup rotation method.

	Monday	Tuesday	Wednesday	Thursday	Friday
All weeks	Media 1	Media 2	Media 3	Media 4	Media 5
Backup type	Full	Full	Full	Full	Full

- *Father-Son:* With this rotation strategy, the same media is used for the first four days of the week. On the final day of the week, a different media is used for the two-week rotation. This method offers some additional flexibility in data retention times and the ability to restore easily. Table 12.2 outlines the Father–Son backup rotation method.

Table 12.2   Father-Son backup rotation method.

	Monday	Tuesday	Wednesday	Thursday	Friday
Week 1	Media 1	Media 2	Media 3	Media 4	Media 5
Week 2	Media 1	Media 2	Media 3	Media 4	Media 6
Backup type	Diff. or Inc.	Diff. or Inc.	Diff. or Inc.	Diff. or Inc.	Full

- *Grandfather-Father-Son:* This rotation strategy has become the standard for business data protection. This method protects your data using the minimum number of media, reduces wear and tear on your backup devices, and allows you to restore individual files or an entire system very easily. This rotation is based on a five-day schedule in which you create one full backup per week. The rest of the daily backups consist of either an incremental or differential backup. The daily backup is considered the Son, the last full backup of every week is considered the Father, and the last full backup of the month is considered the Grandfather. Table 12.3 outlines the Grandfather-Father-Son backup rotation method.

Table 12.3   Grandfather-Father-Son backup rotation method.

Monday	Tuesday	Wednesday	Thursday	Friday	
Week 1	Media 1	Media 2	Media 3	Media 4	Media 5
Week 2	Media 6	Media 7	Media 8	Media 9	Media 10
Week 3	Media 11	Media 12	Media 13	Media 14	Media 15
Week 4	Media 16	Media 17	Media 18	Media 19	Monthly
Backup type	Diff. or Inc.	Diff. or Inc.	Diff. or Inc.	Diff. or Inc.	Full

Putting Backup Techniques to Work

- Learn how often you should back up your data.
- Learn the best ways to store your backed-up data.
- Learn what to back up and what you can skip.
- Learn what to do if your backup fails.

How Often Should I Back Up My Data?

You should back up your data as often as humanly possible. Considering how important your data is to you, why would you shortchange yourself by not doing regular backups? However, there is a point at which you may be duplicating your efforts or just wasting time. To maximize your time and prevent unnecessary wear and tear on your backup tools, follow these guidelines:

- *Business or small home office:* If your livelihood depends on your data, don't take any chances. You should be backing up your data on a daily basis or you risk losing important information.

TIP: If your business is closed on Saturdays and Sundays, this usually means your data will not change on those days. Therefore, a backup would be unnecessary on those days.

- *Student:* Depending on how often you use your computer for course work and how conscientious a student you are, we recommend anywhere from a daily backup to once a week.

- *Casual home user:* The average home user does not create many files or change their Windows settings very much during the course of a day. Knowing this allows us to safely suggest that these people should back up once a week.

- *Power home user:* The more advanced home user more than likely is constantly changing settings and creates a respectable amount of new files. A daily backup would be recommended for this type of user.

- *Business traveler:* You should perform a full backup on all of your devices before you leave on a trip. Leave a copy of this backup at home and bring one with you on the trip. If you lose your device or it is stolen, you will have a copy of your data to restore on another device.

Where Should I Store My Backup Media?

Deciding where to store your backup media is another in a long chain of difficult decisions to make. One word of caution is necessary here: don't store the only copy of your backup in your home or workplace. You need to prevent against theft, fire, and other calamities as much as hardware failure. By keeping your backup media on site and nowhere else is simply asking for trouble. Do yourself a favor and closely examine the following list of alternate places to store your media:

- *Relative's home:* This is a good place to store your backup media, as long as you can trust your relatives.

- *Work drawer:* If you have a locked drawer at work where you can keep personal belongings, this can serve as the perfect hideaway for your backups.

- *Neighbor's home:* If you have a neighbor that you can trust, then go for it. Just make sure there is nothing too personal on the media. Having your backup nearby is your best bet for being able to restore it quickly.

- *Fireproof safe:* Not everyone has a fireproof safe or can afford one, but they are excellent for storing valuable items at home.

- *Safety deposit box:* Financial institutions offer these types of boxes to store valuable property. A small one should be more than adequate for storing backup media safely.

TIP: Do not keep certain types of media in your car. CDs/DVDs, backup tapes, floppies, Jaz, and Zip disks do not do well when exposed to high temperatures. The interior of your car can reach about 140 degrees Fahrenheit on a hot summer day, which will most certainly destroy your media.

How Can I Tell If My Backup Job Completed Successfully?

Unless you happen to own a crystal ball or have ESP, you will have to take steps to determine if your backup job completed successfully. If you neglect this important task, you may find out that your backups are useless. This realization usually happens right after your computer dies. So, to prevent this from happening, here are some ways you can check:

- *Manual check:* Your backup software should keep a list of past backup and restore activity. This is where you can determine whether or not your backup completed successfully.

- *Email notification:* Some higher-end software packages allow you to configure for email notifications. If the backup does not complete or otherwise fails, you'll be sent an email letting you know.

- *Test restore:* This is the only true way of knowing if your backup ran correctly. Restoring from your backup media should be done periodically to ensure that everything is working the way it should be.

Why Is My Backup Taking Forever to Complete?

The time it takes your backup to complete is the product of several different factors. Computer hardware, volume of data, backup software settings, and a host of other factors determine how long it will take. Here is a list of ways to avoid an excessively long backup:

- *Back up only files that change on a daily basis.* Do not back up files that you are not planning on changing anytime soon on a daily basis. Examples of these would be digital photos, music files, video files, and email archives. Backing these files up once a week should be plenty to ensure nothing is lost in case of a disaster.

- *Use differential or incremental backups.* These backups will save you time by not duplicating your efforts. See the section on common backup types for more information.

- *Back up when the computer is not in use.* Try running your backups when the computer is not in use. This will enable your backup software to work unhindered by any other programs and will result in a faster backup.

- *Do not back up unnecessary data.* Avoid backing up data that is not important or critical. See the section titled "What Data Should I Not Back Up."

- *Do not use data compression.* The process of compressing data slows down the entire backup process. This happens because of the extra time involved in shrinking the data you are backing up.

- *Do not verify backups.* Although it is highly suggested that you verify your backup, it is not mandatory. You may just want to verify your backups once a week. This will save you time the rest of the week.

- *Turn off antivirus scanning.* Antivirus software will attempt to scan every file that is backed up during a job. This can add a substantial amount of time to your backup. Disabling this feature will prevent this from happening. Just be sure to turn it back on when you are done.

- *Use better, faster hardware.* If money isn't an option, you can improve your hardware. Investing in a faster backup device will, in most cases, speed up your backup considerably.

- *Check network card settings.* This applies only to cases in which you are backing up data from another computer on your network. Some network cards will not operate at their rated speed unless told to do so. Don't ask why; everyone is tight-lipped about the reason for this phenomenon. We will just have to manually configure our network cards until someone tells us otherwise. Here is how to do this:

1. Open the Windows Control Panel.
2. Double-click System.
3. Click the Hardware tab.
4. Double-click the Device Manager button.
5. Expand the Network adapters section of the tree.
6. Right-click the network device you are using and click Properties.
7. Click the Advanced tab.
8. Select "Link speed and duplex."
9. Make sure that this is set to "100Mbps/Full duplex."

HORROR STORY! I (Peter) was with a client recently and noticed that their backup was taking over 10 hours to complete. I thought this was very odd because the last time I was there, it had only taken about 4 hours to finish. After some investigative work, I discovered that the amount of data being backed up had doubled since my last visit. It turns out that a user had been downloading music and video files onto the file server at an alarming rate. All of this extra data was putting the legitimate company data at risk. The lesson here is to constantly keep an eye on your backup system. Even very small changes in your data can cause large problems with your backup.

What Data Should I Be Backing Up and Where Can I Find This Stuff?

Deciding what to back up is one thing; figuring out where to find it is a different story. Software companies are very good at burying their applications data on your hard drive. Here are some tips on herding all of this data up for backup:

- *System state data:* Microsoft has bunched several items and put them under the blanket of system state data. This contains your Registry information, COM+ Class Registration Database, files under Windows File Protection, and your boot files. It is extremely important to back this stuff up on a regular basis. Most backup software will have this listed as a separate item in a selection list. Figure 13.1 shows the system state data in Microsoft Backup.

- *User profiles:* The user profile folders are pretty much the Holy Grail of things to back up. They contain email program data files, the My Documents folder, program settings, and a ton of other data. There will be a separate folder for each user that logs into your PC. Figure 13.2 shows them in Microsoft Backup.

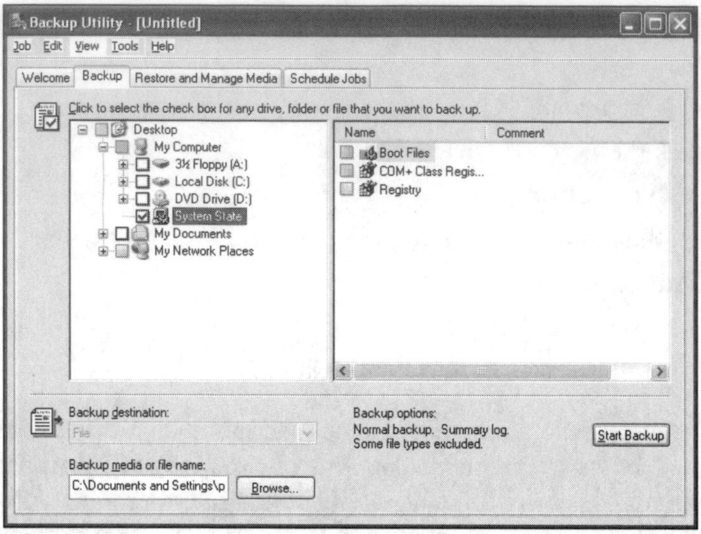

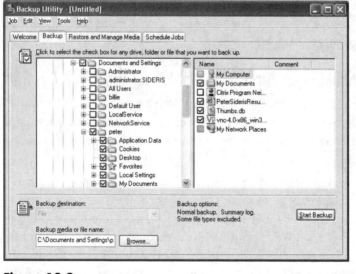

Figure 13.1

System state data.

Figure 13.2

User profiles.

NOTE: *There are some items in the user profile that should not be backed up such as temporary Internet files and cookies.*

- *Program data:* Some applications store their data in their corresponding program files folder. Back up the entire folder in these cases.

- *Financial software:* Programs like QuickBooks and Microsoft Money store their data in files that are put in the My Documents folder. If you are backing up your user profile, you should be in good shape.

WARNING! Keep in mind that every time you install new software that generates data, you must add this data to your backup selection list. It will not happen automatically.

What Data Should I Not Back Up?

Along with all of the important things you should be backing up, there is a host of items that should not be backed up. Going through the trouble of backing this stuff up will add a considerable amount of time to your backup and may cause it to fail:

- *Operating system files:* The operating system should not be part of your backup. The reason for this is simple: Your computer should have come with a restore disk or full version of Windows. This can be used to repair or reinstall the operating system at a moment's notice.

- *Application or program files:* Again, if the application is installed on your computer, chances are you have the disks to reinstall it if need be. Do not waste valuable time and media space by backing these up.

- *Temporary Internet files:* Do not waste precious disk space and time by backing up these unnecessary files. In fact, you should get in the habit of periodically clearing these items from your computer.

- *Internet cookies:* Again, these should not be included in your backup because they will waste time and storage space.

Why Is My Backup Failing?

Backups can fail for a number of reasons, but here are the main ones:

- *Write-protected media:* Make sure that you have not enabled the write-protect mechanism on your tape, floppy, Jaz, or Zip media. These can sometimes be enabled by accident when you handle the media. Usually they consist of a lever or flap that you move in one direction.

TIP: Most locking mechanisms are clearly marked. Look for an arrow pointing toward the locked position to determine where it should be.

- *Permissions:* If you are backing up files from a network, make sure that the account you are logged into the computer with has access to all of the folders and files you are trying to back up. Some higher-end software allows you to specify a user account with which to run the program service. Make sure the account you choose has administrative privileges on your computer.

- *No media:* A lack of backup media in your device will most certainly cause the backup to fail. Make sure that you take care of this important aspect of doing a data backup.

TIP: If you are always forgetting to insert media into your backup device, you can do the following: Set up a recurring appointment in Outlook to remind you to change your backup media. This way, you will have a timely reminder. You could also set your screen saver to display a reminder message or use sticky notes on your monitor.

- *Broken backup software:* If the software you use to do your backups is not working properly, then it only stands to reason that your backups will not work when needed. If you see any signs of your software not working correctly, seek help as soon as possible.

- *Damaged media:* Media does not last forever. Even CDs cannot withstand the effects of time. Damage is the biggest reason why you should retire your media after a certain length of time.

Why Does My Backup Complete, But with Errors?

Some backup software is smart enough to notify you if some items were skipped or could not be backed up properly. These errors will turn up in backup job logs or in job status displays. Most of these errors are caused by data being accessed by someone while the backup software is doing its thing. Some of the higher-end backup products have advanced capabilities that can back these items up. However, these products are expensive and beyond the needs of the average user. Here are some common types of data and the reasons they may have been skipped during your backup:

- *Email data files:* If your email program was open during the backup, the backup will skip any data files accessed by the email software. As a rule, be sure to close your email software before running a backup.

- *Permissions:* Make sure the user account that you are logged into as has full access to all the directories you are backing up. If it does not, the backup software will not be able to touch this data.

- *Financial software:* Programs like Microsoft Money and QuickBooks keep their data in a single file or group of files. Having the program open locks these files and prevents backup software from completing.

Restoring Your Data

- Learn how to successfully restore your data.
- Learn what to do if a restore won't work.

Can I Restore My Data?

The same programs that allowed you to back up your critical data also allow you to restore it. The process requires taking the reverse steps you took to create the backup. See your backup software's documentation for instructions on how to restore your data.

How Can I Prevent Others from Restoring My Data?

Chances are that the data you are backing up is sensitive and should not be accessible to others. It may contain sensitive documents or important financial data. In cases such as these, you would not want someone getting their hands on your backup media and restoring the data. Here is a list of potential ways to keep this from happening to you:

- *Store backup media in a safe.* Store it in a locking safe to which only you know the combination.

- *Hide your backups in a safe place.* Store them in a secret hiding place. Just be sure that you don't forget where this hiding place is.

- *Allow only an administrator to restore your backups.* Some of the higher-end backup programs allow you to specify that the media can be restored only by a system administrator. This will prevent individuals who shouldn't see the data from being able to restore it.

Do I Have to Restore My Files to Their Original Locations?

No. Whether you used a sophisticated backup program or did a manual copy, you will always have the option of restoring your data to an alternate location.

HORROR STORY! Be very careful when restoring data from a backup. I (Peter) had to help bail out a new client who decided to do it themselves. They succeeded in restoring their data, but also ended up overwriting all of the rest of their data with old files.

What Should I Do If I Cannot Restore a Backup?

Even if you had been running your backups religiously, there are no guarantees that your data will restore when you need it. If you encounter a problem, try restoring the backup again. With a little luck, you may find that it works on the second try.

What If I Overwrite an Important File with an Older Version?

Sometimes, in a rush to recover from a disaster, you may happen to overwrite a new version of a file with an older version. This can be catastrophic if you do not have a current version on a different backup. In some cases, this can lead to hours, days, or even weeks of lost work. Just the thought of doing all of that work over again is enough to drive you mad. To avoid making a mistake like this, just follow these tips:

- *Restore on another computer.* Just restore the data onto a different computer. This is a surefire way to prevent overwriting files.

- *Restore to another drive.* Again, location is the key to preventing an unintended overwrite. Restoring the files on a different drive is another excellent way to prevent mistakes.

- *Be extremely careful.* Make sure you double- and triple-check where you are going to restore your files. A little extra time spent up front will ensure that your restore happens without any hitches.

- *Check your software options.* Some backup software programs give you the ability to define their behavior when restoring files. They give you the option of restoring over existing files, skipping the file if it already exists, or keeping the file if it is a newer version.

- *Get a friend to do it for you.* Try getting a friend or relative to help with restoring the files. Just make sure this person is knowledgeable in restoring data or you may run into trouble.

Recovering from a Disaster

Sooner or later the worst possible situation could happen to you. And it could happen when you least expect it. Your system could crash, the data stored on your system could be lost, and you'd feel like jumping out the window of a really tall building.

With your system down, you'd lose all of the programs that you've installed. You'd also lose all the hours you've spent downloading files from the Internet, setting up and fine-tuning your PC, and creating data files. You'd lose all of the photos you've been saving from your latest vacations, and you might even be in trouble at work for losing some valuable data. But all might not be lost, even if you don't have the best backups at your disposal. Fortunately, Windows provides a built-in feature called System Restore that can help you recover from a disaster. So don't throw in the towel just yet. Read on and hope for the best.

What Can I Do If My PC Has a Critical Problem?

In previous chapters we presented worst-case scenarios you may find yourself stuck in, related to total system failures (see Chapters 2 and 3). We'll now tie all of the information together and present it in one place. Here's a summary of the critical problems you could encounter and what you can do:

- *Data files are corrupt.* If you find that data files have become corrupt or are missing, you should take the backup route. Restore your files using backup software. This topic was covered earlier in this chapter.

- *New driver has just broken your system.* If you just installed a new device driver and are now experiencing system crashes and other weird problems, you have a couple of options. The first thing you can try is a driver rollback. You can find information on this topic in Chapter 3. Your second option is to use the System Restore feature. We'll show you how to use this feature later in this chapter.

- *New device has just broken your system.* Installing new hardware is always fun, until something breaks. If your system is acting weird after a new hardware install, you have a few options. The first thing to try is disabling the device in Device Manager. If that does not work, you should give System Restore a try.

- *Drastic settings changes have been made.* I think we speak for everyone reading this book when we say that we have changed a setting in Windows or an application and could not remember how to change it back. Sometimes everything goes well, but other times you may have created huge problems. System Restore is your best friend in situations such as these, as you'll see later in this chapter.

- *Operating system does not boot up.* We covered this topic in Chapter 3. The first thing you should try is Last Known Good Configuration. This will revert all of your drivers and settings to the ones that worked the last time your computer booted successfully. If that doesn't work, try booting into Safe mode and use System Restore. Next on the list would be to use your Windows XP disk to repair Windows. See the next section on instructions for doing this. Your last option is to reinstall Windows and restore all of your data from backup.

How Can I Repair Windows Using the Windows XP Disk?

Windows XP has a neat repair feature that you can access from the installation disk. Many users have no idea it even exists. Here is how to use this feature:

1. Put your XP disk in your CD-ROM drive and start your PC. Make sure your PC is capable of booting from the CD-ROM drive. You can check this setting in the system BIOS.

2. When prompted, press any key on your keyboard to boot from the CD.

3. You will see a blue screen (don't be alarmed; this is normal) and Setup will begin transferring files necessary for this task.

4. At some point, you will be prompted to make a decision. The three options will be Setup Windows XP, repair using the Recovery Console, or Quit. Select the first option by pressing Enter.

NOTE: You may be wondering what the middle option is and why we haven't mentioned it here. This option is called the Recovery Console and it's a pretty advanced repair feature available in Windows XP and 2000. We decided to not cover it here because of the complexity of using it. If you are feeling adventurous, you can find out more at **http://support.microsoft.com/default.aspx?scid=kb;en-us;Q314058**.

---

5. The next screen will present you with another set of two options. It is very important to select the correct option here. Not doing so can potentially erase all of the data on your hard drive. You want to continue by pressing R to repair Windows XP. This screen is shown in Figure 13.3.

WARNING! If at any point you see a warning about erasing data or formatting your drive, you have taken the wrong path. Simply restart your PC and start the process again. Do not continue!!!!!!!!!!!!

6. At this point, the setup process will copy more files to your system and reboot. After it reboots, you will be back to a familiar graphical setup screen. Let the process run its course. You may be prompted for your Windows XP product key, so make sure you have it handy.

7. After your system reboots, you will need to reinstall any updates or service packs.

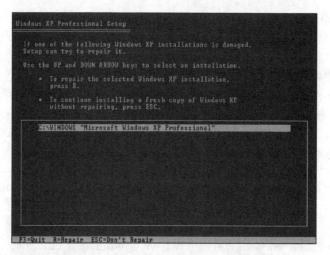

Figure 13.3

Windows repair options.

TIP: This feature can also be of great use when upgrading hardware in your PC such as the motherboard. You can simply replace the motherboard, run through the previous procedure, and be up and running in no time. Without running through this process, Windows would probably "blue-screen" once it realized such a drastic hardware change had occurred.

How Can Windows System Restore Save My Butt?

Microsoft introduced this new feature when it released Windows ME (Millennium Edition) back in 2000. It wisely continued offering this feature with the release of Windows XP. System Restore allows you to roll back your system settings with a few clicks of the mouse. It is kind of like having a virtual time warp built into your PC. Just one click and you are magically whisked back to a point in time before your computer committed suicide. All of this happens without any changes being made to your personal files, email, and browsing history. All of this information is left untouched in its pre-catastrophe state.

What Are Some of the Problems I Can Solve with System Restore?

System Restore might sound a little like voodoo magic, but it's actually sort of like a tape recorder that keeps track of how your system is configured at different intervals. Once System Restore has been activated on your PC (it usually is by default), it will record and save what are called system restore points on a regular basis. These restore points keep track of changes that you've made to your setup, such as when you install programs, when you install automatic updates, and when you install devices such as printers or scanners. The restore points that are saved by System Restore can help you solve problems such as these:

- *Applications that have gone bad:* System Restore can fix serious problems that are caused by applications that don't install properly and cause your PC to go haywire. This is actually a very common problem, especially if you download programs from the Internet. Some programs are created by programmers who aren't especially skilled at designing their creations so that they install properly. A bad program can really make a mess of your system.

- *Downloads that have gone wacky:* You may have downloaded a file that contains a virus, which in turn can corrupt some of your system files.

- *Device drivers that have acted up:* After hooking up a new hardware device, such as a printer or a digital camera, you'll typically need to install a driver so the device will work properly with your PC. Some drivers don't do what they're supposed to do and end up just driving your system crazy.

- *Hardware problems that are lurking:* You may have hardware problems that can cause your system to act up.

Can I Use System Restore If Windows Won't Start Up?

In some situations you can. If the System Restore feature has been previously activated and running on your PC, you might be able to boot up your PC using a back door sort of technique and then use the System Restore feature to roll back your system to an earlier date when it was working properly. Typically, the cause of a problem like this is some software that you might have installed or changes that you might have made to your system that are now keeping Windows from starting up. This seems like one of those catch-22 problems: "If I could only get my car started, I could drive to the auto parts store and get the parts I need to make my car run."

There is one trick that you can use. It involves the advanced startup options we spoke of in Chapter 3 and the black screen known as the command prompt. Here is how you can get System Restore running when Windows won't start up on its own:

1. Access the advanced startup menu by pressing F8 at the appropriate time. It can be a little tricky with a fast computer. Your best bet is to start

pressing F8 as soon as your PC starts up. If you get to the Windows splash screen, you missed your chance and need to try again.

2. Select "Safe mode with command prompt."

3. Log into your computer with an account that has administrative privileges.

4. Type the following at the command prompt and press Enter: **Windows\system32\restore\rstrui.exe**

How Do I Make Sure System Restore Is Activated on My PC?

If System Restore hasn't been activated on your PC, it can't do anything for you. Turning it on is a snap. Just follow these simple instructions:

1. Click Start.

2. Click Control Panel.

3. Double-click the System icon.

4. Click the System Restore tab.

5. Uncheck the box that is labeled "Turn off System Restore," as show in Figure 13.4.

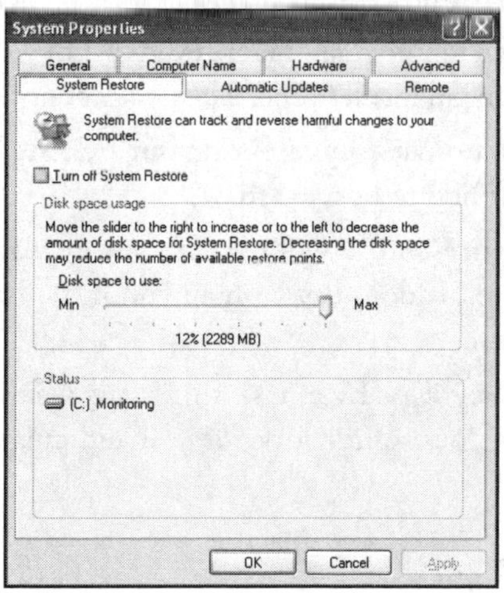

Figure 13.4
Activating System Restore.

If you decide that System Restore is not for you, you can turn it off by unchecking that same little box, although we're not quite sure why you would ever want to turn it off.

> *TIP:* Turning System Restore off also deletes all of your saved restore point information.

You will also notice a couple of other important items on this tab. You have the option of specifying how much disk space you want to allow System Restore to use. If you have anything larger than a 20 GB hard drive, do yourself a favor and set this to the maximum possible amount. In the event of a system failure, you want to have as many options as possible. The other important tidbit of information you will see is what drives are being monitored. System Restore will monitor any hard drive that you have installed in your computer. If you have two hard drives installed, they will both be displayed in this window.

> *TIP:* System Restore requires at least 200 MB of free disk space. Obviously, most computers these days have more than enough free space.

When Does System Restore Automatically Create Restore Points?

System Restore creates restore points anytime Windows goes through a major change to its makeup, as in the following examples:

- *New software install:* Windows creates a restore point before every major software install. This is done to prevent an install from adversely affecting a PC.

- *Auto-update*: If you have enabled automatic updates on your PC, System Restore will create a restore point before every update.

- *Installation of unsigned drivers:* System Restore will create a restore point when you install an unsigned driver. It does this to help you if the driver does something bad to your system.

- *Automatically following 24 hours of inactivity*: Even if nothing major has been done on your PC, Windows does some work for you and creates a restore point just in case.

Can I Manually Create a Restore Point?

Yes. You can create a restore point anytime you want to, but you must have enough hard drive space available. Windows does a pretty good job of creating restore points for you, so this normally would not be necessary. However, you might have a need to do it more often, or you might be performing some operation such as installing new critical software and you want to set a restore point to give you an insurance policy. Here's how to manually create a restore point:

1. Click Start | Programs | Accessories | System Tools | System Restore.
2. Choose "Create a restore point" when prompted.

Type a description of your restore point and then click Create.

How Can I Prevent System Restore from Monitoring Non-System Drives?

By default, System Restore monitors all hard drives in your PC and creates restore points for them. Although monitoring all of your drives seems like a good idea, it isn't necessary. Because all of your system settings are stored on the boot or system partition, monitoring a drive or partition that does not contain these settings is a waste of system resources. A good analogy to this situation would be cutting your lawn twice on the same day. You can stop System Restore from monitoring non-system drives or partitions by taking these steps:

1. Click Start.
2. Click Control Panel.
3. Double-click the System icon.
4. Click the System Restore tab.
5. In the Status window click on the drive or partition that you wish to discontinue monitoring for and then click Settings.
6. Select the "Turn off system restore on this drive" check box.

What If System Restore Doesn't Work?

Sometimes your computer will have gotten so messed up that System Restore won't be able to help you. In such a case, you will get all the way through the restore process, the PC will reboot, and you will then be met by a message stating that the restore process failed. Here is a list of tactics that you can use in this situation:

- *Try again.*
- *Try an earlier restore point.* Keep trying earlier restore points until you get to one that works properly.
- *Use the Last Known Good Configuration feature.* See the next section on advanced startup options for more info on this utility.
- *Restore system state data from backup.* Remember all of those backups you have been making all of this time? Now is the time to use them.
- *Make sure you have the latest service pack.* Windows XP Service Pack 1 contains about half a dozen fixes and improvements for System Restore. Make sure that you have this important update installed on your machine.

Are There Other Recovery/Restore Options Available?

Windows 2000 and XP come equipped with some startup features that can aid you in getting your system back up after a disaster. These advanced features can be accessed by pressing the F8 key at a particular point in the Windows startup process:

- *Enable VGA mode:* This option boots your PC using a standard VGA device driver at 640X480 resolution. It can be extremely handy if you mistakenly changed your display settings to something your monitor does not support.

- *Safe mode:* Windows Safe mode option loads the Windows operating system by loading a minimal amount of system files and device drivers.

- *Safe mode with networking:* This is the same as Safe mode but loads any settings or drivers necessary to get your network interface card working.

- *Safe mode with command prompt:* This option gives you access to the command prompt. You can start programs from here such as System Restore and Check Disk.

- *Last Known Good Configuration:* This option will start Windows by using the last set of system files, drivers, and Registry settings that worked properly. This option can be handy in several situations, such as when you are having trouble booting up after installing a new piece of hardware or updating a device driver.

TIP: You may have difficulty accessing the advanced options menu on newer computers with fast hardware. The screen will load so fast that you may not have an opportunity to press the F8 key in time.

Summary

We hope that this chapter has given you the ability to recover from a variety of disastrous situations. As you have learned so far in this book, there are many forces that are conspiring to ruin your day. But your day will be ruined only if you are not prepared. Having a solid backup plan and knowing what to do in an emergency can save you time, money, grief, and aggravation. So the next time someone thinks you are overly cautious for backing up your files, just smile and relax—you'll be prepared, and a potential disaster won't turn into a big blunder.

14

Digital Lifestyle Hazards

Disasters to avoid:
- Having your PDA stop working for you.

Mishaps and blunders to run from:
- Buying the wrong camera or camcorder.
- Losing digital photos.

t used to be that once you had your PC all set up, you could simply enjoy it. Today, there are a zillion extensions and attachments to your PC so that you can do everything from taking digital photos and playing and distributing music, to keeping in contact when you travel the world with your PDA. It looks as if the "PC as mother ship" idea is here to stay and just about everything else we do in the world is becoming digital and connecting into the mother ship.

Using all of these devices and activities that hook up to your PC in one way or another is becoming known as the digital lifestyle, and in and of themselves they can be sources of real disasters, mishaps, and blunders if you are not careful. In this chapter, we'll take a look at the problems that you may experience if you use devices like PDAs, digital cameras, and scanners. We'll also look at the disasters and mishaps that you might experience using CD-ROMs and DVDs.

PDA Survival

- Learn what to do if your PDA won't boot.
- Learn what to do if you get PDA errors when trying to use your PDA with your PC.

Personal digital assistants (PDAs) are fairly new to the market. The idea is that they provide the functionality of a lower-end laptop but fit in the palm of your hand. Since all this functionality is crammed into such a small space, PDAs are prone to lockups, crashes, and reboots. The following sections will help you troubleshoot your PDA when these errors occur.

What Should I Do If My PDA Will Not Turn On or Boot?

Your PDA is supposed to be the device that is ready to go the moment you need it. As you might imagine, it can be extremely frustrating when you go to use it and it won't turn on. First, use some restraint and don't throw it across the room. Next, check the following conditions to get your PDA up and running:

- *Is the battery charged?* This is the most common cause of a PDA not turning on. Attach power to the PDA and try turning it on. If the battery is fully drained, you may have to let the PDA charge for a few hours before you can turn it on (even if it's plugged in).

- *Are you pressing the right button?* Most PDAs have multiple buttons, one of which is the power button. Some PDAs may require you to press and hold the button. When in doubt, consult your owner's manual.

- *What's that smell?* Does the PDA emit a burning smell? If so, chances are something has burned out and needs to be replaced.

- *Is everything connected properly?* Make sure the power cord and battery are connected firmly to the PDA and to the source of power.

- *Do you have power?* Verify that the PDA is plugged into a power source. If it is plugged into a power strip or uninterruptible power supply (UPS), make sure the power strip or UPS is switched on. Try plugging the PDA directly into a wall outlet to be on the safe side. If all else fails, try plugging a known working device (for example, a lamp) into the outlet to verify that the outlet is working.

- *Does the power button feel funny?* If the power button feels funny or is permanently depressed, chances are it is broken.

- *Does the device need a soft reset?* Soft-resetting a PDA causes the PDA to shut down, discharge all its electricity, and turn back on. Usually this is performed by using a paper clip to press the pin-sized button hole on the bottom of the device. *Do not press too long* because this may perform a hard reset, which erases the contents of your device. Consult your owner's manual for the proper way to reset your device.

- *Are the batteries dead?* If your PDA runs on replaceable batteries, try replacing them.

- *Remove all accessories.* Remove any memory cards, expansion packs, and other connected devices and retry the options listed here.

- *Get help.* If none of these options have helped, you should seek assistance from your local tech support or PDA manufacturer.

TIP: Turn all wireless features off when they are not in use. This will drastically improve the battery life of your PDA.

What Should I Do If My PDA Display Will Not Turn On?

PDA displays have come a long way in just a few short years. They now come in full 64,000 colors with 240×320 resolution and better. The following tips should help you if your PDA display will not turn on:

- *Try adjusting the contrast/brightness controls.*

- *Follow the instructions listed in "What Should I Do If My PDA Will Not Turn On or Boot?"*

- *If you got your PDA wet and now the display does not work, chances are it's gone for good.* PDA display contacts are very sensitive and become ruined when wet.

Why Do I Get the Error "USB Device Not Recognized" when I Connect My PDA to My PC?

PDAs connect to PCs via a serial, USB, or wireless connection. The most common reason for the connection is to sync the contents of the PDA with a PC, but it's also used to install software and even power the device. The "USB device not recognized" error is very common when connecting a PDA to a PC. Here are some tips to help you troubleshoot this error:

- *You need to reboot.* Some PCs do not like the PDA connected and or powered on after the PC is up and running. Connect and power on your PC and then try again.

- *You have too many USB devices.* If you have multiple USB devices connected to your PC simultaneously, they may be drawing more power through the USB port than is allowed. Reboot with only the PDA connected and then try connecting one device at a time to determine the cause of the problem.

- *Use a USB- powered hub.* If you use a USB hub (a device that allows you to connect more USB devices), ensure that the USB hub is powered (has its own power adapter). While you can connect up to 255 USB devices to your PC, your PC does not have the capacity to power more than a few USB devices at a time. By using a powered USB hub, you take the strain off your computer and may eliminate the error at the same time.

- *Check for incompatible cable.* If you bought a replacement PDA sync cable from a company other than the original device manufacturer, it may not meet the full requirements to properly connect the PDA to your PC.

- *Turn off USB charging.* If your PDA software has the option to charge through the USB connection, this may be causing a power surge or drawing more power than is allowed. Turn this option off and reboot your PC to see if the error goes away.

- *Update your software.* This error can also be caused if you are using an older version of your PDA's sync software or if your operating system does not have the latest service pack or patches installed. Obtain the latest software versions and patches and update your system. This may not only solve this problem, it may also help you avoid other problems in the future.

TIP: Microsoft has released several patches that may help with these errors. They can be downloaded at **http://support.microsoft.com/ default.aspx?scid=kb;en-us;838989**.

What Can I Do If My PDA Will Not Sync?

Transferring data from a PDA to a PC is something most of us do at least once a day. Most of us do it by using the cradle, while some of us do it wirelessly. We do it for several reasons, such as backing up data and sharing our calendar information with others. If our PDA stops working, we could be in a lot of trouble, so getting it functional again is paramount. Here are some tips on how to troubleshoot both cradle and wireless synchronizing:

- *Power:* Verify that both your PC and PDA are powered on.

- *Connections:* Verify that the cradle or sync cable is plugged into your PC. If you are using a USB connection, be sure to plug the PDA directly into a USB port on your PC and not into a USB hub.

- *Software:* Verify that the sync software is installed and running on your PC. Microsoft ActiveSync and Palm Desktop both should launch at startup and should be running in the system tray. If they are not, you should begin your troubleshooting here. Reinstalling the software should fix this problem.

- *Soft reset:* Perform a soft reset on your device. This is a great trick for solving a lot of common PDA problems.

- *Wireless connection:* Make sure your wireless adapter is enabled and you are connected to the network. If synchronizing over the Internet, make sure you can access the Internet by opening a web page in your browser. See Chapter 5 for more information on wireless troubleshooting.

- *Authentication:* If you sync remotely to a company network, more than likely you must provide credentials. Make sure you have the right username and password plugged into your PDA. Check with your network administrator to verify your credentials.

HORROR STORY! A client recently called me (Peter) to take a look at his PDA. He said he had not synchronized in quite some time and was having problems. He recently synchronized and lost all of the information on his PDA and could not figure out why. After some investigation, I discovered that he had set his software to overwrite his PDA with the information contained in Outlook. This story has a happy ending though: he was very good about backing up his PDA to an expansion card on a frequent basis.

What Should I Do If My PDA Won't Recognize Expansion Pack Devices?

Expansion packs are jackets or sleeves (not clothes, but hardware) that allow you to connect your PDA to PCMCIA cards, digital cameras, extra batteries, and more. This is the standard interface to add more functionality to your PDA. Here are the steps to take if the expansion pack connected to your PDA will not recognize connected devices:

- *Make sure the PDA recognizes the expansion pack.* Before connecting the device to the expansion pack, make sure the PDA recognizes the connected expansion pack.

- *Make sure the expansion card or device has been pushed firmly and completely into the slot.*

- *Make sure you are using the correct card and that it's in its corresponding slot .*

- *Install any third-party drivers necessary to recognize the card on your PDA.*

- *Reset the PDA with the expansion pack and device connected.*

What Should I Do If My PDA or Expansion Pack Won't Accept an Expansion Card?

Most PDAs include memory slots that accept compact flash, secure digital (SD), or memory stick media. As you learned in the previous section, you can also use an expansion pack to access not only memory media, but PCMCIA cards, cameras, and more. Here's what to do if your PDA or expansion pack will not accept a card or device:

- *Inserting expansion cards into a PDA can be a tricky proposition.* Make sure you are inserting the correct card into the right port and that you aren't inserting it at an angle. For example, do not try to jam a compact flash card into an SD slot. Check your PDA's documentation for compatible expansion cards and where you can insert them.

- *Some manufacturers put a plastic sleeve or "dummy" card into expansion slots.* The purpose is to keep stuff from falling in there and causing problems. Be sure to remove these from the slot before using it.

- *Make sure you have the label on the card facing the correct way.* It should be facing the front of the unit. Most PDAs and expansion packs are slotted so the device will insert only one way. If it requires more than a little push to insert the card, chances are you have it backwards or the card is incompatible.

- *Make sure you are using the right type of card.* While expansion packs do accept PCMCIA cards, most only accept type I and type II. Type III cards are too thick to fit into most expansion packs. Consult your owner's manual to determine what type of card you have and whether your expansion pack supports it.

What Should I Do If I Can't Remove an Expansion Card from My PDA?

Removing a card from a PDA can be as difficult as inserting one. One thing to always remember is to be very careful when removing cards. The pins inside of the PDA that accept the card are very small and prone to bending. Try one of the following options if yours will not eject itself:

- *Push the card in slightly to release the locking mechanism.* Releasing it should allow the card to eject itself from the slot.

- *Use a pair of tweezers or small needle-nose pliers.* Gently grab the card by its edges and pull it up. Do not try to squeeze or force the card because this may lead to damage.

Digital Camera Problems

- Learn how to avoid taking bad photos.
- Learn how to get your digital camera to work with your PC.

How Can I Avoid "Camera Shake"?

This seems to be one of the biggest problems plaguing amateur photographers. You can have the world's best digital camera, tons of training, and perfect lighting and still take a horrible photo. Camera shake happens for one very simple reason. The person taking the photo has moved the camera at exactly the right time to ruin an otherwise nice photo. Before digital cameras, this was an even bigger problem because you did not know you took a bad picture until several weeks later. At least now you have the option of viewing the photo within several seconds and deleting it if you're not satisfied with it. The only problem still left is if you bungled a once-in-a-lifetime shot. Here's how you can avoid it:

- *Use a tripod.* If you can deal with having to carry one of these things around, you can beat camera shake. Who cares if you look like a camera geek or a tourist? At least you will have the best photos.

- *Stand correctly.* Try to stand absolutely still while keeping your legs slightly apart. Keeping your legs apart lowers your center of gravity and prevents you from swaying.

- *Lean against an object.* If you have a wall or fence handy, use it to your advantage. Just don't get lazy and spend the entire day there. No one likes to see five hundred pictures all from the same camera angle.

- *Hold your camera against your forehead.* If you don't have a wall to lean on, use the next best thing. Be careful not to press too hard or you may find the word *Nikon* or *Sony* stamped on your head.

- *Breathe before taking the photo.* Believe it or not, breathing while taking a photo will affect the image. Take a deep breath a few seconds before taking a photo and hold it during and slightly after the camera is done.

- *Relax your grip.* Do not squeeze your camera so tightly that it practically jumps right out of your hands.

- *Press the button gently.* This is what gets the good majority of amateurs. They hammer down on the trigger button as hard as they can. This bad habit is easily avoided by pressing the trigger button gently.

Why Does It Take My Digital Camera So Long to Take a Photo?

You would think that digital cameras would be able to snap photos as fast as a machine gun fires ammunition. It only makes sense that modern technology would be bigger, faster, and better than old stuff. The reality is that digital cameras take longer to snap a photo than traditional cameras. Some digital cameras are so bad that you need to make an appointment just to take a photo. The slow response might make you miss golden photo opportunities while waiting for the camera to reset itself between shots. You will have to carefully plan your shots to get the best results. Digital cameras seem slow because of slow startup and shutter lag. You can't do much about slow startup, but there are a few things you can do to help with shutter lag (the time between when the shutter release button is pressed to when the photo is taken):

- *Know your camera.* Do some tests to determine the delay that shutter lag causes on your digital camera. Try counting how long it takes your camera to take a photo and prepare itself for the next. Once you get a rough idea, you will be able to plan your photos accordingly.

- *Prefocus.* The process of focusing can also add to the time needed to take a photo. Try prefocusing the camera by pointing it at an object that is about the same distance from you as your intended target. Once the camera has focused, turn and take your photo.

- *Turn off the flash.* This can chop some valuable time off of the process of taking your photo. Be sure that you don't need the flash.

- *Lower the resolution.* Taking lower-resolution shots will decrease the time needed to take a photo. This is because every time you take a photo, the image is stored on the charge-coupled device (CCD). When it is necessary to take another picture, this image must be wiped from the CCD. Higher-quality images take longer to remove and increase the time needed to take a photo.

Why Does My Digital Camera Turn Itself Off after a Minute of Inactivity?

This is an infuriating feature with an honest purpose. It is designed to save your camera's battery from being needlessly depleted. However, this feature can ruin some of your best photo opportunities. I wish I had a nickel for every time I missed a prime photo opportunity because my camera had shut itself off. The problem here is that the camera must wake itself up from its little catnap. In some cases, this wake-up period can be longer than just turning your camera on.

You can do something about this, though. Somewhere in your digital camera's configuration menus you will find where you can change this setting. Some cameras even let you turn it off completely.

WARNING! Turning this feature off may not be such a great idea. You will run the risk of having the camera drain the battery if you do not turn it off.

What Is the Best Way to Transfer Photos to My PC?

To the uninitiated, nothing can be more daunting than transferring your photos from your camera to your computer. There are two separate obstacles here. First, there is the problem of physically getting your photos over to the computer. Next, you need to figure out where in your operating system you can accomplish this transfer. There are several solutions to both of these obstacles, depending on your PC setup. Here is the lowdown:

- *Use the interface cable.* Some cameras come with a handy cable that connects your camera to your PC. This allows you to transfer your pictures directly to your PC.

- *Use a card reader.* These handy devices allow you to plug in storage media such as compact flash and secure digital cards. The device is connected to your PC via USB or FireWire.

- *Use optical media.* If your camera writes directly to a CD, you're in luck. You can insert the CD into your PC drive and access it from My Computer.

What Flash Setting Should I Use?

Cameras also have different flash settings. Selecting the right setting can be a challenge for the novice digital photographer. Here are a few tips:

- *Auto:* Here, the camera takes a light measurement, determines how much flash is necessary, and fires the flash accordingly. As with most "Auto" settings, it is designed to provide the best results with the least amount of configuration. It works fine in most cases, but you should not rely on it all the time.

- *Red-eye reduction:* This is designed to reduce the dr2eaded "devil eye" that can plague pictures. See the section "How Can I Get Those Red Eyes out of My Photos?" for more info.

- *Off:* Sometimes you may need to turn the flash off to take a photo. For example, it's best to have the flash off if you are taking a photo through a window or from a car.

TIP: When taking a picture through glass, you can reduce the glare caused by flash very easily. Holding the camera at a 45-degree angle can produce a picture without any nasty glare. It takes a bit of practice to master this technique, but you should be able to get good results if you keep at it.

- *On:* Need we say more?

NOTE: Keep in mind that camera manufacturers may have different names for these flash settings. Check your camera's documentation for the specifics.

Where Do I Plug My Digital Camera into My PC?

If your digital camera came with an interface cable, it must plug into your PC somehow. Where it goes depends on the type of interface cable and how your PC is set up:

- *USB port:* These ports can be found on the back of your computer. Some computers even have these ports mounted on the front of the case for ease of use.

- *FireWire port (IEEE1394):* FireWire is a peripheral standard that was developed by Apple. It is now incorporated into PCs as well. In fact, Apple gets a 25 cent commission on every FireWire port installed.

When Should I Use the Different Scene Modes That My Camera Offers?

Digital cameras have preconfigured modes that offer settings that have been tailored for specific picture-taking opportunities. You should use these to your advantage whenever possible. Too often we become lazy and leave our camera on the "Auto" setting, sacrificing picture quality for ease of use. Think about it for a minute. Everything you use has different settings. Even your electric toothbrush has half a dozen settings. Would you put your toothbrush on "Auto"?

Here is a list of some typical scene modes that you should consider using:

- *Landscape:* This mode is designed to bring both foreground and background objects into even focus. It can come in handy when taking outdoor pictures where you have objects both near you and far away from you.

- *Action:* This mode is designed to capture fast-moving objects clearly.

- *Portrait:* This mode focuses on the subject of the photo. Everything else is put out of focus on purpose.

NOTE: *Keep in mind that camera manufacturers may have different names for these modes. Check your camera's documentation for the specifics.*

Do I Have to Use the Photo Software That Came with My Camera?

When you bought your digital camera, it probably came with software. Unfortunately, the photo editing software included with digital cameras is notorious for being subpar. It provides you with basic organizing and editing features, but it cannot compare with some of the programs that are available. Feel free to use it, though; it may prove to be useful until you outgrow it. Here are a few reasons why this free software is not necessarily worth the trouble:

- *Lacking features:* Because it is free, it probably does not have all of the features you may be looking for. Some even make you upgrade to more features for a price.

- *Designed for beginners:* This is not necessarily a bad thing, but the software that comes with the camera sacrifices features for ease of use.

Why Does My Digital Camera Shoot Horrible Video?

A digital camera has been designed from the ground up to shoot still images and cannot be expected to shoot digital video. It is kind of like expecting a mechanic to be able to fix your plumbing at home. Although mechanics may do some work with cooling systems in your car, that does not make them good candidates to fix your leaky faucet. Digital cameras are limited by several factors in their capability to shoot digital video, including storage, resolution, and optics.

Photo Problems

- Learn why your digital photos print badly.
- Learn how to get red eyes out of your photos.

Why Can't I Find My Digital Photos on My PC?

Whether you transferred the pictures manually or allowed your picture software to move them for you, you may have lost track of all those pictures. Finding them by searching through all of your drives can be a long and tedious process. Fortunately, there is a faster way to find them. You can quickly search for particular file types by using the search feature built into Windows. Here's the procedure:

1. Click Start.
2. Click Search.
3. Click Pictures, Music, or Video.
4. Check Pictures and Photos.
5. Click Search. This will find all pictures and photos on your PC and display them in thumbnail format.

Why Do My Photos Look Good on the Screen but Print Horribly?

Nothing is more of a waste of time and money than printing a photo and not getting good results. Unfortunately, most of us just keep trying to print that picture regardless of the outcome. We may make a few adjustments in the hope that we will finally get that good print. Twenty tries later, the picture still might look just as bad as the first print. Stop printing and check for these problems:

- *Bad printer:* Make sure you have a printer that is capable of getting the job done. Buy yourself a decent ink jet printer or a specialized photo printer for best results.

- *Misaligned print cartridges:* Poorly aligned print cartridges can lead to blurry images. You should be able to realign them using the software that came with your printer.

- *Dirty print cartridge heads:* If the cartridges are dirty, you will get very inconsistent prints. Again, your printer software should have a utility for cleaning the cartridges. It may even have a built-in mechanism for cleaning them.

- *Wrong paper type:* Stick with glossy or matte finish photo paper for printing photos. Do not try to skimp and use normal copy or laser printer paper.

- *Wrong printer driver:* Make sure you have the correct printer driver installed on your PC. The wrong driver can produce unpredictable results and can ruin your photos. Check with the manufacturer as to what driver will produce the best results.

- *Low print quality selected:* Your printer probably has a quality setting that can be adjusted depending on your needs. Figure 14.1 shows an example of this.

NOTE: *The options on your printer may look different or use different terminology for the various print qualities.*

- *Using refilled ink cartridges:* Refilling your own ink cartridges can save you a great deal of money. There are some problems with this system, though. The heads in the print cartridges will wear out after a while. Another common problem is that the ink tanks can leak and make a big mess. You may want to use your refilled cartridges for printing unimportant documents and use the good stuff for the photos.

Where Can I Print Photos If I Don't Have a Printer?

You may be on vacation or otherwise away from home. Unless you cart around a printer in your luggage, you will not be able to print your photos.

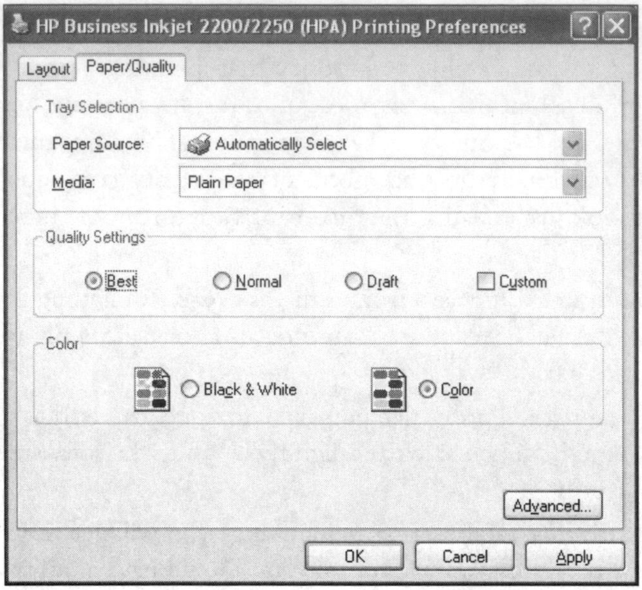

Figure 14.1
Printing preferences.

Your ink cartridge may have just run out of ink, you may have run out of paper, or your printer may have broken. Whatever the reason, here are some options for printing your photos:

- *Camera shop:* Most of these types of stores will be more than happy to print your digital photos for you. Expect to pay a premium for their expert knowledge and personal service.

- *Work:* Keep quiet about this one. If there is a decent color printer at work, see if you can use it. Just make sure you ask.

NOTE: *The authors of this book would never dream of using the printer at work without asking!*

- *Friend's house:* Take your photos to a friend's house. Make sure you ask them first, though!

- *Department store:* Most department stores have photo developing services.

- *Warehouse club:* These stores are just great. Where else can you buy 500 pounds of dog food and 40 rolls of toilet paper and get your digital photos developed?

- *Pharmacy:* Pharmacies have always offered good service with photo development. They have also realized the incredible potential in offering photo printing services.

- *The Web:* There are a ton of services that allow you to upload photos, select the size and number of prints, pay, and have your photos delivered to you. All this can be done from the convenience of your own home.

TIP: Shop around for the best price. The difference in price per print can be substantial from one store to another. Also, make sure they are using quality paper. Paper quality is an important factor in image quality and how long the photos will last.

Why Are Objects Transparent in Some of My Photos?

Transparent objects are abundant in digital camera photos. We are sure you probably have taken at least one of these eerie pictures. By transparent we mean downright ghostly. You can actually see through one or more of the people in the picture. There is a logical explanation for these ghostly images. The person that is transparent actually moved after the flash fired but before the camera was done taking the picture. This can be an easy thing to do. Here is how you can prevent this:

- *Do not use the night mode setting.* This setting on your camera increases the exposure time of the picture. So a shutter time of 1 second can be bumped up to as much as 10 seconds. This means that if anyone moves during this time, they will appear transparent.

- *Don't mess with the exposure settings.* If your camera allows you to change the exposure, don't. Setting it for too long can cause transparent objects in your pictures.

How Can I Get Those Red Eyes out of My Photos?

If you are a Photoshop wizard, you could edit them out. But getting rid of red-eye is much easier if you use the right settings on your camera in the first place. Red-eye is the red tint that ends up in people's eyes when they have their picture taken in low lighting conditions.

The lack of lighting causes the flash to fire and reflect off the retina in the back of our eyes. Something similar happens when certain animals have bright lights shining on them at night. Cats, dogs, deer, and other animals have a reflective film covering their retina that produces a bright white light in the back of their eyes.

The good news is that camera manufacturers have gone to great lengths to give you the tools to suppress your inner vampire. There are also some steps that you can take that will reduce the chance of a photo being ruined:

- *Use the "red-eye" removal feature on your camera.* Most newer digital cameras come with built in red-eye removal. It works by using a sequence of two flashes. The first flash fire is brief and causes your pupil to contract slightly. This initial burst of light is followed by the normal flash that is used to illuminate the picture area. The initial contraction of your pupil reduces the amount of light that reaches your retina.

- *Do not use the flash.* One easy way to completely eliminate red-eye is to not use your camera's flash at all. The only problem here is that there may not be enough light to take a decent picture.

- *Use other light sources.* Try turning on all of the available lighting in a room. This may be enough to make the flash unnecessary.

- Use the "red-eye" removal feature in software.

Digital Camcorder Problems

- Learn how to avoid shooting bad video.
- Learn how to shoot video using the correct settings.

Why Do I Shoot Bad Video?

Shooting good video takes some practice. Just because you like to watch movies doesn't mean you'll know how to make them. Here are some tips on how to shoot better video:

- *Shaking:* None of us can hold the camcorder perfectly still unless we happen to be a tree. If you have shaking problems, try using a tripod until you get better. It may be a little inconvenient to carry it around, but the results will be worth it.

- *Bad zooming:* Try to make your zooms as smooth as possible. Zooming in too quickly can give your viewer a headache. Also, instead of always zooming in, try walking closer to the action.

- *Learn the equipment:* Make sure you take the time to learn about all of its features.

- *Don't talk:* Nothing is more annoying than a camera person who can't shut up. Don't let this happen to you. You will thank us in 20 years when your grandkids ask, "Who is the loudmouth in the background?"

Why Is My Video in Black and White?

As much as you may like to watch old *Little Rascals* or *Abbot and Costello* reruns, having black and white home videos is another matter. Nothing says "amateur" more than black and white video that was supposed to be full color. Don't feel bad though; it happens more often than you think. Here are some ways to avoid shooting black and white video:

- *Camera setting:* Make sure your camera is not set to record in black and white or negative. This will surely lead to frustration. Make sure you read your owner's manual.

- *Cabling:* If your camera's transfer cable is damaged, the video may display incorrectly on your television. This can result in black and white or other weird color combinations.

Why Is My Video All Green in Color?

This is another one of our favorites. It looks as though the video was shot entirely through a submarine periscope. The only things missing are the vertical distance markers. This horrible video is the result of the night vision mode on your camera. Some camcorders put the toggle for this option where you can inadvertently turn it on.

Why Did My Camcorder Fail to Shoot Any Footage?

You've got big troubles if this has ever happened to you. The people being videotaped were counting on you getting the footage, and you blew it. What went wrong? Here are some of the more common mistakes:

- *The lens cap was on.* Some camcorders still use lens caps to protect the lens. Make sure you have removed it.

- *The camcorder was in playback mode.* The camcorder will not record when it is in playback mode.

- *The camcorder was locked.* Some camcorders have a locking feature to prevent recording. It is usually located near the record button.

- *The tape was at the end.* Obviously, if the tape has reached the end, you will not get any footage. One way to avoid this is to make sure the wheels are spinning.

- *The camcorder was turned off.* Another dumb and very avoidable mistake.

Scanner Problems

- Learn how to safely clean your scanner.
- Learn how to properly utilize your scanner.

How Can I Safely Clean the Glass Bed on My Scanner?

During normal use, you may find that the bed of your scanner will become dirty. Everything from fingerprints, crumbs, and stains can affect your ability to get a good scan of a picture.

Here are some ideas on how to keep your scanner clean:

- *Close the cover.* When you are not using your scanner, you should always keep the cover closed. This will prevent any spills or accidents from getting on the scanner bed.

- *Clean your hands.* Cleaning your hands will reduce the amount of natural oils that may be transferred to the scanner bed.

- *Keep food away.* Crumbs and soda belong on your shirt and not on your scanner.

Can the Light in My Scanner Damage My Eyes?

We're not quite sure where this myth started. Perhaps people think doing this is like looking directly into the sun or staring at an arc-welding machine. Both of these activities are capable of permanently damaging your eyes and leaving you blind. Fortunately, scanners pose no such threat.

Why Do My Scans Appear Upside Down on My Screen?

We really hate when this happens, especially after spending a considerable amount of time selecting the proper scan resolution, positioning the picture on the scanner, and performing other pre-scan rituals. Unfortunately, this can be put into the user error category. The problem here is that you put the picture or document on the scanner bed backwards.

Rotate the pictures on your scanner bed 180 degrees. Just rotate your pictures so they are opposite of the way they are currently facing. Then just scan them again. They will be facing the right direction this time around.

TIP: To avoid placing items the wrong way in your scanner, try the technique of putting a sticky note on the scanner with an arrow pointing in the correct direction.

Can I Scan More Than One Picture at a Time?

Most of us scan pictures one at a time. Not only is this tedious, but it is also a waste of time, especially if you have to scan in a large number of pictures.

However, you can put as many pictures on the scanner bed as will fit. All of the pictures will show up when you preview the scan. Just use the select tool in your scanner software when you are ready to actually do the scanning.

CD - ROM and DVD Problems

- Learn why you might be having problems burning a CD or DVD.
- Learn why software sold to let you copy a DVD on a CD burner is a scam.
- Learn how to make sure the CDs and DVDs you use are compatible with the equipment you have.

Ever since burnable CD-ROMs and DVDs were invented, the digital world has changed for the better. *Burning* refers to the process of writing data (files, music, movies, and so on) to a CD or DVD recordable disk. When writing to a CD/DVD, an infrared laser burns the dye (the colored bottom layer of the disk) and darkens microscopic areas that are then read as a 0 or OFF. Areas that are not darkened are read as a 1 or ON. Together, the patterns of dark and light areas form the music, movies, and data we store on the disks.

Recording CDs and DVDs is easy for the most part, but because of the different standards in use, you may encounter problems from time to time.

What Do I Really Need to Know about CDs So I Can Burn Them Properly?

Compact disks (CDs) are currently the most popular media choice for storing music and data. They are typically available in 650 MB data (74 minutes audio), 700 MB data (80 minutes audio), or 800 MB data (90 minutes audio). The type of drive you have and what you are trying to do will influence the type of CD you purchase. Using the wrong type of media can prevent you from reading or writing the disk. Here are the different types of CDs available:

- *CD-ROM:* Stands for Compact Disk Read Only Memory. These are disks that are professionally pressed (recorded) and cannot be rerecorded or erased. That includes the software and music disks you buy (and if you don't buy them, see Chapter 15 for more information).
- *CD-R:* Stands for Compact Disk Recordable. These are the disks most people use to store their data and music. CD-R disks use write once, read many (WORM) technology. This may be misleading. While you

can't erase a CD-R, you can write to it multiple times (so think of it as write many, read many). CD-R should work in most CD players, but expect to have trouble reading them in older, first-generation CD players.

- *CD-RW:* Stands for Compact Disk Rewritable. These disks can be completely erased and rewritten to (think of this as your floppy replacement disk). While the flexibility to erase and rewrite sounds great, not all CD players can read CD-RWs, especially older players. In addition, CD-RWs are marginally more expensive than CD-Rs.

What About DVDs?

Almost everyone knows what a DVD is nowadays. DVDs are essentially the video replacement to VHS cassettes and laser disks. (Remember those? They were these oversized, gold record/CD looking things.) They are also the replacement for CDs for holding data because they can hold over 24 times more data. Here are the types of DVDs in use today:

- *DVD-ROM:* Stands for DVD Read Only Memory. These are disks that are professionally pressed (recorded) and cannot be rerecorded or erased. If you buy, borrow, or rent a movie on DVD, then you have seen a DVD-ROM. These disks can be 9 or 18 GB.

- *DVD-R (DVD+R):* Stands for DVD Recordable. These are the disks most people use to store their data, movies, and music. DVD-R disks use write once, read many (WORM) technology. This may be misleading. While you can't erase a DVD-R, you can write to it multiple times (so think of it as write many, read many). DVD-R disks should work in most DVD players, but expect to have trouble reading them in older, first-generation DVD players. These disks can be 4.7 GB single layer or 8.5 GB dual layer. Dual-layer disks require a dual-layer burner and are typically more expensive than single-layer disks.

- *DVD-RW (DVD+RW):* Stands for DVD Rewritable. These disks can be completely erased and rewritten to. While the flexibility to erase and rewrite sounds great, not all DVD players can read DVD-RWs, especially older players. In addition, DVD-RWs are marginally more expensive than DVD-Rs. These disks can be 4.7 GB single layer or 8.5 GB dual layer. Dual-layer disks require a dual-layer burner and are typically more expensive than single-layer disks.

- *DVD-RAM:* Stands for DVD Random Access Memory. These cartridge-like disks can be completely erased and rewritten to (they look like giant floppy disks). DVD-RAM is an older technology and is slowly dying. These disks can be 4.7 GB single sided or 9.4 GB double sided.

NOTE: *The difference between –R and +R (including –RW and +RW) involves how a disk is set up and doesn't have anything to do with the type or amount of data that can be stored. They are just two competing standards, and the difference really has no effect on the home user other than you need to ensure that you buy and use the right type of media with the right type of drive (i.e., a DVD-R disk should be used in a DVD-R recorder).*

TIP: If you have a recorder that can burn in both –R and +R, try both to see which is compatible with your DVD players.

What Do I Need to Properly Burn Disks?

You'll need a CD/DVD burner and the proper software to utilize it. Most burners come bundled with sufficient but limited burning software. Typically, this software includes features like writing, erasing, and copying disks, while more advanced software can include virus scanning and the ability to make bootable CDs, create ISOs (disk images), burn DVDs, and more. Here is a list of today's more popular or useful burning software:

- *Windows XP:* Windows XP includes the ability to burn CDs. Built into the operating system (notice how I don't use the word *free*), Windows XP provides an easy way for you to burn files to disk (about as easy as placing files on a floppy). While XP does not include the advanced features of a full-fledged burning application, it provides just enough functionality to make audio and data CDs.

- *Nero:* Nero Ultra Edition is a suite of tools that allows you to burn CDs and both single- and dual-layer DVDs. Advanced features include DVD movie compression (fitting a 9 GB movie on a 4.7 GB DVD or even a 650 MB CD), cover designer, audio editor, and more. Nero Ultra Edition is available for $69.99. You can get more information at **www.nero.com**.

- *Roxio Easy Media Creator:* Formerly known as Adaptec Easy CD Creator, Roxio Easy Media Creator is a suite of tools that allows you to burn CDs and both single- and dual-layer DVDs. Advanced features include video, audio, and photo editing, data backup, Napster integration, and more. Roxio Easy Media Creator is available for $79.95. You can get more information at **www.roxio.com**.

TIP: You can also use Windows Media Player 10 to easily burn audio CDs.

Why Am I Have Trouble Burning a CD or a DVD?

If you were one of the early users of CD burners, then you know more than anyone about the challenges of burning a disk successfully. We must have gone through hundreds of corrupt disks with our first-generation CD burner. While the technology has improved since then, it's still not perfect. Here are a few reasons why you may have problems burning a CD or DVD:

- *Buffer underrun:* If you see this error, your burner is writing faster than it can read the data. See the next section.

- *System loaded down:* Burning requires a lot of resources (memory, disk, and possibly network). When burning, you should limit if not eliminate all other activity until the burn is complete.

- *Burner got bumped:* Did you bump the burner while burning a disk? The disk burning process is very sensitive to shock. When a disk is being burned, it spins very fast while a laser burns data to it. The slightest movement of that laser will corrupt your disk.

- *Need to reboot:* Reboot your PC and then start burning. This helps Windows clear memory.

- *Fragmented drive:* If you are burning files from your hard drive to your burner and get an error or erratic performance, it may be caused by drive fragmentation. Drive fragmentation is a normal occurrence that happens when files are read from the hard drive, into system memory, and then put back onto the hard drive. Running the Windows Defrag utility in Safe Mode should help you out in this situation.

What Is a Buffer Underrun?

If you've never heard the term or seen the error "buffer underrun," you're either lucky or have one of the newer burners. When you burn a disk, the slightest interruption can cause an error. If your burner is set to burn at one speed (e.g., 12X) but your data is read at another (9X); the burn process will produce an error (buffer underrun) and ruin your disk. Data can be read at a slower speed than your burner can write for many reasons:

- Slow network or interruptions while reading from a network drive

- Slow or busy drive

- Slow or busy computer

Buffer underruns can corrupt a lot of disks (trust us, we know). To address this, manufacturers have included a technology ("safe burn," "burn proof," "over burn," or whatever they choose to call it) that can dynamically stop and restart the burn process if an error is detected and prevent the error from corrupting the disk. It's included in most of today's burners, but always look for this feature when purchasing a burner.

Does the Color of the Recordable Disk Matter?

You may notice manufacturers selling multicolored recordable disks (green, red, black, blue, and so on). The difference in color is due to the different dyes that are used. Differences can include compatibility (ability to read in various devices), writability, readability, and life span. So which color should you use? There is no clear answer for that question, so you may have to try a few before finding the best one for you and your devices.

Can I Copy a DVD with My CD Burner?

If you've surfed on the Internet long enough, you may have seen software claiming that you can copy DVD movies with your CD burner. You might be tempted to think, "Great, now I don't have to buy a DVD burner to copy DVDs!" Let us say this gently: It's a scam and it would take more than a miracle to make that happen. Here's why it is impossible to copy DVDs with a CD burner:

- *CD drives cannot read DVDs.* They have different lasers that cannot read the data from a DVD.

- *CD burners cannot burn DVDs.* They have a different type of laser than a DVD burner has.

So what do these products do? They compress video. After using these products, you'll end up with a VHS-quality movie on CD (SVCD, VCD, DIVX, and so on). While you may be able to play this movie on your PC, you will need a special DVD player to play this type of video.

Why Does My Burner Say One Speed But I Actually Burn at Another?

Here are a few reasons why your burner might burn at a slower speed than it advertises:

- *Specifications:* Your burner may be rated at different speeds for different types of media. For example, your burner may be able to burn recordable media at 4X but rewritable recordable media at only 2X.

- *Brand of the media you are using:* Different brands of recordable media are rated to burn at different speeds. For example, Jack's DVDs may be rated to burn at 2X but Tyler's DVDs are rated at 4X. The burn speed is usually written on the outside of the packaging or on the website you are purchasing from. Do not purchase any media unless you are aware of the burn speed. You may have a 12X burner but are limited to burning at 2X because of the media you purchased.

- *Firmware:* While your burner may only be able to burn at one speed (e.g., 2X), you may be able to burn at faster speeds with a firmware upgrade. See your manufacturer's website for firmware updates and instructions on how to install them.

- *File location:* If access to the files you wish to burn is slow (network drive, external drive, CD/DVD drive, and so on), your burning software may slow down the write speed because the read speed is so slow.

- *Computer resources:* The speed at which your PC passes data from one source to another depends on its available resources. If your PC is old or slow, has limited resources (not enough RAM, not enough disk space, slow processor), or is just busy, your burning time can slow down significantly.

- *Software:* Your burning software might set the speed at which you read and write data to a slower setting than your burner is rated for. It can change the speed depending on a number of conditions, including the media inserted, the available resources, and the file location.

HORROR STORY!

I (Jesse) remember my first burner (which I affectionately called "Old Smokey") . It was a first-generation CD burner that cost me $800 (CD-Rs were $25 a piece). The burner would burn at 1X on my Pentium 90 MHz, and it took about an hour to make an audio CD. Times sure have changed. PCs are faster, media is dirt cheap, and you can now get a dangerously fast 48X CD burner for practically nothing. But just because your burner advertises one speed doesn't mean it will always burn at that speed. Before buying a burner, make sure you check the reviews and talk to other users.

Why Can't I Write to a Disk Anymore?

CD/DVD burners allow you to burn multiple sessions (areas of data) onto a single disk. This allows you to append data to a previously recorded disk (just as people can leave you more and more messages on your answering machine, until it fills up). Here are a few reasons why you might not be able to write to a disk:

- *Closed disk:* If you closed the disk, then you are no longer able to add sessions to it. You can use your burning software to see if the disk is closed.

- *Out of space:* You may be trying to add data larger than the free space left on the disk. Remember, there is some overhead for each session that is burned. So if you only have 100 MB free on the disk, you will not be able to add exactly 100 MB (probably 99 MB).

- *Max sessions:* You can only have a maximum of 99 sessions per disk.

Why Is My Burner So Damn Hot?

That's why they call it a burner. If you've ever seen the James Bond movie *Goldfinger,* you and Mr. Bond know exactly how hot a laser can get. The laser within a CD/DVD burner can reach over 11,000 degrees Fahrenheit. If you are burning many copies of a disk (i.e., over 10), give your burner a chance to cool down before you burn some more. Your burner may get to the point that it's warm to the touch but never to the point where you can't touch it at all. If it does, you should consider your burner defective and have it serviced or replaced.

Why Doesn't My Device Recognize a Disk?

CDs and DVDs have a high reliability rate but they can fail from time to time. Here's how you can troubleshoot why your device may not recognize a disk:

- *Try a PC:* The drives in a PC are more forgiving than those in traditional CD/DVD players. Try to read the disk in a PC or two.

- *Age:* If your device is old, it may not be able to read (or reliably read) recordable media. We have an older DVD player that used to read recordable media and suddenly stopped.

- *Wrong format:* While your device may be able to read recordable media, it may only be able to read particular formats. For example, you may have a drive that can read DVD+R disks but not DVD-R disks.

- *Wrong disk:* Are you trying to read a DVD in a CD drive? This commonly occurs if you grab the wrong disk (grabbed a DVD when you meant to grab a CD) or have two drives (one CD and one DVD) and stick a DVD in the CD drive.

- *Wrong type:* Did you burn a data disk when you meant to burn an audio disk?

- *Upside down:* Did you insert the disk upside down? It happens. When you use a disk that doesn't have a label and one side is gold and the other is silver, it's hard to know which is the data layer and which is merely the protective layer.

- *Closed disk:* Is the disk or the session closed? One of them needs to be closed in order to read the disk. Use your burner software to examine, determine, and close the disk/session.

- *Premature eject:* Did you eject the disk while it was burning? This may not only cause data corruption, it would also prevent the disk/session from closing properly.

- *Burn errors:* Did you get an error while burning? See the section "Why Am I Have Trouble Burning a CD or a DVD?" earlier in this chapter.

- *Too many burns:* Reliability drops the more times you erase and burn a rewritable disk. Depending on the quality of the media used, a disk can be rewritten from 50 to 1,000 times.

- *Writing on the disk:* If you wrote on the disk (to label it or make a note), you may have damaged it and made it unreadable. See the next section.

- *Cracked disk:* If it's cracked, don't glue it, tape it, melt it, and most important, never insert it into a drive. Today's high-speed drives can spin a cracked disk so fast that it may shatter and shoot shards of the disk out of the drive.

How Can I Safely Write a Label on a Disk?

Writing on a disk with a pen, pencil, or any writing tool with a hard tip can scratch the top surface of the disk, damaging the data layers underneath. For years now, the answer has been to use permanent marker, like a Sharpie. While these markers work fine, there is a chance that the solvents in the marker (you know, the insane smell coming from it) can end up ruining the disk over time (several years). You can now buy CD/DVD-safe permanent markers that do not contain the type of solvents found in conventional permanent markers.

Why Can't I Copy a Video Game?

Unfortunately, most video game manufacturers include copy protection on their disks, preventing you from making a perfect copy (if any copy). Even video games for the PC can and do include copy protection. Typically, the copy protection systems are merely bad sectors placed on parts of the disk that are not accessed when the disk is read but are accessed when a burner is used to try to make an exact copy. When your burner software encounters these errors, the software will cause the disk copy to fail.

WARNING! Under the Digital Copyright Millennium Act (DCMA), it is illegal to bypass copyright protection if you own the disk. Also, copying a rented video game or giving copies to others is illegal.

Why Can't I Play a Video Game I Copied?

Most video game manufacturers include copy protection on their disks. Even if you successfully copy the disk (either by illegally bypassing their copyright protection or just getting lucky), chances are you will not be able to play it. Most video game copy protection is done by special recorders that can insert bad blocks of data onto the disk. If the bad blocks are not present, the video game system will not load the disk. All home recorders are designed to not write bad blocks to a disk; therefore, you never have a perfect copy of the disk.

Why Can't I Copy a DVD Movie?

Most DVDs use a copy protection method called Content Scrambling System (CSS). This protection encrypts the contents of the disk, making copies unplayable. All DVD software companies have been given the key to decrypt the video in order to play it. This is not the same reason the picture is scrambled if you try to plug the DVD into a VCR to record it. DVD-to-VHS scrambling is due to Macrovision copy protection. The copy protection includes extra information in the video signal that instructs the automatic gain control (AGC) chip in your VCR to modulate the gain, brightness, and color, causing the display to be distorted. DVD/VCR combo devices that allow copying from a DVD to a VCR cassette filter out this signal. This signal does not affect your TV because your TV does not listen to this extra information.

How Can I Securely Destroy a Disk?

There may come a time when you have to destroy a disk that contains secure data. Simply throwing a disk in the trash leaves the information available to dumpster divers. You could try to break or cut the disk with scissors before you throw it out, but if you've ever tried, you know that's not as easy as it looks. Just as you shred paper in a paper shredder, you can now shred disks in a new device called a disk shredder. These devices are stand-alone units (no PC required) that can shred 30 disks or more per minute and are available for less than $40. You should be able to buy these devices at major local and online retailers.

WARNING! Attempting to break, snap, or crack a disk by hand is not only a difficult task, but also a dangerous one. Snapping a disk can cause shards of the disk to cut your hands or fly out and cut you or others.

Summary

As you saw in this chapter, technology is all around us. Devices such as cameras didn't change much over the years until they became digital. Now most of us are snapping digital pictures at an impressive rate. Unfortunately, digital cameras are prone to failure unless the user is knowledgeable. We showed you how to get the most out of your digital camera through proper use. PDAs have become very popular in recent years as well. Businesspeople use them for contact management, scheduling, and other tasks. Although they have great capabilities, there is still room for improvement. This chapter showed you how to deal with some of the quirkiness that is inherent in these devices. We also learned of the problems inherent in CDs and DVDs. We reviewed all of the different types of formats and hopefully made the acronyms easier to understand.

15

Piracy

Disasters to avoid:

- Getting caught pirating software and being fined as a result.
- Discovering that you've purchased a PC that has pirated software.

Mishaps and blunders to run from:

- Having file sharing software on your PC that is illegally sharing files without your knowledge.
- Getting in trouble by downloading music or video that has been pirated.

Most things we do these days, from work activities to entertainment, involve digital technology: emails, worksheets, presentations, CDs, MP3s, DVDs, satellite TV, HDTV, you name it. The digital format is both a blessing and a curse for copyright owners (music industry companies, movie studios, software manufacturers, and so on). The blessing of the digital format is high quality, smaller sizes, easy transportation, and exact duplication. The curse is piracy, especially if you are involved in the business of creating electronic products.

Before the digital age, giving someone a cassette recording of a newly released record wouldn't have gotten you into trouble. You likely wouldn't have been fined by a record company or sent to jail. Making and passing out multiple copies would have taken you a few days. Nowadays, you can make an exact copy and distribute it to the world in a matter of minutes. CD and DVD burners, the Internet, compression formats like MP3 and DIVX, and file sharing programs like Napster and Kazaa all make it easy for the home user to set up their own digital duplication and distribution center. As a result, copyright owners have gone on a crusade. Armed with an arsenal of attorneys, they are trying to reclaim what they have lost in revenues over the past five years. This is the reason you should read closely and understand the material in this chapter.

Piracy is the unauthorized duplication, distribution, advertisement, or use of copyrighted material. It is a crime with penalties such as lawsuit judgments, fines, and even jail time. Let's start by looking at piracy, how it happens, how to recognize it, how to prevent it, and what your alternatives are to breaking the law.

Piracy Hazards

- Make sure you understand what piracy is and its legal implications.
- Learn if you are contributing to piracy and how to stop it.
- Learn what to do if you are caught pirating copyrighted files.

Should I Be Worried about Piracy?

Whether it's making their buddy a mixed CD, installing a copy of antivirus software on their brother's computer, or copying a rented movie, most people have performed some sort of piracy in their lifetime. Here's a list of the different groups that should be concerned about piracy:

- *Parents:* Many kids today are more computer savvy then their parents. Since kids have limited funds and judgment but unlimited time and curiosity, parents need to be proactive about making sure their kids aren't engaging in piracy.

- *Business owners:* As a business grows, the temptation to use pirated software increases. Companies often purchase software products and a set of product licenses and then outgrow their available licenses and need to purchase more. This can happen without them even realizing it, especially in a fast-growing company. Besides license abuse, companies have to worry about employees installing pirated software and causing a violation of their current, legal license agreement.

- *Educational institutions:* The dorm room is the birthplace of illegal file sharing. College kids do not have a lot of money to spend. That's why you'll find most of them eating pasta, drinking on "Nickel Night," and downloading pirated software, music, and movies. While most companies sell educational versions or, better yet, provide free trialware (time-limited software), the average student cannot afford the educational version and cannot learn the product in the time allotted (usually 30 days).

- *Anyone who owns a PC:* If you use a PC, you should be concerned about piracy. Even if you don't use file sharing programs or download illegal files, you are using a computer filled with software and files, and some of those may be pirated.

Are File Sharing or Peer-to-Peer Programs Safe?

Peer-to-peer (a.k.a. P2P) file sharing applications provide a simple mechanism for people to share files (music, movies, and more) on the Internet. Napster was the most popular P2P application to date, giving users a way to share, trade, and find music files quickly and easily. As opposed to connecting to one central computer to download and upload files, computers running P2P applications can connect to and download from other computers running the same P2P applications. This allows you to search and download from thousands of computers, providing you with better search results and faster downloads.

Most of the P2P systems now in use are safe as long as you use them properly. Here is a list of some of today's most popular P2P applications:

- *ABC:* ABC (Yet Another BITtorrent Client) is a free, open source P2P client that uses the BITtorrent protocol. The advantage the BITtorrent protocol has over other P2P protocols is that you download bits and pieces from various sources as opposed to downloading the entire file from one source. BITtorrent shares the bits from files that are downloading with other users. This approach maximizes network bandwidth and provides higher availability for popular files. The home page for ABC is **http://pingpong-abc.sourceforge.net**.

- *BearShare:* BearShare is a P2P client that uses the Gnutella protocol, is free of spyware, and contains password-protected filters that can block adult material and visual content (movies, pictures, and so on). BearShare offers both a free client, which contains advertisements, and a subscription-based client that is free of advertisements and costs $3.99 per month.

- *eMule:* Inspired by the eDonkey 2000 client, eMule is a free, open source P2P client that features connectivity to three different networks and is free of advertisements and spyware. The home page for eMule is **www.emule-project.net**.

- *Kazaa:* Recently ruled legal by the Dutch Supreme Court, Kazaa is a fast, full-featured P2P client that has a large user base, allowing for higher availability and variety of downloads. Kazaa offers a free client that is full of spyware, advertisements, and pop-ups, and a $29.95 client that is free of such annoyances. The home page for Kazaa is **www.kazaa.com**

- *LimeWire:* LimeWire is a P2P client that uses the Gnutella protocol, is built in Java, runs on multiple operating systems, integrates with iTunes for the Macintosh, and claims to be faster than Kazaa. LimeWire offers a free client that contains advertisements and nagware and a $18.88 client that is free of such annoyances. The home page for LimeWire is **www.limewire.com**.

- *Morpheus:* Morpheus is an advanced P2P client that features an antivirus plug-in that allows you to use your antivirus software to scan files as they are downloading, includes password-protected filters that can block adult material and search phrases, and provides connectivity to five different networks (including those used by eMule and BearShare). Morpheus offers both a free client, which contains advertisements, or a $19.95 client that doesn't contain ads. The home page for Morpheus is **www.morpheus.com**.

- *WinMX:* WinMX is a free P2P client that features advanced configuration options, skinnable interface, and freedom from advertisements and spyware. The home page for WinMX is **www.winmx.com**.

What Happens If I Am Caught Downloading or Sharing Copyrighted Material?

We believe Mr. John Mellencamp (the artist formally known as John Cougar Mellencamp) said it best, "I fight authority, authority always wins." Heed the words of such an insightful man. We know people who have been caught, and believe us it's no picnic. Lawyers, fines, and settlements can be substantially expensive, to the point where you may have to sell some of your prized possessions (your car, your home, even your Mellencamp record collection). Hopefully, the following scary (but real) scenarios will discourage you from getting involved in piracy:

• *Getting in trouble with your ISP:* The copyright holder informs your Internet service provider (ISP) of the piracy, and the ISP is required by law to terminate your service. Your ISP does not have to divulge who you are at this time. Your ISP may contact you, informing you of what is happening. At this point, you should find out its policy on divulging your information. Some ISPs may fight in court to keep your identity confidential. You should contact a lawyer as well.

• *Getting in trouble with the copyright holder:* The copyright holder could take you to court to have a judge issue a subpoena to your ISP to obtain your true identity. The copyright holder may then contact you to either agree on a settlement or to inform you of legal action to follow.

• *Getting in trouble by breaking the law:* Under the No Electronic Theft (NET) Act, you may be charged with a federal felony, and if prosecuted, you could be fined and or given jail time.

What Should I Do If I've Been Caught Downloading or Sharing Copyrighted Material?

Receiving a notice like this can send chills down your spine. Before you get too anxious and do something stupid, here's what you should consider doing:

• *Verify that the notice is authentic.* Some scam artists send notices (emails, letters) or call you to try to scare you into divulging your social security, password, or other personal information. See Chapter 1 for information on these types of scams.

• *Disconnect your PC from the Internet.* If the notice is authentic and you're using your PC to share files, it is imperative that you stop doing so as soon as possible to limit your liability.

- *Contact a lawyer immediately before discussing anything with the copyright holder.* Definitely do not allow the copyright holder to intimidate you into doing anything (such as admitting guilt or agreeing on a settlement), even if they make it seem like their way is the easiest way out.

What Are the Penalties Associated with Piracy?

The penalties for copyright infringement vary depending on whether you are being prosecuted civilly or criminally. The distinction in the law lies in whether you are just sharing copyrighted materials or duplicating them for commercial or personal profit.

Most people that engage in piracy are in this first group. These are the people that use file sharing programs, burn copies of music CDs, and engage in other similar activities. It seems harmless enough, but these people are putting themselves at a much greater risk than they realize. Unfortunately, this group are the main targets of the Recording Industry Association of America (RIAA) in its crusade to protect the interests of copyright owners. Penalties usually include a lawsuit, but they may also include criminal charges and fines.

The remaining offenders are the die-hard criminals. These people mass duplicate CDs, videos, DVDs, books, and anything else they can make money on. Being convicted of a criminal copyright infringement offense carries a fine of up to $250,000 and five years in the slammer.

How to Detect Illegal or Questionable Material Stored on My PC

You may have illegal files on your computer right now without even realizing it. This is especially true if your PC is used by others (fellow employees, family members, roommates). It doesn't matter who placed the illegal files on your PC; you will ultimately be responsible because it is your computer. Here are some ways to find illegal or questionable material on your PC:

- *Search for media files.* Windows users can do this by right-clicking the Start button and then choosing Find or Search. You can then search for various media file types (*.mp3, *.mpg, *.avi, and so on). Windows XP even provides you with a handy option to search for Music and Movie files without specifying the file types. Once you locate the files, ensure that they are yours or belong to the operating system or software installed on your computer.

- *Search for large, unrecognizable files.* Just because you didn't know what the file was (a file type you didn't recognize) doesn't make you less accountable. Windows XP provides you with a handy option to search for large files.

- *Search for installed file sharing programs.* Windows users can review the list of installed programs by opening Control Panel and clicking Add/ Remove Programs. While file sharing programs are legal to use (when used appropriately), chances are someone has used them to download or share copyrighted files. Look under the download/share directories of each installed file sharing program for copyrighted or questionable files. Most of these directory names include the words *share* or *download*.

What to Do If Your PC Is Sharing Pirated Files

Most people (especially parents) aren't even aware that file sharing programs like Kazaa and BearShare automatically enable and share files on your computer right when you install them. Not only does this present legal problems, but it also sucks up your available Internet bandwidth and slows down your PC. If you find your PC sharing pirated files here's what you can do:

- *Immediately disconnect your computer from the Internet/network.* This is the quickest way to stop your computer from sharing pirated files.

- *Stop the sharing.* Find the program sharing your files and either uninstall it or disable file sharing. See the following section for more information.

- *Permanently delete all pirated files.* See the previous section on how to find pirated files stored on your computer.

How to Stop a P2P Application from Sharing Files

Each P2P application is configured differently to stop sharing files automatically. The methods listed here do not delete the shared directories; they only stop the sharing. The following instructions show you how to stop file sharing in today's most popular P2P applications:

- *ABC:* Because of the nature of the BITtorrent protocol, there is no way to disable file sharing. While files are being downloaded, the BITtorrent protocol automatically shares the downloaded pieces of the files with others.

- *BearShare:* In the File menu, choose Setup and then Sharing. Under the Sharing tab, select each directory listed and click Remove.

- *eMule:* Click the Preferences button. Select the Files icon and select Nobody under "See my shared files/folders." You can also unshare specific directories by clicking the Preference button, selecting the Directories icon, and then clearing that check boxes that are selected under Shared Directories.

- *Kazaa:* On the File menu, click Tools and then Options. Under the Traffic tab, check the check box labeled "Disable sharing of files with other Kazaa Media Desktop users" and then click OK.

- *LimeWire:* On the file menu, choose Tools and then Options. Select the Sharing node, select each directory listed, and click Remove.

- *Morpheus:* Click the Library button. Under the Share tab, select each directory listed and click Remove.

- *WinMX:* Click the Shared Folders button on the top of the application. Click Unshare Folder and select each folder displayed.

Pirated Software

- Learn how software is pirated, how to recognize it, and why you shouldn't do it.
- Learn about the legal alternatives to pirating software.

Software piracy is a crime that involves unauthorized copying, distribution, alteration, or use of copyrighted software. The term *warez* (pronounced "wares," as in soft-wares) is used for a pirated piece of software by underground groups (hackers and crackers) that pirate software for profit, curiosity, and even for bragging rights.

DID YOU KNOW that over one third of the world's software is pirated? According to a 2003 study by the Business Software Alliance, 36 percent of all software is pirated, resulting in a $29 billion loss to the software industry.

How Is Software Pirated?

Software piracy can be as complex as an Internet underground group running a debug program to reverse-engineer a software's security mechanism, or as simple as providing someone with your Windows serial number. Here are a few of the ways software can be pirated:

- *The program is duplicated and given to someone.* For example, you make a copy of your favorite computer game and give it to your cousin.

- *The program is used by more people or computers than the license agreement allows.* For example, you buy a copy of Windows XP Home and install it on multiple computers.

- *A program called a crack is used to bypass the security measures of the program.* This program could remove a time limitation, enable all features, remove annoying registration notices, and so on.

- *A program called a keygen is used to generate a serial number that allows you to register the program as if you paid for it.*

- *A serial number (illegally obtained from a keygen, another user, or a website) is obtained that allows you to register the program as if you paid for it.*

How Can I Recognize Pirated Software?

You may be using pirated software right now without realizing it. Despite how it got on your PC (whether it came with your PC when you bought it or a friend or family member installed the software without you knowing), you are still responsible. Here are a few ways to determine if you are using pirated software:

- *Determine if your copy of Windows XP is being used with a pirated serial number.* The latest service pack for Windows XP will not install on copies using a pirated serial number. When the service pack install begins, it checks the current serial number against a list of known pirated serial numbers. If a match is found, the install is halted.

- *Game consoles.* If playing a video game disc on your PlayStation, Xbox, and so on requires you to install a MOD chip (a device that allows you to play imported or backup games), chances are the disc is pirated.

- *You purchased the software way below the average cost.* The software may be counterfeit, an unauthorized copy, or not intended for resale. See Chapter 1 for more information on this type of scam.

- *You purchased a PC with the software preinstalled and were not given any certificates of authenticity.* More than likely, the retailer is using the one copy of the software and installing it on every computer it sells (which is highly illegal). Computer fairs and smaller computer shops are famous for this. The certificate of authenticity is usually a piece of paper with a hologram on it.

- *You purchase a PC with the software preinstalled and were not given any CDs or mechanism to reinstall the software or rebuild your computer.* While some manufacturers include install CDs or restore CDs, more and more are including the media on the hard drive and provide a mechanism to build your own restore CD via a CD or DVD burner. If there is no way for you to rebuild or reinstall your software, chances are it's because the software is pirated.

DID YOU KNOW that over 50% of software sold at computer shows in the United States is pirated? For more information, you can visit **www.siia.net/ piracy/whatis.asp**.

Why Shouldn't I Download and Use Pirated Software?

The temptation is real: someone offers you a copy of some software you need or you find a copy of the software online, and lo and behold, you have it without spending a dime. Here's why you should not download or use pirated software:

- *It's not free; it's illegal!* You are taking something you didn't pay for and that's called stealing. The days of the lone serial number are over. More and more software manufacturers are using advanced security mechanisms, such as product activation, to prevent piracy and identify the users of pirated software.

- *Quality issues:* Pirated software sometimes crashes from the pieces of code the crackers rip out to bypass security measures.

- *Lack of support:* Pirated software comes with no support from the manufacturer.

- *Missing/incorrect features:* Manuals, audio tracks, help files, and additional features are typical items removed from pirated software to reduce the file size. Sometimes the software version is in the wrong language or is a different version than you expected (educational version, standard vs. professional version, and so on). Imagine trying to work on your PC and not understanding the language (a lot of us feel this way about computers anyway) or playing your favorite game without the sound effects or background music.

- *Aggravation:* Finding, downloading, installing, and testing pirated software can be an involved process. Besides ensuring that the software is intact and functional, you have to ensure that the files are free from viruses, Trojan horses, and other malicious programs. Is all that trouble really worth it?

What Are My Alternatives to Downloading Pirated Software?

Software is expensive, sometimes prohibitively expensive. The problem is you need the functionality of a given software product but can't or don't want to spend the money for it. Here are some ways to get the functionality you love without paying the high price tag you hate:

- *Use freeware.* Why would someone write and then give away software for free? Some do it hoping to be bought out or hired by a large company (like Microsoft). Others do it in an effort to promote other products they sell, and still others do it out of kindness or boredom. Despite the reasons, freeware is a nice, legal way to get software without having to pay for it.

- *Use open source software.* Open source software is community developed, it's free, and its source code is made publicly available. The idea behind open source is to build software that contains the features everybody wants without the fluff and bugs everyone hates.
- *Use careware.* This is a great idea and serves an even greater purpose. Careware (sometimes referred to as charityware) is software developed by someone who then makes it free to the public. In exchange, all they ask from those who use and benefit from it is to make a donation to a charity of the author's choice. An example of this type of software is Kixtart (a scripting language for Windows).

Pirated Music

- Learn why you should not contribute to music piracy and how you can get caught if you do.
- Learn about the legal alternatives to pirating music and how you can protect your music from being pirated.

While audio records (for you youngsters out there, these were vinyl platters with a hole in the middle that were played with a phonograph or "record player") and tapes stored music in analog format, CDs and DVDs store music digitally in large files, typically 40 MB to 60 MB. Compression formats such as MP3 and WMA shrink these audio files to about 1/10th the original size (typically 4 MB to 6 MB) with little to no loss in sound quality. Small in size, high in quality, and plenty of free tools to compress and share these files—it's no wonder MP3/WMA file sharing and players are so popular.

Music piracy is a crime. It is illegal to distribute or obtain copyrighted work without authorization from the copyright holder. Simply stated: Unless Britney Spears tells you its OK, it's illegal to download, upload, trade, or share her music (even though, in our opinion, it's unlistenable anyway). That's why Napster was shut down and why the RIAA is filing lawsuits against anyone (including a 12-year-old girl) who is caught breaking the law.

DID YOU KNOW the music industry loses $11.5 million *per day* due to music piracy? According to the Recording Industry Association of America (RIAA), the music industry loses about $4.2 billion a year due to pirated music. To learn more, go to **www.riaa.com/issues/piracy**.

How Is Music Pirated?

Music piracy can be a complex as running a sweat shop counterfeiting/distribution operation, or as simple as downloading your favorite song without paying for it. Here are a few ways music is pirated by the common computer user:

- *Using a CD ripper program:* Programs like Windows Media Player and MusicMatch are used to read and compress (a.k.a. rip) CD audio into music files (WMA, MP3) that are then uploaded, shared, or traded on the Internet (via Kazaa, FTP, newsgroups, local networks, and so on).

- *Using a stream ripper program:* Just as your FM radio streams music over the airwaves to your radio, music can be streamed over the Internet and to your PC. For each song, the stream usually includes the song title, artist name, album name, genre, and so on (just as most MP3s do). A stream ripper is a program that takes the stream and copies each streamed song to an MP3 on your PC.

- *Making or giving a CD copy to someone else, or receiving a CD copy from someone else:* This includes making a custom mix CD for someone else.

- *Taking or giving a music track to someone else, or receiving a music track from someone else*

- *Downloading music files via Kazaa, FTP, newsgroups, local networks, and so on*

How Can I Get Caught Downloading and Sharing Copyrighted Material?

We often encourage others to stop downloading pirated music (especially bad music) and almost always receive the same response: "How do they (the RIAA) know I'm downloading pirated music?" Here are a few ways you can get caught:

- You are reported by someone. It only takes a disgruntled employee, business competitor, your ISP, a faculty member, or your arch enemy.

- The RIAA installs and runs a file sharing program (Kazzaa, BearShare, and so on), searches for music files, downloads them, verifies them, and then determines the IP address of the computer sharing the files. It can then obtain a subpoena from a judge to force an ISP to reveal the identity of the customer that was assigned the IP address at that given time.

- Someone placed pirated music on a server without the owner's knowledge (company, school, home user, etc.). While you are downloading, the owner spots and reports your activity.

- The company or server you were downloading from was under investigation (by the police, FBI, or RIAA). By examining logs and obtaining client IP addresses, the investigating organization can then obtain a subpoena from a judge to force an ISP to reveal the identity of the customer that was assigned the IP address at that given time.

HORROR STORY!

A single mother, her 9-year-old son, and 12-year-old daughter all lived quietly in a city Housing Authority apartment. They were shocked and frightened to learn that they were being sued by the RIAA for sharing pirated music. While the daughter did not deliberately share pirated music, she did download some through Kazaa (which automatically shares the files on your PC as you learned earlier in this chapter). While it could have been worse, the RIAA settled for a $2,000 fee from the family. Be warned: you are responsible for all the Internet activity that goes on in your home or business, even if it comes from a 12-year-old.

Why Shouldn't I Pirate Music?

Being easy doesn't make it right. And appearing to be free doesn't mean there won't be a cost. (And being able to write these silly sentences doesn't mean we should. Enough already.) The following list will outline a few reasons not to download pirated music:

- *It's not free; it's illegal!* Whether it's a candy bar from a variety store or a copyrighted music download, you are taking something you didn't pay for and that's called stealing. It might be easy, and you might think no one can see you, but that doesn't make it right.

- *The Quality:* Skipping, hissing, low volume, and distortion are just a few of the problems with audio files downloaded or ripped from the Internet. Sometimes the artist or record company will upload or stream bad audio files to frustrate the audio pirate.

- *Aggravation:* Finding, downloading, converting, testing, and listening to pirated music can be an involved process. Besides ensuring that the audio file is intact and acceptable, you have to ensure that the files are free from viruses, Trojan horses, and other malicious programs. Is all that trouble really worth it?

What Are My Alternatives to Downloading Pirated Music?

While downloading and trading music files seems to be the latest fad, there are other ways for you to obtain your digital music easily and legally. The following is just a brief list of alternatives to downloading pirated music:

- *Satellite radio:* The average computer user does not know how to be a DJ and just ends up skipping through their music playlists and listening to a few of their most favorite songs. Sirius.com is a satellite radio service that offers CD-quality, commercial-free music that you can listen to on your PC, satellite radio, and even satellite TV (Dish Network customers only). Combined with quality, availability, variety of stations, automatic DJ, and constant addition of new songs as well as sports, news, weather, TV station audio, and more, satellite radio provides many reasons to choose it over anything else. Pay for radio? Bah, humbug! We said the same thing until we got a little taste, and never looked back.

- *Paying for music downloads:* Sites like iTunes.com and Napster.com allow you to legally buy and download music files. These sites include security mechanisms to prevent you from giving your files to others. At an average of 99¢ a song, this method is more expensive and doesn't provide the flexibility of the following method.

- *Buy CDs and then convert the audio tracks to MP3/WMA files for your own personal use.* Applications like Media Player and MusicMatch make converting your CDs as simple as inserting them into your computer. Additionally, buying retail CDs gives you the benefit of the physical CD (no need to burn your own), CD protective case (hooray!), CD cover and insert (graphics, lyrics), multimedia content, and any other incentives the music industry can dream up.

How Can I and the Music Industry Secure Music Files?

If you currently do or are thinking about converting your audio CDs to compressed audio files, then you should think about security. Not only do you want to protect your music from intentional theft, but you also need to protect it from accidental sharing. The following list contains methods on how you and the music industry can secure music files:

- *Digital rights management:* Windows Media Player, iTunes, and Real Player implement their own versions of Digital rights management (DRM). DRM protects your music files by allowing them to be played only on the computer that encoded the files and or by requiring a license file.

- *CDs with built-in copy protection:* This type of copy protection prevents users from playing or reading the CD in their computers, thus preventing conversion of the audio racks and CD copying. This protection relies on the fact that computer CD-ROM drives can read CDs with audio, data, or video, while standard home CD players can read only audio. When false information is inserted on the CD (disguised as bad data), the computer is tricked into thinking the CD is a data CD with bad data, thus preventing a read. This is a neat trick but it doesn't come without its own problems. Newer car and home stereos are now coming with the ability to read and play MP3s and WMA CDs and would also be unable to read these CDs.

- *CDs with installable copy protection:* These CDs depend on the Windows AutoRun feature to automatically install copy protection software on your PC after the CD is first inserted. This method is a weak attempt at protection because it is easily circumvented by disabling the AutoRun feature. It's also a more intrusive method of protection because it sneakily installs software behind your back when all you wanted to do is listen to music.

Pirated Movies

- Learn about movie piracy and how it occurs.
- Learn why you should not contribute to movie piracy and what the legal alternatives to pirating movies are.

Improvements in digital video compression combined with the spread of high-speed broadband connections has encouraged the practice of pirating movies. Video compression formats like Digital Video eXpress (DIVX) make it possible for a full-length, high-quality movie to be shrunk down to a size that can be downloaded in hours over a high-speed Internet connection. While online movie piracy is a crime, it is becoming as popular as online music piracy. Let's explore how movies wind up on the Internet, why you should stay away, and what your legal alternatives are to online movie piracy.

How Are Movies Pirated?

The process of pirating a movie can be as simple as sneaking a camcorder into the theater to as complicated as cracking digital encryption and copyright protection. While there are many methods pirates use to illegally copy movies, here are the main techniques being used to steal and distribute movies over the Internet:

- *Camcording:* Also known as "cam," this method involves someone sneaking a home video camera into the theater and taping the movie being shown. The video is extremely poor, with things like poor focusing, bad lighting, strange angles (since the camera is looking up at the screen and not at eye level), shaking (lack of tripod), the back of people's heads, and only part of the screen showing (since movies are wide screen and home movie cameras are not). The audio is also poor because it includes mono sound and background noise (hissing and people talking, coughing, laughing, screaming, and so on).

NOTE: *It is illegal to make unauthorized copies of copyrighted material.*

- *Telesync:* Similar to cam, this involves videotaping a movie being shown in a theater but done with professional video equipment. While this method suffers some of the same quality issues as the cam method (strange angle, bad lighting), it does produce better video and audio quality because of the steps taken. Telesyncers use a tripod to prevent shaking, separate record audio through the handicap headphone jack to prevent hissing and background noise, choose a time when there are little or no people in the theater, and sit in the back so the entire screen can be filmed. The equipment is usually hidden in a large bag, purse, or backpack. The camera is then disguised as a person by placing a coat and hat around it.

- *Workprint:* A workprint is a copy of a movie before editing has been completed. These copies are usually stolen from the postproduction houses while they are working on the film. Their quality can vary dramatically, but it is usually average. Since these movies are in the middle of the editing process, they may not contain special effects, sound effects, and background music. Bottom line: this is not a finished product.

- *Telecine:* This method involves obtaining the movie reel and using a telecine device to capture the output to a computer or videotape. This method produces the best quality for movies that are yet to be or are currently in theaters.

- *Screeners:* These are DVDs, videocassettes, or online movie streams intended for the press, critics, actors, censors, and Oscar, or Emmy voters for review or promotion. The screen usually contains a copyright message that is displayed every 15 minutes or so, reminding the viewer that this video is a screener and not meant for redistribution. Screeners are usually leaked to movie pirates by their intended recipient.

- *DVD rips:* Most DVDs include copy protection to prevent copying to DVD, VHS, or a computer file. DVD ripping involves using a computer and DVD ripping software to circumvent or break the copy protection on a DVD and output a digital copy of the DVD to the computer. Some

advanced ripping software even allows you to remove region protection—a security mechanism that prevents DVDs intended for one area
(for example, the United States) to be played in DVD players in another
area (for example, China). Once the DVD is "ripped," the user can place
the files on a recordable DVD (producing an almost exact quality DVD
without the copy protection). Some DVD rips have various features
removed (deleted scenes, alternate endings, director's comments, language
tracks, etc.), so the download is smaller. The quality of these movies
varies based on the chosen compression, but it can be and usually is as
high as the original.

NOTE: *While you have a legal right to make one backup copy of a DVD you own, it is illegal to circumvent the
copy or region protection on a DVD.*

DID YOU KNOW that some movie theaters use night goggles to catch
people video taping? Think about that the next time you go to the movies to
get frisky. For more information, visit **www.cbsnews.com/stories/2003/
04/18/tech/main550005.shtml**.

Why Shouldn't I Download Pirated Movies?

Between the movie tickets, popcorn, soda, and ridiculously priced candy, you
can easily spend $30 for two people to see the latest summer blockbuster
movie. But, if you can see the latest movies "for free" from the convenience of
your home, then why wouldn't you? The following list tells you why:

- *It's not free; it's illegal!* Whether it's a candy bar from a variety store or a
  copyrighted movie download, you are taking something you didn't pay
  for and that's called stealing. It might be easy and you might think no
  one can see you, but doesn't make it right.

- *The quality:* While a movie or a DVD shown in a theater has surround
  sound, rich colors, and clear display, most pirated movies are of extremely
  poor quality.

- *The feel:* The overpriced candy and popcorn, the wide screen, the sta-
  dium seating, the surround sound, and the feel of the audience (just not
  the talking) are just some of the benefits of going to see a movie in the
  theater.

- *Missing features:* Cut-off screens, missing bloopers/extras during the end
  credits, and incomplete movies are typical issues of the pirated movie.

- *Aggravation:* Finding, downloading, converting, testing, and displaying a pirated movie can be an involved process. Besides ensuring that the movie is intact and acceptable both visually and audibly, you have to ensure that the files are free from viruses, Trojan horses, and other malicious programs. On top of all that, downloading a high-quality movie over a fast Internet connection could take days and hog up your connection. Is all that trouble really worth it?

What Are My Alternatives to Downloading Pirated Movies?

Being able to see the movie they want when they want for little or no cost is what people first find attractive about downloading movies. The following list outlines your alternatives to illegally downloading copyrighted movies (that is, it outlines how you can watch quality movies with ease and without breaking any laws):

- *Video on demand:* This is as close as you can get to illegal movie downloading, but legally and without all the negatives. Typically provided as a service of digital cable and satellite providers, video on demand allows you to select and watch the movie of your choice while including control features like pause, rewind, and fast forward.

- *Movie streaming:* Services like Movielink.com and Starz Ticket! at Real.com allow you to watch movies over your Internet broadband connection. Because the movie streams (as opposed to downloads), you can start watching a movie in minutes.

- *Online rentals:* Besides your local video store, you can now have the latest movies delivered to your door (Netflix.com, DvdAvenue.com). These services send you the DVDs of your choosing in self-addressed envelopes. There are no late fees and no specific due date for your movies. You can keep them as long as you want and return them whenever you want. When you are ready to return, just place the DVD in the self-addressed envelope and stick it in the mailbox. In addition, these services have an extensive library of available movies (way more than all of your local video stores combined) and fast delivery (usually two to three days).

- *The matinee:* Almost every theater has a matinee. Some have them on the weekends, others every day until a certain time, and others even have "matinee days." If you pick the right time combined with the right movie, the matinee is the best way to avoid crowds and disruptions.

Pirated Subscription Services

- Learn about subscription service piracy and how it occurs.
- Learn how subscription services are pirated, why you shouldn't do it, and how to prevent it.

Cable, satellite, and the Internet are among the most common services the average person subscribes to. We have grown dependent on them. Today, the average person spends $90 a month or more for both television and Internet services. That's over $1,000 per year, not exactly chump change. Cost is just one of the reasons people take "shortcuts" to obtain these services and pay as little as possible. No matter how it happens, if you use a service you did not pay for or provide others with a service they did not pay for, it's a crime and is punishable by fines and jail time.

How Are Subscription Services Pirated?

Piracy has grown from simple subscription fraud tactics such as giving false information to advanced methods such as reprogramming access cards to decrypt an encrypted signal. Here are some of the more common techniques that PC users are employing to pirate services:

- *Video capture/tuner cards:* These cards allow you to watch and record TV channels on your PC. This is perfectly legal, but some pirates upload the recorded shows to the Internet, sharing everything from the last episode of *The Sopranos* to the latest pay-per-view movie.

NOTE: *Even if you pay for the original broadcast of the service, it is illegal for you to give that service to others outside your home and it is illegal for them to receive it.*

- *PVR download:* Personal video recorders (TiVo, Replay, UltimateTV, Windows Media Center PCs) record television programs in digital format, using the same or similar compression used for DVD video. Some pirates "hack" their PVR, connect it to their home network, download the video from the PVR, translate it into viewable files, and upload them to the Internet. Companies like HBO (Home Box Office) make their money from people subscribing to their channel for programming like *The Sopranos* and *Six Feet Under.* When others upload every episode to the Internet, they are bound to lose existing and potential subscribers.

- *Reprogramming satellite access cards:* An access card (also known as a smart card) is a credit-card-like piece of plastic that contains the software to decrypt and display only the satellite channels you pay for. A pirate reprograms the access card via a smart card writer, modifying the software to allow viewing of all channels.

- *Satellite access card emulators:* Besides using access cards, pirates use computer programs to emulate the functionality of an access card, which would allow the viewing of all channels. An emulator can be any PC that connects to a satellite receiver and uses this software to allow viewing of all channels.

- *Internet access sharing:* Depending on the terms of your contract or customer agreement, you may or may not be allowed to share your Internet connection with more than one PC. You should know your agreement to make sure you are in compliance. Even if your agreement allows sharing, it most certainly does not allow sharing outside of your residence. This includes sharing by using a wired or wireless network connection.

HORROR STORY!

A friend of ours decided his satellite service was too expensive and he was going to start pirating it. He purchased all the equipment and downloaded all the software he needed to do it. He enjoyed this service for a few months until he received a phone call. The phone call was from the satellite company's lawyer. The lawyer stated that they knew he was pirating service and that they had all the evidence to sue and prosecute him. They gave him a choice of paying a $5,000 settlement and turning in all his equipment or taking his chances in court. Wisely, he paid the settlement. So, in his quest to save a few dollars, he lost $5000, the cost of the pirated equipment, and his satellite service.

Why Shouldn't I Pirate Subscription Services?

While it's easy to see "the benefits" of subscription piracy, sometimes it is not so easy to see the costs. Here are a few reasons why you should not take part in subscription piracy:

- *It's not free; it's illegal!* More and more providers are using addressable (trackable) receivers, private security firms, and fancy techniques to find exactly who is stealing their services. If you cheat, you could easily be caught.

- *Quality:* Regardless of which service is pirated, quality is almost always degraded. Internet access sharing not only provides weaker signals due to distance limitations, wireless strength, and added resistance when the cable is split, but because you are sharing your bandwidth with others, your download/upload speeds will be dramatically reduced. Most cable descramblers provide weaker signals, resulting in reduced video and sound quality. Descramblers may not only cause you to have a weaker signal, they may also cause all customers downstream (from your home to the end of the cable) to have a weaker signal. Finally, programming captured using a computer or PVR and shared over the Internet are of reduced quality due to the way these devices capture and the compression used to reduce their size for Internet access sharing.

- *Raids:* If you purchase equipment to pirate a service, chances are you will ultimately be caught through the sales transaction. For example, a cable or satellite provider might discover that a company is manufacturing devices to descramble/steal their service and inform the police. The manufacturer is raided and arrested. The manufacturer then cuts a deal by providing the police/cable/satellite provider with its customer list. If your name and address is on the list, expect a visit.

- *Possibility of it costing you:* Besides possible jail time, legal bills, fines, and lawsuits, pirating services may actually cost you. Some descramblers decode pay-per-view movies without you having to call, order, or pay for them (at least at first). The box may actually send an "order" signal to your provider and you may end up having to pay for all those movies you thought you were getting for "free." This bill can be huge.

- *Faulty equipment:* Cable descramblers are prone to "signal leakage." Also known as signal bleed, this occurs when the device unintentionally emits radio frequency (RF) signals. Most of these devices are cheaply built and do not follow the strict regulations set by the FCC regarding RF emission. Not only can the cable/satellite provider detect your theft because of this emission, but the emission can actually interfere with police, 911, aircraft, emergency and other radio signals.

- *Missing features:* If you pirate a service, you may not be getting the full feature set. Channel guide, parental control, and tech support are a few of the possible items missing when you pirate a subscription service.

HORROR STORY! We recently heard about a person who was caught stealing from a cable provider and was fined a considerable amount of money. The person was caught by a clever technique that the cable provider was using to check for pirates. It created channels that paying subscribers cannot see but people who pirate can. It then advertised some amazing deals (top-of-the-line computer for $300, vacation package for $500, and so on). The unsuspecting pirate calls in to get the deal, the provider takes their information or minimally gets the phone number through caller ID, and the pirate gets fined.

How Can I Prevent Subscription Piracy in My Home?

As the subscription holder, a parent, or a guardian, you are ultimately responsible for any piracy that takes place in your home. Here are a few ways to prevent piracy in your home:

- *Protect your wireless network.* Sharing a subscription service with others outside your home is illegal regardless of whether you knew about it or not. The best way to protect your wireless network from others is to use encryption. See Chapter 5 for more information.

- *Use the equipment from the provider.* Providers usually charge rental fees or charge more for their equipment than third-party retailers would. To avoid paying rental fees or being overcharged, or to simply use different equipment that has more features, some people purchase their own equipment. Besides compatibility and performance issues, third-party equipment may circumvent subscription security, allowing you to get more than you pay for. By using the equipment (unmodified) given from the provider, you can rest comfortably knowing you will get only what you pay for at the best quality. This includes receivers, modems, and access cards.

- *Report service problems.* If you are experiencing slow service delivery, poor quality, or interference, you should report it to your provider to have it corrected. As mentioned in the previous two sections, poor service can be a symptom of subscription piracy either in your home or in your neighborhood.

Summary

With all the advances in technology recently, it seems as if you can make a perfect copy of just about anything (music, movies, software). And now with high-speed Internet, you can quickly search, share, and download these copies. In this chapter, you learned how files are pirated and how they may even be pirated from the PCs in your home or business. You also learned how the movie, music, software, and service companies are aggressively seeking, suing, and prosecuting anyone who tries to pirate their products. Getting something for free always seems like a great idea, except when it involves stealing. In the end, it's just not worth it. Be smart and don't take what doesn't belong to you.

Index

Degunking Your Email, Spam, and Viruses
By Jeff Duntemann
ISBN 19321193-X
340 pages
Available Now!
$24.99 U.S.

Overwhelmed by spam?

Plagued by pop-ups? Ever been hit by a virus or Trojan horse? Wasting time sorting through your huge pile of email? If so, *Degunking Your Email, Spam, and Viruses* is the book for you! Jeff Duntemann, co-author of the best-selling book *Degunking Windows*, shows you how to keep annoying email clutter at bay, how to quickly organize your email so you can find what you need, how to eradicate and prevent spam and pop-ups, how to protect yourself from Internet scams, hackers, and dangerous viruses, and much more. A great book for anyone who needs help keeping their PC safe and free of spam and email clutter.

Degunking Microsoft® Office
By Christina Palaia and Wayne Palaia
ISBN 1-932111-95-6
320 pages
Available: April 2005
$24.99 U.S.

Make Microsoft Office run like a dream!

Battling constant mishaps with Microsoft Office? Does PowerPoint hog your memory? Does Excel or Word crash without warning? Do these applications load at a glacial pace? Are temp files running rampant? Do you have problems finding the really important documents that you need? If these problems are frighteningly familiar, you need to degunk your Microsoft Office applications and files! Having a gunked up system with Office can really impact your productivity, especially if you don't have a method to keep everything organized and clutter-free. The solution is to use *Degunking Microsoft® Office* to streamline all your Office applications, better organize your data files, and take advantage of the applications' built-in time-saving features.